THE GAME MUST GO ON

ALSO BY JOHN KLIMA

Bushville Wins!

Willie's Boys

Pitched Battle

THE GAME MUST GO ON

HANK GREENBERG, PETE GRAY, AND THE GREAT DAYS
OF BASEBALL ON THE HOME FRONT IN WWII

John Klima

Thomas Dunne Books
St. Martin's Press
New York

To my mother and her mother—
and to my grandfather,
who loved them both

THOMAS DUNNE BOOKS.
An imprint of St. Martin's Press.

THE GAME MUST GO ON. Copyright © 2015 by John Klima. All rights reserved.
Printed in the United States of America. For information, address St. Martin's
Press, 175 Fifth Avenue, New York, N.Y. 10010.

www.thomasdunnebooks.com
www.stmartins.com

Designed by Omar Chapa

The Library of Congress Cataloging-in-Publication Data is available upon request.

ISBN 978-1-250-06479-0 (hardcover)
ISBN 978-1-4668-7108-3 (e-book)

St. Martin's Press books may be purchased for educational, business, or promotional use. For information on bulk purchases, please contact the Macmil-
lan Corporate and Premium Sales Department at 1-800-221-7945, extension
5442, or write to specialmarkets@macmillan.com.

First Edition: May 2015

10 9 8 7 6 5 4 3 2 1

CONTENTS

TO THE FRONT
A Note to the Reader

The story of the war and baseball is the story of us. If you care about baseball, everything you know about baseball comes from what happened during World War II. If you care about World War II, this is a new version of the war story you have never read. The war created who we are and it created modern baseball, and from that came the evolution of modern professional sports today, because the games we play changed because of the battles we fought.

I set out to write this story because I thought that the people who write about baseball don't know much about World War II, and the people who write about World War II don't know much baseball. I grew up with both in my life and always felt that the grand story of baseball and the war had never been told in a cohesive, narrative style that explained why the two are connected, and how we can see it, even if we don't realize it, in our lives today.

When I would find the few books written about baseball during the war, I couldn't stand the lack of knowledge about the war's basic campaigns, personalities, or machines. As for the war writers, they're interested in the war, so they never stopped to ask what baseball meant to the soldiers and to the home front or who was involved. But this connection between baseball and the war was part of our national identity and remains a pivotal part of our history.

Back in the war, pilots had maps printed on their silk scarves in case they were shot down. So in this note, I'd like to provide the reader with a short road map of what to expect, a comfortable fit, one that welcomes you into the world of your parents and grandparents, so that you can visit them again, whether they are here with you or not.

The basics: Pearl Harbor was bombed on December 7, 1941, in the baseball off-season. Nobody knew if baseball would be permitted to continue because the war was going to require millions of men. We needed them for the Army, the Air Force, the Navy, and the Marine Corps. Somebody had to build all the equipment. That meant millions more men and women working in factories at home and a tremendous strain on the resources that made possible baseball and everything else routine in American life.

The baseball commissioner was Judge Kenesaw Mountain Landis. He asked President Franklin D. Roosevelt what baseball should do. Landis wanted to know if baseball was important enough to continue during the war. This was a complicated decision. After much pondering, FDR wrote a note called the Green Light Letter, saying, in effect, the Game Must Go On.

The reader should be introduced to three principal characters before we begin this story. They may or may not be known to you. One man is Hank Greenberg. He was a big-time home-run hitter for the Detroit Tigers. He was the first major league baseball star to enter the Army, and soon, every other significant star followed him into the war effort. One by one they left the majors: players such as Bob Feller, Ted Williams, Joe DiMaggio, and Stan Musial. So did lesser-known ballplayers, who are well worth meeting: Buddy Lewis, Phil Marchildon, Jake Jones, Bert Shepard, Hank Bauer, Bill Greason, Warren Spahn (he was a nobody when the war began), and others introduced throughout this story.

Another player you should all meet is Pete Gray, who lost his arm at age six when he was essentially run over by a truck. He played baseball his whole life, longing for a chance to play professionally, but because he was an amputee, he was rejected and often ridiculed. The war's manpower shortage created his opportunity, and he got to play in the big leagues for one year because the Army would not take him because of his disability. He became the symbol of the imperfect players who kept the majors going on the home front. He was also an inspiration to wounded servicemen everywhere. Pete's story resonates especially now, as a generation of amputees have come home from Iraq and Afghanistan to become wounded-warrior athletes who prove the power of determination.

The final player is a boy named Billy Southworth, who, for the young parents reading this, could have been just like your son. He was a promising ballplayer headed to the big leagues. He had it made because his father was the manager of the St. Louis Cardinals, the best team of the war years. But Billy wanted to fly and wanted to serve, and he got his wish, quitting baseball, then flying and fighting aboard a B-17 bomber in the skies of Europe.

I wonder if the culture of vanity and narcissism we have created in this country today would permit such wide-scale selfless sacrifice at the cost of money, fame, and career. In the war years, thousands of athletes from all sports, amateur and professional, from all nations, decided that winning the war, a collective goal, was more meaningful than individual accomplishment. Playing a professional sport, while requiring great commitment, effort, and dedication, is not the same as fighting a war. The level of sacrifice and commitment from the World War II generation was far more substantial than wearing a flag pin on the lapel or singing the national anthem as if it were a tryout for a TV talent show.

Professional athletes have become an untouchable class in modern American society. In the war years, they were also celebrated, but they were not permitted to put career above country. The president of the United States, Franklin Delano Roosevelt, said so. The result was the baseball manpower shortage of World War II, the greatest crisis the game has ever faced, the price to be paid for keeping baseball going as a morale booster for the war effort at home and at the front. It is also why modern professional baseball looks the way it does, and because the other American sports, namely football and basketball, have copied baseball's evolution, which adapted to the manpower shortage, so, too, can it be said that the modern sporting landscape we have as Americans can be traced to what happened to baseball during the war. The manpower crisis changed the entire way modern athletes are bought and sold, placing a focus on youth. Now, the zest to discover and celebrate adolescent athletes borders on disturbing.

Most of what Americans know about baseball, or their other favorite sports, comes from what happened to baseball in World War II. The amateur draft, the integration of African-American and Latin players, unionization, free agency, big media deals, franchises changing cities, construction of new stadiums, rapid economic expansion and growth, all came from baseball and the war. The war made the country come of age and took the games we play with it. This is that story, too.

The war is the dividing line between baseball as it developed in America from the 1860s until the 1940s, and baseball and modern American sport as it has developed from 1941 to 1945 and into the twenty-first century. The saga of baseball and World War II is the earth's crust of baseball history. Nothing matches its wide-scale influence—not gambling scandals, not drug and steroid scandals, not labor stoppages or skyrocketing salaries, not any one era, not the achievements of any individual player, team, game, or series. Baseball in the war belongs with the ages.

History is best told through human experiences and human emotion. Therefore, this is not a textbook or a reference book. I wanted it to be the first book to put baseball players into combat, and to let the reader discover the magnitude of their contributions by making them experience how out of place they felt, yet how they rose to the occasion at the cost of personal sacrifice. I wanted the reader to feel the bullets coming at them, to smell the cordite, to see what they saw and feel what they felt. I wanted the reader to hear these ballplayers turned soldiers and sailors and airmen talk, walk, breathe, hope, and eventually play the game they left behind. I wanted readers to walk in the shoes of Hank Greenberg, Pete Gray, and Billy Southworth, who all fought the war in different ways.

With that said, this one is dedicated to everyone out there who grew up with the war the way I did, and to my parents and grandparents, who lived it. Take your time to savor it, and may it connect you to your family's past as it does me to my own. It's meant to be enjoyed. It is a long book from a long war, but, hey, it has a good ending.

I'm fascinated by World War II, having been a participant. I read everything I can and everything that's ever written about it. I must read it, you know?

—HANK GREENBERG, 1980

PART I

The Green Light

1941

CHAPTER 1

Good-bye, Hank

Hank Greenberg walked up the corner of Michigan and Trumbull one last time. He strode with his head down and a fedora pulled low above his eyes, a travel bag firmly clenched in one hand and the other pressed deep into the pocket of his overcoat. His wing tips skipped past torn ticket stubs, burnt cigars, and other trash on the cracked sidewalk until he passed beneath the overhang, reading BRIGGS STADIUM.

The empty ballpark slept in the morning, hours before fans arrived for the afternoon game. Hank walked up the ramp into the stadium, smelling scents of cooking grease and mowed grass. The ballpark was Hank's home, and he knew well her rhythm and moods, and though she was deserted in the early chill, Hank knew all that made her breathe.

He got to know her as a twenty-two-year-old kid in 1933, fresh up from the minors on a morning just like this. The old, blue pillars holding the double-deck stadium together framed her charms, the ghosts, and his memories. The wind blew in from above the left-field roof, pushing against Goose Goslin's shirt and stirring the infield dirt where Ty Cobb had left footprints. The breeze swirled near second base, where Charlie Gehringer spent the years methodically stealing singles when he wasn't quietly hitting them. The tobacco-stained pitching rubber on the mound, where Schoolboy Rowe, Tommy Bridges, and Elden Auker baited batters, led to the runway at home plate, where Babe Ruth once blasted a ball clear over the right-field wall.

Day after day Hank ducked into the tiny, bomb shelter–like home dugout, which was clearly not built with the intention of housing a six-foot-four right-handed slugger who played first base and then left field, hitting home runs into the left-field wind, off the recently added right-field, upper-deck grandstand, even into the barren reaches of deep center field.

Every ballpark is a theater, and every theater has its star. Hank had become part of this place's soul. Hank smiled at the ballpark workers, who made pennies sweeping the stands while he made thousands hitting balls into them, with never a thought that he was somehow better than they were. He had seen them every day for the last seven years, and they knew each other by heart. Good-byes were never easy, and his walk through the stadium in the morning sun was only the first farewell of the day.

Hank pulled open the door to the home clubhouse. The overhead lamps were turned off, and the only light came through the big row of windows above the room. Across the room, a small lamp was burning inside the manager's office. Hank bypassed his locker and walked straight to the light.

Del Baker was sitting in a folding chair behind a small card table that he used as his desk. Baker was always smoking, and his ashtray was a cigarette graveyard. He liked his office to be Spartan, musty and stale. He was crusty and crabby, but as sharp as the nail where he hung his hat. The daily newspapers were scattered across his desk, but Baker had gone right to the sports pages and pulled out the commentaries from the *Detroit News* and the *Detroit Free Press*. Hank saw the blank lineup card and a fountain pen on top of the papers. Baker only had one question, but Hank answered before he could ask. Yes, he was playing on his last day before he left the Tigers to join the US Army.

Then Hank turned and walked away. He was usually the first one in the clubhouse, and today was no exception, especially since last night was his going-away party. He stepped up to his locker stall, the one in the front corner of the room always assigned to the team captain, the locker he inherited from Mickey Cochrane. Hank flipped the fedora off his head and put it on the rack. He eased out of his overcoat. He looked into his stall. The bright white jersey with the big number 5 on the back was staring at him, almost pleading with him to stay.

Hank slowly dressed in silence. A few minutes later, he wore his baseball pants with the belt unbuckled, slippers over his dark blue sanitary socks, and a long-sleeved T-shirt. He sat on his stool and contemplated his career. All ballplayers know their numbers, even if they don't admit it. Their production was directly linked to their value on the field and their self-worth as men. He had 247 career home runs over eight full seasons entering 1941. He hit 30 home runs or more in a season five times, including 58 home runs in 1938, when he fell just two shy of Babe Ruth's single-season record. But Hank's selflessness was larger than the silence in the room. He would never once draw attention to two simple facts that made his decision to leave the major leagues at the peak of his ability staggering in its significance: Hank was the reigning American League MVP, and he was the highest-paid player in the game, who was putting his annual $55,000 salary on hold to earn $21 a month working for the US Army.

Hank was a businessman who knew his value. He was never afraid to represent himself and negotiate with ownership over his salary when he was convinced he was right. He was never afraid to push back when he believed the owner was wrong. He knew his ability would never be so prized again. He was coming off a season in which he almost won the Triple Crown, hitting .340 and leading the American League with 41 home runs, 150 runs batted in, and 50 doubles. He was a hitting machine who scored well more than 100 runs a season, almost always flirted with 200 hits a season, and had even so effortlessly moved from first base to left field that he won two Most Valuable Player awards at different positions. He was the rock of the Detroit Tigers, but he never saw himself as much more than that kid from James Monroe High in the Bronx.

Everyone saw Hank as the kind of guy one wanted to be as a ballplayer. He was talented, dignified, and intelligent, but he also worked incredibly hard, saw himself as a guy who could hit but had ordinary skills otherwise, and sought no attention. His modesty endeared him to the humble, hard-working fans of Detroit, who, in the lean Depression years, knew he was as predictable as the smokestacks and as reliable as the factory horn bellowing at nine and five.

His teammates loved and respected him as much as the fans did. One by one, the players sauntered into the clubhouse, hiding their hangovers. They all knew he was leaving for the Army, even if most of them couldn't understand why he had to go. Croucher and McCosky could have cried. York wanted to hug Hank, so he did, and the big Indian squeezed hard.

Campbell and Higgins shook his hand. Tebbetts laughed off his sorrow, promising Hank that once Hitler found out Hank was in the Army, no enemies would ever dare mess with the Americans. Gorsica came last and promised Hank he would try to pitch him a farewell victory. The two kid pitchers, Trout and Newhouser, were usually cocky and obnoxious, but they were moved by the moment and too shy to say good-bye.

Then Hank buckled his belt, put on his spikes and tied the laces, picked up his outfielder's glove and first baseman's mitt he had specially designed a few years before, took two bats, and headed to the field. He was the first man on the field that day, as usual. Today he wanted to be the first so he could be alone, and his teammates knew why. Everyone was saying good-bye to him. Hank needed to say good-bye to himself.

The Army was getting a surefire future Hall of Fame slugger, while the Detroit Tigers were bound to get nowhere. Hank led them to the World Series in 1934, 1935, and 1940, three times in seven years. He prided himself on being one of the few players who could put a team on his shoulders and haul them past the Yankees. The only time the Tigers won, when they beat the Cubs in 1935, Hank broke his wrist and only had six at bats. That was just one of the regrets he had on his last day in 1941. Someday, he wanted to play in the World Series again, and he wanted to do it here at Briggs Stadium, in front of these fans, and he wanted to be healthy enough to play.

He stayed optimistic, hoping he could serve his time and be discharged in time for the 1942 season. He would still have a lot of career in front of him, as long as the war didn't get in the way. He was only thirty years old and he was the first star player of his magnitude to be drafted. The war had been going in Europe since 1939, and Americans wanted no part of it. That didn't mean war wasn't a possibility. Hank wasn't happy about leaving, but his desire to do what he felt was right outweighed his self-desires. Teammates were astonished that a man with so much talent could be so selfless.

But Hank knew his time had come. He had a low draft number from the time he registered with Selective Service in 1940, and when he took his first Army physical later in the year, he was disqualified because of flat feet. Hank was roundly criticized, and he resented that some newspaper guys put out a street rumor that he bribed the doctor to fail the physical. Hank smelled bullshit. He thought it was anti-Semitic. Hank never considered himself an overly religious Jew, nor did he see himself as someone carrying a mantle for the religion, but he vehemently opposed bigotry and oppression. His conscience always guided him. When he refused to play on Yom Kippur in 1934, he became a hero. He didn't do it for the headlines. It was a simple matter of principle: he wanted to honor the beliefs of his parents.

Oh, but there was an edge to Hank. He grew up in baseball hearing the nasty taunts from the rubes sitting in the stands. He'd get sheeny, Jew, and kike all the time. Hank knew it was because they feared the unknown of a huge six-foot-four kid with a Jewish last name who never seemed intimidated by intolerance and wouldn't put up with it. He remembered the time he had to explain to a Southern teammate named Jo-Jo White that a Jew was not a person with horns growing out of his head. Hank became guarded over the years, and he took great pride in his work. He pushed himself to be great because he knew when he was simply human, he'd hear names raining down from the stands, even from the fans that supposedly loved him.

He learned how to stand up for himself at an early age. He grew up in an immigrant neighborhood where English was the second language and most people spent their entire lives in the Bronx. When Hank signed with the Tigers in 1929, he quickly developed a thick skin when he went to the minor leagues, and he learned to fight back. A big brawl occurred during the Three-I League play-offs at Illinois in 1931, and again at Dallas when he was playing for Beaumont in 1932. Hank never forgot how, in a sort of comically dysfunctional way, "everything was focused on that dirty Jew on the field, you know?"

When he broke into the big leagues, Hank made it a point to teach any ballplayer who gave him trouble a lesson he would never forget. Hank made it simple. You kept your mouth shut or he would come see you. The Chicago White Sox had a mouthy manager named Jimmy Dykes. One of the ballplayers on his bench howled, *YELLOW JEW BASTARD!* When the game was over, Hank tore off his spikes, put on his shower slippers, and marched to the visiting team's clubhouse in Briggs Stadium, pushing open the door clearly marked POSITIVELY NO VISITORS so violently that the door banged against the concrete wall. Hank stormed to the center of the room and stood in front of a bunch of half-naked men, demanding, "I want that guy who called me a 'yellow Jew bastard' to get on his feet!"

Nobody stood up.

So when his draft number came up again in 1941, Hank knew the only way to silence the critics was to stand up again, to do the unthinkable, and walk away from baseball. Besides, he didn't really have a choice, so doing it now was the closest to doing it on his own terms. He was ready to get his Army hitch out of the way, even if it cost him the season. Yes, it hurt, but he was doing so because it was his duty to serve his country as called, and because he wanted to quash the rumors that he had weaseled out of duty in 1940. You could take Hank's uniform and his bats away, you could take away his salary, you could transplant him from the batter's box to the barracks, you could make him march a hundred miles with his flat feet, but you could not take away his sense of dignity. He owed it to the country that he called home, that had allowed him as the son of Romanian immigrants to chase baseball instead of following his father into the textile business. Hank had a very real sense, shared by the sons of European immigrants, that America had given his family their lives. Now it was his turn to return the favor. It was as simple as that. Hank never made the Army a complicated decision. What is right is right.

His manager, Del Baker, respected that about him, but he was worried that it would do more damage to Hank's ability than he realized. Baker remembered World War I, when the war shortened the 1918 season, and he knew that even a short period of Army time away from baseball could hurt a career. He watched Hank take batting practice that morning, heard the balls exploding off his bat like gunshots, and prayed that the war wouldn't come any closer than it already was. Baker knew that the longer Hank didn't play, the harder it would be for him to be the player he was. Hank was aware of the risk, too, but he was a ballplayer living in the moment. Ballplayers in the moment can't think years ahead. Baker was flat-out terrified that the big man would never again be the same.

It was an otherwise mundane Tuesday-afternoon game, May 6, 1941, the nineteenth game of the season. The defending American League champion Tigers sported a dull 10-8 record, tied for fourth place. The Yankees were in town. The night before, the Tigers had thrown a farewell party for Hank, and it had been one hell of a blast. The club gathered at the Franklin Hills Country Club. The night was full of booze, cigar smoke, and probably some girls. It was more like a bachelor party, and you knew that because a lot of the guys from the Yankees were there, too, including Joe DiMaggio. Now, everybody knew Joe D didn't go anywhere unless some blondes were involved, but Hank Greenberg was his favorite brunette. "I do remember hearing about that going-away party," pitcher Virgil Trucks recalled. "All I'm going to tell you is everybody had a great time."

Before the game, Hank was presented with a gold watch by his teammates, inscribed with their names. Hank could look at his wrist in the Army and remember all the old buddies who were going to miss him when he was gone, and it read like the lineup card Del Baker filled out. With each name he wrote on the lineup card, he groused and bitched and moaned. *1. Croucher SS; 2. McCosky CF; 3. Gehringer 2B; 4. York 1B;* then, when he wrote *5. Greenberg LF,* he was whiskey numb and hoped for the best; *6. Campbell RF; 7. Higgins 3B; 8. Tebbetts C; 9. Gorsica, P.*

Hank had played with so many of these guys for so many years—the position players, Charlie Gehringer, Rudy York, Birdie Tebbetts, and Barney McCosky, who taught him how to play left field when he moved from first base—and the veteran pitchers, Tommy Bridges and Al Benton, and the crazy young and cocky hurlers, Dizzy Trout and Harold Newhouser. He didn't know when he would see them again. Hank didn't anticipate how many of them would eventually follow him into military in the coming years, how the war would change them all.

Yet when Hank spoke to the press, all that came out of his mouth was red, white, and blue. He made it seem as if no worries had entered his mind, when in truth baseball was his living, his income, and his identity. He was making more than even DiMaggio. By this stage in Greenberg's career, a number of historically significant career milestones were within his reach. One in particular stood out: he wanted to become the third player in baseball history to hit 500 career home runs. Only Ruth and Jimmie Foxx had made it that far. He thought it would be nice if he could hit three more home runs in his final game and leave for the Army with the nice round number of 250. It wouldn't surprise anyone if the starting pitcher for the Yankees, a right-hander named Ernie "Tiny" Bonham, adhered to the old code of the honorable ballplayer and grooved a few farewell fastballs.

Only one other major league regular had been drafted and entered the Army, an unlucky Philadelphia Phillies right-handed pitcher named Hugh Mulcahy. He'd twice lost 20 games in a season, led the league both times, and earned the sobriquet Losing Pitcher. Hank was a different bird. He knew all eyes were on him. He knew he was being held up as an example to all future ballplayers who would be called to service. Ballplayers were glad it was Hank, not them. He was a big man with big shoulders, and they knew nobody else could handle the pressure or conceal the frustration like Hank.

War was dangerous business for a ballplayer. A ballplayer could never face a shot, never so much as hear a gun go off, and he could still be a casualty. He could spend his career peeling potatoes, scrubbing latrines, playing ball on the camp to entertain the troops, and still wind up a dead man as far as baseball was concerned. A farmer, a cabdriver, a doctor, a lawyer, a high school kid, a college boy—those guys could all resume their lives when it was over, if they survived. Not the ballplayer who needed time on his side. A ballplayer who spent any prolonged period in military service risked losing it all, and worse yet, he risked that the talents that made him special in life might never come back. He could be forgotten in the eyes of baseball, and for many, that possibility was just as awful as seeing their name carved into a white marble cross.

"I have been ordered to report May seventh and I will do so," Hank said. "I want no favors and I ask none." Thankfully, the Tigers planned no embarrassing ceremonies to honor him before the game, but the grounds crew gave him a special pen-and-pencil set. Hank genuinely appreciated that. He stopped his pregame routine and thanked the guys who raked the dirt and watered the grass. He graciously accepted the writing set and shook each man's hand. That was authentic, not some newsman sticking a camera in his face. The groundskeepers worked hard and didn't make a lot of money, but they chipped in to give a guy who was much wealthier than they were something he could have purchased a thousand times over. Hank was moved and made sure every one of the guys knew how much he appreciated their thoughtfulness.

The Tigers front office expected a nice kick in ticket sales from fans coming to say good-bye to Hank. It was reasonable to think a few more fans than usual would skip work on a Tuesday afternoon to see him play for the last time this season. Del Baker emerged from his office and concealed his foul mood as he posted his starting lineup, while a disappointingly small crowd meandered through the turnstiles. The front office was dismayed and concerned. Before television, ticket sales were the lifeblood of any club. Without fans putting down money at the box office, there were no concession sales, and that hurt business. Without Hank, there wasn't much incentive for Tigers fans to buy tickets. The theater was losing its star.

When he came to bat in the second inning, the crowd of 7,850 gave him a warm welcome. He gently tapped the brim of his navy-blue Tigers hat in acknowledgment, then stepped into the box as if it were any other game. The Yankees were fanned out in front of Hank, with Joe DiMaggio in center field resting his hands on his knees. Tiny Bonham was on the mound, as stocky as DiMaggio was slender. Bonham was six foot two and built like a bathtub. He threw high and hard fastballs to set up his sinking forkball. Hank liked it. He wanted his last game to be against a guy with a good arm.

Tiny rocked into his windup, drawing his hands back behind his head and kicking hard as he pushed down, his front foot pushing against the dirt as if his spurs were kicking a horse, and the good fastball came flying out of his hand. Hank watched the pitch rocket into catcher Bill Dickey's glove with a leathery snap. Hank was going to miss that sound. Strike one. Then Tiny cranked it up again, and Hank's muscles sparked into action. He took his fast, violent, and aggressive swing, as if funneling all his frustration into tormenting the baseball, and he heard the other sound he would miss so dearly, the crack of the bat, the gunshot echoing on the corner of Michigan and Trumbull.

Hank knew when he got one good, and nothing else felt quite like it. Nobody could put backspin on a ball like him. As the ball carried into the blue seats of the left-field upper deck, he dropped his bat and began to trot as with any other home run, but he wasn't immune from emotion. Every step said good-bye. He passed Joe Gordon playing first base, Jerry Priddy playing second, and little Phil Rizzuto playing short. The crowd cheered for Hank as he headed to third, past Red Rolfe, as a few stray newspapers fluttered down from the upper deck. Hank crossed home plate. Like so many times before, his home run gave the Tigers the lead.

Hank came to bat in the third inning, again facing Tiny Bonham. Rudy York was on first base. The crowd cheered louder, sensing time slipping away. Hank always possessed the reflexes of a regular man; that is, until somebody was brave enough to throw him a fastball.

The bat started forward in a flash, and again, that good sound of bat on ball, the gunshot on the corner. The ball was gone in a blink, soaring almost into the same spot as before in the upper deck in left field, where kids sat on baby-blue bleachers on sunny days and dreamed of playing with Hank. Hitting home runs was the one thing Hank made look easy, the great physical intangible that could not be taught and was only given, the loose explosiveness of his strength. He wasn't nearly as pretty when he ran the bases, chugging and puttering around like an old Model T with smoke coming out the front, but he savored every sweet stride until he spiked the plate.

As Hank trotted home, the thought occurred to him that now he had 249 career home runs—and it was only the third inning! He had at least three more at bats left in the game to hit his third homer of the game and reach the magical 250 mark. It wouldn't be against Tiny Bonham, who was lifted from the game and replaced with Atley Donald, a soft-spoken, swampy Southern right-hander.

Hank could smell his third home run, but he got greedy and his swings got long. He admitted it would be a hell of a send-off to wind up with three home runs in the same game. But Donald got him the next two times he faced him, and in the eighth inning, Hank came up for the last time. He stopped to hear his name announced. He almost never did that, but he knew the meaning of the moment, in the memory of the fans, and in his own life.

The small crowd felt large and loud, standing on its feet cheering for him, as if sending him a long good-bye kiss. But now it wasn't just the fans, it was the Tigers, who all stood on the top step of that little bomb shelter of a blue dugout at Briggs Stadium to applaud Hank. Bill Dickey, the Yankee catcher, lifted his mask onto his baseball cap and extended his hand to Hank. Hank touched Bill's hand and doffed his hat to the crowd, some of whom were in tears. Del Baker, the manager, was on the top step of the dugout cheering with the rest of his players, crying and raging on the inside.

Atley Donald stood on the mound with the ball in his hand. He watched Hank soak in the moment and decided that the man who asked no favors deserved one anyhow. Donald wound up and threw Hank a first-pitch fastball. He took something off it, but he shouldn't have. Hank took an explosive and violent cut, missing enormously, corkscrewing his knee into the ground and nearly falling over. Strike one. The fans whooped it up, they loved it, and Hank gingerly got up with a big dirt splotch on his pants.

Hank dug back in. For this split second, everyone forgot Hank was joining the Army. There were no armies, no nations, no soldiers, no war, no nothing. There was just a right-hander with a baseball in his hand, and a batter wringing the bat tightly in his hands. Atley Donald rocked back and threw another fastball, the sharpest kind, where Hank could hear the seams hissing, and he swung as hard as he could.

The swing sounded like a guillotine swishing the air, but Hank hit nothing, trying as hard as he could. Strike two. The good-bye kiss had no tongue. Donald could be a mean bastard right here and waste a fastball in the dirt or even knock him down with two strikes.

But Donald had too much dignity for that. Bill Dickey, the catcher, wouldn't put down a sign. The Yankee manager, Joe McCarthy, had no orders. Donald decided to throw Hank a belt-high fastball. And somehow, Hank knew all along what was coming. Donald rocked into his windup and threw one more heater. Hank took his last swing and twisted himself into an empty knot. Strike three. Hank struck out and the Army had a new recruit. Now it really was official—World War II came early to Detroit.

Hank slowly walked off the field, but he was in no hurry to take off his uniform. After another round of good-byes, he was tired and wanted to leave. The entire day had been emotionally draining. He said, "I appreciate everyone's efforts in giving me a send-off, but it's a relief to get it over with." When he was finally dressed, someone snapped a photograph of him in street clothes mournfully hanging up his jersey in his locker for the last time, the big number 5 facing the camera. Hank looked huge, but his jersey looked small. Hank looked as if he were turning his back on an old friend.

He told the reporters that he was upset about how much publicity his enlistment had garnered. He didn't think being a ballplayer warranted special treatment. The Army had offered him a one-day grace period to participate in Detroit's pennant-flag-hoisting ceremony the following afternoon, but Hank had declined. He said good-bye to his manager, Del Baker, and the owner, Walter O. Briggs. He emptied out his corner locker and left his career book marked at 1,049 major league games.

As he put his fedora on and draped his overcoat over his shoulders, he lifted his travel bag and took a deep breath, muttering aloud to nobody in particular, "I wouldn't want to go through this again." Then he walked out of the home clubhouse for the last time, turning out the lights above him.

CHAPTER 2

Ghost on His Shoulder

Pete Gray told the story like this, remembering the basics as steadily as he held the bat with his only arm. "When I was six, a huckster come into town. He was selling stuff—you know, potatoes and apples—and he said he'd give me a quarter or something if I'd go house to house to tell them about the potatoes and apples. After he was done, and he give me the quarter, I was on the running board of his truck and he said, 'Jump off.' And I slipped. In those days, trucks had wooden spokes in them wheels, and my arm got caught in the spokes."

Pete had a way of making the accident and the injury sound like nothing more than a bad sneeze, but this bloody mess had ripped a little boy's arm off his body. Pete remembered how the driver didn't pay attention after Pete jumped off the moving truck. The driver stayed on the gas, twisting and shredding the arm, snapping the elbow, and allowing the bone to impale the skin. Pete left out the details best not imagined. He rolled to a stop with his arm in an unnatural position, hanging like a thread and gushing blood. Pete said the driver stopped once he saw Pete in his rearview mirror. Pete couldn't remember how he got home, but he thought the driver took him home and left him on the front porch. Most of these memories were cloudy and disjointed, distorted by trauma and youth. Pete knew he went to the hospital; he thought a neighbor rushed him over. He didn't remember any of the doctors or when exactly he blacked out, but medicine being what it was in about 1920, he knew that when he woke up, the doctors had cut away his right arm above the elbow. Pete didn't talk much about the accident the older he got. He simply didn't think there was much worth saying.

From the moment he woke up in his hospital bed with his arm bandaged, baseball was survival. Pete had lost his arm, but not his passion for playing. He was just a little boy and baseball was his world, and to give it up would be to surrender a normal life. He wouldn't give up on himself, and if he ever thought about it, his father would make sure he never did.

Pete senior taught Pete junior how to live all over again. Years later, Pete remembered how his father firmly burned these lessons into his mind. Pete senior did not know how his boy would support himself as an adult. He knew the coal companies would never let anyone inside the mine shaft with only one arm. Pete senior saw it as a blessing that his son would never have to smell the grime and cough up the black phlegm. He only knew that his boy was going to have a harder time than the other boys his age, so he pushed his little boy as soon as he was out of the hospital and back on his feet.

Pete junior was born a right-hander, but as soon as the arm was gone and the stump had healed, Pete senior taught him how to do everything left-handed. He helped him learn how to write, how to eat with a fork and a knife, how to comb his hair, brush his teeth, and clean himself. When Pete junior got angry and frustrated at the difficulties of learning anew, Pete senior questioned his toughness and manhood, even though he was only a boy. When he failed to complete one of his tasks, Pete senior pushed him harder. When Pete junior got angry, Pete senior did not relent. Pete junior may have resented his father, but over time he understood why the old man challenged him. No matter what Pete did in the following years, it always seemed as if his father were never far away. Pete learned never to hold back because of his disability; he finished difficult tasks out of sheer defiance and developed the enormous desire to prove himself daily. He lived his life the way his father taught him to, hard and determined with unrelenting, serious commitment.

Pete heard his old man's voice in his head long after the coal miner was dead, barking words he told the parents of the handicapped kids he often met: "If the kid falls down, don't pick him up. Don't let him ever feel sorry for himself. That's the way my father treated me." When Pete ventured to the baseball field again, the other kids asked him if he wanted to be the batboy. Pete laughed in their faces. He was always cocky that way. He refused to be a spectator. He thought he was a better ballplayer than they were, even with one arm cut off. He believed he had a better batting eye than anyone else, but he hadn't tried to play ball again since losing his arm. He realized he wasn't ready yet, and he wouldn't be fully healed from his traumatic accident until he learned to play baseball again. He knew very well that he was starting from scratch, but he heard his father's voice shouting in his mind, and he vowed to push himself as hard as his father had pushed him.

He undertook his quest in solitude, journeying far out of town, following the railroad tracks where nobody could find him. He searched for a long stick, one with just enough weight and balance, one that spoke to him, and then, all with the same hand, he would toss up a rock to try to hit it. "I'd spend hours just flipping up rocks and tin cans and hitting 'em with a club. I'd do that for hours and hours every day to develop a quick wrist," Pete said. He was developing superior hand-eye coordination and quickness.

Then there was the question of how to field, catch, and throw. He realized that his days as a shortstop were over. Ground balls ate him up because he couldn't react to bad hops. So he tried a new position, center field, where his speed and his quick reactions could compensate for the split second he needed to properly position his body to field the ball, drop the glove, transfer the ball to his throwing hand, and get rid of it. When he struggled to field the ball, transfer the glove, and make a clean throw, he heard the words of his father. *If I fall down, don't pick me up.*

With time and practice, Pete figured it out. If he removed the padding from the glove and wore it at his fingertips with his pinkie sticking out, he could catch the ball, move the glove under his armpit, squeeze the ball out, then bare hand and throw. It only worked because Pete's pinkie was crooked and bent up at a right angle. He could sling the glove off his fingers, hook it on his pinkie, and then swing it under the stump, freeing his arm to throw, all in one fluid motion. This took tremendous athletic engineering and creativity, balance, strength, and coordination. He looked like a bicycle peddling itself.

"I had a shoemaker make that glove for me special," Pete said. "He'd take out most of the padding and I'd use it like a first baseman's glove, keeping my pinkie outside. It helped me get rid of the glove quicker. I'd catch the ball, stick the glove under my stump, roll the ball across my chest, and throw it back in. No big deal. It was just grounders that gave me some trouble."

When Pete emerged from his self-imposed solitude, he was a brand-new ballplayer and an even more focused person, older than his years. Soon, he was the best ballplayer in town. Pete was hitting leadoff and playing center field for his neighborhood team. He constantly wanted to prove himself. Childhood friends remembered how fiercely competitive he became. He had no patience for intolerance or sympathy for his condition. You could look the wrong way at Pete Gray and he might pick a fight. He became the kind of ballplayer that teammates loved and opponents hated. Everything was tit-for-tat. It was difficult to tell when he was trying to beat you and when he was trying to kill you.

Once, Pete tried to score from second base on a single, challenging a sturdy Russian catcher guarding home plate as if it were the Tomb of the Unknowns. Pete flew past third base, lowered his shoulder, and rammed the catcher into the ground, knocking the ball loose. The Russian jumped to his feet and towered over Pete, shouting words to the effect of *If you weren't a one-armed son of a bitch, I'd kill you*. Pete looked at the guy and jawed back. Then he threw a quick punch and knocked the Russian back down. This time, the Russian didn't get up so easily. Kids in coal-mining country learned quickly that if you messed with the stump, you got the horns.

By the time he was a teenager, Pete was making $100 a week playing semipro ball for teams in Pine Grove and Scranton. He was well on his way to making his living as a ballplayer, easing his father's fears of his future profession. "I never worked a day in my life at nothin' but baseball," he said in later years, and he was happy that way. Pete was determined to be the next discovery from the ballplayer country of the coal towns, where for decades scores of major leaguers had emerged. Bird-dog scouts noticed Pete and turned his name in, and he heard that a dozen scouts recommended him. Nothing ever came of it. Pete thought it was because the scouts reported that he had only one arm, disqualifying him from the start. He decided that if the only way he would be discovered was to protect his chances by omitting his disability until the last possible moment, he would wear his lies as proudly as the empty sleeve on his shoulder.

When he was sixteen in 1931, he showed up at a local St. Louis Cardinals tryout camp in nearby Minersville. No other club signed as many prospects as the Cardinals. Branch Rickey's blueprint was to build quality through quantity, but even his minor league system had no use for a one-armed ballplayer. "I still remember the guy gave me number forty-eight," Pete said. "And the scout asked me my real name."

Because he was underage and wanted to sign illegally, Pete created a new name. He was born Peter J. Wyshner on March 6, 1915, and grew up on a spec on the map called Nanticoke, Pennsylvania. Wyshner didn't have much of a ring to it, so he lied about his age and modified his name: "I told them Pete Gray." The reasoning was small-town simple: "My brother boxed under the name Whitey Gray, and that was good enough for me."

No matter the name, the Cardinals said no and sent Pete home. On behalf of all of professional baseball, the St. Louis Cardinals had made an enemy in Pete Gray, the coal miner's son, the brother of a scratch boxer, the guy with one arm. As infuriated as Pete was when he was dismissed, his resolve become firmer. He sensed his road would be long and filled with a great deal of heartache, but he was willing to suffer to prove that he was a complete person possessing enormous pride, not an incomplete ballplayer missing an arm.

When Pete was a kid, a young ballplayer could break into organized baseball another way. That was through small-timers who ran freelance operations commonly called baseball schools, which frequently offered their services in the classified section of *The Sporting News,* the national baseball newspaper. Baseball schools took on aspiring minor league ballplayers and trained them to the point where they could be sold. Pete found a baseball school in Hot Springs, Arkansas, run by one Ray Doan. Pete took his earnings from the coal-miner league and hitchhiked to Doan's doorstep.

Doan's first impression of Pete was no different from that of many others. Here was a tall and thin kid with narrow bones and only one, very long arm, with his glove slung over the barrel of the bat on his shoulder and a satchel around the knob. Pete explained he had come all the way from Pennsylvania for a tryout. He told Doan he was a good country ballplayer who wanted to play professionally. Pete never mentioned the ghost on his shoulder, but he always knew the eyes of strangers went straight to his empty sleeve. Only Pete's conviction broke their gaze, the intensity of his words overmatching their curiosity at seeing a one-armed ballplayer arriving unannounced on the front porch. "When I showed up, he looked at me like I was crazy," Pete remembered. "I told him I'd hitchhiked all the way, so he sent me out onto his field."

The baseball school operators raised ballplayers like crops to sell at market. Doan's business partner was a former big league outfielder by the name of Johnny Mostil, who spent ten years with the White Sox. Johnny had his doubts, too, so he mercilessly smashed balls at Pete, who astounded Johnny with his speed and range. Pete ran so well that Johnny forgot that the kid had only one arm. "He hit a hundred flies to me, mostly to my right side, figuring I couldn't get my glove over in time," Pete said. "But I caught everything in sight." Pete remembered Ray Doan's look of astonishment. "He just kept rubbing his eyes. Finally he said, 'Kid, you can stay here all summer.'"

Pete was Johnny's grasshopper. He drilled lessons from his career into Pete's head. Johnny taught him to hunt the fastball. They worked on Pete's one-hand bunting and baserunning. Johnny taught him how to read pitchers and identify the curveball. They worked together to solve the positioning problems Pete's disability caused. Johnny gave Pete exactly what he needed at this stage of his life and career—he treated him like a player with two arms. Pleased with Gray's development, Ray Doan made phone calls to Class D minor league teams, but in his eagerness to make the sale he made the mistake of being honest. "He'd say, 'I've got this one-armed outfielder named Gray,' but they'd scream back, 'Are you nuts?' and hang up real quick," Pete said. Even decades later, one could sense Pete rolling his eyes at how stupid Doan was to be honest.

Disappointed, Pete returned home to play for a town semipro team called the Hanover Lithuanians. In the roughneck league, brawls between unionized and nonunionized coal-mining teams were vicious. Sometimes he was heckled, but he decided he didn't care what anybody else thought. He was determined to play in the majors, even if he had to slide spikes-high to do it. "I dreamed of playing in the major leagues, but I thought it was out of the question," he said. "After all, who ever heard of a one-armed ballplayer? So I said to myself, 'Pete, the whole trick is confidence in your-self. If you are sure you can do it, you will do it.'"

Then he got a letter of introduction to Philadelphia Athletics manager Connie Mack, who loved signing local boys for a pittance and putting them to work in the minor league coal mines. Pete was putting up great num-bers, but Mack didn't know he had one arm. When Mack realized Pete's disability, Pete remembered Mack's cold rejection very well: "Son, I've got men with two arms who can't play this game." Pete may have wondered, *Well, you're the guy signing all the players, and you're supposed to be a genius, so how come none of them can play?* Pete could tolerate rejection, but what he hated most was when people wouldn't let him try out because of his dis-ability. "Connie Mack never even let me on the field," he said. "That was the biggest problem and it wasn't just Connie Mack. It was all the scouts. They'd never give me a chance to show what I could do."

In 1938, a coal-mining ballplayer Pete knew recommended him to a semipro team in Quebec called Les Renards de Trois Rivières, the Three Rivers Foxes. When he arrived at the train station, the manager discovered Pete had one arm. Pete vividly recalled the conversation:

"What's your name?" the manager asked.

"Gray."

"What's the matter with your arm?"

"I don't have any."

"Jesus. Say that again? What's your name?"

"Gray."

"What are you coming here for?"

"To play ball."

"Oh . . . I'm in trouble."

When they arrived at the field, they did not give Pete a uniform and they would not let him take the field for pregame batting practice. Pete sat in the stands and wondered why he had to come this far just to get rejected yet again. In the middle of the game, one of the club owners told Gray to suit up. He sat on the bench until there were two out in the bottom of the ninth with the bases loaded and Three Rivers was down by a run. A batter came up and took strike one. Then the manager, who had hours earlier stared at Pete in disbelief, pointed at Pete and told him to grab a bat. Pete knew exactly what this was—they were trying to weed him out. Pete jumped off the bench and grabbed his bat with conviction.

Pete stepped out of the dugout and loosened up as he always did, by swinging two bats over his head with one hand. All the attention in the ballpark was on him. Nobody had seen a player like him before. They were immediately captivated and began chanting his name in French, *Gree! Gree! Gree!* Three Rivers was losing to Quebec, 1–0. Pete took two pitches for balls and the count was 2-and-1. *Gree! Gree! Gree!* Then he got a pitch he could handle, a fastball. Pete flicked his strong wrist, as if he were whacking tin cans on the railroad tracks back home, and laced the ball hard down the right-field line. Two runs came racing home. The local fans went crazy.

The Quebec players stomped off the field, muttering nasty French profanities. Pete stood at first base and loved the cheers. For the first time he could remember, he doffed his hat to the fans, who showered the field with pocket change. Nobody needed to ask Pete to scoop up the tip money. He collected it all in his hat and years later said he made $100 that night. Then Three Rivers signed him to a $500 contract to play the remainder of the season. The memory lasted longer than the money. He had been searching for acceptance. He hoped the feeling would never leave him. "I figured this game was meant for me," he said.

Pete hitchhiked to Brooklyn in 1939 with every intention of playing semipro ball for a team called the Bushwicks, a notorious outfit of baseball mercenaries who couldn't shake the dirt out of their blood. Their roster was twenty lies deep, names printed on nickel scorecards and sold to clueless fans sunning on rotting wooden benches. The Bushwicks were the most infamous team in the Metro League, which, given all its seedy charm, was firmly the subway floor of New York City baseball.

Pete thought playing in the Metro was the perfect place for him to be seen, scouted, and signed. The Metro was for young players on the way up and old pros on the way down. The Metro was a question-mark league, where all varieties of suspicious backgrounds existed, playing in uniforms with no names and numbers and concealing true identities and birth dates with vague surnames such as Black, Brown, and Gray. Everyone was here for a reason, and almost everyone had a secret to hide.

Pete was missing his right arm, but not his sense of certainty. He played his way out of the coal-mining country and was now convinced he would play his way out of Quebec, but the promoter of the Brooklyn Bushwicks, Max Rosner, greeted him with hearty skepticism and dismissal. Over time, years of such cold and harsh rejection had swelled inside Pete, changing his cheery and cocksure attitude into something deeper, darker, and surlier. Nothing made Pete angrier than the notion that he was asking for a playing job simply because he had one arm. He lived in the age of the traveling circus, the door-to-door salesman, and the carnival con man, so a lot of people thought Pete was a guy looking for a clever way to take advantage of his disability.

Pete detested that notion, but he lacked the schooling, the social skills, and the patience to refute it with anything but a willingness to squarely punch a guy in the jaw. His conviction was sharper than his spikes. You could call him a one-armed son of a bitch; hell, you could even call him a goddamned cripple—but don't call him a horseshit ballplayer, especially if you'd never seen him play. When Pete showed up in Brooklyn, he was as hot as the innards of the coal mines he'd left behind in Pennsylvania. He hadn't come to Brooklyn to be rejected, but that's just what happened.

Rosner saw the ghost on Pete's shoulder and told him to take a hike, refusing him a tryout and scoffing, "That's the best gate-crashing stunt I've ever heard." Pete wouldn't take no for an answer. He handed Rosner a $10 bill, the rest of the traveling money in his pocket, and told him, "Keep it if I don't make good." Impressed by the one-armed ballplayer's bravado and perhaps amused by his cockiness, Rosner gave Pete a workout but never expected anything good to come out of it.

He was wrong. When he saw Pete catch-and-throw with one arm, handle balls hit hard to his right where he had no arm, and take batting practice, where he proved he could hit these bush league, vagabond pitchers and run like hell, Rosner reconsidered. He was astounded that a man with one arm could make so many things on a baseball field look easy. Maybe Gray had some ability after all, even if it was strange ability. It was most certainly a sellable ability. Rosner knew right away the astounding one-armed ballplayer would be a big hit at the box office. That's what Rosner really cared about, so he offered Pete a contract. Pete didn't think twice. He asked for the pen, signed his contract, and stuck his hand out. Rosner shook it. That was well and good, but Pete wasn't asking for a handshake. He wanted his $10 back.

Word traveled fast through the city that the Bushwicks had a fantastic one-armed outfielder. Soon the locals flocked to Dexter Park. Rosner paid Pete $25 to play on the weekends. Pete was stunned to see big crowds show up, a product of Rosner's flashy advertising around the neighborhoods. In later years, Pete's imagination got the better of him, when he said there were crowds as big as ten thousand to see him in the little Metro. Truth is, the Brooklyn Dodgers were lucky to get that many. It wasn't where people went to be seen, it was where they went to hide. In either case, Pete realized that people would pay good money to see him play, and as long as he got his cut of the action, he was happy. When he saw how he packed the fans into the stands, he refused to play again until Rosner raised his salary to the princely sum of $350 per month. The promoter cringed and relented.

Rosner realized he had a great story on his hands, so he recruited a sports reporter from *Newsweek,* the national newsmagazine, to venture from Manhattan to come visit the sticks and see Brooklyn's miraculous one-armed man. It wasn't every day that a player from the Metro got his picture in *Newsweek,* but there was Pete, posing with his bat ready to hit and that ghost hanging below his right shoulder.

"ONE-ARMED SLUGGER," read the *Newsweek* photo caption. "Pete Gray, who lost his right arm at the age of 6 in an auto crash, now plays centerfield for a semi-pro team in Brooklyn, not because of his box-office value as a curiosity but because he is really an asset. Up to last week he had accepted 34 chances without an error and, as leadoff man in the line-up, he was batting a lofty .449."

Most ballplayers smiled in photos, but Pete seldom did. He looked stern and committed in his *Newsweek* photo, bat cocked as if he were ready to punch the next bastard who called him a name. There was truth and fable in the nation's introduction to the mysterious, quiet, and quirky one-armed ballplayer. Yes, he had lost his arm in a freak automobile accident, but it happened when he was so young that years and trauma had wiped clean the exact date of the injury. Six was the most common age given, but in later years Pete confessed he couldn't remember if he was four or five when it occurred. Pete had a good thing going in Brooklyn, where he could have played his entire career and been remembered as a local legend. He could have turned his local celebrity into a job or his own liquor store or boxing gym and managed in the Metro when he was done playing.

But Pete didn't want to settle for small-town fame. He could not accept anything less than his ultimate goal of playing major league baseball. That was his father talking; Pete would not dare let him down. Pete couldn't easily explain to strangers why losing his arm and playing baseball were deeply connected in his psychology, but he knew the loss of one facilitated the need for the other. Nobody kept good records in the Metro, but he later said he hit about .350 that summer. Pete knew Rosner made big money selling contracts up the ladder to professional baseball, and he wanted to be next. For that to happen, Pete had to be scouted by someone with the power to sign a ballplayer on the spot.

Only one scout mattered in the Metro, Paul Krichell. A tough and shady son of a bitch, he was a former catcher with the sore knees and crooked fingers to prove it. Krichell was so stubborn that he was once hit in the head with a foul ball and refused to see a doctor for months. When he finally submitted to an X-ray and was told he had a fractured skull, Krichell didn't care. He downed some aspirin with a shot of whiskey and went out and caught nine innings.

He briefly tasted the big leagues, but nobody remembered him for anything else except the time Ty Cobb almost sliced off his manhood. Cobb came flying around third on his sharpened-spike tiptoes, slicing the corner of the bag like a witch on a broomstick. Krichell had the ball first and squared up to block the plate, but Cobb soared directly into Krichell's crotch, spearing him with his spikes, making Krichell wince for the camera, knocking the ball loose, and shredding the lower flap of Krichell's chest protector. Krichell never lived down the indignity of baseball's first recorded groin kick and rarely walked straight again, but at least he still had a deep voice.

Krichell caught the rest of his career in the minors for little money and lots of pain, but he was good at making friends. When he finally finished playing, Ed Barrow, the business manager of the New York Yankees, liked his smarts and hired him as chief scout in 1920. He was great at signing kids for nothing and telling their parents it was a great deal. When he robbed Lou Gehrig by signing him for $1,500 and a $400 bonus, the front office loved him. Krichell's reputation grew until he became known as baseball's first superscout. He received two thousand letters a year seeking his attention. Word got around that the Bushwicks had a left-handed-hitting center fielder who could run and was hitting .350. That was a player Krichell knew he needed to see.

Nobody told Krichell that Pete Gray had only one arm. When he saw him, he was furious. His enormous scouting ego was insulted to be asked to inspect such an inferior player. Krichell only wanted players who would make him look good. He didn't care if Pete had more heart than any ball-player he had ever seen. He thought Pete was a joke, a waste of his time. Pete wasn't surprised. But he had a long memory and he carried each rejection with him for years, putting far more thought, emotion, and effort into his rejection than Krichell ever put into it in the first place. Not everyone was as disillusioned. One astounded spectator was sportswriter Whitney Martin, who wrote Gray was "tall, raw-boned, can run like an antelope, catch fly balls with amazing dexterity and speed that matches that of a two-handed player. He uses a large bat, swinging the 36-inch, 37-ounce bludgeon like a war club. He takes a vicious cut at the ball." Yet as inspired as Martin was, he concluded Gray "probably will never see the majors."

The greatest challenge of Pete Gray's life was not losing his right arm. It was the fear of losing his shot at playing in the big leagues because he lost his right arm. Some fans rooted for him for that very reason, but Pete never went out of his way to bond with them. After the *Newsweek* story, he started getting letters. But Pete didn't care about notoriety simply because he had one arm. He saw himself as a ballplayer who grew up in a small town in Pennsylvania called Nanticoke. That was a great place for a kid with one arm to grow up playing ball because there were fields all over town, and after a while the neighborhood folk forgot Pete had one arm. He was just a good ballplayer who did things a little differently, but anywhere else Pete went in pursuit of his dream, he was deemed a freak. He fought against it constantly and developed a strong sense of guarded skepticism. Pete played again in the Metro in 1940 and 1941, bouncing between a few teams, always playing for the highest bidder. He succeeded in making a name for himself, but not in sparking the interest of professional baseball. To them, he was just that one-armed busher in Brooklyn. He was a non-prospect. To the young Pete, that was a worse fate than death itself.

When the summer baseball season was over, he loved coming home to Nanticoke because it was the only place in the world where he was just plain old Pete, not the guy with one arm. He had come a long way, but how much further could he expect to go? He was home in Nanticoke in winter 1941, drinking with the coal miners on a Saturday night. He woke up slowly on Sunday morning. It was December 7, 1941.

CHAPTER 3

Billy and the Kid

Billy Southworth forever heard he was too little to play baseball for a living, but he never believed it for a second. He was generously listed at five feet nine, but he had a smile wider than his height. From the day he started, he knew exactly what kind of ballplayer he wanted to be. He was one of those lefty-hitting, righty-throwing slightly built outfielders with small bones who would never grow much bigger or put on much muscle. He would never hit the ball far or hit many home runs, but he could always run. There would always be guys more talented than he was, but that never scared him. He was convinced he could play smarter, work harder, and that he wanted it more than the next guy. He played with modesty and glee, and with no desire for attention, so much so that nobody in his adopted hometown of Columbus, Ohio, ever knew very much about him.

He grew up off the land in Columbus, born in 1893 in Nebraska before his family moved, when the town was mostly open-expanse, Midwest farmland. When Billy grew up, the Pennsylvania Railroad had a machine station at the center of town, and a streetcar line connected the neighborhoods. When the new homes were built, the backyards had so much land, a family could till the soil. Immigrant parents from Europe always knew how to feed the family with nothing but a small sack of seeds, hard work, and a hoe. A family could survive on potatoes, cabbage, and carrots. The Rickenbackers, the family with a kid named Eddie who was three years older than Billy, made their own sauerkraut. Families kept a chicken coop for eggs, owned goats for milk, and sold the excess to help pay the bills.

Sometimes, Billy and his brother would race Eddie down the streets in homemade soapbox derby cars. It was great to be a kid back then, when plywood, tin cans, bicycle tires, and a hammer and nails could provide all the entertainment in the world. Both Billy and Eddie wanted to win, but the much-desired results of these soapbox derbies are lost to time and memory.

Billy and Eddie wanted to carve out their own niches in life. They respected their hardworking parents, who taught them to love America, the country with the big French lady in New York Harbor who blessed their entry and gave them everything they had. But the boys wanted to create their own destinies, and each fell in love with something as new and distinctive as their growing country.

Billy Southworth fell in love with baseball the way Eddie Rickenbacker fell in love with cars, engines, and flying machines. People had played town ball in Columbus since before the Civil War, and the town's first recorded professional team arose in 1877. Since the turn of the century, the minor league Columbus Senators had played in town, an American Association team one notch below the big leagues. Columbus was peppered with semipro leagues, and a kid could grow up playing sandlot ball. Billy fashioned himself into a slick-fielding, fast-moving center fielder who could make everyone forget his lack of height. He hooked on with his first minor league club in 1912 at the age of nineteen. He got his first prolonged crack at the big leagues in 1915 at age twenty-two as a member of the Cleveland Indians, just as World War I was starting. Billy only hit .220 and was rightly terrified that he would never play in the big leagues again. He drifted back to the minors with a thousand other guys. He was already an old pro at twenty-four years old, playing for the Birmingham Barons in the Southern Association when his first and only son, Billy Jr., was born, June 20, 1916 or 1917, depending on the source. He remembered it as the happiest day of his life.

The war caused the minor league season in Birmingham to be cut short, allowing Billy to come home to Columbus to spend time with his wife and the baby. America was in the war that summer and Billy heard the news that his old buddy Rickenbacker, who everyone called Rick for short, had turned his passion for speed, motors, and machines into a career with the newly formed American Air Service, where he proved to be a quick study in the cockpit. Planes, in the early years of American aviation, were flying coffins. The Air Service was so new that it had no formalized training, and pilots often joined the front after a scant number of hours, where they were usually decimated in days. The average untested pursuit pilot in World War I had a lifespan of about two weeks, but Eddie was different. When Billy heard about Rick's exploits, he smiled, because he understood and related to his courage. Billy understood that competitive nature and fearlessness were two and the same, no matter the occupation or walk of life.

While Billy was planning to play another summer at Rickwood Field in Birmingham in 1918, Eddie joined the 94th Aero Squadron, one of the first American air units deployed to the Western Front. The 94th soon gained fame back in the States with serialized newspaper adventures chronicling the squadron's duels with Baron von Richthofen's Flying Circus. While Rick was gunning down Germans, Billy finally got another shot at the big leagues with the Pirates in 1918, and he got it because of the war. The draft forced many ballplayers into the Army or left them scurrying to join the Navy. Billy didn't profile as much of an infantryman, with his newborn baby and his history of baseball injuries saving him from the trenches. This time, he left the fighting to Eddie and let the bullets fly off his bat instead. He hit .341 and stole 19 bases, proving at last he belonged in the big leagues.

In the summer, the famous photo of Rickenbacker leaning against the fuselage of his SPAD XIII was published around the country. There was old Rick, grinning with his service cap just a touch pushed to the side, his elbow just above the Hat-in-the-Ring squadron insignia boldly painted where no German could miss it. Rick and the boys of the 94th wore their Class A's dressed to kill and meant it. When the war was over, Rick had shot down twenty-six German aircraft to become America's Ace of Aces and firmly entrench himself into the American heroic consciousness. Maybe Billy senior read newspaper stories about his old childhood friend Eddie Rickenbacker to Billy junior. And in the coming years, boys of Billy Southworth Jr.'s age wanted to do one of two things more than anything else in the world: to be big league ballplayers or to be pilots.

Billy junior grew up watching his dad live his dream as a big league ballplayer. There was no better way for a boy to grow up. Billy senior was never the flashy guy, and he was never very famous outside of baseball, but inside the game, he earned the reputation as a smart ballplayer who was so positive and sunny that everybody loved him. The Pirates kept him until the end of the 1920 season, when he was part of a big haul of players sent from the Pirates to the Boston Braves for shortstop Rabbit Maranville. Billy played three years in Boston, hitting .300 each season in Braves Field, then was part of a package of players traded to the New York Giants in exchange for Casey Stengel and others.

Billy got the biggest break of his career on June 14, 1926. He was traded to the St. Louis Cardinals, where he became a key addition to the first Cardinals team ever to win the World Series. At age thirty-three, Southworth was never better. He hit .317 in 99 games down the stretch, helped the Cardinals beat the Yankees in seven games, and hit .345 in the Series, including a game-winning home run in Game 2. The World Series victory defined and invented the Cardinals. They were baseball's first champion built on players signed and developed in the farm system, influencing how the Cardinals built, played, and won for decades.

Right next to him was his boy, Billy junior, who turned nine years old the season the Cardinals won it all. Dad was "Billy the Kid," and junior was "Billy's Kid." Billy's Kid grew up taking batting practice with Rogers Hornsby, Sunny Jim Bottomley, Chick Hafey, and the other Redbirds at Sportsman's Park. He was the team batboy. He learned how to hit and curse, roll, chew, and spit tobacco, and win with them, and his world was baseball. Billy junior was there during that memorable World Series when Pete Alexander came in from the bullpen to strike out Tony Lazzeri with the bases loaded and saw Babe Ruth thrown out attempting to steal second base to end Game 7. Billy junior was in the dressing room when the Cardinals celebrated with victory cigars. He watched as Hornsby poured beer over his dad's head, dousing him with loving profanity as the foam dissolved on Billy senior's shiny, thinning hairline.

Billy senior wanted to become a big league manager, and he got his chance with the Cardinals in 1929, but he wasn't ready. Billy junior turned twelve that summer and got a taste of how hard and cruel life in professional baseball can be. Billy senior was too closely connected to his fellow players to command their respect. Owner Sam Breadon had zero patience for growing pains and the second division. He fired four managers in four years, starting with Hornsby after he won the World Series in 1926, and ending with Southworth, who struggled in his first stint, finishing in fourth place in 1929.

Getting fired was a rough blow. Billy senior floated back down to the minor leagues with hopes of returning to a big league bench quickly, but it wasn't meant to be. He won 105 games in Rochester in 1930, one step below the big leagues, but nobody called. For the next few years, he was stuck managing in the minor leagues, where he was a forgotten man. But those long hours in the desolate minor leagues, surrounded by excited kids on the way up to the big leagues and disgruntled veterans on the way down, provided ample opportunity to help forge his son's path. Billy senior found happiness in teaching his son how to play like a pro. The boy was receptive to the teachings and immersed himself in a baseball future.

Billy senior taught baseball the Cardinal Way. A ballplayer must be technical and efficient. A hitter must know his strike zone. When he gets his pitch, he must not miss it. He must display discipline at all times, yet be aggressive when the time comes. He must run the bases, close the gaps, make good throws, position himself, keep his teammates in the game, and be a leader and a good teammate. Under Billy's watchful eye, junior became quite a prospect.

But away from the field and the loving moments of developing his son's baseball talent, the early thirties were rough, torturous years for Billy senior both personally and professionally. He was fired from managing his hometown minor league team in Columbus in 1932, and in 1933 his wife died unexpectedly. The father and son grew closer in tragedy, and as the elder Billy's baseball career fell apart, his relationship with his son tightened. His love for his son was his saving grace, and in those difficult years he remembered Billy junior as "the closest friend I had."

Billy senior stayed home in Columbus in 1933 and 1934 while Billy junior was playing high school baseball. Billy senior had a job as a coach for the Giants in 1933, but ran afoul of manager Bill Terry and was fired before the start of the season. For a time, Billy senior left baseball and worked an ordinary job to pay the bills. His real job was making sure his son was ready to play pro ball when he graduated from high school in 1936. When Billy junior received his high school diploma in Columbus, many scouts were at his graduation ceremony trying to swoop in to sign him, the way scouts operated before there was a player draft. But they had no chance. Billy Southworth Jr. was born to be a Cardinal, and he signed immediately with the organization he grew up with. The years helping Billy junior prepare for pro ball helped Billy senior get his life back on track. He remarried and fathered a daughter and dreamed of a new goal, of managing his son in the major leagues.

Billy senior went back into baseball when Branch Rickey brought him back to the Cardinals organization, but instead of starting him with an assignment in the upper minors close to the majors, Rickey sent him back to the bushes. Ordinarily, a baseball man with Billy senior's level of experience might have protested, but he knew Rickey offered him a golden chance. Starting at the bottom of the Cardinals chain would inevitably allow him to manage Billy junior, who started his pro career in 1936 and batted .340 in Martinsville. That earned him a promotion to Class B Asheville, where his manager was his father. Father managed son for 29 games that season. Never was there more love between a manager and a minor league outfielder with a pedestrian .253 batting average.

The time with his father served Billy junior well. Their paths drifted apart, with Billy senior managing in Memphis in the Southern Association in 1936 to 1938, while Billy junior hit his way up the baseball ladder. By 1939, with the Rome Colonels at the age of twenty-two, he had his best minor league season, hitting .342 with 15 home runs and 25 doubles. Those kind of numbers got a guy to the big leagues. Billy junior was named MVP of the Class C Canadian-American League. Strapping and good-looking, he had the big-league bloodlines baseball teams loved, and when Branch Rickey promoted Billy senior to manage the Cardinals in 1940, it seemed natural that the kid would soon be playing outfield for his old man.

But Rickey was just kidding. After all, Billy junior was another piece of chain-store inventory to be sold for profit. Rickey did just that, selling Billy to the Toronto Maple Leafs in the Class AA International League, one step below the majors. Maybe Rickey was trying to do Billy a favor by selling him, because the Cardinals were loaded with talented young outfielders. Toronto's working agreement was with Connie Mack's Philadelphia Athletics, which meant that if Billy was going to be a big leaguer in 1940 or 1941, it would be for Mack, not for his father.

Perhaps disarmed by the whole ordeal, Billy started with a slump, then shook it off and got his bat going. But it wasn't enough to save him and he was sold yet again, this time all the way down to Class B, another full notch down the ladder. For an aspiring young ballplayer, it was a tough pill to swallow. It was easy to wonder if he would ever play in the big leagues, so he wondered what else was out there. He had already found the answer in the clouds.

War was in the air when Billy joined Toronto in spring 1940. Canada was already in the war against Germany. The Battle of Britain raged from summer into the fall. Canadian boys all hated the Hun with a passion, and tales from World War I fathers sprinkled the countryside. The stories of Billy senior's childhood with Eddie Rickenbacker planted firmly in Billy junior's consciousness years earlier came home to roost. Baseball had always been his love, but the war was coming, and if American boys were naïve about its inevitability, the Canadians were not. Billy junior saw and sensed it before other American ballplayers his age. Here was Billy, so close to the big leagues he could almost count the money, hitting .280 in his 15-game look with the baseball Maple Leafs, instead being lured to fight the war in the sky because Connie Mack dumped him all the way back to the Interstate League.

Billy heard the war calling. The ballpark in Toronto was located near a Royal Canadian Air Force field where prospective fighter pilots took Initial Training School. While Billy took batting practice or patrolled the outfield during games, pilots training in Tiger Moth, Stearman, or Fleet Finch biplanes buzzed overhead and then graduated to the monoplane Harvard trainers. Billy spent a lot of time with his neck kinked to the sky. But when he heard the Spitfires, something changed.

Nothing sounded as good as a Spitfire. Sometimes they would fly low near the ballpark, flaps down, gliding home. Other times they would open throttle at treetop level and could be heard for miles around. Pretty soon, Billy stopped thinking about hitting fastballs and starting thinking about chasing Germans. This was part of his boyhood mythos, his having been reared on tales his daddy told him about Rickenbacker, and now it was Billy's turn to throw his hat into the ring.

The lusty growl of the Spitfire's supercharged Merlin engine seduced him. The Spitfire was the Joe DiMaggio of British pursuit fighters—long and elegant, streamlined, it made everything look easy, and once Billy saw and heard the Spitfires, he dreamed of becoming a pursuit pilot and thought his life had a higher purpose than playing baseball. His time and place called for more than balls and strikes and after 62 games in Wilmington in 1940 Billy decided the bush leagues were a dead end.

Airplanes called to many ballplayers of Billy's age like a siren song, the generation of boys reared on tales of World War I flying aces, chance encounters with barnstorming and mail pilots when they were kids, and Lindbergh's flight across the Atlantic. Ballplayers, especially hitters, were natural candidates for flying—they had good hand-eye coordination, excellent vision, and superior athletic ability, and they were hotly competitive, well conditioned, and suited for the hostile environments and physical rigors of military combat aviation. Like the best of the aces, they possessed a fierce desire to win in one-on-one combat. That was the mark of excellence shared by the good pilots and the good ballplayers alike.

With the Spitfires swirling and Europe burning, Billy inched closer to his decision. That off-season, he thought hard about quitting baseball. This was a huge decision and one not immediately understood by his father, the baseball lifer who had spent so much time grooming his son to follow in his own hard-earned footsteps. Their conversations are lost to time, but it is not hard to imagine Billy senior's initial hesitation or even disagreement with his son.

Billy junior was close to the big leagues, and in the winter of 1940, with thousands of minor leaguers clamoring to get a chance on one of the sixteen major league clubs, even getting close was no easy feat. Billy had certainly seen the struggles his father endured in his own baseball career and had to appreciate the risk he was taking if he quit baseball now. America wasn't even in the war, and Hank Greenberg was several months away from being drafted. There was no rush for Billy to give up baseball, but he wanted to, and that was evident. He was making a career choice—flying airplanes versus playing baseball. And he was only twenty-three. Billy senior would surely have warned him that if he quit playing now, and America got into the war, he might never get a second chance. If he did survive, his playing career would almost surely be gone, the window to succeed as a major leaguer closed.

But what Billy senior might not have understood was that in teaching his son the Cardinal way of playing baseball, he had also taught his boy how to think like a pilot. Just as a hitter must know how to execute in a certain situation, so, too, must a pilot. A ballplayer must know his body. A pilot must know his plane. A ballplayer must be disciplined and controlled in the face of adversity, as a pursuit pilot should be.

And perhaps Billy senior could have thought back to those long-ago days in the streets of Columbus, when he and Eddie pushed their Soap Box Derby racers to the edge of their rickety limits, trying to win, trying to be the best. Billy senior had always strove to implant his competitive spirit in his son, and here it was manifesting itself with a stick and a rudder instead of a bat and a ball. It wouldn't have been hard for Billy senior to spot the dashing in his son and think, just for a moment, just maybe, *Dammit, he reminds me of Rick.* You could almost imagine Billy junior leaning against the fuselage of a Spitfire.

Then there was something else, a common fear among all parents in the coming years, that of letting a beloved child go to war, especially the only child from a deceased mother. Billy senior had been through the first war, and the guys who were old enough to remember the Great War sensed the Americans would be in this one, too, even if they were late to the party as they had been the last time around. No parents wanted to see their children go, but they would, and they did. Maybe that hurt Billy senior the most—not that his son was giving up his chance to play in the majors, but that he was doing it to fight a war. Billy senior knew it was his son's decision, and how could he be critical of his son for following his heart and convictions, and making what he felt was the right choice, even if it was not the easy choice?

Billy junior made his mind up in December 1940 when he enlisted in the Army Air Corps and began flight training at Parks Air College in East St. Louis. The story was big news around the country: son of the Cardinals manager, probable future major leaguer, gives it all up to train for the coming war. He was the first notable minor leaguer to quit playing baseball to join the military. The story was a sign of things to come, but at the time, most people didn't read it that way. A quote from Billy senior that hinted at his reluctance, offering a small window into those private conversations: "It looks to me like he's passing up a swell chance to go places." Billy junior's heart was already in the cockpit, and though he still loved baseball, the father could tell his son had chosen a different path. "I am certain I have made the wisest choice," Billy junior told news reporters. "I'm rarin' to start Army flying."

Before Billy junior left, his father had one request. He wanted the two to remain as close as they possibly could. Billy junior knew it wouldn't be easy, but like other war sons, he vowed to write plenty of letters home, especially after he shipped out. Billy senior was rightfully worried. He had seen World War I permanently change some of the ballplayers he knew, especially pitcher Pete Alexander, his teammate on the '26 Cardinals, who came back from the Western Front a shelled and scarred man who was a fragment of his former self. Billy junior wanted to fly single-seat pursuit planes and flame the Germans, but his father sensed that his son had no idea what he was really asking for. When the reporters asked Billy senior what he thought of his son's decision, he absolutely refused to criticize his son, but the best he could offer was the lukewarm "I'm pretty much sold on Army aviation myself now."

Billy senior's boy was a man now, and if this was what he wanted to do, this was what he would do. Who was his father to stop the whims of a twenty-three-year-old? How could Billy senior criticize his son for putting his country over his baseball career? Isn't that what Billy senior's parents, and Rickenbacker's family for that matter, had taught him all those years ago in Columbus? Billy Jr.'s future seemed so secure with baseball in it. But then again, no baseball future was written in stone anymore, was it? Billy senior knew baseball was going to change gradually now, one player, one person, one team, and one family at a time. He had no idea what baseball in World War II was going to look like, but he couldn't imagine its being very perfect, not if an entire generation of boys like his son were willing to walk away from the major leagues. The war was coming. How long it would take, the father did not know. Where it would take his son, he also did not know. Billy senior knew the moment his son walked onto the airfield that the war for both father and son had just begun. The father would worry each and every day about his son, even as he tried to manage the Cardinals back to the World Series.

CHAPTER 4

War!

On Sunday morning December 7, something was wrong. Eight minutes into the first quarter of the Washington Redskins football game at Griffith Stadium in DC, emergency requests for Pentagon and War Department officials from the Army and Navy were announced over the public address system. In the press box, sportswriters were told to keep their game stories short because big news was coming. Getting sportswriters to shut up for a few minutes was no easy feat, but there was good reason. The Pearl Harbor bulletins reached the press midway through the first half, but the Redskins decided not to announce it to the crowd for fear of panicking the fans. One reporter remembered finding out when his wife wired him in the press box, WAR WITH JAPAN.

When the game was over, the 27,102 fans hit the streets and heard what the rest of the country had been hearing on the radio. The Japanese surprise attack on Pearl Harbor inflicted heavy damage and casualties. Americans were stunned and outraged. Among the burned bodies and burning battleships was a baseball field riddled with bullet holes and bomb craters. When the Japanese fighter pilots covering the dive-bombers met no American planes rising to challenge their attack, the fighters dropped to treetop level and hunted for easy targets. The baseball field at Hickam Field, set just aside from the flight line, was raked. A *Christian Science Monitor* story reported, "The heaviest concentration of bomb craters is on the baseball diamond, which apparently was mistaken for buried water or oil storage." Nobody knew if the Japanese intentionally flamed the baseball field, but a lot of people took it personally anyhow. A shot-up baseball field seemed like an insignificant loss, but not one lacking symbolic damage to American society and pride. The Japanese pilots had unknowingly poked the Americans anew. The Yanks were at war with Japan, and soon, baseball was, too.

The bombs were felt in Chicago at the winter meetings. The titans in baseball power began preparing for war when the Selective Services Act took effect in October 1940, but the baseball owners did not know how to prepare for a crisis they had no idea of how to anticipate or manage. In 1940, baseball people wondered how the draft would affect the sport, but they were sure it was going to eventually damage the quality of the game. Every player had a number of factors to determine his war worthiness. Suddenly, every ballplayer's personal information was as important as his baseball statistics. Was he married, did he have children, would he be excused for a physical deficiency, would he be allowed to serve in the off-season only or would he be gone for the duration of the war? What would happen to the 1942 baseball season? While Pearl Harbor burned, the owners feared their business would go up in smoke along with it. "These ifs," *The Sporting News* wrote, "rest in the laps of the gods."

The ear of God was pressed to the radio on the afternoon of December 7 at the Chicago Palmer House. All eyes were firmly placed on Judge Kenesaw Mountain Landis. He listened carefully to the news bulletins coming out of Honolulu. His face was etched with concern and worry. Owners, writers, and fans always looked to his wise old face for guidance and security, but for the first time anybody could remember, Judge Landis looked as angry, terrified, and confused as any ordinary man.

Landis was the first baseball commissioner. He was also the last commissioner the owners would ever fear. He ruled the game like a czar and made it clear that while he worked for the owners, he would not hasten to discipline them if he felt their actions were detrimental to what he termed "the best interests of the game." At the age of seventy-five in 1941, his shaggy hair was still as white as marble columns, but he was showing his age and vulnerability. Having been sick for weeks when he pulled himself out of bed to preside over the winter meetings, he expected business as usual and instead got the greatest crisis of his baseball career, surpassing even the 1919

World Series scandal. Landis rose to power in 1920, appointed from the federal bench in the wake of the Black Sox scandal, and since that time, he had dictated the momentum, direction, and shape of baseball, treating it as an American institution to be protected by his guidance. Landis had no fear of disciplining owners or players and acted with complete authority. He banished players and he also liberated them. When he listened to the news from Pearl Harbor, he knew this war would not permit him to act as autonomously as he usually operated. Millions of voices were involved, not just his. He knew at some point that he was going to have to do what he hated most. He was going to have to contact the White House.

Landis huddled next to the radio with William Harridge, the president of the American League, and William G. Branham, president of the National Association, the governing body of the minor leagues. They looked to Landis for wisdom, but like other Americans, the Judge was shocked and could not readily develop his thoughts. Nobody knew what he was thinking. Landis could always speak like a street-tough Chicagoan, so the best he could offer was a ragged and rugged denouncement of Japanese aggression. "Don't it beat hell," he finally groused. "They attacked us without warning as they did the Russians years ago."

Reporters circled Landis, but he gave them nothing. Landis was always accessible, but he generally liked to stonewall the press. He believed it was his charter to stay out of the papers, even though he never seemed to miss a good photo opportunity. "I won't comment until I have more information," he snapped. "I have been ill and am trying to pull myself together." Landis retreated to his room, but the reporters tailed him. They believed baseball's future was in his hands, but for the first time Landis didn't have a clear vision. His elusiveness was telling. His uncertainty made baseball owners nervous. He was asked what would happen to baseball during the war. "No one can even guess," he said. "I would be going way out on a limb if I ventured an opinion."

When the Judge wouldn't offer a definitive answer, Harridge tried to soothe the owners. That was like the second-stringer trying to put the crowd at ease. Predictably, it lacked the desired effect. "While the nation's welfare is our first concern and we will do whatever is desired by the government, I am sure baseball will carry on as it always has—completing its 1942 schedule and those of other years," he said. The baseball writers knew Harridge was stalling. How could baseball plan a season schedule if the government and the military had jurisdiction over the players, ballparks, and transportation? "This is baseball's dark hour, with the impact of the war clouding the game's future," Shirley Povich correctly wrote in the *Washington Post*. "If you miss your baseball next summer, that's another item you can blame on the Japanese."

Immediately after the declaration of war on December 8, the age limit of twenty-eight for draftees was revoked. That meant just about every major league baseball player was subject to the draft. It also meant that the first wave of big league ballplayers who were already classified 1-A, registered with low draft call numbers, and fit for duty, such as Hank Greenberg and third baseman Buddy Lewis and shortstop Cecil Travis of the Washington Senators, would be among the first called to duty. In the days immediately following Pearl Harbor, baseball players of all ages and talent levels across the country suddenly saw their futures change by the hour. Ballplayers stopped seeing themselves as ballplayers first; rather, in the spirit of what amounted to an American youth movement to get into the war and win it, they saw themselves as excited warriors ready to do battle. They found a new hero in an old one. The first ballplayer to step forward after the war began was the one who had been drafted first.

When Hank Greenberg walked out of Fort Custer, Michigan, on December 5, 1941, two days before Pearl Harbor, he felt the pain of a bad toothache, but carried a wide smile. His seven-month hitch with the Army was over. He was a proud but altogether weary veteran of the Fifth Division, Second Infantry Anti-Tank Company. The Tigers couldn't wait to get him back in the lineup in 1942. Without his home-run power, the Tigers had fallen all the way from winning the pennant to fourth place, 26 hopeless games behind the Yankees. The writers wanted to know how Army life had treated Hank. He could have joked that his root canal was the result of eating Army chow, but big Hank was too big of a guy for that. He was, after all, proud of his service, but it had taught him that he never wanted to be a foot soldier again. When he was asked if he could still hit the way he did in the old days, Hank beamed and said, "If it weren't for the tooth, I'd be in one hundred percent shape."

Hank came out of the Army in great physical shape, but it wasn't baseball condition. A lot of people expected Hank to go into the Army and just play service ball games for the entertainment of the troops, but he thought playing Army ball to get out of hard work would make him a fraud. When he was offered chances to swing the bat, he decided not to because there was no good competition that could keep him sharp. He was convinced that such superficial service would have wasted his time and embarrassed him.

One of his fondest memories was a spring march through Cincinnati, where residents lined the streets to hand the sweltering soldiers mugs of cold beer that the troops chugged as they marched. The troops were on their way South to war games. Hank, born in the Bronx and a city boy all the way, had never walked so far in his life. His flat feet had to be killing him, but he never complained. He was already used to rural Southerners alarmed at the sight of a six-foot-four Jew. If some education was required on their part, Hank was happy to quietly dispense such wisdom far away from public eyes. The superior officers were astounded at how a guy with such money, fame, talent, and prestige could be so modest, going about his business as though he were just another poor bum drafted into the Army business.

Everyone who encountered Hank in the Army usually had a good story to tell about him, and it always had nothing to do with baseball. A career officer vividly remembered one episode, after Hank had finished the march to Alabama for training and his unit was camped in the sweltering summer heat in Tuscaloosa: "I was standing in a clump of woods on one of the hottest afternoons I ever saw in my life, watching some troops from the Middle West work out a tactical problem. There was a mortar detachment just ahead of me, and I walked up to look their emplacement over while waiting for the real show to start. Just as I came abreast of 'em, I heard the sergeant say, 'I don't like it. I'm afraid, for all this work, we've got it too close to the road. I'm afraid the umpires will say we can't fully control that crossroads from here. Let's dig it up and put it about one hundred feet up that hill. If we hurry, we can get it done in time!'

"'Okay, Sarge,' a husky voice responded from underneath the leafy camouflage the crew had pulled over the gun. A cigarette butt came spinning through the air, and out from under that brush crawled the biggest, the sweatiest, and the most tired-looking soldier that I ever saw in my life. A half dozen other fellows followed him. They began to dig and shove and lift, and with the big fellow's shoulders doing most of the pushing, they bunted and bucked the thing up the hill with the pick and shovel, hastily filling the new position.

"Another officer came by about then and we were discussing the change—which, incidentally, was an intelligent one—and he said, 'Do you know who that big soldier is?' I told him I didn't. He said, 'That's Hank Greenberg, the ballplayer!'"

Hank Greenberg was a ballplayer again on Saturday, December 6. He was single but discreet, and there was always a lady in his life. On his first night of freedom from the Army, he took the company of his date and thought not of Army life, baseball life, or the war. Some nights, a guy just had to be a guy.

That night, owners and general managers at the winter meetings weren't expecting anything out of the ordinary on December 7. Though they were worried, war planning never entered their thinking. They were baseball men and they knew only baseball. Sure, Selective Service would probably take a few players here and there, but, look, a guy like Hank was already on his way back to the Tigers, how bad could it be? As long as there were good ballplayers and the fans to pay to see them, all would be business as usual. They wanted to talk trades, buy and sell ballplayers, light cigars and smoke, drink and banter. Those were the perks of their lives as baseball executives, all expenses paid. The big rumor in town was that the Cardinals and the Dodgers were talking about a blockbuster trade to send Johnny Mize to the Dodgers for Dolph Camilli and the rich sum of $65,000. The other vague rumor in the lobby of the Palmer House was that the St. Louis Browns, long the doormat of the American League, wanted to move to Los Angeles. The owners and executives laughed out loud at the Browns. How would you transport teams from coast to coast in a timely, cost-efficient manner? The Browns were twelve years ahead of the Boston Braves leaving for Milwaukee and seventeen years in front of the Dodgers and Giants abandoning New York, but on the first night of Hank Greenberg's freedom, the only worry in the house was making sure there were enough matches for the cigars.

Then the world commenced burning on Sunday morning. The flames spread all across the country, curling the edges of ballplayers, who never saw it coming. Hank Greenberg's exit from the Army did not last long. When he heard the news, he was moved to action. He was on reserve and knew damn well he was going to be called back soon, so he decided not to wait. He could not see the value in returning to baseball in the time of need, nor could he stomach the idea of another hasty departure from the game he loved. So once more, he made the tough decision look easy. The day after Pearl Harbor, Hank enlisted on his own. He was never trying to become a role model, but in doing what he knew was right, he became a greater hero than he ever thought he was. "I have not been called back," Hank said. "I'm going back of my own accord. We are in trouble and it is the only thing to do."

Hank's words were a call to action for young men everywhere, but it wasn't the only option he had. He had served 180 days and earned sergeant's stripes. He could have gone back to the Tigers and awaited recall, hit that 250th career home run in 1942, put a few more home runs next to his name, cashed a few more paychecks, and everyone would have called him patriotic. He was a huge star and nobody would have blamed him, but when Hank made up his mind, there was no changing it. He could not find the practical value in delaying the inevitable.

And he wanted to leave right away for another reason. Hank never forgot the resentment he felt in 1940 when he was first classified ineligible for the draft. When he enlisted after Pearl Harbor, he did it because he wanted to cut off the head of the snake. Hank carried a personal vow that when his time came to fight for something bigger than baseball, bigger even than himself, he was going to do it. He didn't give a damn how many home runs or how much money it cost him to do the right thing. He cared about his pride, and he was a good son who wanted to make his family proud. "I came to feel that if as a Jew I hit a home run, I was hitting one against Hitler," he once said.

When he reenlisted, nobody dared criticize him again. The silence was rewarding. Hank always knew that if he stood up to bigotry, he'd always come out on top. That fueled his motivation to return immediately after Pearl Harbor. *The Sporting News* wrote, "Hank completely silenced his critics, not only by performing his duties like a good soldier, but by voicing his intention to return to the Army voluntarily after his recent release."

Hank was in control of his Army career this time and had the power to change something he couldn't when he was drafted. Having served in the infantry and experienced the muck and grime, he decided to join the

Army Air Corps. He wanted to serve with the airplane crews, not the rifle squads. Hank Greenberg looked to the sky, and though he might never say it often during the war, as a Jewish boy from the Bronx, he would be damned if he would go to sleep under a Nazi moon and wake beneath a Rising Sun.

When Hank announced his decision, the baseball writers wanted to know if he was willing to accept the possibility that this time his career might really be over. Hank grimly acknowledged the possibility, but he was willing to accept his career as a casualty. "This doubtless means I am finished with baseball," he said. You could almost feel his heart breaking before composing himself again. "But all of us are confronted with a terrible task: the defense of our country and the fight for our lives."

Bob Feller was not interested in backing down from the fight. He was driving on a country road in Iowa on the way to sign his contract for the 1942 season when the Pearl Harbor news came over the radio. Feller did not hesitate. He spun his convertible into a U-turn and headed home. He remembered this moment for years to come, never forgetting the terrible fear of war on the doorstep and the overwhelming resolve to join the fight. Feller's sense of patriotism and action was as heated as his fastball, which by the age of twenty-two had made him the most intimidating right-handed starting pitcher in baseball. "I thought we were losing," Feller said. Years later, it was fitting that he wasn't thinking about his own wins and losses. "You see what you can do. You got to get going to protect your country."

Feller took action with little regard to how he would protect his arm and his future. He would enlist first and worry later. He was an unmatched workhorse in the time of the durable pitcher, leading the American League in victories, innings pitched, and strikeouts from age twenty in 1939 to age twenty-two in 1941. Nobody threw a fastball harder than Feller, but what made him dominant was the hard, sharp, late-breaking, swing-and-miss curveball. Hank Greenberg hated facing Feller. On days Feller had his curveball going, the game was over before it started.

Feller hoped he would still be good when the war was over, even though he was eight years younger than Greenberg. He had won 107 games and struck out 1,233 batters in the six years since he broke in as a seventeen-year old rookie with the Cleveland Indians. He was a three-time 20-game winner. Without the war, he was young enough to make a run at 300 wins and 3,000 strikeouts. He knew some of these milestones were going to go by the wayside, but how long would the war last? Would it be a year, two, three, four, five, or even six? That was a lifetime for a ballplayer, eternity on the line.

Feller worried about losing the war before it started. He enlisted in the Navy in a highly publicized ceremony on December 8. Feller, like Greenberg, had the popularity to stay at home and pitch for the people, but he wasn't interested. He was classified 3-C as the sole supporter of his family because of his father's terminal cancer. Feller could have stayed with the Indians and pitched for the $32,500 he made in 1941, but the money did not motivate him. Pride did.

Feller was as combative off the field as he was on it. The fighting words spilled out of him, and at that moment he was not a star pitcher, he was just another angry young American kid who wanted to take on the enemy by himself. When he was an old man, he was still fighting mad: "We wanted to take those guys on and beat the living hell out of them, and I wanted to be a part of that."

Sworn in by Lieutenant Commander Gene Tunney, the retired boxing champion, Feller's oath was broadcast over national radio waves and filmed by newsreel crews. The staged photo of his induction was published in every newspaper in the country. You couldn't miss Feller, decked out in a pristine pinstripe suit and a colorful silk tie, standing in front of a big American flag, accepting his duty with a devilish little smirk. He traded his princely salary for $89 a month. Feller knew he was the best recruiter the Navy ever hired. He was a born salesman who believed it was his duty to encourage other boys to get with the program. He pitched the war as if it were the biggest game of his life and immediately recognized the connection between sacrificing playing baseball and motivating the country. When the microphones were on him, he eagerly announced three lines, beamed into living rooms around the country like bullets across the outside corner: "I am glad to make whatever sacrifice is necessary. We've got to win this war to keep baseball on the map. I'm jumping in to help people wake up." The Navy loved this guy.

Feller kept a 12-gauge in the trunk of his car and boasted that he had better control with a shotgun than he did with his fastball. Judging by the number of his walks, he was probably right. But it was also an extension of his personality, the same combativeness hitters feared. Feller was living his words when he said, "I'm glad to make whatever sacrifice it may be. We've all got to sacrifice from now on."

Feller possessed a very real sense of revenge and hatred for the enemy. They had attacked his nation and robbed him of his precious innings, and by God, if they were going to steal years away from his pitching career, he was going to make the bastards suffer. There was no mistaking that Feller wanted to get behind the barrel of a gun battery, and he had no qualms about devising creative ways to stay in shape, even if it meant playing catch on the deck of a destroyer.

Feller reported to the Norfolk Naval Training Station and quickly devised his plan. He was going to fight, of that much he was certain. But he was going to keep his moneymaker in shape while he was in service. That was part of his reasoning behind joining the Navy, which led the way in recruiting athletes from different sports to lead physical fitness details and put on exhibitions for soldiers and sailors. The Navy offered the best service ball teams. Feller recognized early on that as an athlete he had to fight a personal two-front war: one to fight, and one to stay in shape while he fought. He talked about whipping the Japanese while keeping his whip in working order.

Feller set an example for scores of ballplayers who wanted to find ways to keep playing baseball even as they risked everything. They followed Feller and Greenberg, willing to sacrifice not only their careers but their lives, even if they privately hated the idea of losing out on some of their best years of athleticism and surrendering nice salaries for puny war wages. They would perform their duty and hope that they did not lose everything they once were.

Greenberg and Feller were symbolic as baseball's early wartime fighters, connected in the public memory the way Eisenhower and Patton would become later in the war. From day one of the war effort, baseball and victory were connected, and Greenberg and Feller were leading the charge. While the boys marched away, the baseball industry followed two of its biggest stars to war. Then on December 11, Adolf Hitler declared war, and when he did, he declared war on baseball, and the American way of life.

When Nazi Germany declared war on the United States, baseball fit into everything Hitler hated about America. For years, the Nazis had been using baseball as an example of why the Americans were an inferior culture and society. At the 1936 Berlin Olympics, when baseball was a demonstration sport, the quality of play was so rough that an entire generation of Germans came of age believing the Americans were as stupid as baseball. A crowd of one hundred thousand came to see the game, but by the second inning, the Germans, in the words of reporter Grantland Rice, were "bored, dazed, baffled, and thought it terrible."

When fans started leaving the stadium, the Germans enticed the crowd to stay by announcing that a marching display would take place at the end of the game. The only time the Germans cheered was when men went sliding into the bases, but the overall concepts of balls, strikes, outs, innings, singles, doubles, triples, home runs, bases on balls, strikeouts, errors, and wild pitches were completely foreign to the nationalistic German audience. The American ballplayers were nobody special, not professionals, and for some reason weren't good college players, either. The crowd was thought to be the largest to see a baseball game in world history. Rice called the event "a complete flop," and the memory stayed in the collective German consciousness as an example of the American dullards. The fans, however, loved the goose-step drills and lustily saluted the brownshirts marching in unison, the sound of their boots much more rewarding to the Nazis than the crack of the bat on the ball.

Hitler wasn't much of a sports fan when he first came to power, but had been convinced that athletics had a place in his ideology at the Berlin Olympics. But Hitler saw baseball as a gypsy of a sport, played by the dirty blood of Europe, something invented by the British, played by the Irish, copied and transposed to America, then venerated as a team sport played by filthy immigrants. That was the crux of his argument against the Americans: Hitler thought baseball was a game played by a lower-class people, the steerage of society, who did not conform to his ideals. Hitler believed that athletics could help build an army of men molded in the master-race image, so for the most part the Nazis exalted individual sports, such as fencing, boxing, equestrianism, and running. The only team sport was soccer, where Hitler's team wasn't quite as good as Mussolini's.

When the Olympics ended, the Nazi's use of baseball to denigrate the United States continued into the 1940s. At institutions of higher learning all around Germany, including Heidelberg University, courses studying American government, culture, and society used major league baseball as an example of its flaws. The Nazis believed that the reserve clause of the major leagues, which permitted major league owners to control players as property in perpetuity, was proof that slavery still existed in the United States. The Nazis also pointed to the hypocrisy of the segregation of American baseball, asking why such a democratic and free state celebrated a game that rigidly imposed racial superiority.

CHAPTER 5

The Green Light

Pete Gray wanted to fight back. He thought of himself as just another young ballplayer willing to sacrifice for the greater good when he decided he would quit baseball to join the Army. The coal miners in town were fuming hot at the Pearl Harbor attack and ready to get into the war. Pete wanted to join them, and a few days later he was standing in a long line of eager recruits at his local recruiting station. When his turn finally came to remove his shirt, the Army doctor sized him up the same way baseball scouts did— no arm, no chance. Go home.

The Army rejected Pete despite his vocal objections. He was embarrassed and angry, turned away in front of everyone he knew, discarded as a cripple, humiliated to hear Uncle Sam say he was garbage because he had one arm. He was hurt and sullen, excluded again, banned from his generation's great call to action.

The Army refused to take any man missing an arm or a leg. Pete didn't know about regulations and didn't care. He grew testy when he sensed discrimination. His Army rejection only diminished his already thin patience for anything he deemed derogatory. "I never deserved the 4-F classification," he steamed years later. "If I could teach myself how to play baseball with one arm, I sure as hell could handle a rifle."

Pete's disdain for his 4-F classification spoke volumes about how he viewed himself. He never thought of himself as handicapped. His best friend was also his worst enemy, a stubbornness that belonged with the greats, unwilling to accept anyone else's definition of his limitations. He knew he would have to find another way to fight the war, but he didn't know how. He had no idea where he was going to play in 1942, or if there would even be a bush league for him to play in. All around the country, teams were disbanding as players rushed to enlist. He hated the feeling of being left behind.

The major leagues were well aware that the hundreds of minor league teams and thousands of semipro teams were watching their rosters of young players dry up. The majors saw a looming manpower crisis, but they could not put their business model above the nation's war effort. So in the hours after Pearl Harbor, baseball decided to act, even if it could not know for certain what the future held. Team owners awaited clarification from Judge Landis about the course of the game's future, but knew it was bad business to do nothing.

The driving force behind baseball's early war drive was Clark Griffith, the owner of the Washington Senators. Griffith knew his way around wartime baseball. During World War I, he'd organized baseball's war-bond drives, equipment drives, and encouraged his players to serve the country. Griffith was also a good organizer, and in those early days after Pearl Harbor, his fingerprints were firmly stamped on baseball's first response to World War II.

Baseball committed $25,000 to a ball-and-bat fund for Army and Navy outfits and promised to raise $100,000 more at the All-Star Game in July. Baseball vowed to use all its promotional power to raise money by selling war bonds and committed its ballplayers to public relations. The ballplayers were as much a wartime resource as steel, wood, nylon, and rubber, which promised to be in such short supply that actually manufacturing baseballs consistent with prewar standards might prove difficult. From now on, fans would be asked to return foul balls for the good of the war effort, rather than take them home as lucky souvenirs. Even if you could find new baseballs, who was going to be left at home to play the game? Where would the fans come from?

In those dark and terrifying early days, ideas were forming about baseball's part in the war effort. Cardinal general manager Branch Rickey never missed a chance to blow into the wind. "Our entire country is war-minded," he said. "I feel our people will need diversion, normal relaxation, and out-door recreation while we are at war. While our boys are fighting for de-mocracy, we should not overlook the stay-at-homes. Industries are booming. Thousands and thousands are moving from rural districts to larger cities. Sports should play an important part while this war is going on. We must do our part in keeping up the spirit of the non-fighting class."

Rickey's statement in the January 1, 1942, *Sporting News* was the clear-est statement yet on the meaning, power, direction, and role of baseball during the war. He was prophetic, envisioning massive geographical mi-grations and manpower shortages reconfiguring baseball for decades to come. It would not only take the best players from the game today, but the boys leaving would return as washed-up warriors, and then the game would re-quire new talent. Many ballplayers would miss starting their professional careers entirely. They would be playing softball when the war ended. Rickey asked himself the fundamental question that led him to integrate baseball five years later: Where were new ballplayers going to come from? But be-fore any of that could happen, baseball had to soldier on in 1942.

Rickey indirectly helped build baseball's wartime manpower supply when he created the massive Cardinals farm system in the 1920s and 1930s. By the time the war started, his format had been copied throughout base-ball. By 1939, the Cardinals had twenty-eight minor league teams, twice as many as its closest competitor, the Brooklyn Dodgers. In the American League, the Cleveland Indians had seventeen minor league teams and the Yankees had sixteen. Professional baseball participation experienced a marked upswing in the years leading up to the war. In 1939, the year the war be-gan in Europe, American boys were lining up to play pro ball.

The boys going to war grew up in the 1930s, when the Depression made work tough to find. They wanted baseball jobs and knew how to pay their dues. They hustled through tryout camps and baseball camps desperate to hook on to a paying playing job and signed minuscule contracts at unpre-cedented rates. For five consecutive seasons, the number of active players on the minor league baseball reserved list spiked, peaking at a new high of 4,357 in 1939. The forty-one minor leagues ranged from Class AA to Class D, the very top to the very bottom rungs of the minor league ladder. Mi-nor league teams were in virtually every town in America, with twenty-one Class D leagues, which was entry-level professional baseball. Thousands of the first waves of American volunteers came from the low minor leagues and semipro leagues. These were ballplayers nobody ever heard of. When they vacated, those leagues were shut down. When the owners in the majors observed this begin after Pearl Harbor, they trembled. If the minors could go out of business, perhaps they could, too.

Before the war started, nobody realized that baseball players provided a ready-made army of tough kids well adjusted to doing a different kind of battle. As America prepared to raise a new army to fight a new war, the future fighting boys had been bred on baseball. Their worldview was shaped by years of scraping away in the low minors, toiling on dusty diamonds instead of in coal mines or on farms. They knew how to work hard, asked for no favors, and understood performance ensured survival. They saw themselves in Hank Greenberg and Bob Feller, but still, they waited to hear from Judge Landis. His silence was long, worrisome, and, worst of all, completely unlike him. Through December, he stayed in seclusion, making no public statements. He pondered the future of baseball and shared his thoughts with nobody. His winter of silence confused and conflicted everyone in baseball, from the wealthiest owner to the lowliest minor leaguer. Finally, with the first month of the war going poorly for the Americans and making it obvious that this was to be a long engagement against formidable enemies on many fronts, and with spring training looming a month away, Landis moved.

He was aware that his age and health would make this the most significant decision of his final years, one that would conclude his career. On one end of the Judge's docket were the eight White Sox players banned for life for fixing the 1919 World Series. On the other would be how he handled baseball during World War II. Landis realized that it was a larger decision than for his office alone. A man of action, he recognized that baseball's role in the war effort must be dictated by the federal government. That was how it worked in World War I, and that, he reasoned, was how it should work in World War II. To gain the required guidance to lead his game, Landis knew the time had come to do something he didn't want to do. He had to get involved in Washington politics, though he preferred not to get his hands dirty. Landis despised politicians, though many would have called him one of the greatest politicians ever to rule the game. Landis, a man of ego, went right to the top. He wrote a letter to President Franklin D. Roosevelt.

Landis wasn't interested in working out baseball's problems through the newspapers and didn't want to talk to Roosevelt's staff, either. He didn't care if the president didn't call him, but he wanted a directive from Roosevelt himself, not a statement from his office.

Everybody knew that it took a lot of guts for Landis to swallow his disgust for Roosevelt. The Judge was a hard-right conservative Republican who loathed Roosevelt's New Deal Democratic policies. Their disagreements were plainly visible over the years. Once at the 1933 World Series, Roosevelt and Landis were in box seats a few feet away from each other, yet clearly went out of their way to avoid one another. Baseball people loved to have their picture taken with Roosevelt. Not Landis. He didn't want any connection of his office to the president's, and he certainly didn't want to muddy his hands with this "socialist" Democrat. But other than that, he loved the guy.

Such pride Landis must have swallowed when he put pencil to paper on January 14, 1942. The Judge wrote with broad, sloppy, sharp strokes; you could feel the animosity coming out of his hand. But in this crisis was something amazing. Landis decided that what was best for the entire country was more important than his personal and political beliefs. So he wrote:

> *Dear Mr. President,*
>
> *The time is approaching when, in ordinary conditions, our teams would be heading for spring training camps. However, inasmuch as these are not ordinary times, I venture to ask what you have in mind as to whether professional baseball should continue to operate. Of course my inquiry does not relate at all to individual members of this organization, whose status, in the emergency, is fixed by law operating upon all citizens.*
>
> *Normally we have, in addition to the sixteen major teams, approximately three hundred and twenty minor teams—members of leagues playing in the United States and Canada.*
>
> *Health and strength to you—and whatever else it takes to do this job.*
>
> *With great respect*
> *Very truly yours,*
> *Kenesaw M. Landis*

Landis's offer was monumental and significant and unparalleled in base-ball history. He was willing to shut down all sixteen major league teams and all minor league teams at the same time. By essentially firing every single player signed to a professional contract at any level in baseball, Landis would have handed all manpower to the draft and war effort immediately. He was willing to do so without regard to baseball's business interests, which meant he was volunteering to shut down the game without the owners' permission. Landis's suggestion was unthinkable at any other time in the game's history, except for the outbreak of the war. He would close the gates, moth-ball the ballparks, and baseball would not take a dime during the war if Roosevelt wanted it that way. It was a grave, courageous, selfless offer by a son of the old Republic whose name was taken from a Civil War battle-field, the Republican who disliked the president so much that he never once willingly permitted himself to be photographed with the Democrat from New York, to shut down his entire industry if the president he so strongly disliked told him so.

When the letter reached Roosevelt's desk, his first thought was to let baseball temporarily sunset so the country could focus on the war effort. Roosevelt's thoughts were far from baseball in the early days of the war. Hundreds of items crossed his desk daily. He was adjusting to the pace of life of a wartime president and the maddening, stomach-churning stress. Every industry was downsizing and contributing its best talent to the war effort. Roosevelt initially thought baseball wasn't important enough to keep alive, but he was forgetting that he had the soul of a fan. At first glance, saving baseball wasn't as important as building the war machine. The game's well-paid athletes would survive and would eventually be drafted anyhow.

But somewhere in Roosevelt's inner thoughts was the image of sus-pending the games and shutting down every ballpark in America. That didn't sit right with him. There were practical reasons, yes, but there were also sentimental reasons. Shutting down baseball would be like taking a dream away from a kid. For some of the boys under fire, their survival and nar-row life experiences would be fiercely connected to baseball. Shouldn't all Americans have a reminder of what they were fighting for? Wasn't it his job to help motivate them? Roosevelt's thoughts began to sway. He wondered if shutting down baseball would do more harm than good. He knew better than anyone else how long this war was going to take, and he knew there would be massive redistributions of population and resources. He thought people needed something to watch to relax and enjoy. He understood that the war was going to have to be won at home *and* on the road, but he needed to find a way to do this without appearing to compromise the overall commitments and sacrifices made by the rest of the nation.

Roosevelt was conflicted but concluded that he did not want to take baseball from the American people during the war. But he also resented that one industry alone and its workers should enjoy privileges that other Americans in other occupations did not. Roosevelt was too democratic for that. He sought counsel in baseball from someone he trusted and called him.

Clark Griffith was getting his team ready for the 1942 season. He was worried because his two best hitters, Buddy Lewis and Cecil Travis, had already been inducted. But in one respect, Griffith was looking forward to the lean war years. He believed he could win multiple pennants because he thought he was more capable of doing more with less. Griffith was correct in that respect, though his players didn't think he was a genius. They just thought he was a dirt cheap, penny-pinching old man who lived in a horse-and-buggy mind-set. When word reached Griffith that Roosevelt had summoned him to the White House, Griffith didn't hesitate. The two had been friends for years. He also didn't tell the other owners he had been asked to speak to the president, and he certainly didn't care to tell Landis. The president wanted to see him personally, and this was a plum for Griffith, who saw the once-in-a-lifetime opportunity to more deeply forge his relationship with a sitting president. He also recognized that at this moment he had more power than any other owner in the history of baseball.

Griffith most assuredly grinned in pleasure. He was in his element and couldn't wait for the self-righteous anger he would accrue from the other owners. Griffith did not mind one bit, and nobody should ever have wondered why his nickname was the Old Fox.

Griffith arrived in the Oval Office to a warm welcome from the president. The Old Fox must have been a pleasant sight for old eyes. Roosevelt had plenty to worry about. German U-boats were hunting in waters off the East Coast. The Japanese offensive in the Philippines intensified with the first waves of attacks on Bataan. One of the precious few American aircraft carriers, the *Saratoga,* was crippled in a submarine attack near Hawaii. Only days before, Roosevelt had submitted his first wartime budget to Congress, a massive appropriation of $59 billion calling for the production of 60,000 planes in 1942 and 125,000 more in 1943; 45,000 tanks in 1942 and 75,000 more in 1943; 8 million tons of shipping in 1942 and 11 million tons more in 1943.

Given the huge parameters of Roosevelt's war life, something as simple as baseball must have felt insignificant. Roosevelt needed Griffith to help remind him why ordinary people wanted baseball and how the major leagues could operate in a depleted manner that would still somewhat resemble normalcy. The letter from Landis was on Roosevelt's desk when Griffith arrived. Griffith was the only person in baseball Roosevelt felt comfortable enough to trust, to welcome into his office at a time like this.

They had known each other since World War I, when Roosevelt was Assistant Secretary of the Navy and led ballplayers in marching drills across the field. Griffith had always welcomed sitting presidents to his ballpark on Opening Days. Griffith always considered Roosevelt something of a good-luck charm. Now Roosevelt needed a friend, someone he could trust, to help him sort out what to do with wartime baseball.

Their trust was formed over many April days. Roosevelt threw out the first pitch at Griffith Stadium for eight consecutive years, a record for sitting presidents. FDR always seemed so happy and jolly at ball games, and he even got to see a World Series game at Griffith Stadium in 1933, when the Senators won their only game in the Series against the New York Giants. Griffith spoke fondly and proudly of his time with the president. "I used to see Roosevelt frequently," Griffith said. "When I have gone down to the White House, no matter what administration is in office, I seem to be one of the people who can walk in at most any time."

But this time was different. This wasn't a courtesy call. It was to be a significant discussion about the future of the baseball business. Griffith long understood the value of mixing baseball, politics, and public relations. When he first became part owner of the club in 1912, he talked William Howard Taft into coming to the ballpark, and even though he didn't like baseball, he liked the food. Griffith had better luck with Woodrow Wilson, who liked to sit in his open car down the right-field line. Instead of a

Secret Service man, Griffith assigned his backup catcher to stand guard and shag any big flies before they put Wilson in harm's way. Warren G. Harding had no personality, but he kept a perfect scorecard. Herbert Hoover came once, but never came back after the fans booed the hell out of him. When Roosevelt became president, Griffith found the guy he was waiting for. He needed a president with the heart and soul of a baseball fan. It seemed so long ago now, but when Roosevelt summoned Griffith to the Oval Office to discuss the Landis letter, the old memories must have come flooding back.

Roosevelt never lost his passion for baseball, though in the early days of 1942, he might have forgotten how much he once loved the game. He wrote in 1937, "When it comes to baseball, I am the kind of fan who wants to get plenty of action for his money. I have some appreciation of a game, which is featured by a pitcher's duel and results in a score of one to nothing. But I must confess that I get the biggest kick out of the biggest score—a game in which the batters pole the ball into the far corners of the field, the outfielders scramble and men run the bases. In short, my idea of the best game is one that guarantees the fans a combined score of not less than fifteen runs, divided about eight to seven."

Roosevelt liked the big boppers—Ruth, Gehrig, Foxx, DiMaggio, Williams, and, oh, yeah, Greenberg. Griffith and FDR became good friends in the 1930s. Everyone knew it. But their discussions were always private and confidential. *The Washington Post* noted, "Griffin has worn a beaten path to the White House and the results of his labors have given to local fans the most glamorous opening days in history." Roosevelt and Griffith were synonymous with each new spring and each start of the new baseball season. "When the president flashes that million-dollar smile of his, it is bound to help my boys get off to a good start in the race for the flag," Griffith said.

Roosevelt, in turn, learned how baseball helped the morale of the people through the rough Great Depression years. He was eager to link his image to baseball. The *Post* noted, "The Nation's first baseball fan dispensed a rare presidential blessing upon the game yesterday when Franklin D. Roosevelt, manipulator of the New Deal, told Clark Griffith that baseball had done as much as any one thing to keep up the spirit of the game." It was smart politicking, smart marketing, and good old-fashioned common sense.

If people loved baseball, they ought to love the president who loved baseball, too.

Roosevelt and Griffith shared another ritual. Every April before the start of the season, Griffith visited the White House to present Roosevelt with his American League seasonal pass. As the years went by, Griffith extended that practice into bringing two passes, one for the president and one for the first lady, always encased in a new handbag. Griffith became Roosevelt's baseball version of Winston Churchill: a friend, adviser, and confidant.

Griffith was indeed FDR's baseball man, so thoroughly entrenched that his name appears in the president's date books. When the two got down to business in 1942, Roosevelt's ideas were clear. His first question was if baseball could survive with replacement players at the major league level, assuming the armed forces would draft away the best ballplayers. Griffith answered a resounding yes. For years, Griffith fielded teams with many inferior players cobbled together from all walks of American life. He could get by, and if other teams didn't know how to do it at first, they would adjust—or lose. Griffith thought there would be enough 4-F players—former players who were too young for the last war and too old for this one, ballplayers who worked factory jobs, and guys with medical abnormalities—to fill the reduced rosters of all sixteen major league clubs and play a full season schedule. Griffith conceded the quality of play would suffer, and that Hank Greenberg's and Bob Feller's enlisting was just the beginning of the talent exodus that was sure to drain the major leagues, but there was no avoiding that. The question was if there were enough ballplayers left at home to keep the game going and, more important to Griffith and his fellow owners, to keep selling tickets and concessions. Griffith assured Roosevelt that baseball would scrounge up enough misfits to keep the majors going.

Next, Roosevelt wanted to know how else the baseball industry could contribute to the domestic war effort and adhere to wartime restrictions at the same time. Roosevelt recognized baseball had value on the home front for the workingman and woman. While one army was raised to fight, another would be conscripted to build and fill Roosevelt's massive production orders. These workers would benefit from baseball, Roosevelt reasoned. Ball games would stimulate the domestic economy because workers would have a place to spend wages, even if wartime meat rationing made that ballpark favorite, the hot dog, more expensive or even impossible to find.

Griffith vowed baseball could survive even in the face of daunting logistical challenges. Griffith pledged the cooperation of his fellow owners, even if they didn't know he was committing them to the president. He was certain they would go along with him in order to keep the gates open. Baseball would donate bats and balls by the thousands to servicemen around the world. Griffith promised to use his own Washington Senators as an example. His team would play countless war-bond games and host charity drives. The Senators would play service teams for the entertainment of troops based stateside. Creative scheduling, such as the frequent use of double-headers, could help ease the travel burden and maneuver around gasoline rationing.

Roosevelt raised a finger. He wanted more night baseball games, which many owners, including Griffith, opposed as a money-losing proposition. Roosevelt made it clear that this was not a negotiation. He wanted night baseball because factories would run on twenty-four-hour shifts during the war, so people on the odd hours would have a better chance of catching a ball game (and putting some of their money back into the economy) at night.

Griffith did not push back against Roosevelt's wishes. The owner wasn't a fan of night baseball because the electricity was costly and the lights so dim that he thought hitters couldn't see the ball well. But Griffith agreed and told the president that baseball would ration all essential materials in accordance with the War Production Offices. Wood would be rationed so much that the Louisville Slugger Company stopped making bats and started making M1 rifle stocks. The rubber core used in baseballs could be replaced with something cheaper. Teams wouldn't produce scorecards because of the paper shortage and baseball cards wouldn't be printed.

Roosevelt was satisfied. Griffith was certain Landis would adhere to Roosevelt's directives. Roosevelt's letter was carefully crafted. No mention was made of the meeting with Griffith, which never formally existed. The rough feelings between Roosevelt and Landis were not acknowledged, but the president threw the ball squarely into Landis's chest. Saying his letter was not a formal request, and that the ultimate decision must rest with Landis, Roosevelt made it perfectly clear that he was unofficially making the decision. If Landis went against him, he would have to take the consequences. One politician to another, it was no wonder Landis hated Roosevelt, who got his way without even asking. Roosevelt's reply to Landis, dated on January 15, 1942, became known as the Green Light Letter. With these words, President Roosevelt decreed that the game must go on:

My dear Judge:

Thank you for yours of January fourteenth. As you will, of course, realize the final decision about the baseball season must rest with you and the Baseball Club owners—so what I am going to say is solely a personal and not an official point of view.

I honestly feel that it would be best for the country to keep baseball going. There will be fewer people unemployed and everybody will work longer hours and harder than ever before.

And that means that they ought to have a chance for recreation and for taking their minds off their work more than ever before.

Baseball provides a recreation which does not last over two hours or two hours and a half, and which can be got for very little cost. And, incidentally, I hope that night games can be extended because it gives an opportunity to the day shift to see a game occasionally.

As to the players themselves, I know you agree with me that individual players who are of active military or naval age should go, without question, into the services. Even if the actual quality of the teams is lowered by the greater use of older players, this will not dampen the popularity of the sport. Of course, if any individual has some particular aptitude in a trade or profession, he ought to serve the Government. That, however, is a matter which I know you can handle with complete justice.

Here is another way of looking at it—if 300 teams use 5,000 or 6,000 players, these players are a definite recreation asset to at least 20,000,000 of their fellow citizens—and that in my judgment is thoroughly worthwhile.

With every best wish, very sincerely yours,
President Franklin D. Roosevelt.

Finally, all of baseball, and every major league player, minor league player, semipro player, high school player, and all manner of fans had their answer. Baseball continued but the government was taking the stitches off the ball. Instinctively, baseball people understood that Roosevelt's edict presented a manpower shortage that the game had never before seen. Kids under twenty were going to get a chance to play in the majors before they were ready. Players over thirty would be recycled and pressed back into service. Misfits, miscreants, and players with strange physical ailments would find places to play.

Roosevelt masterfully succeeded at selling wartime baseball to the public despite the difficulties the major leagues were soon to experience. His letter was widely distributed and published in newspapers across the country. It was reprinted in its entirety on the cover of *The Sporting News*. The response was supportive and in unison. Roosevelt was right—the game must go on—and players such as Hank Greenberg and Bob Feller were the trailblazers.

Writing in his *Sporting News,* publisher J. G. Taylor Spink carried the party line for the baseball industry: "Well in advance of the 1942 pennant season, baseball could designate Franklin Delano Roosevelt, President of the United States, as its Player of the Year. Without even waiting for the national executive to throw out the first ball in Washington in April, both major leagues would make no mistake in naming Mr. Roosevelt their most valuable man in all branches of their specialized endeavor. For in writing to Commissioner Kenesaw Mountain Landis that the White House wanted baseball to go right on through the war, in giving to our National Game that priceless executive sanction and presidential approval, F. D. R. already has done more for the game than any of its most brilliant exponents possibly could hope to contribute through the 1942 season—and the 1943 campaign to boot."

Clark Griffith was at his Old Fox finest when news hit the streets. He complimented Landis, even though he knew his influence weighed more heavily on Roosevelt: "Commissioner Landis is to be complimented for his direct action. The fact that we were ignorant of his plan is not a bit disturbing to us. As the Commissioner, the guidance of the game is in his hands and Mr. Landis again has justified his wisdom."

Landis decided he didn't need to wield his wisdom. He was confident he had made the right decision by letting Roosevelt decide. Maybe in his old conservative heart he was bitter that his actions led to such accolades for Roosevelt, but when it came to baseball, business was first, politics was second. "I hope that our performance will be such as to justify the President's faith," he said.

The politicians reflected Roosevelt's faith. "Professional baseball has a place in the country, even in a time of war," Representative Walter G. Andrews, from Roosevelt's home state of New York, said. He didn't care if the guys in the majors in the next few years were of unremarkable quality. "They may not play as good ball, but what difference does that make?" Baseball owners heard that and cringed. You try selling tickets without Joe DiMaggio. "I think that the example set by two of the game's greatest players, Hank Greenberg and Bob Feller, is a good thing for the country."

If Judge Landis possessed the ear of God, then Connie Mack was the voice of God. When he spoke, it was as though calm and acceptance swept through the land. The longtime owner and field manager of the Philadelphia Athletics had recently turned seventy-nine years old. He was already a national institution for his longevity and presence, and he was every bit a part of the nation's baseball self-identity as was Babe Ruth. Mack always spoke in slow, caring tones, both to his players and to the press. When FDR's letter became public, Mr. Mack as he was called, eased the nation in his own special way.

"We are in for a long war, and there is no use trying to make ourselves believe anything else," he said. "Baseball is a national institution now. The fans want it, the soldiers will want it, and we are going to give it to them. They'll want something to see, and those lads in faraway camps will want something to read about besides the war."

But Mr. Mack had been around long enough to realize that turbulent years were coming and offered a warning: "Now that this country is at war, we're going to have our troubles. It will purely and simply be a matter of getting players."

Connie Mack was the first person to say definitively that baseball was going to have a manpower shortage. His age and experience allowed him to quickly envision just how much of an impact the manpower crisis would have on millions of lives, the future of baseball, and, in turn, the shape of American professional sports for decades and generations to come. Mr. Mack realized so many men were going to be required to win the war that he tried to put it in modern terms. If a boy was a teenager or a young man in his early twenties and wanted to play professional baseball, no matter if he was in the minors, college, semipro, or high school, he wasn't going to play pro ball anytime soon because the war had to be won, and he was going to be drafted. What was left of them whenever the war ended was their problem. The big leaguers entering service were all going to give up large amounts of salary, skills, and prestige just to be treated the same as everyone else. Mack said this before anyone else, before Branch Rickey, and nobody doubted him, even if people didn't understand the magnitude of these changes just yet.

Clark Griffith got to work right away, using his connections in the sporting-goods manufacturing industry to shake loose the goods. Countless GIs played with balls and bats that originated from Clark Griffith's efforts to spearhead equipment donations to the servicemen. "Everything we send them will be the finest available," Griffith boasted. "The baseballs they get will be identical with our official big league balls, and the bats will be Louisville Sluggers of the Hillerich & Bradsby Co."

There were different baseball kits for the fighting man: Kit A would contain three bats and a dozen balls. Kit B would contain a complete catching-gear set: mitt, mask, and chest protector and shin guards. The assumption was that most fighting boys would never leave home without their baseball glove, so the kits did not include them. Besides, production of baseball gloves would be curtailed during the war because of a shortage of leather, needed for vital goods such as bomber jackets, rifle straps, and boots. If the guys could scramble together bits and pieces of the two kits, they could play a ball game anywhere they could find enough flat dirt to dream. Griffith's former third baseman Buddy Lewis recalled, "Your glove was about the most precious thing you had during the war, even if you rarely got a chance to use it. Things could be terrible and lonely, you could be homesick, but you could always have a catch with another guy if you could get your hands on a ball. I didn't care if the guy got cut from his high school team. It didn't matter to me—if you had baseball out there in the middle of nowhere, somehow, some way, you didn't quite feel as far away from home."

Roosevelt's green light gave meaning and place to baseball during war. Americans spread across the globe in the long struggle ahead carried baseball with them as a reminder of home. Many of those boys would play baseball on bomber fields and battlefields, in jungles and in deserts, in Europe and Asia and the Pacific, in bitter cold and unforgiving heat. They used the balls and bats Clark Griffith collected, the permission Franklin Roosevelt granted, the spirit Hank Greenberg and Bob Feller provided, and the courage of Billy Southworth Jr. and Pete Gray. The game would go on, until the war was won.

PART II

Over the Hump

1942 – 1944

CHAPTER 6

Earn It

Hank Greenberg sat quietly in the ballroom audience of a Manhattan hotel, looking completely out of place. He wore his Army Class A dress uniform and picked around the food on his plate as a couple of baseball reporters stumbled up to the makeshift stage for the annual follies at the Baseball Writers' Association of America dinner. The baseball writers around him were dressed up, which for them meant ironing their shirts and making sure a season's worth of mustard stains were rubbed out of their neckties. A couple of jolly and half-drunk hacks in a better mood than they had any right to be sauntered up to the stage and performed a horrendously scripted comic bit re-creating President Roosevelt's writing the Green Light Letter. Nonetheless, the act got big laughs.

The annual dinner was a January tradition and unofficially marked the countdown to spring training. Thanks to Roosevelt, everyone finally knew there would be a 1942 baseball season, and his go-ahead was the talk of the night. The get-together was always a big deal in New York City, where a dozen daily newspapers and an army of sloshed reporters covered the Yankees, Dodgers, and Giants. The commissioner's office might have been in Chicago, the author of the Green Light Letter might have resided in Washington, DC, and *The Sporting News* might have been published in St. Louis, but the heartbeat of baseball was in midtown Manhattan, and ink was the game's blood.

Even with bad comedy, the mood wasn't as light as it usually was be-cause of the big man in the Army uniform sitting in the center of the room as modestly as a mess cook. Writers and players were separated by money as far back as the 1940s, but not by camaraderie, access, or proximity. In the days before electronic media, the only voices that mattered were those of the men with the pencils and notepads patrolling the clubhouses. A level of trust and some degree of friendship existed, and certainly a sense that they were all lucky to be drawing a paycheck to be working in the big leagues. A guy like Hank, even when he got angry with them, was usually nice about it. He was a big star with a big personality, but he never acted that way, which further endeared him. He came to the dinner at their in-vitation because he had a weekend off from the Army. In the month after he reenlisted, he had spent New Year's Eve at home with his family in Crotona Park and slipped so quietly into Fort Dix that nobody knew he was there.

Having grown up in the Bronx, Hank was always a hometown favor-ite in New York City even though he played in Detroit. The first off-season of the war was a time of great patriotism and breathless excitement, a pep rally that didn't truly reflect how arduous this road would be. Hank, how-ever, sensed differently from the inebriated writers, who paused long enough from their vaudevillian sketches portraying FDR to honor Hank with a spe-cial award. Hank didn't need the trophy, but the camaraderie and friend-ship of the baseball world was easy to miss. Even if they were baseball writers, at least they were still baseball people, familiar connections and regular faces from the normal life he'd left behind.

Roscoe McGowan, a longtime baseball writer for *The New York Times*, presented Hank with a plaque for being the first professional ballplayer from the city to enlist in the armed services. The last time Hank accepted an honor from the baseball writers was following his first Most Valuable Player award in 1935. After a brief introduction outlining his numerous achieve-ments for the Detroit Tigers, Hank was called to the stage. He rose from his table to thunderous applause, but even as he walked to the front of the room, he wondered at all the commotion. The extra attention always both-ered Hank. He never got over how strange and uncomfortable it made him feel. He stepped to the podium and the room fell silent. He was a com-manding presence wherever he went. "This is the second time I've been honored on this dais. I honestly feel there was some provocation for the first time in 1935," he said.

What he said next personified why he was the model soldier for baseball's war: "But I have yet to earn my right to this honor." Hank was right, because he was saying that America and baseball hadn't earned anything in this war yet. A recognition of the truth was in that statement. The applause came in waves, one after another, until finally even Hank broke down and smiled. He raised his hand to acknowledge them and realized that when he'd left the Tigers, he hadn't had a chance to say good-bye to the baseball writers. Everyone deserved a proper farewell, so Hank let the writers have theirs. A few days later, he left Fort Dix for Bolling Field in Washington, DC, where his new career in the Army Air Corps was about to begin, but at that moment on that night in Manhattan, it was as though Hank Greenberg stood on a train as it pulled away from the platform, growing smaller in the distance as he waved good-bye to his old friends with the pencils and notepads.

Once Hank vanished from public view, baseball settled into the new normal. The war was here, famous ballplayers would be leaving for the services, but the game would go on for the good of morale and patriotism, if not for better baseball business. Ed Rumill, the longtime columnist for the *Christian Science Monitor,* saw the industry rapidly changing. "There will be spring training, opening days, home runs, pitching battles, umpire debates, peanuts, popcorn and chewing gum, just as there has been down through the years. But it hardly will be the same. How could it be the same with boys like Bob Feller and Hank Greenberg missing?"

At Boston's Fenway Park, a letter arrived on the desk of Red Sox general manager Eddie Collins. In it, his star left fielder, Ted Williams, notified the club that he was classified 1-A for the 1942 draft, a change from his 3-A status in 1941. Just as the Tigers had lost Greenberg and the Indians had lost Feller, the Red Sox were sure to lose Williams sometime in the near future. From a young age, Williams understood how the war was going to damage every ballplayer's value. "Your income spirals if you're a lawyer, an insurance man, or a doctor, but a ballplayer just has so many years and then his goes down," he explained. But Williams also refused to renege on his obligation to the country and the war effort when his time came. He was ready to fight and honed his eyes by shooting out the lightbulbs on the left-field scoreboard with his gun, much to the great annoyance of owner Tom Yawkey.

When *The Sporting News* printed Joe DiMaggio's home address it obtained from his draft card, it was enough to make the Yanks jittery. There was no easy way to replace their resident center fielder from 2047 Taylor Street in San Francisco. When DiMaggio filled out his draft questionnaire, he didn't know the legal name of his employer, so he wrote, "American League Baseball Club of New York." DiMaggio figured the draft would eventually get him, too, though he planned to play for the Yankees in 1942.

Every single major league ballplayer's draft status was newsworthy because it might affect his career, his major league team, the pennant races, and even the outcome of the World Series. Teams had to consider the war as a factor when building their clubs. The war leveled the playing field, exposed organizations without depth, and rewarded those who had signed enough young players so that the draft couldn't get them all at once.

A ballplayer's draft card was now vital: his age, height, weight, previous medical conditions, bats left, throws right, married or not, children yes or no, shoots and marches when and where? Every major league player was at the mercy of the local draft board when he was registered with Selective Service, and it would be this way from now until the end of the war. It was up to a doctor's exam to decide his fate. Some doctors were baseball fans who didn't want to see their team tank when the war was on, so one might look the other way if a ballplayer had so much as a hangnail. In time, this caused much speculation and resentment that some players might have been given a free ride. If the player passed his physical, he would be drafted into the Army, but many took the Bob Feller route and joined the Navy once they passed their Army draft boards.

The manpower shortage was felt acutely in the minor leagues in the immediate months following Pearl Harbor. Around the country, entire minor league and semipro town teams joined up. For those players who didn't immediately volunteer, operators of minor league clubs were all too eager to offer them up. "If Uncle Sam wants some of our players, he's more than welcome to them," Fort Worth general manager Zeke Handler said. He didn't say how he would keep his team alive in the coming war years, mainly because the appropriately named Handler, like other minor league operators, had no idea how he would stay in business during the war.

The answer was, by any means necessary—using underage kids who weren't ready for the level of baseball they were thrust into, or, more commonly, taking retired minor leaguers who were working wartime factory jobs and recycling their baseball careers. They would also employ players without any previous professional playing experience, which before the war was unheard of for most upper-level minor league teams. The plan would keep a pared-down version of the minor leagues alive during the war, but in the majors, the owners hoped it would never get that bad. What it actually did was provide a model the majors eventually copied.

Privately, even as they rallied behind Roosevelt, major league owners worried how they would market an inferior product. They feared the war would kill attendance. In the years before television generated billions of dollars in revenue, walk-up ticket sales and concession sales were the primary income for major league teams. Owners, while often accused of being greedy, still priced even the best seats within reason because they feared pricing out ordinary fans would push children away from the game, thus cutting off the industry's future talent supply and fan base. Owners saw fans as customers, not as TV viewers or electronic data, and they lured them as individuals, and not ratings. The fans, young and old, had to have a reason to keep coming, to keep the turnstiles clicking during the war. The star players had been the reasons, the star attractions. Take away the good players, and even if FDR insisted the game go on, owners wondered if fans would pay good money to see the scraps left behind. Wartime baseball presented another unknown. How would fans react to players who weren't serving in the armed forces for one reason or another? After all, if they were healthy and strong enough to play in the majors, why couldn't they gear up and join the fight? Attending a major league game could become an ethical question.

The thought terrified the owners, who weren't about to go against the wishes of a popular president in wartime. Compared to their giant corporate descendants, the major leagues of the war years were mom-and-pop stores. Most teams were family operated, and the game had been organized and controlled that way since baseball rose to popularity at the turn of the century. Wartime baseball would be a shell of itself, and nobody knew if the shell would sell. The war had just started, but it already had the makings of an All-Star team of players in the service, especially in the American

League. In addition to Greenberg, Feller, Cecil Travis and Buddy Lewis of the Senators, outfielder Sam Chapman of the Athletics, and first baseman Johnny Sturm of the Yankees enlisted. Teams began to ask a new question: How do you win a wartime pennant?

The Yankees could find someone else to play first base in place of Sturm and still defend their 1941 World Series crown as long as they had Joe DiMaggio, Joe Gordon, and Charlie Keller playing every day. Tommy Henrich, the third member of their highly productive outfield, was classified 1-A and was expected to enter service sometime during the coming season. Another future Yankee outfielder, Hank Bauer, played his rookie season in 1941 for Oshkosh in the Wisconsin State League. He was a tough St. Louis kid who hit 10 home runs that year, but he quit baseball to join the Marines after Pearl Harbor. "I had high hopes of moving up to the major leagues after a few years in the minors," he said. But at the time, Bauer echoed the sentiments of many youngsters who thought the Marines offered a pretty good deal. "I swapped my seventy-dollar per month job and lousy meal money for twenty-one bucks a month, good food, and great medical care. It was not that bad a deal even if they took six and some change out of my pay every month for life insurance."

As long as DiMaggio was milling around center field, all seemed right in the Bronx. Casey Stengel thought he had seen everything in baseball, but then he saw what the war would do to the game. "The draft can make these two pennant races a big scramble," Stengel predicted. "The main American League scramble will be to keep somewhere in sight of the Yankees."

Stengel was right. Without the humorous mutilation of the English language that characterized his career as Yankees manager a decade later, Stengel spoke with convincing elegance about the war's influence on the forthcoming season. "Any baseball club that has DiMaggio, Gordon, and Keller doesn't have to bother much. But there can be a big scramble for second and third places. We might find out whether the loss of Ted Williams hurts the Red Sox more than Feller's absence hurts Cleveland. The Yanks suffer no such destruction."

The American League missing Greenberg, Feller, and possibly Williams while the Yankees retained DiMaggio as well as the other core members of the 1941 team that finished 101-53 promised to be a one-sided affair. DiMaggio was the heart of the team, hitting with cold dignity. He led the league with 125 runs batted in and hit .357 with 30 home runs in 1941. DiMaggio was proud that he never bragged about anything, but his 56-game hitting streak that season was something else. "If I say it myself, that fifty-six-game hitting streak was a good trick," he said. "That's one job the boys are not going to beat while I'm around."

DiMaggio won the 1941 AL Most Valuable Player award, easily outdistancing Williams and Feller, and if there was anything DiMaggio knew, it was how to ask for a raise. He was sitting pretty in the early days of the war. His son was born in October 1941, and his hometown San Francisco draft board bestowed a 3-A classification on him in light of his family status. When he went to see General Manager Ed Barrow, DiMaggio had his eyes set on a raise from the $37,500 in 1941 to $50,000 in 1942. Barrow had teeth even DiMaggio did not anticipate, humiliating him in public, using the very newspaper men who venerated him to denounce him.

Industries across America cited the war as an excuse to freeze or lower wages. Barrow was the first baseball executive to use the war as the reason to keep a player's salary depressed. Barrow froze or reduced salaries on every player from the '41 champs. The wealthiest team pleaded patriotism to play poor with their prized players. The only guy with the clout to challenge Barrow was DiMaggio, but even he was just another player with no collective rights. Why pay more? Barrow argued. Greenberg and a million just like him were making $21 per month, $99 if they were as smart as Feller and joined the Navy. DiMaggio couldn't live on thirty-seven grand?

Barrow blasted DiMaggio, saying that no player should expect "a big raise while American soldiers are making twenty-one dollars a month." DiMaggio didn't like being portrayed as greedy, even if he was the one being bullied. If he disliked anything more than looking bad on the field, it was being embarrassed off it. He backed down and accepted Barrow's contract with a slight raise. Joe D privately sulked and hated that son of a bitch with every bone in his valuable body. But at least he got to play in the majors in 1942, and the war didn't touch the core of the Yankees pitching staff—Hank Borowy, Tiny Bonham, Red Ruffing, Spud Chandler, and Lefty Gomez—not yet, at least.

As easy as it was for Stengel to predict the Yankees would run away with the American League race, he couldn't decide who would win the National League. "The Dodgers and Cardinals will be about as strong as they were a year ago," he said. The Cardinals and Dodgers engaged in an epic pennant race through the 1941 season that ended in the final week of the season with the Dodgers winning the pennant by 2½ games. One of the closest races in years had the Cardinals alone in first place for seventy-three days, and the Dodgers alone atop the standings for seventy-eight days. Seven times, the teams were tied, and eighteen more times they were deadlocked by virtue of a few percentage points. They played each other 23 times and each won 11 and tied the other time, jostling through the summer, withstanding injuries and pitchers head-hunting hitters.

The war wouldn't stop the Cardinals. Manager Billy Southworth Sr. took over the Cardinals 44 games into the 1940 season and began his first full season in 1941 while Billy junior made his first solo flight that January while based at Parks Air College, Illinois. Even as he embarked on his military aviation career, Billy junior emulated his father. Asked to describe his father's influence on him, he said, "The first thing I can remember is sitting with a bunch of ballplayers, big leaguers that played hard and played to win. My father was one of them. Not a big fellow, but full of scrap and determination." Billy went about his new career the same way. He wanted to be the best combat pilot he could possibly be. No new pilot learned to fly without a few bumps in the air, but Billy had a steady hand, never cracking up any of his trainers.

Billy senior's Cardinals were full of skinned knees and raw talent. The old man was at his best when he was a father figure to many of his young ballplayers. One of them was outfielder Enos Slaughter, a small-town kid from North Carolina whose worldview stretched no farther than the miles of tobacco plants around where he grew up. He wanted to play in the majors, but wondered if he was from too small of a town to make it big. Getting a hold of him in the minor leagues, Billy changed all that in a hurry.

Southworth convinced Slaughter he was a major leaguer waiting to happen. Billy gave him the confidence, and Slaughter ran with it, turning himself into a left-handed, slash-and-burn, contact hitter who rarely struck out. He was a hell-raiser on the base paths, barreling into the bags with his spikes flying. Slaughter played the outfield with abandon, diving for every ball within reach, and he loved to dare guys to run on him. Slaughter was athletic enough to play all three of the outfield positions, but his arm strength made him a natural right fielder. He picked up one of those derogatory nicknames bestowed upon ballplayers who make opponents absolutely furious. At the age of twenty-six in 1942, "Country" Slaughter played with burning abandon and was Billy senior's favorite ballplayer, the kind of man he hoped Billy junior would become.

Another baby Cardinal was shortstop Marty Marion, a twenty-three-year-old kid who signed when he was seventeen. He was as graceful a shortstop as anyone had ever seen, ranging far to his left and right to glove balls few other shortstops could reach. He reached so many balls that so few other shortstops could reach that he accrued large numbers of errors, but he could turn a double play and dodge a base runner like nobody else. Billy trusted him from a young age and gave him confidence when he had none, another example of his fatherly touch with his young ballplayers.

Billy senior got his hands on a young, mountain of a catcher named Walker Cooper, who had baseball smarts and a real rough side. Billy liked that Coop was a natural leader; he thought he would make a fine field manager one day. Coop became Billy's eyes on the field, telling him when his pitchers were spent and when their stuff was gone. He had a big arm and made it known that he wasn't afraid to use it. He took a pounding behind the plate, but he couldn't wait to swing the bat. Billy thought he had the makings of the best catcher in the game.

Then on September 17, 1941, a new rookie arrived in the second game of a doubleheader against the Boston Braves. The boy was a skinny and spry, smiling twenty-year-old with a swing you couldn't miss. He had been tearing up the minor leagues, and Billy was waiting for him. He knew it wouldn't be long before the kid was hitting in the middle of the batting order. History and timing were on Billy's side. How lucky he was to be the manager at the right place and time, thanking his lucky stars to be penciling in the first lineup card of Stan Musial's career. The rookie unleashed his corkscrew batting stance and whipped a double to right in his second major league at bat. Musial kept right on going, hitting .426 down the wire and making it look easy, killing the Cubs with a 6-for-10 day in a doubleheader. When it was over, Cubs manager Jimmy Wilson fumed, "Nobody can be that good!"

Billy senior was excited to have this ball club. He never liked the way his stint as player-manager of the Cardinals unfolded in 1929, and after so many years of waiting, he was eager to get another shot. Now he had it, with a group of young players with incredible talent that was his to mold. It should have been the greatest time in his life, but his excitement was always tempered by worry for his son, whose flight training continued.

Billy kept a close watch on his son in the summer of '41. He transferred to Brooks Field, Texas, where he learned that he wouldn't become a fighter pilot like Eddie Rickenbacker. Instead, he earned his bomber's pilot wings. Billy junior's dream of flying the nimble pursuit planes was over— he was destined for the heavies, the trenches of the skies. In February 1942, he transferred to Pendleton Field, Oregon, to join the newly activated 303rd Bomb Group. Everybody knew they were headed to England to open the air war against Germany. They were already waiting to take delivery of their new B-17 heavy bombers. In his daily life with the Cardinals, Billy senior was always calm, confident, and happy-go-lucky, but privately he was worried. In February 1942, news of the first professional-baseball casualty rattled him. The boy was an inexperienced pilot killed stateside. It was easy to envision his own son in the young airman's coffin.

Billy senior didn't know how much the war would change everything he had ever known. In the next few years, the faces from his Cardinals would vanish one at a time . . . Slaughter, Marion, Cooper, even the kid Musial . . . and the rest of the league, even the Dodgers, wouldn't be the same . . . and somewhere over Europe would soon be a piece of himself, Billy junior, the skipper of a B-17, the brave son of the nervous father, who captained his Cardinals into the 1942 season and needed baseball to keep him steady in his worried mind.

CHAPTER 7

A New Contraption

Clark Griffith loved the first day of spring training. He flocked South, eagerly greeting his players as they arrived. He bounced around the ballpark like a spindly old man in a candy store, directing his ballplayers this way and that. He was the boss, so the ballplayers nodded and appreciated his insight or at least gave him that impression so he would continue signing their paychecks. But when they saw the unusual mechanical device set up on the pitching mound, the ballplayers wondered what Griffith was thinking this time.

Griffith was frugal to the point of annoying his players, but he traditionally signed up plenty of extra pitchers for spring training. Their purpose wasn't to win games for the big club, but to throw endless batting practice to the hundreds of players in his organization. Griffith didn't mind that in peacetime, but war is hell, and so was feeding and housing all those extra guys. So he reached deep into his pockets, which alone was newsworthy, and paid the princely sum of $1,500 for a first-generation pitching machine, which was eventually dubbed Iron Mike for the way it hurled baseballs with an overhand motion.

Nobody had ever seen a pitching machine on a major league field before. *The Sporting News* described it as a "new fangled contraption that looks like an anti-aircraft weapon." Griffith loved his new acquisition, because of its soulessly cost-efficient, robotic qualities. "Ordinarily we'd bring a lot of rookie pitchers down here knowing they weren't worth their keep as prospects," he said. "We're out from under that expense. Nobody has to feed the machine."

But somebody had to feed the propaganda machine. Griffith claimed the device could hurl a baseball 240 miles per hour, much faster than the 180 miles per hour Bob Feller threw. Yes, in 1942, German scientists were developing rockets, jet engines, and assault rifles that could cut a man to pieces, but the Americans couldn't figure out how to realistically measure fastball velocity. It was going to be a long, long war.

It already felt like a long war to Hank Greenberg. His transfer to the Army Air Corps officially went though, and he transferred from Bolling Field in Washington, DC, to MacDill Field, near Tampa, where he was within driving distance of the Tigers spring-training camp in Lakeland. Hank wasn't stupid. His motivation for transferring to the Air Corps was simple: "I had my fill of the infantry and decided that if I was going to serve, at least I would serve in the Air Force, where I thought I could do just as much for the country and do it in a much more pleasant way."

Greenberg was assigned to a physical-fitness detail while he was in training to become a bombardier. The training for a bombardier was rigorous and scientific, requiring men to learn how to operate the complicated Norden bombsight. There was strategy in Hank's service. He wanted to see action, so the best way was to learn a job skill that could be put to good use and had high demand. Of course, someone in command would have to let the two-time MVP off the ground. But even as he trained for bombing missions he wasn't sure would ever come, people wouldn't let him lose sight of his still being a star baseball player.

He took dinner one evening with J. G. Taylor Spink, the longtime editor and publisher of *The Sporting News,* and one of the institutional voices of baseball. Spink was eager to regale his audience with tales of dinner with Hank. He wrote, "Greenberg looked to be in perfect shape. In fact, I figured he had taken off 15 pounds, he was so thin, and his face was so lean. But he told me he had not lost a pound since he left the Tigers. He said that ballplayers did not know what condition meant until they got into the service with its simple food, early hours, and hard work."

GIs enjoyed Hank's interview and could relate to a guy who was in the Army same as them. The war had only just begun, and already Spink wanted to know if Hank was getting ready to play baseball again. Hank apologized and said he didn't mean to let the guy down, but, no, he hadn't picked up a ball or a bat in any meaningful way since he hit his two farewell home runs and left the Tigers. When Hank finally did relent to take a few hacks in a camp game, he was alarmed at how slow he felt. "I felt like knocking those fat pitches out of the park," he said, "but I couldn't connect anymore. My timing was gone and my muscles wouldn't work fast enough." Then he offered words that made everyone sad: "Make no mistake about it, I won't play a lot of ball afterwards."

The Army Air Corps didn't care if Hank never played again. They had excellent use for him in the team's publicity department. Hank was never thrilled with the amount of photo opportunities he had to perform, but that was the price of fame. A few days after he arrived at MacDill, the Army posed him in the cockpit of a bomber, looking down on his old friend Joe DiMaggio, who was in town for a USO gig. The headline read:

IT'S A GREAT LIFE, HANK SAYS TO JOE!

One can only imagine what the two ballplayers actually thought about the stunt, though Joe, fresh off having his hat handed to him in his salary dispute, was in no mood to run against the Army. Another time, Hank, dressed in his Army uniform, posed with a bat in front of a P-40 Tomahawk and a group of airmen. The photograph received national run, with the *Chicago Tribune* blaring:

OKAY ADOLF, TRY TO STRIKE HIM OUT!

Baseball was a constant reminder in Hank's life during the spring of 1942, even though he wasn't playing. He met up with Hugh "Losing Pitcher" Mulcahy of the Phillies, the first major leaguer drafted the year before. The two strode down the walk of the base, caught by eager Army photographers, with Hugh carrying his leather Phillies travel satchel. Hank looked pleased to be in the company of another major leaguer. Such moments made him feel closer to home.

Eventually, being so close to the Tigers camp was too much for Hank to resist. He got permission to visit Lakeland, where he walked into the dressing room and saw his old friends. He borrowed a uniform and took batting practice; after a few labored swings, he managed to blast three mammoth home runs. His teammates loved it, but Hank warned them not to get too excited. He knew it was not as easy as he made it look. For the first time in his baseball life, he felt like an old man with diminishing skills whose time was passing.

A few days later, he played an exhibition game for the Air Corps, on loan to the Tinker Field baseball team against the Washington Senators. Clark Griffith was eager to greet the slugger, but Hank wasn't sure he was ready to face live pitching. Griffith told him he had just the trick to get him loose. Hank could come to Senators camp anytime he wanted to take batting practice against the pitching machine. Hank laughed, smiled, and sucked it up, got three hits, and drove in the only runs against the Senators, but he felt slow. Really, it wasn't fair to throw him into the fray, where he faced a young pitcher with a big fastball named Early Wynn, who was nasty and mean and bound for 300 career victories. Hank tried, but trained eyes could tell he wasn't the same.

The game was witnessed by many sportswriters and was the first sign of how not playing because of the war sapped what a player could do. Poor Hank started the war as the symbol for the ballplayer brave enough to put his career on hold. Now he was the symbol for the guy who might never get it back at all. The first speculation that Hank was finished surfaced. "Hank Greenberg is sure the war is going to last so long that he will never be able to play big league ball again," the *Hartford Courant* wrote. His days hitting cleanup might be over.

Hank was the Air Corps's favorite PR cleanup hitter, and his inclusion in exhibition games for servicemen was a sign of baseball's new way of life. The first wartime spring training was marked by an addition to the regular baseball wartime calendar, the frequent games against Army and Navy bases. The Cardinals, for example, pledged to keep open dates on the schedule and would donate any admission sales to the Army athletic fund. The Dodgers created an organization-wide drive requiring all employees, from the lowly secretaries to the club president, to purchase defense bonds. The Dodgers, like other teams, left ample room on their slate to play service teams. They pledged donations to the ball-and-bat fund and allowed all servicemen to attend their major league games for free. These practices became common in both leagues and a regular part of the wartime American landscape.

As more and more young Americans hurried to join the war effort, service baseball teams rapidly organized around the country, offering professionals who were in the services the chance to stay fresh by playing other professionals on Army and Navy base teams designed and promoted to whip up the morale of the different branches of service.

At Jacksonville Naval Air Station, former Philadelphia Athletics pitcher George Earnshaw, who retired from baseball in 1936 with 127 career victories, managed a team of naval aviation cadets against the Atlanta Crackers, the most popular team in the Southern Association. "For two hours, officers, aviation cadets, and sailors relaxed together," *The Sporting News* reported. "Overhead, formations of great flying boats occasionally added to the stirring picture. No outsiders are allowed at the games in the Naval Air Station, but there wouldn't be anything but standing room if they were. The station personnel are not required to go to the games, but try to keep the boys away. They seem to enjoy getting in the swing of that old Navy spirit."

Mickey Cochrane, the former Tigers and Athletics All-Star who was one of the greatest catchers of the 1930s, entered the Navy and was commissioned a lieutenant at Great Lakes Naval Center and would be charged with building the most formidable team in the Navy. In the next few years, major leaguers clamored to join the Navy and play for Cochrane at Great Lakes rather than take their chances in the regular Army. Cochrane was the best baseball man in the Navy, and in time he influenced the playing careers of many servicemen, filling the gaps of professional development missed during the war years.

Some players hated wartime baseball already, but could never complain in public. Was it fair for a major league team to barnstorm all over to play service teams of inferior quality? The grind of a major league season was rough enough without having to play two months of ball games for nothing. Other players simply thought resuming their baseball careers in wartime was unethical. Perhaps it was not a coincidence that three of those who enlisted were Detroit Tigers, former Hank Greenberg teammates Pat Mullin, Fred Hutchinson, and Bob Uhle. By some counts, the Tigers already had more players in the service than any other team in the majors.

Pat Mullin especially had been influenced by the baseball's wartime economics. He played outstanding baseball as a rookie in 1941, batting .345 in 54 games, but when he arrived in early 1942, he learned the Tigers had given him a small wartime salary reduction. Joe DiMaggio wasn't the only ballplayer nixed on the money. Mullin entered the Air Corps, telling friends he had planned to enlist all along, figuring his draft number would come up soon anyway. But players were starting to wonder if owners would use the war as an excuse to suppress salaries, knowing players could not argue for fear of antagonizing the public.

Detroit Tigers owner Walter O. Briggs slashed first baseman Rudy York's salary in half, calling his performance weaker in 1941, despite York's hitting 27 home runs and driving in 111 runs without Greenberg protecting him. Briggs also cut veteran pitcher Bobo Newsom's salary in half, ignoring the burly right-hander's 250 innings pitched and hammering him for his 12–20 mark on a fifth-place team. Few players got lucky. Pitcher Johnny Gorsica went 9–11 and asked for $9,000, getting $5,000 instead, a slight raise from 1941. Players sensed owners were using the war to hide behind unwarranted salary suppression. Players hated it but could say nothing, but the seeds of their desire to fight back against the owners were planted in the early months of the war.

Cost cutting was in full force around the majors and the minors, and sometimes it wasn't even management offering the sacrificial cut. Veteran minor league pitcher Wayne Osborne of the Pacific Coast League's Hollywood Stars offered to return his 1942 contract unsigned and take less money in return for what he considered a below-average 1941 season, and with the expectation that baseball was in for an uncertain year. "I don't figure that I'm worth that much dough again this season until I can prove myself again," he said. "It is my belief that if baseball in general and Hollywood in particular face an uncertain year, I want to go along doing my part." Osborne was a break-even pitcher in 1941, 12 wins and 12 losses, and the Stars refused to accept his offer of a pay cut, even though many Coast League teams considered cutting spring-training games because so many players worked in the shipyards. Osborne reluctantly signed his deal and left the office wondering why the Stars didn't accept his offer. The Stars shook their heads, wondering why any wartime ballplayer felt guilty about getting a raise.

As Opening Day neared, excitement gathered in the air. Even, perhaps, a little bit of swagger. The shock of Pearl Harbor had run thin, replaced by a fierce craving for revenge. In Washington, DC, a joint Army-Navy strike was planned against Japan and kept so secret that not even the pilots volunteering for the mission knew the target. The Japanese were the enemy with the face. Baseball old-timers scorned them. Ty Cobb snarled, "I never did like them." He still blamed a Japanese boy for once stealing his cleats and glove.

War was on the mind of everyone in baseball no matter the context. When sixty-six-year-old Kid Elberfeld, a former Cobb teammate and Yankee shortstop who finished his career with the Senators, visited Clark Griffith's spring-training camp in Orlando, he displayed the scar on his leg caused by Cobb's vicious sliding decades ago. "He went out of his way six feet to give me this," Elberfeld said. The reporters who saw it commented that it was a "swastika-shaped spike wound."

New York City mayor Fiorello H. La Guardia practically waved his fist at Nazi Germany and dared Hitler to disrupt the 1942 season. "If we are to be hit, I'd just as soon get hit in Yankee Stadium, the Polo Grounds, or Ebbets Field as I would in my apartment. Baseball is going to be my only source of entertainment this summer. It is perhaps more important now than ever. The Nazis will not give us a systematic bombing, they will send over suicide squads for token attacks. If we get panicky, if we start making changes, we will be doing what the Nazis want us to do."

Truth be told, Adolf Hitler was probably more obsessed with the fifty-one German Army divisions invading Russia than he was with who would win the World Series. American citizens needed the start of the baseball season to get here quickly because the war news was still grim, especially from the Pacific, where in April, a few days before the start of the season, US forces unconditionally surrendered on Luzon. Only a small force of American troops held out on Corregidor. On the mainland, seventy-five thousand prisoners of war, about fifteen thousand of whom were Americans, began the dreadful Bataan Death March. Six hundred Americans were shot, beheaded, bayoneted, or beaten to death as they succumbed to exhaustion and malnutrition. American hatred for the Japanese soared, while patriotism and love for baseball flourished. Though Americans didn't pay attention to the Japanese baseball leagues, many of their star ballplayers, just like Americans, put down their playing careers to heed the emperor's call. Baseball was a bone of contention between the Americans and the Japanese, as if the two nations were fighting for the game's soul.

When Jimmy Doolittle piloted the lead B-25 bomber on his low-level bombing run over Tokyo designed to frighten the Japanese people and boost morale on the American home front more than actually inflict any meaningful physical damage, he buzzed a field where the Japanese were playing a baseball game. Later he claimed that he was low enough to see fans shake fists at him, though that may have been a bit of aviator hyperbole. But Doolittle really did buzz the ball game after dropping his incendiary bombs. His after action report read, "Lowered away to housetops and slid over western outskirts into low haze and smoke. Turned south and out to sea." A year later, Doolittle told the *Chicago Tribune* the story of the famous "Thirty Seconds over Tokyo" raid, leaving the paper breathless. "Whatever the score, the game was called. Was the game suddenly called at just about that moment on account of rain? Or was it hail? Whatever, it was supplied by Doolittle himself. The Japs were pretty sure about the way their ballgame was broken up."

Morale building on the home front was job number one. The Doolittle raid succeeded in lighting up willpower more than the Tokyo streets, and the new baseball season was on the way. Baseball was proving to be a morale builder already, and the heavy fighting hadn't even started. A lonely soldier wrote to *The Sporting News,* his clever humor disguising boredom and worry, killing time with pen and pencil. He plotted out a pennant race, only the participants were the warring nations, and "world champion" took on a new meaning. In war as in baseball, this GI picked the Yanks to win it all:

"First place: USA. Nickname: Yanks. Manager: Roosevelt. Predictions: Will be in for Stretch Drive. Second place: Britain. Nickname: Limeys. Manager: Churchill. Predictions: Pennant threat. Third Place: Russia. Nickname: Reds. Manager: Stalin. Predictions: Not worse than third. Fourth Place: Germany. Nickname: Huns. Manager: Hitler. Predictions: Manager trouble. Fifth place: Japan. Nickname: Japs. Manager: Hirohito. Predictions: Will have a rough trip. Sixth place: Italy. Nickname: Black Shirts. Predictions: Definitely second division. Seventh place: China. Nickname: Chinks. Manager: Chang Kai-shek. Predictions: Long center field wall hurts. Eighth

Place: France. Manager: Petain. Predictions: Hopeless farm club for Germany."

Opening Day in the majors meant President Roosevelt making his annual appearance at Griffith Stadium in Washington, DC. But like shortstop Cecil Travis, sworn into the Army at Fort McPherson, and third baseman Buddy Lewis, stationed at Fort Knox, FDR wouldn't make it either because of his wartime commitments. That didn't stop fans from asking. A letter to the White House begged the question:

> *Dear Pitcher Frank:*
>
> *Now I realize that there's a big game going on right now that we must, and ARE, going to win. But here at home, for the sake of morale, let me congratulate you for your ideas on the continuance of professional baseball. Which brings me to the inquiry: How does your arm feel for pitching at Washington come opening day, pitcher Frank?*
>
> *We think you'll have a lot of strikes on the present opposing team when spring rolls around. If so, will you try and come out to the baseball lot and pitch the first one for us again? Good luck, pitcher, with every ball you throw!*

The answer was no. On April 14, the Senators started the baseball season against the World Champion New York Yankees. The empty presidential box signified just how much had changed since the war started. Clark Griffith took one look at the crowd of thirty-one thousand, many of whom were servicemen decked out in full uniforms cramming to the creaky rafters of Griffith Stadium. They were admitted free, but at least they bought concessions. About two thousand fewer fans showed up than when Roosevelt came. Griffith figured he would never see a crowd this large here again during the 1942 season. He was right, though he hoped to make up some of that attendance with night baseball, if he could get the other clubs to go along with the president's wishes.

Nobody came to the ballpark to see Vice President Henry Wallace toss out the first ball, but it was the first big crowd at Griffith Stadium since the Redskins football game on December 7. This time, there was no mistaking a nation at war. "Several thousand service men, officers and enlisted men were in the crowd, with the white hats of the Navy as standouts," *The Washington Post* noted. "The runway which comes under the grandstand and empties near the presidential box was boarded up. In place of 'Hail to the Chief,' the Army band played 'God Bless America.'" A band played "The Star-Spangled Banner," and the crowd sang in unison.

Buddy Lewis, of course, wasn't in the lineup. Playing third base instead was rookie Bobby Estalella, a thirty-one-year old Cuban journeyman in his second stint with the Senators. Griffith had traded for Estalella from the St. Louis Browns in September specifically to replace Lewis and provide veteran stability at third. The age of the wartime replacement player had begun—out was the younger, fresher Lewis. In was the older, less gifted Estalella, who had batted only .241 for the woeful Browns.

An old hand, Red Ruffing, pitched a 7–0 shutout for the Yankees on Opening Day, limiting the lifeless Senators to 3 hits. Clark Griffith could probably tell this was going to be a long year. It looked to be a long year for everyone except the Yankees, Cardinals, and Dodgers. All of a sudden, finishing in last place, or in the second division, wasn't quite as end-of-the-world as it used to be.

Casey Stengel would know. He was fifty-one years old, entering his fifth season managing the Boston Braves, and he had finished next to last every year since Hitler invaded Poland. He didn't have much to look forward to in 1942. He shipped his best young left-handed pitcher, Warren Spahn, back to the minor leagues a few days into the season because he thought Spahn lacked the courage to pitch in the majors. He called Spahn a "cherry pie," which was a polite way of calling him another crude name. Spahn resented Stengel for doubting his courage, especially when he already knew he was going to join the Army.

When asked if he thought the Braves would improve any, Stengel muttered, "I hope we do." That wasn't exactly a rousing vote of confidence, but it showed how quickly the war was changing everything. He could see the game transforming from teams with stars to teams with replacements, from those with legitimate talent to those with hard-to-fit-yet-convenient ability. The question about every player in the future wasn't going to be if he had major league ability. It was going to be if the government would leave him on the playing field. Stengel called the season "unimportant compared to winning the war. There are many years left when we'll have peace after we've won this scrap, but there won't be any peace worthwhile unless we do. Baseball will have its share in keeping a great American game going along, a game that will last a long time after we have mopped up the Germans and the Japs, who will finish far lower than the Phillies and Browns." Stengel was kind enough to omit his own Braves from the blood roll of bad teams.

Stengel understood something that owners and baseball men were thinking and worried about, but not discussing out loud, as the 1942 season started. The question was not what the game would look like during the war. Everyone knew baseball would get worse as the war moved along. The real question was where would the replacements come from and what kind of players would they be?

CHAPTER 8

Bad Check

Pete Gray wondered if any baseball team would take him. He was home in Nanticoke playing in the sandlot leagues, going nowhere fast. Even the town leagues weren't so good anymore. So many young boys had left town for jobs in the Army and Navy that old men kept the local leagues alive. Pete was left behind and he hated it. The quality of play was no good, but at least he could make a few bucks. He supposed he could go back to the Metro again, but he didn't like that thought. He had already proven himself there and he knew the scouts weren't going to touch him. So he spent his time watching the world pass him by.

The war was the worst news for many ballplayers, but for Pete, it was his lucky break. The manpower shortage was first acutely felt in the minor leagues, leaving leagues scrambling to field enough teams to remain in business. Drastic times called for drastic measures, and in a move that would have been unheard of before the war, certain semipro teams were granted lower-level professional classification in order to keep some leagues operating. One of those semipro teams that became an official minor league team was the Three Rivers club in Quebec, which was admitted to the Class C Canadian-American League. Pete had played for the Three Rivers Foxes in 1939 before he departed to play for Brooklyn and other clubs in the Metro. He had fond memories of his first hit there, when the fans chanted his name and showered him with loose change. When Three Rivers received the news that it was now officially a professional minor league team, Gray was one of the first players they called. They didn't need to ask him twice. "They knew what I could do," Pete said. "So they sent me a contract." Pete was on the first train out of town, and at long last, after years of rejection, he was finally going to play professional minor league baseball.

When Pete arrived, Mickey O'Neil was ready to help. A tough Irishman, he had been playing professional baseball since 1917, an itinerate catcher who saw life through his birdcage mask. Mickey played nine major league seasons and then bounced through the minor leagues, where he nurtured aspiring ballplayers. Mickey took an immediate liking to Pete and recognized why he was good. It wasn't his raw ability but his capacity to cope with his limitations. Pete had always searched for somebody in professional baseball who believed in him. Mickey was that guy.

Pete played ball as if there were no reason not to smile. He was an old man in the Canadian-American League, but at least he wasn't as old as Mickey. Pete didn't make much noise, except with his bat, hitting .381 in 42 games. Mickey could dream on him—he knew the war was going to cripple the majors in the next few years—and he thought Gray would be a suitable replacement outfielder.

Mickey liked Pete, but discovered a trait that worried him. It wasn't that Pete was antisocial—hell, some of the best ballplayers were—but that he drank like an angry coal miner. He hated when people drew attention to his handicap, and when they did, he became touchy, defensive, and surly. But a guy like Pete needed all the friends he could get. Mickey tried, and when the season was over, he planned an attempt to smuggle his moody understudy to the majors.

The majors already looked different as the 1942 season progressed. How to fill the seats was constantly discussed. Everybody needed a player fans wanted to come see, and that was just as true of Three Rivers as it was for the Detroit Tigers or Cleveland Indians. Without Greenberg, the Tigers drew roughly 104,000 fewer fans, and without Feller, the Indians pulled 286,000 less. Pete helped his little franchise draw 30,000 spectators even though they finished in sixth out of eight teams. "Gone is the sure-fire box office click, Bob Feller," a Cleveland reporter wrote in *The Sporting News,* undoubtedly mournful that Feller was pitching for the Navy and not the Indians. "Gone is the fence-shattering, popular and personal exponent of batting power, Hank Greenberg." Then, as if writing with Pete in mind, a player he had most likely never seen and never met, he wrote words Pete feared: "No freak attractions can baseball offer this summer."

Pitchers in the 1942 American League certainly had it easier without Hank anchoring the Tigers lineup, but the government wanted him hitting cleanup for war-bond sales. On the Fourth of July, the Yankees held a 4-game lead over the Red Sox, while the Dodgers were running away with the National League pennant race, with a 9½ game lead over the Cardinals. A Yankees-Dodgers World Series rematch seemed inevitable.

A few days layer, Hank was invited to join the service All-Star team to play the winner of the major league All-Star Game. Hank's former teammate Rudy York hit a 2-run home run to win the All-Star Game at the Polo Grounds, but Hank declined the chance to play for Mickey Cochrane's Military All-Stars in Cleveland. Instead, he continued his intensive courses at Officer's Candidate School in an effort to do something more substantial than pose for pictures.

In August, he graduated OCS with a second lieutenant commission and was made director of sports for all Army bases throughout the nation, a big administrative job. Hank was happy for the responsibility if his beaming image in the press photos were to be believed. But deep down, Hank believed preparing the men to fight wasn't the same as fighting himself. Posing for photos wasn't fighting. He was a glorified cheerleader in 1942. That was hard to take. He could have been a glorified cheerleader if he was playing for the Tigers, but at least baseball had managed to salvage the season with a story line everyone loved. For that, they could thank manager Billy Southworth's Cardinals and the National League pennant race, one that was remembered for years to come.

Billy Southworth was at his best when he was leading the charge from the top step of the dugout. He was an excellent field manager and game tactician, but he also had the energy of a little kid and was a bold and loud, lovable leader whom his players respected and responded to. After the first few months of the 1942 season, his team slumped, but in July, the Cardinals clicked. They went 22-9 but still only picked up ½ game on the first-place Dodgers. His team was demoralized after playing so hard and gaining so little, but Billy refused to let them quit. When his young shortstop Marty Marion watched his batting average nosedive to .180, Billy talked him out of leaving the team. Marion listened to his manager, and soon the Cardinals began to believe in themselves, even if it took every last bit of Billy's charisma.

Southworth knew the Cardinals had always been a great second-half team in the years they won the pennant. They bottomed out on August 8 when ace pitcher Mort Cooper was hammered for 5 runs in 2⅓ innings in Pittsburgh. The Cardinals rallied to tie the score, 5–5, and the game went 16 innings at Forbes Field before it was halted by curfew, resulting in a draw against the dreadful Pirates. Southworth knew they didn't have the look of a winning team, despite the obvious talent. He always had a knack for knowing when to verbally kick his team's ass.

Nobody ever talked about what Billy said when he lit up his team behind closed doors, but he sure was good at it. On the morning of August 9, the Cardinals were 9 games behind the Dodgers. To get back into the race, the Cardinals needed to get hot right now. It was hard to ignore Billy when he got going. Voice raised and arms tucked at his sides, his words packed an Irish-whiskey punch. He woke his team up. The Cardinals swept a doubleheader from the Pirates and began to get hotter than any team had ever before been.

While he was waiting to ship out, Billy Southworth Jr. kept a close eye on his dad's pennant race. During most of the 1942 season, Billy junior shuttled from California to New Mexico to Texas in various stages of flight training with the new 303rd Bomb Group. The summer was spent between beer halls and the ball fields as the crews awaited the delivery of the new B-17 bombers they were planning to ferry over the North Atlantic to England within the next few months. Every day was an adventure in the newly forming American air armada—and the bombers were a mixed bag of bad parts.

Billy showed his natural ability for flying and leadership when he experienced an in-flight crisis. The first B-17 Billy got his gloves on was a hand-me-down crate that lost its number two engine on his maiden flight. Billy nursed her home through some nervous moments. When Billy landed with hardly a bounce, one of his gunners, Sergeant Lucian Means, said, "You are good, aren't you, sir?" Billy jawed back, "Hell yes, Means!" You could almost feel the cocky smile hanging off Billy's lips. He was, after all, Billy's kid.

What he saw was his dad's boys busting off a 14-3 tear, with an 8-game winning streak, leading up to a showdown with the Dodgers. Because of his closeness and his constant worry for his son, Billy senior knew better than any other manager in baseball that no team could stay intact for the duration of the war. Winning seasons were always scarce and precious, but the war made winning this year even more urgent. Besides, what could be more satisfying than wiping that stupid smirk off the face of the Dodgers blowhard manager, Leo Durocher?

When the Dodgers arrived at Sportsman's Park on August 24 to begin a 4-game series, the Brooklyn Bums were treated as unholy enemies on sacred ground. The hometown fans bestowed a lusty roar when the Cardinals took the field. Dizzy Dean, the former pitcher who turned his big mouth into a career as a broadcast personality, wore a ten-gallon hat and chewed bubble gum and slurped from a beer bottle as he described the action. Baseball games like this made it easy to forget the war.

At Biggs Field in El Paso, Billy Southworth Jr. and his bomber boys crowded around the radio to listen to the night games and pull for his daddy thanks to a signal so loud and crisp it could be heard clear down to the Gulf of Mexico. Billy could tell the other guys all they wanted to know about the Cardinals, all the inside baseball dope he learned from his dad. He could tell you what brand of tobacco Walker Cooper chewed, how light of a bat Stan Musial liked to use, or how Marty Marion liked to poke his index finger out of his glove. The two Billys were intensely connected, and as surely as he told his squadron mates about his dad's ballplayers, Dad told the ballplayers about Billy and his bomber boys. Their connection was deep and personal, even when they were not face-to-face, linked together in baseball and in war as no other father and son. Besides, Billy junior was the best salesman the Cardinals ever had. He single-handedly converted the entire 303rd into Cardinals fans.

Billy senior's ballplayers wanted to win it for the city, for the manager, for the son and all the boys he served with. Stoic southpaw Max Lanier started the first game of the series on the twenty-fourth and beat the Dodgers 7–1 with a 4-hitter, disposing of pitcher Larry French in two hours flat and never cracking a smile. The next day was the main event, ace against ace, Whit Wyatt against Mort Cooper. Wyatt was a crabby bastard whom Joe DiMaggio called "the meanest guy I ever saw." In turn, Wyatt promised, "If DiMaggio was batting in our league, he'd be doing most of his hitting from his ass."

Cooper and Wyatt were two of the best wartime aces in the National League. Wyatt blossomed with the Bums and was so good in '41 that he led the league with 22 wins and 7 shutouts, including a memorable 1–0 shutout against Cooper and the Cardinals in St. Louis on September 13, a victory that sealed the pennant for the Dodgers. Cooper fumed all winter after losing that game.

This season, Cooper wanted his revenge against Wyatt. He beat him 1–0 in Brooklyn in May and again in July in St. Louis on a day when Wyatt didn't have his stuff. Cooper, knowing Wyatt would be better today, planned to be on his game. Cooper always had a sore arm and never complained about it, but you could always tell he was hurting when he chewed aspirin tablets on the mound, grinding them with his molars and swallowing them dry to dull the pain in his elbow.

Cooper and Wyatt fought the best pitching duel of the '42 season in front of a record night-game crowd of 33,260, matching zeros through 9 innings. Each man pitched as if he would be damned if someone else had to come in and replace him. Cooper didn't make a mistake until the ninth inning, when Dolph Camilli roped a double against the right-field screen. But Cooper caught a break when Camilli got greedy. He tried to stretch it into a triple, but right fielder Enos Slaughter played the hop, spun, and fired to shortstop Marty Marion, whose perfect relay throw nailed Camilli at third. The crowd exploded and the Cardinals danced off the bench. Who needed the World Series? What was better than the Cardinals against the Dodgers?

The pressure was starting to show on the Dodgers in the twelfth inning when, with the game still scoreless, Leo Durocher's temper finally flared. When Leo lost it, nobody could cuss like he could. John Lardner, writing in *Newsweek* with his father's flair for the funny, thought Leo was "the most polite and clean-tongued gentleman in the national pastime when his mouth is shut." With Dixie Walker at the plate, Leo thought plate umpire George Barr's strike zone was absolute horseshit. Barr told Leo to settle down, but that was like telling a lion to sit. Leo kept coming, his voice rising, the spittle spewing, his little jaw outstretched into the big man's chest. Finally George Barr had it, and in the middle of the inning he ran Leo out of the ball game.

Leo went berserk and the Cardinal crowd egged him on. In the summer of '42, thousands of American boys arriving in Newfoundland, Ireland, and England were exposed to the colorful phraseology of the British Isles, bringing out the profanity in an entire generation of boys. But if they had kept the microphone close to Leo's lips, he could have taught them all they needed to know about cussing profusely. The arguing Durocher was a thing of profane beauty, his lyrical and symmetrical berating of umpire George Barr likely similar to these exasperated tones: *"Jesus fucking Christ, George! Are you trying to fuck me? Where the fuck was that fucking pitch? My guy can't hit that fucking pitch with a goddamn broomstick! How the fuck is my fucking guy supposed to fucking reach that? How fucking long do you think his fucking arms are? That's a fucking horseshit fucking call, George, a fucking horseshit fucking call!"*

You could probably hear Billy junior's bomber boys laughing it up and trying hard not to let the beer come throttling through their noses. Leo stormed off the field, and while he stood on the mound, Mort Cooper probably didn't even try to hide his amusement. He chewed a few more aspirins and went back to throwing them. Cooper was never better. He pitched into the thirteenth inning, locked up in a scoreless game against Wyatt, and nobody cared if the bomber boys were going to go to sleep late tonight. But Cooper finally cracked in the top of the thirteenth when he gave up a two-out slap single to Lew Riggs, scoring Mickey Owen to give the Dodgers a 1–0 lead. The Bums jumped off their bench in excitement. Cooper kicked the dust. The crowd fell silent. The bomber boys felt despair.

Billy Southworth Sr. was at his best when the boys around him thought all was lost. He looked down his bench and saw his tired kids, who thought they were beaten again. But he refused to let his team think the game was over. He had infused them with his spirit, same as he had with his own kid, and he had learned something about this club in the past few weeks. As Leo Durocher might say, they just had no fucking quit. Billy wouldn't let them. In the bottom of the thirteenth, the Cardinals responded to their little, plucky leader. Slaughter drew a one-out walk, and Stan Musial lined a single off the glove of the leaping shortstop, Pee Wee Reese, scooting

Slaughter to second and bringing up Mort's brother, the catcher, Walker Cooper.

Walker Cooper against Whit Wyatt in the bottom of the thirteenth, Cardinals down by a run against the Dodgers. Hell, it wouldn't have shocked anyone if FDR was staying up late listening to this ball game, too. This was the kind of ball game boys like Billy and the bomber boys would remember in the flak-filled days ahead. Walker Cooper was just as sinister as Whit Wyatt. Coop was rawboned and rangy and used to spit on a hitter's socks if he caught the bastard peeking at his signs. Wyatt challenged him and Coop responded with a single back up the box to score Slaughter and tie the game. He was the last batter Wyatt faced. He pitched 12⅓ innings and gave up 1 run on 7 hits. He battled for each and every pitch in his longest outing of World War II.

Mort Cooper was still in this ball game, pitching a scoreless fourteenth. He might have been running out of aspirin. In the bottom of the fourteenth, Billy senior's boys were finally able to put Billy the Kid's bomber boys to their bunks. A bunt, fielder's choice, and a walk loaded the bases with two outs for Terry Moore, the old veteran. Moore slapped one at third baseman Lew Riggs, who knocked the ball down but couldn't make the throw in time. Marty Marion scored and the Cardinals had a 2–1 win, trimming the Dodger lead to 5½ games. It was Mort Cooper's sixteenth victory of the season, on his way to the best year he ever had. The victory was a turning point in the Cardinals season.

The following day, manager Billy's wartime revelation, twenty-four-year-old, rookie, right-handed pitcher Johnny Beazley, won his sixteenth game, and the Cardinals again won in their last at bat. This time, Coaker Triplett from Boone, North Carolina, hit a little dribbler not thirty feet, but it was enough for Jimmy Brown to come sliding across the plate with the winning run, finishing another 2–1 win.

The Dodgers managed to beat Max Lanier in the fourth game, 4–1, and the Cardinals fell to 5½ games back, but they felt a lot closer than that. "Leo Durocher's cockiness has probably vanished by this time," *The Washington Post* believed. Two games were still left on the schedule against the Bums, this time at Ebbets Field, and manager Billy plotted his pitching rotation so that Mort Cooper and Max Lanier would again face Brooklyn.

This pennant race had an urgency. On August 28, Southworth's star right fielder, Enos Slaughter, enlisted in the Army Air Corps and was sworn into the reserves, allowing him to finish the season before being called to duty as an aviation cadet. At least Stan Musial seemed safe for the 1943 season. Billy knew again that this was the year to win it all, while all his players were still here. All they had to do was keep the race as close as he kept the letters from his son.

A stranger could tell the National League standings just by eavesdropping on Billy senior singing in the shower. He had a distinct tradition. The soft sound of his Irish tenor meant the Cardinals had won. Silence amid running water meant a loss. He had been singing a lot lately. Southworth made a habit of never predicting pennants, even when he was convinced his boys would win. The Cardinals charged into fall and arrived in Brooklyn to start a 2-game series on September 11 on the verge of catching the Dodgers. The pennant race provided a happy distraction from the daily war news coming from Guadalcanal. The Cardinals trailed by only 2 games. Southworth bluntly told his boys, "If you can't win both games at Brooklyn, you don't deserve the pennant."

Sixteen games had passed since the Cardinals took three out of four from the Bums. In that time, the Cardinals had only lost twice. They were 35-9 since August 9. Both Southworth boys were on a roll. On September 4, Billy junior was promoted to captain in the 303rd Bomb Group, prompting a party at Biggs Field. A few days later, the bomber crews were issued flight plans containing routes across the North Atlantic. By September 11, when the Cardinals came to Brooklyn, the 303rd had flown to Chicago.

The Brooklyn fans booed the hell out of Mort Cooper when he warmed up at Ebbets Field, but Mort loved every hiss, howl, and scowl. Mort was always a little demented, but he took his goofiness to a new level during the pennant race. He wore number 13, a jersey digit thought so unlucky most sane pitchers avoided it, but since winning his thirteenth game, he had been trading up one jersey number at a time with a different teammate to correspond with the win he was going for. So here he was, wearing number 20, trading his 13 to Coaker Triplett for the day, but when you have a 1.96 ERA, nobody calls you crazy.

Mort relaxed in the dugout before the game with his brother, the catcher Walker, and their kid brother Jimmy, who was wearing his sailor uniform, one of 2,501 servicemen admitted free of charge, scattered among the 29,774 fans. Mort pitched a masterpiece, a complete-game 3-hitter, shutting out the Dodgers 3–0 to slice the lead to 1 game and becoming the National League's first 20-game winner. Mort was so good that two of the three hits were cheap, and he never allowed a runner to reach second base. He demoralized the Dodgers with each pitch and once more beat their ace, Whit Wyatt. Mort even helped his own cause, collecting 2 hits and scoring 2 runs, one of which was on Enos Slaughter's two-out, two-strike, sixth-inning single to give Mort a 1–0 lead. When Mort came to bat in the eighth inning, even the Dodgers fans applauded him.

The Cardinals could pull even in the race with a win on September 12. Many wanted rookie Johnny Beazley to pitch. He had 19 victories and hadn't lost since July 26. But manager Billy went with the veteran hand and his instincts. He wanted lefty Max Lanier, who, two starts earlier, on his twenty-seventh birthday, shut out the Cubs. Lanier didn't have the same good fastball Beazley did, but Billy was certain savvy would beat swagger. "I can usually tell when Lanier's right," he said.

Billy wasn't wrong. Lanier mowed down the Dodgers and beat them 2–1, at long last pulling the Cardinals even with the Dodgers in the first great pennant race of World War II. Leo Durocher wasn't in a giving mood. He snapped, "All right, they caught up. It took them five months to do it." But everyone else thought the Dodgers were finished. Gladys Gooding, the Ebbets Field organist, grimly played "The St. Louis Blues." Lanier never pitched a more meaningful game.

Owner Sam Breadon ordered the Cardinals to print World Series tickets. The next night, the Cardinals kept rolling, splitting two with the Phillies while the Reds beat the Dodgers, pushing them ½ game behind. The race was over. The Dodgers went 11-7—and while winning the last 8 games of the season gained only ½ game. The Cardinals finished the season 14-2, 12-1 in the final 13, and won the pennant by 2½ games, practically pushing the war news from Guadalcanal off the front pages. The Cardinals went 21–4 in September and finished the regular season as the hottest team in baseball history. They went 42-8 from August 9 until the end of the season on September 27, a feat no team matched in a fifty-game span for seventy-one years.

It was Billy Southworth's finest managerial moment. He brought a team back from the dead to win the pennant, and now the Yankees awaited them in the World Series. "They are singing the praises of Billy Southworth, the Redbird pilot," *The Sporting News* wrote. "They used to speak of him as a great guy who was a good manager. Now they say he has proven that a great manager can be a very decent sort of fellow."

While his father readied for the World Series, Billy Southworth Jr. knew his war was just getting started. The 303rd had been stationed in Chicago far too long for his taste. Too much downtime, too many beers, too many girls flocking to boys wearing pinks and greens. As his father guided the Redbirds, Billy discovered he had a natural touch for handling his own bird, the B-17, and he tried to coach other pilots. His crew struggled to come up with a catchy name for their bomber. They kicked around a few ideas and decided on *Bad Check*, figuring the bomber, like a bad check, would always come back to the table.

Billy dated around, but hated it when the girls came on too strong or were too stupid to understand the war he was getting into. Even though guys in his crew were getting hitched left and right (including one who proposed by telephone), Billy decided not to get married. "I'd like to get into this damn war and return so I can settle down."

The only drama he was interested in was baseball. He followed the pennant race and noted his dad's team's comeback in his diary. He had circled the date for weeks now, an September 20 doubleheader at Wrigley Field in Chicago. Billy senior made it out to the airfield to visit his boy and his crew. "Dad paid me a visit," Billy junior wrote. "Autographed my plane. He's the grandest guy I know." Billy got a pass and went to see the Cardinals split the doubleheader against the Cubs. He was thrilled to see all the players he had been reading about and listening to on the radio, especially Musial, who batted .315 with 52 extra-base hits and was only hinting at his potential.

The next day's paper featured a photo of Billy senior and Billy junior, prompting 303rd pilot Ehle Reber to note in his diary, "Billy will surely get the needle when he comes back. We put his picture up on the wall of group operations. 'OUR BOY SMILIN'" was put above the picture! Some fun!"

But deep down, Billy knew his day at Wrigley Field (admitted for free in his service uniform) was going to be his last day at a park for quite some time. The bomber boys were combat rookies going up against the Luftwaffe, the hard-nosed, experienced German pursuit pilots who had fought from

Spain to Africa to the Eastern Front. He was worried about the condition of the new American bombers, their lack of suitable frontal defenses, and the inept chain of command in the Eighth Air Force. Billy had already seen guys wash out or die in stateside accidents. He was growing impatient. "Sure tired of sitting around," he wrote. "I want to go into combat. That's where the real work lies and where things must be accomplished."

The real work for the Cardinals was to beat the Yankees in the World Series. Though the Cardinals had completed the hottest run in baseball history, and though they were younger, fresher, and stronger and had been playing meaningful games since August while the Yankees were counting the days until the World Series, the Cardinals were heavy underdogs. To the Yanks, the Cards were a cute little threat from that other league. Hell, most of the Yanks had been rooting for the Dodgers because it meant a bigger pot of gate money to win. The Cardinals were a bunch of kids, and though they had cut down the Dodgers, they played Game 1 like scared bushers. The Yankees were elegant and experienced. The Cardinals didn't score until the ninth inning when the game was out of reach, playing tight and losing 7–4, with their ace pitcher, Mort Cooper, shellacked, and their star rookie, Stan Musial, hitless.

Manager Billy Southworth was the only guy on the bench with any World Series experience. Billy taught his players to never give in. On the field before the game, he met with Hank Greenberg, who was dressed in his uniform and on hand to promote Army Air Corps recruiting. They had much in common thanks to Billy junior's impending deployment to England. The reporters gave them space before the game, so nobody could tell if Hank secretly confided to Billy that he, too, wished he could be assigned to a bomber unit. All the publicity work Hank had to perform during the war had a graceful uneasiness about it. Maybe he was a little jealous of Billy junior, though Billy senior probably would have told Hank to be careful what he asked for. Hank wished manager Billy luck and maybe he told him that although he was an American League guy through, and through and Joe DiMaggio and Red Ruffing were two of his best friends, he still respected the job that Billy had done on the Cardinals bench this season.

Billy handed the ball to right-hander Johnny Beazley and named him starting pitcher for Game 2. The rookie 20-game winner answered the call by pitching 7 fearless innings. He tied up the Yankees with hard fastballs inside and soft changeups away, shutting out the Yanks and carrying a 3–0 lead into the top of the eighth.

Then Johnny the Beaz, as his teammates called him, made mistakes when it mattered most. He gave up two-out singles to a pair of veteran hitters, Roy Cullenbine and Joe DiMaggio, cutting the lead to 3–1, and bringing Charlie Keller to the plate. "King Kong" Keller was fearsomely strong with 30-home-run power. Beaz threw him a hanging curveball and regretted it. Keller blasted that loopy breaking ball over the right-field wall, a 2-run home run that tied the score 3–3, silencing Sportsman's Park, and nearly extinguishing the youthful Cardinals' fighting spirit.

Manager Billy Southworth refused to worry. He was out on the top step of the dugout, clapping for his boys, even with two out in the eighth inning. The Cardinals were desperate and needed a spark, a sign of life, not in a few batters from now and not in a few minutes, but right now. There was no other hitter Southworth wanted at the plate than Enos Slaughter. Musial might have been the best pure hitter, DiMaggio might have been the best pure ballplayer, but "Country" Slaughter was the greatest clutch player on either team.

Everybody wanted to see Slaughter against DiMaggio in this series, this storied study of opposites, the city slicker versus the barnyard ballplayer. Slaughter did not disappoint. He lined a double down the right-field line and ran like hell, flying around first with his hat flying off and sliding into second, rousing the dirt and raising the crowd, bringing them to their feet and reviving them, a two-out double in a tied game.

When Yankee shortstop Phil Rizuto muffed right-fielder Roy Cullenbine's incoming throw, Slaughter smelled blood. He bounded to his feet and charged to third to take the extra base. He dove face-first into third, much to the invigoration of Cardinals fans. The winning run stood at third base, shaking the dirt out of his uniform. Musial was coming to the plate. The Cardinals fans were crazy loud.

Lieutenant Hank Greenberg sat in the radio booth at Sportsman's Park with play-by-play man Red Barber, who described the action to a nervous nation. During the Game 2 broadcast, Hank was pumping recruiting by dutifully telling fans that baseball teamwork was just like teamwork in the Air Corps. Hank's heart was in a different place. He wished he could be on the field, sizing up these Cardinals, instead of in the damn radio booth.

He noted the Game 1 Cards as flat and "too little, too late," but he knew they wouldn't quit, not if manager Billy had anything to say about it.

Hank sensed the Cardinals coming alive, sparked by Slaughter and flogged by Billy, their charming little pilot, who rallied his boys on the bench. This was the teamwork Hank was talking about, a shining example for the war effort, the reason baseball was selling victory. "The pilot is no more important than the navigator, the bombardier, the radiomen, and the mechanics," Hank told the listeners. Though he was talking about the captain of a plane and not the manager of the Cardinals, it was just the same.

Stan Musial walked to the plate with uncanny composure. He had done a whole lot of nothing in the Series, though you'd never know from his body language that he was 0-for-7. A young player, he carried himself like an old pro. You couldn't tell if he was batting with the season on the line or if he was playing his harmonica. He was facing Ernie "Tiny" Bonham in relief, a familiar nemesis for Hank. The St. Louis fans rose to their feet, but Musial wasn't jittery in the least. He just stood there in the loud silence, coiled up and ready to hit, when a low rumbling came from the distant horizon.

Bonham, a 21-game winner, wasted no time coming right after the kid. He threw Musial a fastball. Musial attacked as if he'd been sitting on a fastball all along, twisting his hips into his swing and bouncing a slow-hit ball over the head of second baseman Joe Gordon. It wasn't hit hard and it wasn't pretty, but it was enough to send Slaughter scurrying home with the go-ahead run, clapping and hooting as he came. The Cardinals had a 4–3 lead the Cardinal way: a two-out double, an extra base by going for the jugular, and then a timely hit by a kid older than his twenty-one years.

The 34,255 Cardinals fans at Sportsman's Park were wild and loud, but they weren't alone. Nine more fans came to the party last minute: pilot, copilot, navigator, engineer, bombardier, and four machine gunners. As the faithful cheered the Cardinals, their voices were drowned out by the loud rumbling of the four turbo supercharged Wright engines churning three massive propeller blades each, powering the B-17 bomber nicknamed *Bad Check,* piloted by Captain Billy Southworth Jr. and recently autographed by manager Billy Southworth Sr.

Billy's kid was inbound from Battle Creek, where the 303rd was temporarily stationed, one day before the scheduled flight to England. The crew was in a great mood, with payday in the morning and the flyby later in the afternoon. Everyone in the 303rd thought Billy was the best captain. His once-in-a-lifetime sortie showed why. Perhaps the crew was listening to the radio and heard Hank Greenberg. The fans were too excited to ask how Billy junior knew how to calculate his trajectory so that he passed over Sportsman's Park exactly on cue, like an angel on the Cardinals shoulders, trumpeting Musial's triumph.

The bomber growled across the St. Louis sky at around a thousand feet and 137 miles per hour with its landing gear retracted, wing flaps neutral, and hopefully frightening the New York Yankees the way the crew hoped to terrify Nazi Germany. Southworth flew under the strictest guidelines of the War Department's acceptance-performance tests of the B-17F Flying Fortress. Billy could recite all the specs of his Fort as surely as he could rattle off the batting averages and earned run averages of his father's ballplayers.

Hank Greenberg had a perfect view of the incoming bomber and swore he felt a shiver run down his spine. He was an Air Corps man, and he could feel *Yeah, this is my team now!* The fans stood and roared as the bomber crept over center field, flying clear and directly over the grass, the long shadow of the four-engine beast passing over Joe DiMaggio's head and for a split moment blocking out his sunlight. The rest of the boys rushed to the open machine-gun portals in the center of the plane to look out the openings. The air rushed into their faces; they were low enough to smell the cigar smoke. As Billy's bomber soared over the field, he wiggled his wings toward the right, to the third-base side, where the Cardinals dugout was. Manager Billy knew exactly what his boy was saying: *This is good-bye.*

Billy Southworth Jr. didn't want to get married before the war because he didn't know if he was coming home, but he wasn't leaving without one last flyby. As far as he was concerned, this was his first and only appearance in a major league game, though it was never recorded as such. He had long since decided to give up his baseball career to sit behind the controls of an airplane, and there were no regrets. His life was entering a new phase now, and the rest of 1942 and the start of 1943 promised great danger, as it did for the rest of the country. The flight was Billy's own decision and didn't make the daily papers because of wartime confidentiality restrictions.

Maybe manager Billy told the writers, *For the love of God, please don't get my kid court-martialed!*

Yet the flight did happen, coverage limited to a small item on page 14 of the October 14, 1942, *Sporting News,* reading only, "An Army bomber soared over the field a moment after Stan Musial drove home Country Slaughter with what proved to be St. Louis's winning run in the eighth inning. It almost seemed the symbol of victory." A 1943 *Washington Post* column confirmed the flight, with Billy conveying enough information for the reporter to conclude, "He circled his fortress over Sportsman's Park during the tense moments of the second game of the World Series."

The fans never forgot the moment the B-17 flew low overhead and banked for one long circle around Sportsman's Park. Most people had never seen a B-17 up close before, much less heard the rumble of the Wright engines. Billy junior flew while wearing his favorite Cardinals hat, a gift from his father. It was coming to England with him. "Pop said it was a lucky cap and he wanted me to have it," Billy junior said. The brim was pressed over his aviator's sunglasses, and his earphones were pressed over the flannel lid.

Hank Greenberg watched the bomber rumble over. He wondered when it would be his turn to leave the States. He had heard much about the industrial war effort back in Detroit, where Briggs Manufacturing, owned by the family that owned the Tigers, produced the ball turret on the B-17s, the bubblelike machine-gun emplacement under the belly of the beast.

As quickly as Billy junior arrived, he was gone. After his final pass, he pulled the nose up and started climbing. The bomber crawled into the distance, becoming a little brown speck before *Bad Check* vanished into the horizon. In the dugout, Billy senior never showed his emotions. He watched the plane until he could see it no more. He knew his boy was leaving. In the cockpit, Billy never showed his emotions, either. His father had trained him well. The old man finished one job. Now it was the kid's turn to help finish the other. And just like that, Billy junior was off to the war.

The Cardinals found the inspiration they needed to win it all. Enos Slaughter threw out Tuck Stainback at third base in the top of the ninth to complete the Game 2 victory and even up the series. The Cardinals then finished off the unthinkable, sweeping three games at Yankee Stadium to win the World Series. The war was the reason the '42 World Series was the first one broadcast over shortwave radio, allowing American GIs across the globe to follow the games. That helped results of the World Series travel faster than ever, even to the Philippines, where American POWs held at Santo Tomas University in Manila followed the games with the help of local sympathizers. "We got full reports on the 1942 World Series through our underground system in Manila," one veteran told *Yank* magazine. "The people on the outside would pick up the game on the shortwave and slip us the pitchers and catchers and inning-by-inning scores through the fence. The Japs never did catch on."

Five games wasn't anything compared to five months. That's how long it took manager Billy Southworth's Cardinals to seal their reputation as America's team during World War II. The '42 World Series stayed with Americans more than any other Series during the war. The Cardinals were like the war effort itself, young and homegrown, in need of veteran leadership to topple an enemy with stuffy leaders and a significant numerical advantage early in the game. That archetype resonated with the American people. It wasn't just the story of the 1942 baseball season, but the story of the war.

CHAPTER 9

Billy's War

Nobody wanted to see the first pitch of the next baseball season more than Billy Southworth Jr. He brought the lucky St. Louis Cardinals hat his father had given him before he managed the Cards to the World Series title with him and liked to wear it instead of the traditional "crusher" style officer hats the B-17 captains wore. Pretty soon, bomber captains in all the groups spread across the Eighth Air Force were requesting soft baseball hats from the quartermaster. Billy unknowingly started a fashion trend, but he was only wearing the Cardinals hat because it was soft and comfortable and helped keep the sun out of his eyes when he was in the cockpit. Besides, he wouldn't dare tamper with lady luck.

Luck was the only thing a bomber crew thought could save them in the early days. When the 1942 baseball season ended, the air war began. Billy Southworth Jr.'s war finally arrived at dawn on November 18, 1942, a little more than a month after the end of the World Series. The bomber crews were nervous and excited, and as much as baseball was part of Billy's blood, the game felt much more distant than an ocean away. The B-17s taxied up the grass at Molesworth, one after another, roaring loudly as they went. Billy was in the cockpit of *Bad Check,* part of the 427th bomber squadron of the 303rd Bomb Group. Finally, it was Billy's turn to kick his rudder and line his nose up on the runway. He took a deep breath; this was it. He pushed forward the throttles and opened up the engines. His B-17 rumbled down the field and lifted into the darkness.

"I felt just like a rookie ballplayer going into Yankee Stadium for the first time," he wrote. The targets of their first raid were the German submarine pens at St. Nazaire, France. The American bomber crews, including Southworth himself, were kids who were too dumb to know the danger. "We were so young, we didn't realize what we were getting into," Southworth's waist gunner, Sergeant Bill Fleming said.

Twenty German fighters jumped *Bad Check* twenty minutes from the target. Billy had never seen anything so fast. The bullets shocked him. "We were outnumbered and outweighed, and it was just like standing up there at the plate watching three fast ones whiz by," he said. They were also horribly outgunned. It was the first time Fleming and the other gunners had ever fired their .50-caliber machine guns in combat. All told, the crews only had about thirty hours of operating experience, including Southworth's flyover of Sportsman's Park. The Germans had been flying for years.

Southworth flew his B-17 through German 88mm flak filling the sky with angry puffs of black smoke and shrapnel. Billy didn't give a shit how the approach looked as long as he stayed in formation and reached the target. He flew like there was no way in hell the bastards could touch him. Southworth didn't think he was flying scared. It was bombs away at 19,400 feet, and Southworth turned the lumbering B-17 for home. "The plane felt loggy and flew like a truck," Billy complained. It took all his strength to keep the control wheel in a straight line, especially under attack. The job done, his copilot took a nap and missed the two German fighters tailing *Bad Check* home looking for an easy kill. The gunners got the fighters to scram, but when Billy landed, his walk-around revealed something he hadn't imagined: "We counted thirty flak holes in our ship."

Southworth, however, thought the mission was a rousing success. He thought his bombs hit the target, journaling, "They were excellent hits." But the high command, especially Colonel Curtis LeMay, scornfully nicknamed Iron Ass by the airmen, did not agree. It was a sloppy raid showing inexperience. The Germans thought the Americans were a joke, so LeMay ordered the bombers to fly tighter formations, to not take evasive maneuvers, and not threaten the integrity of his pinpoint-bombing doctrine. Billy quickly lost the boyish cockiness. The war took away his jubilance.

On December 12, Billy learned for the first time exactly what he had quit baseball for. The 303rd took off for Romilly-sur-Seine. The mission was a snafu from the start. Twenty B-17s took off and six aborted. Southworth was the second bomber from the front of the formation. There was little flak because the primary target was fogged in. But then the fighters came, dozens of them, bearing the distinctive yellow noses of JG 26, the feared German squadron the bomber boys nicknamed the Abbeville Kids. The engine spinners of their Bf 109s and Fw 190s were painted bright yellow. Southworth had never seen anything like it. He never told his father about the yellow-nosed bastards spewing 20mm armor-piercing cannon fire. The shells could kill a man on impact or destroy an engine. If the shell exploded on your lap, you were dead. The Germans were expert marksmen and fearless fliers against kids who had learned how to fly and shoot yesterday. The bullets and shrapnel knocked against the bombers, shaking the men inside, who furiously poured machine-gun fire out the windows. The war movies at home made the bomber boys look cool and collected, but inside the bombers it was sheer madness, profanity, blood, hatred, anger, and angst. Southworth realized how the Americans' lack of experience and preparation placed them at a disadvantage. He hated being unprepared. It went against everything his father had taught him.

"Two minutes over the French coast and here come the Jerries," Billy wrote in his diary. "Six of our ships took positions on our right and an even level (piss poor). Another bunch was on our left and level—stinks. The Huns bore in. Here come four at me, firing across my nose from one and two o'clock. Our guns, top turret and more guns blasted a steady stream. My window, already cracked, became streaked with cracks at which I became furious at Sergeant Means (top turret) for disobeying orders, firing forward as his zone was rear. The ball turret was reported out of order."

The Germans were fearless and terrifying. The 190s and 109s would pull up even alongside the bomber formations, just out of range of the guns, then throttle up and turn sharply, head-on toward the bombers. The early B-17s had virtually no protection in front, only a puny 30mm machine gun the crews called a peashooter. The Germans pelted the bombers with 20mm cannons, trying to kill pilots like Southworth and keeping on a collision course until kicking hard on their rudders, flipping over, nosing away from the bomber at the last moment, then diving through the formation so quickly that the machine gunners couldn't track them. This went on and on. It caused pilots to panic and gunners to make bad decisions. It scared the American kids shitless.

Southworth's fear came out in anger and impatience with the men around him. Southworth didn't care if they hated his guts as long as he got them home alive. As Southworth kept his bomber in formation, the B-17 next to his was hit and floated out of the box. Southworth moved his bomber at the last moment to avoid a collision. But the other bomber hit Billy's on the way down. Billy, somehow, kept his bird steady. "This numbskull slid fifty yards out of his formation and into ours. I skidded out of danger, extremely lucky to avoid a terrible crash. He hit our horizontal stabilizers, putting a damn good dent in it. I'll take a bow for being on the alert and saving our necks there." Billy later described the encounter to a sportswriter like this: "Another Fortress, out of control, came roaring towards us. I caught sight of it in time to turn and dive my ship violently. His wing put a large dent in my horizontal stabilizer. It was too close for comfort."

Billy was a good pilot. A big dent in his horizontal stabilizer made flying the bomber extremely difficult. The mission was a disaster. Two crews were lost. The bomber that hit Southworth made an emergency landing in the French countryside and became the first B-17 captured by the Germans. Southworth managed to dump *Bad Check*'s payload near the railroad yards in Rouen. Now he had to turn for home and survive.

The Germans resumed their head-on attacks in a running firefight all the way back to the English Channel. Southworth believed he had to remain composed. He knew that if his emotions got the better of him in the cockpit, he was dead. So he internalized everything and made his war methodical. "Continual attacks were made by the yellow-nosed FW-190s, often from the nose," Southworth wrote. At long last, the blessed Spitfires arrived to chase away the 190s and take the bombers home. Southworth just tried to keep his bomber straight. Men—who were really kids—cried at the sight of the Brits. The bomber boys prayed and kissed the tarmac when they landed. They inhaled the sandwiches and cigarettes the Red Cross girls handed them. Then they went out and got extremely drunk and looked for some easy British girls.

Southworth never said a damn thing. He was determined not to show a single ounce of feeling. The worse it became, the tighter he held on to baseball. Other men needed booze and broads, but Billy couldn't stand the local girls. "English girls just aren't that sharp," he complained. Billy wanted spring training to start so his dad could send him letters about the Cardinals. He needed the 1943 baseball season to begin. Nothing could take his mind off flying quite like baseball. In pensive moments, Billy knew he could ask himself a realistic question: Would he really live to see the 1943 season?

That was a daily question. On the afternoon of January 3, 1943, the bombers of the 303rd flew into the fiercest flak storm they ever experienced. The weather was cold, crisp, and clear—hunting season for the gun crews below. "Over the target the antiaircraft fire was very heavy and it was hitting the planes," Bill Fleming, Southworth's waist gunner, wrote. "We started to realize somebody was really shooting at us. The plane on our wing took a direct hit and completely blew up. Pieces of it flew all over our plane, knocked holes in the wings and the stabilizer. It was a terrible shock. None of us could believe what had happened. By the time we got off the target we knew this was no playground anymore."

When that happened, pilots often saw blood and guts splatter their windshields or pieces of human flesh pass their cockpit window. That night, Southworth did not write in his diary. Instead, he went out to get drunk. He *never* drank.

He sought baseball to keep his sanity. Superstitious as all hell, he started playing catch with his crew before takeoff, even if it was still dark outside. He'd play catch by the soft glow of the lamps the ground crews used. Playing minor league baseball must have felt a lifetime ago. The close calls were adding up. On a January 23 mission to the Lorient Port and Brest U-boat pens, Southworth wrote intensive flak "sounded like rain blowing on a tin roof, or a limb cracking, a bolt of lightning." *Bad Check* dropped its bombs at twenty-three thousand feet and found itself in the battle of its life, a running firefight against about forty-five fighters. Southworth's nervous eyes thought he counted "fifty to one hundred fighters in the area." The head-on passes began, mostly Fw 190s, including one pass that riddled Southworth's cockpit windshield so badly that Southworth wrote, "Bent my head slightly in case she let go." That was Billy's calm way of saying, *I almost got my fucking head blown off.*

It got worse. Billy raised his head in time to see the 190 still coming in at point-blank range with no intention of diving away. Terrifying. The 190 kept firing and Billy thought the guy was ramming him: "Looked as if we would crash head-on, so I raised my nose to allow my lower turret to fire back but instead pulled up too violently, throwing everyone on the floor as the enemy grazed beneath us." The gunners fell on their spent .50-caliber shell casings like kids slipping on banana peels. Southworth's copilot, John Dillinger, pushed the controls down to level her out. But the ship next to him, *Susfu,* was not so lucky. Pilot Harry Robey was killed instantly by another fighter pass, the same tactic meant to kill Southworth. Robey slumped over his control wheel, thrusting his bomber into a steep dive, narrowly missing taking *Bad Check* with him. Billy saw the tail gunner firing defiantly as the bomber went down.

More fighter passes. The radio went dead. The ammo and fuel ran low. More flak. Southworth lost engine number three. Two more bombers were hit, causing one to spiral to its death and the other to slowly sink to its fate. It reminded Billy of a morbid scene between two of his favorite ballplayers, one slow and one fast: "They pulled way from us like [Ernie] Lombardi and [Terry] Moore in a footrace."

Southworth and what was left of the bombers crowded together to limp home and fend off the attacks. The Germans kept coming until the Americans were safely near England. Finally, Southworth made a safe emergency landing at Exeter and returned to Molesworth the next day. When he did, Southworth learned that one of his good friends, Ehle Reber, and his entire crew from *Jerry Jinx* had been shot down and ditched in the Bay of Biscay. All aboard were killed.

The Germans made taunting broadcasts to American air crews, telling them they were going to keep attacking head-on. Billy and the other crews demanded that the Air Corps add forward 50-caliber machine guns to better defend the B-17s against head-on attacks, but he was cautiously superstitious in his writing, unlike Reber, whose words invited fate. "We will soon have twin .50s in the nose," Reber wrote days before his death. "Hopefully it won't be too late for someone." The loss was as close as the empty bunks. Billy, as always, kept it terse. Emotion was his enemy. "Learned of Reber's tough luck," he wrote. "Hate to lose the lot of them."

Billy kept his baseball rituals alive. He kept a ball and a glove with him on his missions so just in case he was shot down and interned in a

POW camp, he would have something to do to pass the time. There was no other time like the early months of the bombing campaign over Europe. Later in the war, when numerical superiority and fighter escorts were prevalent, some B-17 crews went entire tours without firing a shot in defense. But in those miserable early months of Billy Southworth's war, it was trench warfare at twenty thousand feet.

Inside the bombers it was freezing and not pressurized. The windows were wide-open for the guns. Men wore four layers of electrically heated, heavy-leather flight clothing that took on a permanent reek after a while. It was no wonder that boys back in the States couldn't get new baseball gloves—the bomber boys were making all the fresh leather smell like elephant shit. Frost accrued on men's eyebrows and on the windshields. Frostbite was rampant among the crews. If the electric heating went out inside a flight suit, a man could freeze to death. Everyone had ear and sinus troubles. Everyone got sick.

Billy Southworth Jr. had a baseball in his pocket when the curtain was pulled back on the big target board in the briefing room on the early morning of January 17, 1943. A collective silence struck the crews. The flight plan showed that for the first time in the war, the target was Germany itself. He felt terrible that day, but he had waited a long time to drop bombs on Germany itself, and he wasn't about to tell anyone how awful he felt for fear of being grounded. His head throbbed with a sinus headache and a nagging cold, but like the old ballplayer he was, Billy couldn't wait to get after it. "I was tired and sore," he wrote. "Taxied like a bat out of hell into position, my crew jumping into ship as I pulled on to perimeter track."

As usual, Billy wore the lucky Cardinals hat his dad had given him during the 1942 World Series. The raid on Wilhelmshaven was uneventful by 303rd standards, with erratic flak and greenhorn German fighter pilots. It was bombs away at twenty-three thousand feet. But Billy had a special delivery all his own. When he was over Germany, Billy reached into his pocket and pulled out a baseball. He slid open the pilot-side cockpit window. His copilot, John Dillinger, thought Billy was crazy. Then he smirked with that cowboy Cardinals grin of his and dropped his personal payload on the Third Reich, a Spalding baseball bearing the signature of National League president Ford Frick. Say hello to Hitler, from the St. Louis Cardinals.

The raids kept coming as the 1943 baseball season approached. It looked like Billy might just make it to Opening Day, as long as FDR gave the green light again. Billy was eventually grounded because of his sinus trouble and missed another month with an appendectomy. His original bomber, *Bad Check,* had been to hell and back, so a new B-17 was christened *Winning Run.* One of the mechanics came up with a sketch Billy and his crew loved. "We're going to paint a guy in a Cardinal uniform, tough-looking mug, with one foot resting on a baseball that has a time fuse attached to it," Billy said. What they got instead was a redbird, a Cardinal, perching on an over-size baseball.

Billy began getting letters from his dad about the Cardinals and how wartime baseball looked at home—which was to say, a little bit shoddy. But even wartime baseball was baseball, and Billy needed it, as badly as he needed his bomber and his gunners and the rest of his crew, as badly as he needed to keep tossing baseballs out the window to plant in the soil of Nazi Germany. Every ball he dropped meant he was one mission closer to rotating home. His original crew from *Bad Check* had long since been broken up, and many of the men he'd known when the 303rd first arrived in Molesworth were dead. Billy was a veteran now, who saw inexperienced pilots killed by the same mistakes he had instinctively avoided. "Lost one of the group in Lorient," he wrote when the weather thawed and springtime caressed the English countryside. "He was new, didn't even know him. Head-on attack. He wasn't experienced. His formation flying was poor. Too bad."

Billy knew discipline would keep him alive. But while he waited to fly again and the baseball season started, he didn't know that one of his most terrifying ordeals lay just in the offing, or in Billy's time frame of the war, around the time the Cardinals next played the Dodgers. He finally seemed tranquil again. He knew for sure he would live to see the start of the 1943 baseball season, but he did not know if there would be a 1943 baseball season.

The winter months following the Cardinals triumph in the World Series had been long. Anxiety grew as the Americans mobilized and entered the war on a much greater scale. Billy Southworth Jr.'s experiences with the Eighth Air Force typified the new air war over Western Europe. Three Allied task forces, including five carriers, landed thirty-four thousand US troops near Casablanca. An additional thirty-nine thousand US and British troops landed near Oran, followed by thirty-three thousand more near Algiers. The newly appointed Allied supreme commander, General Dwight D. Eisenhower, was once a semipro shortstop in Kansas. *Newsweek* noted, "Baseball is a passion for many of the men in General Eisenhower's Army." Ike himself was a big baseball fan, but right now his first priority was to open a second front against Rommel in North Africa to push the Axis clear off the continent. In the Pacific, fifty thousand US troops made the final push to secure Guadalcanal, while fighting raged in New Guinea. In February, the brutal Guadalcanal campaign finally resulted in an American victory, but with the realization that island-hopping through the Pacific would be tedious and costly.

Roosevelt and Churchill met at Casablanca in January and agreed to jointly invade Sicily when North Africa was secured, and they committed to the unconditional surrender of the Axis powers. Roosevelt wanted an invasion of northern France to finish Germany, but acknowledged such an effort would be more than a year away. So he reluctantly accepted the Sicily invasion, though his generals warned him of enormous casualty rates against rugged terrain and fortified mountain positions.

When Roosevelt came home to Washington, he was tired. As spring training neared, there was no official word from the White House concerning the start of the 1943 season. Baseball would not proceed without another green light from Roosevelt, or at least a gesture that another season had his blessing. A letter was waiting for him from a Marine vet, who spoke for many grunts when he wrote:

> *There has been considerable comment lately in newspapers and over the radio about the possible termination of professional baseball. I have discussed this matter with several other Marines and we all feel that baseball should continue this year and if possible, for the duration of the war. Baseball keeps our spirits up, gives us something to talk about and promotes sportsmanship. It is my belief baseball would greatly aid servicemen overseas. I served in China and Guam for almost three years before the war and always eagerly read reports of scores and games. It brought the States to me*

very pleasantly. We hope that baseball will continue to operate this year.

The genuine fear was that the war would make a 1943 major league season impossible. Newspapers and fans speculated the season would be canceled because of the excessive manpower demands. All one had to do was read the newspapers to see the huge numbers of American troops deployed to North Africa and the Pacific. In addition, travel and resource restrictions controlled everything from where spring training could be held to whether a fan could buy a hot dog at a game.

Without a clear response from Roosevelt, Clark Griffith again took it upon himself to schedule a visit to assure another wartime baseball season. Griffith tried hard to get on the president's schedule books, but he found that getting an appointment during the war was much harder than it used to be. Writing to Stephen Early, the president's secretary, in March, Griffith asked, "Steve, when you and your pal get around to the point where you can pass out the 'green light' for the coming season, please don't fail to make mention of the fact that baseball played on weekends and at night would not at all take the war worker off the job and absenteeism would be curtailed to the smallest degree."

With the winter thawing and spring training nearing, Griffith's patience was rewarded. About six weeks after Roosevelt returned from Casablanca, Griffith was finally admitted to the White House. He believed appearances were everything, so on occasion of his annual visit in early April to present FDR with his ceremonial American League pass, the Old Fox polished his shoes, slicked back his silver hair, dry-cleaned his Sunday suit, and melted when Roosevelt greeted him with his informal, friendly, and folksy "Clark!" thickly coated with that famous aristocratic New York accent.

Griffith was pleased to learn that Roosevelt absolutely wanted baseball to continue, but he evidently did not want to make another public statement about the issue. Bigger things were on his mind, things he could not tell Griffith, such as the planned invasion of Western Europe, a bombing campaign against Japan, and top-secret nuclear-weapon-technology research in the New Mexico desert. Griffith could take something as simple as the baseball word back to the people.

Roosevelt did have one request. He wanted more night baseball. Griffith told him that he had run into stubborn opposition from Judge Landis and the owners. Griffith explained how he had been rebuffed when he tried to start a few Senators games at twilight. Roosevelt didn't care that Landis wasn't going to go to any great lengths to accommodate Roosevelt's wishes. He was aware that Landis had said during the winter, "I will not go to Washington, nor will I ask a favor for baseball from anyone."

But Landis had been on the phone to Washington, and his conversations in part helped Griffith get what he wanted. Landis's conversations with Joseph Eastman, head of the Office of Defense Transportation (ODT), a cabinet-level position charged with monitoring all transportation in the United States, resulted in a planned baseball schedule that would include a record two hundred doubleheaders in 1943, designed to cut down on travel. Exhaustive doubleheader schedules, which starved players, who couldn't get proper meals between games because of meat rationing, became a regular habit for the rest of the war. Landis also allowed morning baseball to be played for the first time, permitting occasional 10:30 a.m. games, thereby acknowledging Roosevelt's desire for war workers on odd hours to be able to take in a ball game.

The war didn't change Landis's dislike of Roosevelt, but the commissioner was pleased to quietly get the 1943 season locked down, even if Griffith thought he was doing all the work. Landis had his own way of doing business. He summoned reporters to announce, "I received a letter signed by five men in the Army. They wanted to be sure that they would be at the next World Series. I sent them assurance that they could be at the next World Series as my guest!"

To Griffith, Roosevelt made it clear that he was not interested in baseball's political infighting. He had enough of that in his job as wartime president. Griffith's visit, therefore, was somewhat ceremonial, but Roosevelt was a politician in his own right. His cabinet communicated to Landis the president's domestic demands for wartime baseball, while keeping Griffith, a man FDR genuinely liked, the public face for his green light. The game must go on.

Griffith was proud to do his part. Roosevelt again made Griffith his baseball version of Churchill, the man who would help him fight in the streets. Nobody else in baseball followed the war as closely as Griffith. The

Senators owner was proudly descended from soldiers who fought the red-coats and marched in the federal army during the Civil War. Griffith fancied himself a wartime general. His office walls were plastered with war maps and red, white, and blue pins signifying American, British, and Canadian troops, with black pins for the Germans and (predictably) yellow pins for the Japanese.

Griffith didn't just follow the war news. He tried to predict it, antici-pating tactical moves before they occurred, living the war in his own strange way. "He moves American forces in North Africa and the Southwest Pa-cific according to his own strategy and then waits for Generals Eisenhower and MacArthur to catch up with him," *The Washington Post* observed. The *Post* thought Griffith brazen enough to share war advice with the president of the United States.

Really, the only piece of tactical news Griffith wanted to know was if Roosevelt would be able to revive his tradition of throwing out the first pitch on Opening Day, which was April 20 against the Philadelphia Athletics. Griffith was ready to show off the wartime uniforms he had for his ball-players, which featured red, white, and blue stirrup socks. Roosevelt told him he'd think about it, but Griffith knew that meant no. He left with a handshake, a photo opportunity, and his signature move—another new handbag for the first lady with her season pass enclosed. A few days later, Griffith got the news he was expecting: Stephen Early informed him that the president's war duties would "prevent him from hurling the first pitch." But it was a small price to pay for the new season.

Fighting men around the world rejoiced when they heard the news, as did fans, players, and owners on the home front, who quickly geared up for the second wartime season. All that was certain was that it promised to be harder than the first. Roosevelt had always been right to let the people keep baseball. The time when they needed it most was not the time to take it away. When word reached the Molesworth airfield in England, Billy and his bomber boys celebrated, just like boys in foxholes or the girls working in factories. For Billy senior and the Cardinals, the feeling was shared, and father and son could look forward to another season of exchanged letters chronicling the pennant race and life in the air war. Everybody was happy to know that Roosevelt had once again decided that the game must go on.

Billy junior couldn't wait to see his dad again when his tour was over to find out if Billy senior could manage the Cardinals to another World Series. The war was a long way from over, and everyone knew it. But there was hope. Baseball was back in 1943.

CHAPTER 10

Too Tall, Too Short, Too Young, Too Old

President Roosevelt made the cover of the April 15, 1943, *Sporting News*, heralding the arrival of the second wartime major league season. The cartoonist depicted Roosevelt alongside an eager American soldier ready to charge into battle, his M1 rifle pointed at the ready. The GI boasted, "Yes, Sir! That's my America! It's one of the important parts of my way of livin' I'm fightin' for. . . . I'm givin' up a lot for th'time bein'. . . . But THEY could let me keep baseball!"

Actually, they could let him keep what was left of baseball, but what was left was more than enough to keep morale going at home and abroad. The simple and secure thought of baseball as a steady constant in the tired days ahead meant everything to the war-weary nation. A sailor wrote a moving letter to sportswriter Grantland Rice, who penned a sentiment summing up the arrival of the new season: "The deck of a destroyer is hardly the place to whistle 'Take me out to the ballgame,' but this blue jacket wants his baseball!" The need for the game in the darkest hour sparked the beginning of the three longest, strangest years it had ever known, and the game's wartime manpower shortage caused changes that shaped the game for decades to come.

The signs that the war was transforming baseball and its role in American life began as the war entered the second baseball season. Commanding officers saw how much the game meant to the boys in service. At the

Baseball Writers' dinner before spring training, a message from Lieutenant General Brehon B. Somervell summarized the Army's position on the value of baseball to the fighting man, no doubt reflecting what officers lectured to their troops:

> *I wanted to tell you how important a factor baseball is in the winning of the war. It has been said that the success of the British Army can be traced to the cricket fields of Eton. I say that the sandlots and big league ballparks of America have contributed their share to our military success. A great percentage of all major league players at the time of Pearl Harbor are wearing military uniforms and giving a splendid account. A million and a half kids from the junior sandlot teams sponsored by the major leagues and the American Legion are in the armed services. They are good soldiers. They learned teamwork early and it takes teamwork to win a battle or a war. Baseball also teaches realism. We never dare forget that a battle or campaign can be upset by a ninth-inning rally. We take no chances. We dare not slow down. We dare not relax until the last batter is out.*

Since the soldiers and sailors clearly wanted and needed baseball, the remaining major leaguers were going to have to deal with a new lifestyle far removed from anything they had ever before encountered. Traditional hallmarks of the game were temporarily altered in order for the game to proceed with the government's approval. The first concession was moving all spring-training camps from Florida and California to locations closer to the major league clubs, without concern for the usual creature comforts. Travel would be more difficult from now on because fuel restrictions meant no more coast-to-coast adventures until the war was over. A Pullman train reservation could not be made more than twenty-four hours in advance and was subject to change based on military needs. "The strangest baseball training session in the game's century of progress," *The Washington Post* announced. "Gone are palm strewn fields, to be replaced by Turkish baths and winter fields."

The Cardinals froze in Cairo, the Dodgers shivered at Bear Mountain, the Giants used John D. Rockefeller's former country club and golf course, the Reds had Indiana University, and Detroit was in Evansville, among other obscure locations. Every team was somewhere strange and different. Cold rain and mud-flooded fields made regular preseason workouts nearly impossible. Drinking and smoking were rampant among bored ballplayers. These unusual spring camps presented their own sets of difficulties throughout the war, but until it was over, such anomalies would be routine.

Even the ball was made differently. To conserve rubber, the new ball was now made with a balata core, which was a cheaper, rubberlike substance used in place of real rubber because of material rationing. It was a terrible experiment. *The Sporting News* featured a photo of a dissected baseball, reporting, "This cut-away view of a baseball shows the center consisting of two layers of reclaimed balata compound, covering pill of cork, compounded with reclaimed balata compound as a binder to hold shape." The ball just didn't play true and was discarded a few weeks into the season. Pitchers couldn't make it move, and hitters couldn't make it jump off the bat. Players thought it was lifeless.

On Opening Day at Griffith Stadium in Washington, DC, Clark Griffith got his ceremonial first-ball pitcher from the White House, but it wasn't Roosevelt. The best the White House could offer was Paul McNutt, a former college pitcher and the chairman of the War Manpower Commission. That selection was as fitting as it was frustrating. Every ballplayer knew McNutt's name. He was the grim reaper, the guy who had your draft number. When McNutt lobbed the first ball, the ballplayers did not scurry for the baseball as they always had for Roosevelt, perhaps for fear that if they told McNutt their names, they, too, would be drafted into service and join the swiftly increasing numbers of major leaguers in service.

Opening Day was quite a letdown, foreshadowing the struggles to come. The biggest problem was becoming apparent. The glaring manpower shortage took its first toll of the war, with the ranks of active major league players in service swelling from 71 in 1942 to 219 in 1943, including Ted Williams, who left the Red Sox for Naval flight training before selecting Marine aviation, and Joe DiMaggio, who left the Yankees for the Army. "It becomes evident each day that enlistments and Selective Service are picking the cream of the major league baseball crop," the *Hartford Courant* wrote. "There is no comparison between this war and the last one in the matter of big name players entering the service."

Baseball executives believed the player shortage would balance the 1943 season, giving teams who otherwise couldn't compete with the Cardinals or the Yankees hope for close pennant races. "The manpower proposition can be the great equalizer," Clark Griffith hoped. Branch Rickey, freshly fired from the St. Louis Cardinals and now the general manager of the Brooklyn Dodgers, predicted, "Every team has lost vital players, but the competition will be there, and that's the important thing." But a few weeks into the season, it was clear that wasn't true. The Cardinals and the Yankees took off early and never looked back, but the standings were much less of a priority in war than in peace. Most fans didn't care as long as they had ball games. The '43 pennant races were no races at all, but that never bothered soldiers and sailors. They were just as interested in the ballplayers joining them in the fight as they were in the fights for the pennants.

Ted Williams and his friend and teammate Johnny Pesky entered Naval flight school together, with dreams of shooting down Japanese Zeros instead of gunning down the Yankees in 1943. Williams vowed, "I'm not batting .400 in this flying stuff yet, but I'm going to do it." Missing Williams, Pesky, and center fielder Dominic DiMaggio, who joined the Navy, the Red Sox fell to seventh place. The only time Williams played at Fenway Park in 1943 was in July when he faced Babe Ruth in a staged home-run contest. Williams already felt slower than he thought he would. He managed to hit three homers, while the exhausted and embarrassed Bambino couldn't understand why he was too weak to loft even one lazy ball into the stands.

Joe DiMaggio never swung the bat once for the '43 Yankees. He was utterly miserable and in poor health. His marriage and ulcers were a wreck, and he knew he was earmarked for somewhere in the Pacific. Joe was a glorified show pony. Some guys fought the war behind a rifle. DiMaggio fought his in front of a camera. A few months removed from playing the Cardinals in the 1942 World Series, the best center fielder in the major leagues was quartered at Santa Ana Army Airfield playing against such low-level talent as Fullerton Junior College. He had a 27-game hitting streak he didn't care much about.

The Army rolled DiMaggio out for photo opportunities at every turn, and he talked endlessly about baseball with servicemen and reporters. That was his job, but for Joe, that was no job at all for a real ballplayer. Yet those moments were the only connections to the life he'd left behind. If nobody asked him for his autograph, he might forget who he was. The generals who requisitioned him for service teams never risked putting him in harm's way, even when they eventually shipped him out of Santa Ana. Joe knew how to use them. These guys were all about prestige, and as long as he smiled and winked, he could have it better than ordinary Joes. He freely moved around at night, driving into Hollywood to flirt with all the blondes he could handle, even when he was making $50 per month. Joe figured it out— the Army was just trying to sell tickets. If his best contribution to the war effort was getting kids to sign up, so be it.

Joe D had company when the Yankees lost veteran right-handed pitcher Red Ruffing to the Army. He was a four-time 20-game winner with 258 lifetime victories who was hoping to make it to 300 wins, but the war killed that dream. Ruffing was a screwball and in his later years a screwup. He was drinking heavily, mostly this homemade purple hooch he kept in his flask, getting plastered and fat, and pitching for the Sixth Ferrying Command in Long Beach, just up the road from DiMaggio in Santa Ana. A game was arranged pitting the two Yankee greats against one another. Ruffing pitched a gem and struck out 9, including DiMaggio. This baseball-at-war business was so screwed up that it took joining the Army for Ruffing to finally pitch a no-hitter. He shook his head at such bum luck.

With Williams and DiMaggio gone, the emergence of Stan Musial of the St. Louis Cardinals saved the season and established a rising young hitting star for years to come. Playing in his first full season, the harmonica-playing kid proved that his rookie season in 1942 had been no fluke. The boy could swing the bat and was here to stay. He won the batting title with a .357 average and hit 13 home runs, also leading the league in hits (220), doubles (48), and triples (20), an indicator of his overlooked speed. Musial played each of the outfield positions and recorded 15 assists, an indicator of his arm strength, instincts, and athleticism. Musial won the first of his three Most Valuable Player awards in the decade. Nobody thought he was less of a hitter just because the pitching was thinner. At long last, Musial was the young star the National League had been waiting for to match the magnitude of DiMaggio and Williams, the young stars of the American League.

A description of the twenty-two-year old Musial in the *Christian Sci-*

ence Monitor captured him perfectly in his times: "He can run with typical Cardinals speed and do it intelligently. He can hit with power against any kind of pitching. He can run down a fly ball and when he gets to it, he knows where to throw it. He hustles and has love for the game. He wants to be a great ballplayer." Boston Braves manager Casey Stengel put it bluntly: "That Musial! You're going to wake up one day and discover that he is the best player in the big leagues. I'm not sure he isn't already."

Musial was one of the rare lucky ones, classified 4-F, who were permitted to stay in the majors in 1943. He was the heart of the Cardinals, especially after outfielder Enos Slaughter enlisted. Slaughter wanted to be a pilot, but washed out of aviation cadet school. "The doctors told me I was color-blind and they told me that I would have to find another way than I had expected to serve Uncle Sam," Slaughter said. For the next two years, Sergeant Slaughter ran calisthenics at Lackland Field in San Antonio. He was the right fielder for the San Antonio Cadet Center Warhawks, where for two years he played in the eight-team San Antonio Service League, where he hit .498 and watched in admiration as the 4-F Musial moved into his old right-field turf for the Cardinals and produced the best season anyone had ever seen during World War II.

The Cardinals and the Yankees were the only teams strong enough to survive the manpower crush of the 1943 season, proving that in war or peace, the only two ways to build a winning baseball team are with a lot of cash or a lot of young players. The Yankees lost All-Stars Joe DiMaggio, Tommy Henrich, and Phil Rizzuto, but bought their way out of trouble, purchasing first baseman Nick Etten from the dreadful Philadelphia Phillies. Etten came out of nowhere, a 4-F star who belted 14 home runs and drove in 107 runs, precious power in a season in which total home runs fell below 1,000 for the first time since 1927. Another outfielder, Johnny Lindell, won 23 games as a pitcher in the minor leagues in 1941, but hit his way into the lineup and drove in more runs than Roy "Stormy" Weatherly, a crabby outfielder who was purchased from the Indians to replace DiMaggio.

The Yankees ran away with the American League pennant, while across the River, the Brooklyn Dodgers disintegrated by design. Veteran pitcher Larry French and young stars Pete Reiser and Pee Wee Reese were lost to the services, but the real story was Branch Rickey's rise to power. Derisively called the "the father of the chain store," he grew wealthy selling his excess player inventory, but his percentage of the profits fueled his conflict with Cardinals owner Sam Breadon. Hired in Brooklyn to build the Dodgers into a generational contender, his first stage was to let the club bottom out during the war. The Dodgers finished 23½ games out of first place, not exactly what was expected of a front-office boss who was touted by the Brooklyn press as a "master psychologist, nifty news generator, spell-binding orator, keen talent scout, sagacious executive, charming personage, passionate patriot, and rock bottom Honest Abe." Rickey never did admit to the public how far he was thinking ahead, but his fingerprints make it difficult to imagine that he wasn't already thinking of signing Negro League players as early as 1943, the first devastating season of the wartime manpower shortage. Rickey launched the embryonic stages of his complete overhaul of the organization that eventually changed baseball for years to come.

While Rickey dismantled the Dodgers, the Cardinals had the horses, and manager Billy Southworth guided them to 105 wins and a runaway NL pennant. The Cardinals and Yankees fittingly met in a World Series rematch, but this time the Yankees had their revenge. Veteran pitcher Spud Chandler, the AL MVP in '43 owing to his 20-4 record and league-leading 1.64 earned run average, beat the Cardinals twice, including a shutout in the final game. The Yankees won the series in a 5-game snap punctuated by a B-17 Flying Fortress making a flag-level pass above Yankee Stadium. The Fort's flyover was a patriotic push to sell war bonds and a read-between-the-lines payback for Billy junior's memorable pass over Sportsman's Park in the last World Series.

The season made great entertainment for the boys in service, but it did not begin to tell the entire story of all the ballplayers who put their careers aside for the good of winning the war. Most of these players were not as famous as Hank Greenberg, Bob Feller, Ted Williams, or Joe DiMaggio, but they were good professional ballplayers, and their stories composed the fabric and meaning of major league baseball at war.

One of Clark Griffith's favorite players was gone for the second consecutive year in 1943, Buddy Lewis, a good-natured country boy from North Carolina. His hunting eye was as keen with a shotgun as it was against the fastball. He played ball at Wake Forest and established himself in the big leagues at age nineteen in 1935, hitting .300 three times in the next six seasons before he turned twenty-five, collecting 210 hits in 1937 and hit a career high .319 in 1939. He enlisted and took basic training at Fort Knox in 1942 and hoped for a transfer to the Air Corps. He thought his chances of flying were gone when he never heard back. On the night before he was supposed to ship out to the invasion of North Africa for Operation Torch, his transfer came through. Lewis couldn't believe his luck. He missed the invasion and instead spent the 1943 baseball season in flight school at Lawson Field, where he trained to fly transports. Transport pilots were in great demand, and Lewis knew he'd eventually be shipped out.

Buddy orchestrated a memorable farewell in 1943. On his way out of Washington, he flew his C-47 so low over Griffith Stadium that its draft blew the hat off the batter, George Case. Case remembered looking up at the plane. He knew it was Buddy. Case picked up the rosin bag and tossed it high into the air, his way of bidding Buddy good-bye.

When Buddy flew out of town, he was the second significant Senator missing, joining shortstop Cecil Travis, who joined the Army infantry at age twenty-seven following the 1941 season, when he led the American League with 218 hits and finished second in the league with a .359 batting average. Travis spent 1943 playing Army ball and wondering when he would see combat. Buddy Lewis had All-Star ability, and Cecil Travis had Hall of Fame potential. Peace had never been kind to the perpetually hapless Senators, but the war promised to be hell.

Flight training a crow hop away from Buddy Lewis was Bert Shepard, a former minor league pitcher, who was qualifying to fly pursuit planes at Daniel Field. In 1939, he was a teenager who hitchhiked from Indiana to Southern California in the hopes of being discovered. He worked odd jobs and played semipro ball until 1940, when a White Sox scout signed him to a $60-a-month contract. Shepard thought he was the richest kid in the world, but the contract had a catch—an option that it would only pay if Shepard could make the cut at the White Sox minor league camp. Shepard didn't make the grade and headed home with his head down and his pockets nearly empty, but he turned his look with the Sox into work in the Evangeline League and Ohio State leagues.

When the 1941 season ended, Shepard pitched a few innings for a Class C team in Anaheim, which was a minor league team for the Philadelphia Athletics. Shepard met Connie Mack, who had no use for him. The rejection furthered Shepard's resolve, but he thought the war was more important than playing in the minors, which he did in 1942. "I wanted to keep playing," he said. "When the war started, I think everyone was waiting around to see what Landis was going to do. There was going to come a point when you had to decide if you were going to play ball, or if you were going to get into the fight."

James Murrell Jones was on the fast track to the big leagues in 1939. He was tall and strong, six foot three and nearly two hundred pounds, cut from rugged Louisianan stock. In his rookie season, playing for Monroe in the Cotton States League, he flashed hometown home-run power, hitting .321 with 14 home runs and 103 runs batted in. In 1940, he advanced to Shreveport in the Texas League, which was a man's league, a place for older players, where ballplayers rarely jumped to from the lowly Class D leagues. Jones, whose determination was as cut on his face as it was on his muscles, hit .301, with 16 home runs and 75 runs batted in. At Shreveport again in 1941, he came into his own with 24 home runs. Major League scouts were all over him. Shreveport valued his contract at $25,000 for his power bat and superlative first-base defensive skills. It didn't take long for the Chicago White Sox to purchase his contract. *The Sporting News* christened him "one of the most promising of this year's players."

James Murrell Jones wanted two things in his young life: one was to play in the majors, and the other was to be called by the nickname he much preferred over his given name. He loved the sound of Jake Jones. It was a tough guy's name, the kind of name you would fear, if he had anything to say about it.

At the age of twenty in 1941, Jake broke into the big leagues long enough to smell the grass. He made his major league debut on September 20 at Comiskey Park against the Hank Greenberg–less Detroit Tigers. The Tigers gave Jones a rude awakening. The first pitcher Jones faced was Bobo Newsom. They didn't have nibblers with big mouths and bigger curveballs like this in the Texas League. The next Tigers pitcher to hold Jones hitless was Tommy Bridges, who was one of the great Tigers aces of the 1930s. He was older and savvy, had a drinking problem, and saw the holes in the boy's long swing. Another hitless day for the Louisiana rookie led to another one when Al Benton shut him down. When the series was over, Murrell Jones was 0-for-11 and had played himself out of the Opening Day plans for the 1942 Chicago White Sox.

But Jones, like Bridges (Army) and Benton (Navy), the two Tigers pitching stalwarts who soon followed Hank Greenberg into the service, had no idea what the war would do to his baseball career. Jones had seen enough big league time to realize he wasn't ready yet. He realized it might be a while before anybody knew the name Jake Jones. He left for the Navy in 1943, determined to learn how to be a fighter pilot. Unlike many of the other ballplayers who wanted to fly fighters, this kid had a chance to make it in aerial combat. His baseball career would have to wait.

Another player notably absent from the American League was Philadelphia Athletics right-handed pitcher Phil Marchildon, who joined the Royal Canadian Air Force in November and started training for duty in a bomber crew. When he was pitching, Marchildon flashed great stuff with bad control and engaged Williams and DiMaggio on many memorable occasions. He had one of the best young arms in the league, but he decided the business end of a machine gun in a bomber would be a better way for a star pitcher to take it to the Germans.

His story was special because he was from rural Canada, from a place where major league scouts did not dig. Marchildon was so isolated that he said he didn't even know the major leagues existed until he was in his twenties. In 1939, he was an unknown twenty-five-year-old pitcher on a coal-mining team in rural Ontario with a good fastball, a great curveball, and a terrible dose of wildness. He was tall and slender with committed eyes and sleek black hair. Finally, a birddog scout sent a letter to the Toronto Maple Leafs, the nearest minor league team, and soon Marchildon was granted a tryout, where he struck out 7 of the 9 hitters he faced. He coaxed a small bonus and signed his first professional contract to pitch Class C ball. He won all six decisions and was promoted to Toronto before the end of the season, where former big league catcher Johnnie Heving predicted, "That boy has a curve that is a one-way ticket to a major league club."

Marchildon started the 1940 season with Toronto, coming as fast as the Spitfires buzzing the field, but the fighters did not tempt Marchildon as they had Billy Southworth Jr. Marchildon never dreamed that a Royal Canadian Air Force career was in his future. All he wanted to do was pitch his way to the big leagues. Marchildon could be dazzling and maddeningly inconsistent, often simultaneously. He once struck out 10 and walked 10 in the same game. He was on the fast track to the majors in 1940, finishing 10-13 with a 3.18 earned run average.

Connie Mack purchased his contract from Toronto for $10,000 and promoted him to the Philadelphia Athletics for two major league starts in September. Facing the Washington Senators with Buddy Lewis and Cecil Travis and the Red Sox with Ted Williams taught Marchildon that he was not yet ready to win, but gave him proof that he belonged.

"I always thought I could pitch in the majors if I got the chance, and I didn't think it mattered where I was from or where I grew up," Marchildon said. "I just wanted the chance and I knew I could make good because I had the quick curveball. I got it to a point where I felt good throwing it against anyone, anytime. I wouldn't say I had an overpowering fastball like [Hal] Newhouser or Feller, but I could keep you honest."

Marchildon started the 1941 season in Philadelphia and made his first start on May 3 against Newhouser and the Detroit Tigers. This great pitching matchup featured two of the best young arms in the talent-rich American League. Newhouser beat Marchildon, 4–3, but the Tigers were impressed with the Canadian right-hander's stuff. Hank Greenberg doubled and struck out against him and three days later left the Tigers to join the Army.

Marchildon established himself as one of the most promising starting pitchers in 1941. He went 10-15 and pitched 204 innings, posting a 3.57 earned run average. He knew he would eventually have to make a decision about the war. After a solid 17-14, 4.20 campaign in 1942, he decided to join the RCAF when the season was over. A few months later, he thought that getting his tailor-made flight officer's outfit in that royal blue was just as incredible as the first time he wore his royal-blue Philadelphia Athletics hat in the majors. He knew he would soon be in the skies over Europe.

Another minor league player who vanished in 1943 was Warren Spahn, who pitched the 1942 season in Casey Stengel's Boston Braves doghouse and won 17 games with a 1.96 ERA for Class A Hartford. Spahn's arm was so durable that in August he pitched a shutout in the first game of a double-header and came back a few hours later to pitch the final 6 innings of the second game, picking up two wins in the same day by throwing 15 innings.

The *Hartford Courant* suggested "our nifty southpaw" was "knocking on the door of the baseball Hall of Fame."

Spahn joined the Army in December 1942 and spent 1943 learning infantry skills and pitching for Camp Chaffee. He harbored no grand illusions of aviation. He knew that he was just a rank-and-file minor leaguer and that nobody would do him any favors. He knew he was bound for Europe. He met a Cherokee girl and thought he would marry her when the war was over, but he decided to wait to see if he survived.

He wasn't long removed from the boy who was a high school pitcher in Buffalo in 1939 who discovered he could throw a rainmaker curveball. He decided his future was on the mound, where his quirky, cocky, and combative personality took shape. He wore number 13 and thought it was lucky for him alone. He ignored the scouts who thought he was too small. The Boston Braves signed him for $80 per month in 1940, and in 1941, Spahn went 19-6 with a 1.83 earned run average for Class B Evansville in the Three-I League.

Spahn established himself as a major league prospect playing for manager Bob Coleman, one of the finest minor league managers and talent developers in his era, who a decade before had mentored young Hank Greenberg. When the war started, Spahn was twenty years old and too damn stubborn to worry about it. He wanted to get to the majors—and he thought 1942 would be the year it would happen—if only the baseball season would carry on as planned. By the time 1943 arrived, he knew he was no different from a guy like Hank Greenberg, even though he was much younger, hadn't proven anything in the majors, and had next to no money. He already knew that whenever the war was over, whenever he got out, he would never be the same.

While Warren Spahn wondered if he would ever pitch in the major leagues again, Bob Feller asked himself the same question. After he pitched a 5-inning war-benefit game at the Polo Grounds in June 1942, he was angry and made it known that he wasn't in the Navy just to sell war bonds. He wanted to get his sea legs, so the Navy finally consented and sent him to gunnery school at Norfolk, where he learned to command a 40mm gun crew. In September 1942, Feller was assigned to the battleship USS *Alabama BB-60*.

In January 1943, his father passed away from cancer, and Feller returned to Iowa on emergency leave for the funeral. The loss had been coming, but it still hurt. Feller believed his father was the biggest reason he had turned into a successful major league pitcher. In March 1943, a famous photo of Feller posing with his Quad-40 gun battery was published in newspapers around the country and became one of the iconic photographs of World War II baseball. More than ever, Feller longed to fight. He embarked to the North Atlantic with the *Alabama,* which spent most of the 1943 baseball season escorting Allied troop convoys through U-boat-infested waters. The *Alabama* returned to Norfolk in August and set sail for the Pacific in November, where she promised to earn her battle stripes and give Bob Feller the fight of his life.

The Pacific theater was already the overlooked one of the two major theaters of operation, and many of the ballplayers who became Marines ended up in the shit first. One of them was minor leaguer Hank Bauer, the lowly Yankee farmhand who joined the Marines after Pearl Harbor. Bauer cut his teeth in combat as a machine gunner in a Marine raider battalion in 1943. His first taste of action was a three-day hike to beat the Japanese to Segi Point in the Solomon Islands. After trudging through swamps and jungles on nothing but canteen water and candy bars, Bauer showed he wasn't afraid of anything. "We reached a point where we could look out on this bay," he recalled. "We spotted this barge, full of Jap soldiers, out on the bay—hell, never did see a barge on land, did you? Me and this other machine gunner opened up on them with crisscross fire. We just shot the hell out of this barge with everything we had. Do you know, we sank the damn thing—with machine-gun fire, and that's no bullshit!"

The war stories the ballplayers accumulated were no bullshit, but they weren't in it to brag. Players like Bauer were supposed to be baseball's next generation, but instead of growing the game they were fighting the war. All of the players in the service at the major and minor league levels, such as Hank Greenberg, Bob Feller, Ted Williams, Joe and Dom DiMaggo, Buddy Lewis, Cecil Travis, Enos Slaughter, Pee Wee Reese, Pete Reiser, Larry French, Phil Marchildon, Jake Jones, Warren Spahn, Bert Shepard, and Billy Southworth underscored baseball's manpower crisis. Fans following the majors at the time had no concept of how badly the war devastated scouting and player development. The lifeblood of baseball is finding and developing young players, but the war took so many men and boys that it ruined the traditional pipelines. Baseball had to find new ways to find new players both in the minors and the majors. That struggle became a war of its own and influenced the game for decades to come.

When it became apparent that replacing major leaguers was going to be a serious problem during the war, baseball general managers and evaluators begin to understand just how drastically the war undercut their traditional player procurement routes, and how it would force them to change the way they scouted, signed, and developed young players. The war made baseball ask new questions, which eventually helped to transform it into a modern business.

The war didn't just drain baseball of contemporary major league players in their twenties and thirties; it was robbing the game of the younger generation of teenage boys who either lied about their ages to enlist or would be drafted as soon as they reached eligible age. Minor league players who were already in their early twenties and went into the service would return home as damaged goods in the eyes of professional baseball. From the wartime generation came many older ballplayers who later became scouts, who would sign players that shaped baseball's landscape in decades to come. But in 1943, a new sense of urgency permeated baseball—how to develop talent when all the manpower was needed elsewhere. Baseball teams began considering players that before the war they would never have considered. Discards were suddenly in demand, but even getting some of them to commit to playing ball during the war was no easy feat.

The first problem was that many minor leaguers did not want to be playing while the war was going on. They sensed they were missing out on the biggest event of their lives. At six feet eight inches and 225 pounds, Mike Naymick was one of the largest pitchers anyone had ever seen. When the Army rejected him, he gave the Marines a try, but they turned him down, too. "Do you mean to tell me that I have to go back and tell everyone I'm still 4-F?" he griped. For many young men, *4-F* was a four-letter word.

Naymick thought he was turned away because he was simply too large to be an infantryman. His size-17 feet were so large that he was told he couldn't get another pair of baseball shoes made until after the war. Naymick was dejected. His reward was a pitching job for the Cleveland Indians, where he took Bob Feller's roster spot and went 4-4 with a 2.30 ERA. What was a plum job in peace was thought by some players to be a waste in war.

If Mike Naymick was the tall of it, Mickey Haefner was the short of it. He had everything going against him, except that he was left-handed. Haefner was generously listed as five feet eight, a knuckleball pitcher who couldn't throw hard enough to splash water, and never played minor league ball until he was twenty-five years old. He should have been the easiest player in the world for scouts to bury, but he could eat innings with a rubber arm and a callous determination, which had value during the war. "He has heart, but the boss likes 'em big" was the explanation one scout gave *The Sporting News* about why Haefner was trapped at Minneapolis from 1940 to 1942, winning 44 games. He was thirty in 1943, the perfect age for a wartime rookie in the estimation of Clark Griffith, who paid $20,000 for Haefner's contract and assigned him to the Senators pitching staff, where within two years Griffith assembled the most unique pitching staff in baseball history.

Haefner was too old, too short, and too slight to be a solider, so he gladly took his 4-F status and set about establishing himself as a wartime major leaguer. But it was going to take more than old men to keep the game going, and this was the problem. A long-term fix was needed for discovering baseball's new generation, and if possible, some teams would try to glimpse the future by using the war to run out players entirely too young for the majors.

That's how right-hander Carl Scheib got to pitch for the Philadelphia Athletics, becoming the youngest player in baseball history at sixteen years and 248 days, when he quit high school and pitched 2/3 of an inning against the New York Yankees on September 6, 1943, mopping up in the ninth inning of a lopsided loss. He was so young that his parents signed the contract for him. Scheib remembered being too young to be nervous, but "we were losing, which we did quite often." The Athletics lost 105 games, finished dead last, and Connie Mack nursed Scheib through 5 more mop-up outings. He pitched in 15 more games in 1944 and 4 more in 1945, joining the service at the end of the war.

Carl Scheib's record was made to be broken and on June 10, 1944, fresh from nearby Hamilton High School, Joe Nuxhall became the youngest player in major league history when he pitched one game for the Cincinnati Reds and made the sixteen-year old Scheib practically look like a geezer. Nuxhall was too young to register for the draft, but old enough to pitch in the majors at 15 years and 316 days. He was left-handed and threw hard, offered hope for good box office, and it seemed like a good idea at the time.

There was only one problem. The kid was 15 years and 316 days old.

Frankly, the kid was terrified and he shouldn't have been there. The week before he's pitching against altar boys, next thing he knows, he's facing the St. Louis Cardinals, the best team of the war years. Manager Billy Southworth, compassionate fellow that he was, might have thought the Reds had taken this whole wartime replacement thing a little too far. The game must go on, sure, but can this kid finish puberty first? Nuxhall was bench jockeyed just like any other rookie would be, and that didn't help the poor boy's nerves any either.

His inning started when he got George Fallon to ground out to short. It was good to know that a high school boy with no professional experience could walk into a wartime major league game and retire a lifetime .216 hitter who also happened to be a replacement, even though he was about to turn fifteen years older than Nuxhall.

That's where the fun ended for the poor kid. Then he walked the pitcher, Mort Cooper. Nuxhall threw a wild pitch, he walked another guy and Stan Musial was at the plate. As far as teenage pitchers go, this is the nightmare where you pitch naked, or at least in nothing but a jockstrap. Musial singled and the kid didn't wake up.

Take the boy out? Not a chance! Let him learn the hard way! The hitters all ran together for poor Nuxhall: walk, walk, walk, single . . . and now they took him out. The final score was Cardinals 18–0, but who was counting? The good news was that this outing was nothing that age, pitching experience, and several years of therapy couldn't heal. But Little Joe wore it like a pro, even when he was an old man and people asked him more about that one game when he became the youngest player to ever play in the majors, more than they ever wanted to know about the pretty good career he salvaged, or the 135 career victories or all the great decades he enjoyed broadcasting for the Reds. His fate was tied to one line score until he died at the age of 79 in 2007: 2/3 of an inning, 2 hits, 5 runs, all earned, 5 walks, no strikeouts, nine batters faced and no home runs. As Nuxhall liked to point out: "Hey, I kept the ball in the park."

As strange as it sounded to start pitchers so young in the majors and then farm them out, the war actually began teaching professional baseball how to better develop young pitchers by not rushing them just because they throw hard. Of course, the game always struggles to be patient with young power arms. They aren't all going to be Bob Feller and walk from high school to the majors. Teams just like to think their guy will.

The career paths of Scheib and Nuxhall showed that pitching requires patience. Connie Mack kept Scheib, sent him back to the minors after the war, made him a regular in 1947, and watched him blossom into a 14-game winner in 1948 who pitched in the majors until 1954.

It took Nuxhall ten years to figure it out as a big leaguer, but he got it going as a 12-game winner for the Reds at the age of twenty-five in 1954, and became an All-Star in 1955 and 1956. Some years later, he showed Nolan Ryan how to throw his change-up.

The war permanently changed how and when amateur players were scouted and signed. America was a rural nation, so most talented town players migrated to independent minor league teams, where major league scouts signed them to play higher-level minor league ball. But the war drained the manpower from the minors and put many of those teams out of business. For the first time, scouts began searching for high school players to sign before they ever played minor league ball for an independent club. That idea, now accepted practice, was then revolutionary. Scouts shifted their focus to teenagers playing high school and American Legion ball and to young men playing for Army and Navy teams. Then they devised new and sinister ways to sign them. The Yankees allowed high school players on their top farm team in Kansas City to work out with the Blues under the unwritten provision that the boys would be signed when the war was over. Baseball was really losing three generations of ballplayers to the war: the current players serving, the players who would have replaced them because they would have been of signing age during the war, and the players one class behind them, who would populate the minors.

Jack Zeller, the general manager of the Tigers, explained how baseball was changing: "A great many of the players who have gone into the armed forces and who are yet to go will be lost to the game forever. They may be too old when peace is restored, and many of them will be unable to come back." He promised Briggs Stadium would be used as a training facility for adolescent players when the Tigers were on the road. "If we are to have baseball after the war, we must start right now. We'll have to develop players for the postwar era that must be lads of twelve, thirteen, or fourteen years old. If they are good prospects, we'll offer them contracts. Then if they go into service, they'll have baseball jobs to come back to after the war."

To combat the talent drainage, teams took drastic measures that created institutionalized changes. Before the war, no major league team would have considered spending extravagantly for an untested amateur player. But when the Tigers lost Hank Greenberg in May of 1941, they overspent for a college outfielder named Dick Wakefield, paying the record sum of $52,000 for a boy who had never played professional baseball. The Tigers believed they needed to buy a young bat to replace Greenberg because they could not predict when Hank would return or what kind of hitter he would be when he did. It was the first time in baseball history that an unproven player was paid better than existing major leaguers, simply on his potential. It was a radical idea in 1941, and it earned Wakefield the derisive nickname that survives today for any player of any sport who earns large money before stepping foot into the highest level. Dick Wakefield was the original *bonus baby.*

He panned out in 1943, leading the league with 200 hits and hitting .316 with 38 doubles. But opposing players resented the former University of Michigan star for his instant wealth while the rest of them suffered and bled for paltry annual contracts. Wakefield was flamboyant, and players thought he didn't work hard after getting paid so handsomely. He won no friends when he suggested he was a better hitter than Ted Williams. Wakefield recognized the perils of becoming baseball's first bonus baby, but "I had to take the money," he protested. "I was a poor boy. I wouldn't have been a better ballplayer without the bonus. But when you're going badly, they get on you more than they would the average ballplayer. The bonus baby is all right, as long as he's having good years."

The bonus babies boomed after the war, reaching a peak of criticism when pitcher Paul Pettit became the first $100,000 high school bonus player in 1950, but the seeds were planted when baseball saw its first player shortage in the war. To combat the bonus boom, an amateur draft was created in 1965.

When the Tigers signed Wakefield, they let the genie out of the bottle— they created the concept of high-priced bidding wars among rival teams for amateur players. During the war, economics restricted the practice, as did the potentially bad public relations of turning young men who should have been in the service into wealthy juniors. Wakefield's big season in '43, paired with the sudden lack of talent that rushed players young and old, short and tall, skinny and fat, odd and misplaced, to the majors, showed that baseball was ready to learn from the war when it was over. Baseball's first experiment with cradle robbing led to the draft, which was created to curtail spending, but instead created rampant inflation for all future bonus babies. The next time you see a high school kid get more money than you can possibly imagine, think back to the day the US Army took Hank Greenberg away from the Detroit Tigers.

Throughout all the madness, one old, former ballplayer wanted to get in the war. He was the guy all the ballplayers at war grew up watching, and now he wished he could be serving alongside them. But Babe Ruth was never going to be allowed to fire a shot. He would have to settle with being a symbol. When Japanese soldiers taunted American Marines on New Guinea, they shouted, "Fuck you, Babe Ruth, go to hell, Bob Hope!" When Ruth heard that story, he delivered his most famous wartime quote: "I hope that every Jap that mentions my name gets shot. And to hell with the Japs anyway!"

The Babe, though beloved, was bloated from years of booze and bingeing. His throat was shot from cigar smoking. Ruth still had his old spirit and swagger, but his strength was sagging. He remained wildly popular, though he knew he was blacklisted from ever managing a major league team, payback from all those owners he embarrassed and infuriated while he was saving their industry in the 1920s and 1930s. If baseball wouldn't let him do his job, he hoped the Army would. He arrived unannounced to register at his local draft board in April 1942 and wheezed, "This where the old guys sign up?" Ruth wore reading glasses perched over his nose and cringed when photographers snapped images of him filling out his information card. "No pictures with these cheaters on," he grumbled. "I'll run you all outta here." One newsman egged him on, saying, "But, Babe, all of us can beat you running now." The Babe lowered his glare. "Yeah," he reluctantly lamented, "I guess you can."

Ruth gave his age as forty-seven (accurate), weighed in at 240 pounds (his playing weight was 215), and listed his work status as unemployed. He called his complexion "dark," which the clerk quickly changed to "ruddy." Asked his hair color, Ruth replied, "Getting gray." He signed autographs for everyone around him. His wavy signature was still as pretty as his swing. Asked what kind of Army job he had in mind, Ruth said, "I don't care. Whatever and wherever they think I could do some good for the country. Personally I think I might be able to do some good in that morale work. You know, going around to different camps, talking to the boys."

The Army rejected Ruth, who found ways to do a lot of good for the war effort. He visited many hospitals and spent time talking to wounded boys, doing most of his work without newsmen around. He couldn't understand why in the hell his throat hurt so badly. He waited all summer to be summoned for something bigger, but the call never came until August 1943, when he was asked back to Yankee Stadium for the first time in years.

In his younger days, Ruth might have hoped it was for an interview to manage the Yankees. But he knew he would never get that shot. Instead he was asked to appear in a war-bond benefit between games of a Yankees-Senators doubleheader. He donned his pinstripes yet again and walked to the batter's box, where the villain reprising his mound role would be none other than the great pitcher Walter Johnson, a 417-game winner who was now a farmer living in peaceful retirement. The old smoke was gone, but Johnson could still throw the ball with that sidearm motion as gracefully and effortlessly as ever.

Nearly seventy thousand fans crammed to the rafters of Yankee Stadium to see Babe in pinstripes again. Ruth and Johnson strolled out to the field to thunderous applause. It was just like old times. Before Ruth went to the box, Johnson muttered, "Hey, Babe, do me a favor. Don't hit any back to me." Ruth chortled, "Hell, I'll be lucky to hit one at all." Johnson thought Babe was joking, but then quickly realized that he was serious.

The ground rules were simple. Johnson would throw twenty pitches. Babe would try to hit them out. From the first swing, Johnson knew Ruth was in pain. He had seen him so many times over so many years. He knew everything was wrong. Babe was labored and tight. He wheezed when he swung the bat. Johnson eased up and grooved slow, straight balls down the middle, trying to give Ruth something he could hit, trying to give the fans something to get into. Walter didn't want to embarrass him, but Babe couldn't do anything anymore. Walter sensed his old friend's sadness. Finally, on the seventeenth pitch, Johnson grooved one just right and Ruth lofted a soft line drive over the short right-field wall for a home run. The fans roared. A few pitches later, Ruth hit a high, long ball into the upper deck in right field. The ball curved foul, but it was enough to look like an old-style Ruth home run.

That was close enough for Babe. He dropped the bat and hobbled off for one more home-run trot around the Yankee Stadium bases, listening to the applause once more. He waved his hat, as was his old custom, but he didn't realize that he was beginning his good-byes. Walter Johnson was waiting to meet him, and when the Babe crossed home plate, Walter gave him a hug. Ruth said something in Walter's ear. The fans didn't realize that he was asking Walter to hold him up.

A few moments later, Ruth vanished from the field as the fans chanted, *"We want Babe, we want Babe!"* But he was hiding alone in the dressing room, and nobody knew how bad he looked, how awful he felt, how skinny he looked naked. The early stages of the throat cancer were showing. "Mr. Ruth is taking a shower right now and can't come out," the public address announcer said. The Babe was nowhere to be seen. But deep in the caverns of Yankee Stadium, with the help of the old clubhouse guy, the Babe sat alone, crying, his old friends protecting him, his voice croaking. There was nothing they could say. Babe Ruth was slowly dying.

CHAPTER 11

Plasma for the Soul

The war raged on after the pleasant diversion that was the 1943 baseball season. After the World Series, the Italian campaign slogged on, and a few weeks later in the Pacific, the US landings at Bougainville in the Solomon Islands began, followed by the bloody landings at Tarawa. October in Europe was a costly one for the American bomber crews, especially on the infamous day when a massive formation of 291 B-17s from the Eighth Air Force flew without fighter cover deep into Germany to strike Schweinfurt. The bombers were hammered, with 60 losses and 121 limping home, in a day so devastating that it finally forced a change in American bombing doctrine.

Billy Southworth Jr. did not fly in the Schweinfurt raid, and when he heard about it, he might have thanked his stars and wondered if he had been on the mission, would he live to see the 1944 baseball season? As his father's Cardinals ran away with the pennant during the 1943 season and lost a World Series rematch to the Yankees in five games, Billy ever-increasingly relied on baseball news from home to help keep his sanity as he inched closer to completing his tour. Baseball became his bond with reality, his connection to home, and something steady and dependable, plasma for the soul. Nobody died, nobody's bomber exploded in midair, nobody shot at him, nobody cursed him in German, and he didn't have to curse anyone. He kept an extensive diary that became known only years after the war, so nobody knows how much about his air combat he told his father. The best guess is nothing, as if leaving the war on the pages would appease the ghosts.

Billy never forgot the mission on May 19, 1943, over the shipyards of Kiel, when he flew into the dragon's teeth. The Germans protected their primary U-boat port with everything they had. Billy commanded a bomber ironically nicknamed *Son*. The spring weather allowed him to wear his lucky Cardinals hat, which was as much a security blanket as a sun visor. The target was smoke-screened by the Germans, but Southworth dropped his four thousand pounds of incendiary rounds with relative ease. Then the shit hit the fan.

Southworth and his crew were in the rear formation of six bombers and flew as the center of the box, or the eye of the storm. A gaggle of forty to fifty FW-190s and ME-110s interceptors jumped the bombers off the German coast. They had avoided the flak field over the target, but were waiting to jump the bombers after the payload was dropped. Flying in the rear meant Southworth and his section got the brunt of it, and Billy swore he had never been in a running firefight so bad. The 303rd claimed ten destroyed, seven probable, and eleven damaged. "Fighters greeted us at sea and a continued two-hour battle ensued," he wrote. "Before it was ten minutes old, I saw two fighters and three B-17s shot down. The fight out was fierce, ME-110s shooting from the front, side and rear, FW-190s bursting in from head-on. What a day."

But in the mayhem and the trauma of seeing bombers burn and flying through flak and cannon fire, of dodging shitheel-crazy German ME-110 pilots who knew how to take down B-17s from their blind spot, Billy closed his eyes and reverted to baseball. He needed to think about it if he was ever going to get home. "Cards lost to the Dodgers, 1–0," he wrote after the raid. "Henderson shot down one at 200 yards."

Billy's foxhole was his cockpit, but he was utterly terrified that the guy next to him would be an incompetent rookie pilot who would get him killed. As his tour neared completion, he was counting the missions. The magic number was twenty-five to be rotated out. He was lucky. The later the war went, the more missions were required for rotation. Billy pondered how he was ever going to get out alive. Now more than ever, his diary revealed how baseball served as his psychological glue:

An interesting question asked of me, 'Do you feel the same before each mission?' The answer is no. It used to be a big thing like the opening game of the season with the bases loaded, only more so. As we taxied down it was all business. The night before it was on one's mind, anxious to go but sleeping light as a mouse. First over enemy territory seemed like a new world waiting for the big fight to follow. Once it came, I worked harder than ever before and keen as a razor. It's all the same now, except preceded by sound sleep, mindful of the crew, target position in formation and characteristics of the ship scheduled to fly. Mind on the new boys on my wing. Are they new? Green? Fly close? Stick in on evasive action? Do they understand their job and their ship? He bears watching or I can count on him. Today, I heard from Dad. The Cards beat Brooklyn.

Finally, Southworth made it. He flew his final mission on July 17, 1943, a relatively easy hop over Hanover. Before his final mission, Billy posed with his crew. He had turned twenty-six a month before, but he looked many years older. He draped his arm around Staff Sergeant Bill Fleming, the right waist gunner who had flown with him on the majority of his missions. Billy wore his lucky Cardinals hat just astray. As a nod to Southworth, the 303rd asked him to fly lead in a ship called *S for Sugar,* with the rest of the bombers forming up behind him. Three bombers off to left wing was his old ship *Bad Check,* and in the rear was another of Billy's old crates, the one he nicknamed *Winning Run.* All his old girls flew with him one last time.

The last raid didn't have much of a Hollywood ending, but that was perfectly fine for Billy. Everybody wanted a boring hop for their twenty-fifth and final mission. The target was socked in, so most crews aborted, including Billy. But before he exited German airspace, Billy dropped one last five-ounce, regulation Spalding payload on Nazi Germany. "Took a trip to Hanover and brought bombs back due to an overcast target," he wrote rather jovially. "Dropped one of my baseballs on Germany and another on the field." When his B-17 lumbered back to the base, Billy buzzed Molesworth and threw the last pitch out the cockpit window. He was going home. He knew he would never play baseball again, but he didn't care. He was still

in the Army Air Corps. His entire life was in front of him for the first time
since he quit baseball.

There was no quit in the boys who wanted to play baseball on the home
front during the war. The game desperately needed ballplayers, regardless
of imperfections, to help keep major and minor league teams alive and to
encourage the kids too young for the war to keep playing. Team rosters
could potentially change daily, so nothing was ever set in stone. That's when
Pete Gray realized he did have a chance to play in the majors after all, even
if he was just another nobody looking for another job. But for Pete to make
it to the majors, he needed to accept what he hated the most. The baseball
world saw his value only in that he was permanently flawed. Pete could accept being accepted only because he had one arm, or he could never play
in the majors, ever. So Pete accepted the challenge. When the story about
Babe Ruth hitting the home run against Walter Johnson made the papers,
it was easy for Pete to remember why he believed he could do this. He loved
telling the story because it was a reminder of beating the odds, which, just
as for any other soldier in combat, was the essence of Pete Gray.

Pete never forgot the time he hitchhiked (in his memories, he was always hitchhiking) to Wrigley Field in Chicago to see a game in the 1932
World Series, Cubs against Yankees. He swore he was there the day Babe
Ruth called his own shot and hit a home run. The story is part of baseball's collective book of fables, but Pete always swore it was true, and he
never forgot how much the Babe inspired him. He said watching Babe silence those hecklers with a home run was the moment he discovered that
the secret was to have confidence in himself. No matter what, if Pete would
just believe, it would all work out.

Pete had been through the wringer over the years, and if the Babe had
ever met him, he would surely have told him, "Good job, kiddo, you're doin'
more with one arm than most guys do with two!" The war made Pete a
professional when he played for Three Rivers in 1942, but he moved up
the ladder and played the 1943 season for Memphis. How he came to be
in Memphis was a story in itself, a testimonial of survival, of the one-armed
ballplayer's dogged determination and the weird world of wartime baseball.

After he finished playing at Three Rivers, Pete barnstormed the countryside (possibly hitchhiking) along with his friend the catcher Mickey

O'Neil. There was no fame to Pete. He was just another ballplayer looking for a job during the war. Mickey and Pete were a two-man act looking for a contract. Mickey believed in Pete. He told all his baseball friends that Pete was as graceful a defender as Joe D, but there were no takers. "I don't like to use the word *crippled*," Mickey said. "He didn't play like any cripple. He was better than nineteen of twenty men his age. I'd look around and not a damn person from the club was there to watch him work out. My heart went out to that kid."

Pete took the rejections until Mickey lined up the day he had been working on for months. He brought Pete to Braves Field, to work out for the Boston Braves brass, including General Manager Bob Quinn and field manager Casey Stengel. Mickey played for the Braves, so his word carried some weight, but of course he admitted that his young prospect lacked his right arm. When Stengel saw Pete for the first time, he almost fell out of his chair laughing. Mickey felt bad for Pete as he heard Casey bellow, "A one-armed ballplayer? Who are you kidding?" Mickey maneuvered Pete into a tryout anyhow, finding a diplomatic way to tell Casey that his Braves had finished next to last in four consecutive years under his majesty's astute leadership.

Mickey knew Pete just had to impress Quinn, not Casey. Pete put on his usual show, hitting line drives with excellent baserunning and center-field defense. Quinn was impressed at how Pete compensated for his shortcomings, but he wasn't biting. "If he flops, the public will think we're playing them for suckers," Quinn explained. "Besides the American League would make a laughingstock of us."

That's what infuriated Pete Gray. The player who survived on courage alone could never find anyone in the big leagues brave enough to believe in him. No matter what he did on the field, no matter how well he did it, there was always going to be someone who lacked the guts to let him play. Pete didn't show his disappointment, but when Mickey was asleep, Pete drank hard and often. The winter was long and despondent, until the weather thawed, and Mickey O'Neil got Pete one more break. This time it was a tryout with Toronto, one of the big outfits in the International League, one step below the major leagues.

Pete was thrilled because he played three exhibition games against the Philadelphia Athletics, and Connie Mack, the manager who'd rejected him a few years before. By all accounts Pete played well, making a charging catch in center field and doubling off runner Jo-Jo White at second base, an established major leaguer. Pete might have wondered, *Which one of us is the busher?* But something between Gray and manager Burleigh Grimes didn't sit right. When the brief trial was up, Pete was cut once more, and with the folding of the Canadian-American League after the 1942 season, his prospects seemed bleak. Nobody would touch him, especially after it was rumored that Gray told Grimes where he could stick his goddamn spitball.

When the 1942 season ended, 1,011 minor leaguers were reported in the armed forces, but the number may well have been higher and promised to grow each year during the war. The number of departing players was climbing daily. The dwindling numbers of players created a shortage of catchers, which benefited O'Neil. When Mickey heard Memphis needed catching in 1943, he thought Pete could ride his coattails.

Doc Protho was manager of Memphis and one of Mickey's old friends. One last time, he stuck his neck out for Pete. "Mickey told him, 'Get that guy,'" Pete said. "Protho told Mickey, 'You must be going nuts.'" Mickey's devotion to Pete's career caused some baseball men to believe that Mickey had finally taken one too many foul balls off the kisser. But Mickey didn't care. In Protho, he finally found somebody who understood what he was trying to accomplish. "In about four days, [Protho] sent me a check and told me to come out to Memphis," Pete said.

When Pete arrived, he went out to center field. He had been abused and was jaded and thought this was another close call going nowhere. "Doc sent me to the outfield with some big, chunky kid," Pete said. "I caught everything, but the kid kept having flies bounce over his head or fall in front of him. I kept yelling instructions at him, but he had two left feet. Protho called us in and said, 'Don't worry about the kid. He ain't never going to be any good at baseball. That's my son, Tommy.' Yeah, it was Tommy Protho, who wound up coaching pro football."

Protho told Pete the good news. He was offering him a contract to play for the Memphis Chicks during the 1943 season. Pete could have cried, but chances are he hardly cracked a smile. Then, Doc Protho, who was a legend in Memphis, where he had played and managed for many years, in addition to his major league stint managing the Phillies and playing parts of five seasons in the majors, handed Pete a contract and a fountain pen.

Protho believed enough in Pete, who hadn't even played an inning for him. Protho correctly scouted Pete's strengths instead of overthinking his weaknesses. When he heard all the stories about the fool scouts burying him, he scoffed. He thought the scouts were scared. He was sure they were talking themselves out of a big leaguer. He realized, as Mickey O'Neil did, that if this guy was going to play in the big leagues, it was going to be during the war. That would be his only opportunity, and he would be gone when the war ended. He decided he would try to help this boy. Protho knew all the unwritten rules of the game and did Pete another favor. "Before I signed my contract, he told me to add a few years on to my birthday so I would appear to be younger than I actually was," Pete said. "Then when the big league clubs saw the roster, I was listed at twenty-six instead of twenty-nine."

This was Pete's best shot and he knew it. After years of letdown and rejection, he was playing for somebody who had recently managed and played in the majors and who wanted to move him up. It was all up to Pete. He began the 1943 season on the roster of the Memphis Chicks, a downtrodden team that needed a wartime attendance boost and a reason to feel good about itself. He batted .289, playing as a pinch hitter at first, before clawing his way into the starting lineup with the help of a 4-hit day in June that garnered national attention. Papers around the country followed his progress. He drew large crowds throughout the Southern Association and helped the league stay in business. Mickey O'Neil grinned behind that birdcage catcher's mask. *See that kid playing center field with one arm as good as two? That's my guy, Pete Gray.* The war was the best thing that ever happened to Pete Gray.

When the story of a one-armed outfielder playing in the minors started filtering down to the big leaguers in the service, most of them assumed that the game had gone to hell. Hank Greenberg was still in the States during the 1943 season, but he was incredibly sick of waiting around. He wanted to get into a combat zone, and he didn't care what the brass thought of his intentions. Clearly the command wasn't eager to get a star ballplayer killed, but Hank resented his favored status, and he was prepared to protest. He was stationed at the Army Air Force training center in Waco, Texas, for fifteen months, from October 1942 through December 1943. He was in charge of physical-fitness programs for pilots, bombardiers, navigators, gunners, and technicians. He was also sent around the country to check on other base fitness programs and never played baseball, unless the Army summoned him for the occasional war-benefit game, such as a war-bond game at the Polo Grounds in April, when he played alongside Enos Slaughter and Johnny Beazley from the Cardinals.

Hank kept track of the Tigers. Del Baker, his former manager, was fired and replaced by the pudgy and affable Steve O'Neill, who caught in the majors for seventeen years and was considered among the best at his position from 1913 to 1922. O'Neill correctly predicted that he had a pretty good hitting team. Rudy York led the league with 34 home runs and 118 RBIs, finishing third in the MVP voting. The bonus baby, Dick Wakefield, had his exceptional rookie year, and another outfielder, veteran Doc Cramer, hit .300. O'Neill dreamed about Hank in the middle of that lineup, especially when Hank dropped by Briggs Stadium before a game against the Indians on June 24.

The newly promoted Captain Greenberg was touring the Midwest inspecting athletic facilities for servicemen. He walked into the dressing room at Briggs Stadium unannounced several hours before a doubleheader and traded his officer's khakis for his old flannel uniform. It must have felt strange to Hank to swing the bat again in his old ballpark. They were very much like old friends who missed each other a lot. These were his first swings at Briggs since he'd left for the Army in May 1941. Hank hit a few batting-practice home runs, but he felt sluggish. O'Neill, ever agreeable and optimistic, would have loved even the half-speed Hank in the lineup. "We sure could use big Hank out there," he sighed.

The next time Hank saw the Tigers was in August at Yankee Stadium, where another war-bond game was scheduled before a Tigers-Yankees doubleheader. This star-studded affair had seven of the twelve living Hall of Famers in uniform, and when Babe Ruth hit one of Walter Johnson's grooved fastballs out of the park, Ruth proved he was still America's favorite heavy bomber. The Army dispatched Hank from Waco to lead "Hank Greenberg's Army All-Stars," but the newspapers knew about it before he did, which greatly annoyed him.

Hank wasn't happy when he learned the Army wanted him in New York City to play in a war-benefit game. He had not picked up a bat in a few months. Now he was being asked to strap it on and give forty thousand cheering fans a piece of what the majors were missing? Hank hated how the Army handled him as a professional baseball player and thought they were idiots. Did they really think a guy could just pick up a bat and hit, look good in front of a full house at Yankee Stadium, just like flipping a switch? The guys running the Army were fans, and fans don't know anything about the time, work, effort, and commitment it takes to be a top-notch ballplayer. Hank cringed at the thought of being rusty in front of so many people. His irritation was heightened when he got to the ballpark and discovered there was no Tigers uniform for him to wear, so he had to squeeze into Yankee pinstripes to be paraded in front of the cameras. The reporters thought Hank did it on purpose, as a tactic to get traded to the Yankees after the war. Hank spent the rest of the day explaining to the press that he had no desire to leave the Tigers and that he felt embarrassed wearing another uniform while his teammates were in the same ballpark.

But Hank had no say. He was simply a GI following orders, and he certainly was not the first soldier to think his orders were Situation Normal All Fucked Up. This was Army propaganda at its best, wearing thin on him. "I don't care where I play in the game or whether I just sit on the bench," he said, and that was no lie. Hank preferred not to play. When he did get onto the field, his swing had no timing, no ease. The Army had 14 hits, but Hank didn't do enough to make the game story. His contact was weak and labored, though if he struck out, the writers were kind enough to let it slide. Hank was completely embarrassed. He should never have been on the field playing in front of that many people. It called to memory the time in an Army game in front of a small crowd that he bowed sarcastically and apologetically after striking out three times. Hank was only thirty-two, but he felt as ancient as the old-timers.

Hank's day was so dismal that reporters asked him if he could play in the majors when the war was over. That was a big statement: they were telling him he looked awful. *Thanks for the newsflash.* He hated moments like this, when he figured he had given it all away to pose for pictures for the Army. "I figure my baseball days are over," he said. "I'm thirty-two years old, and after you're out of the game two or three years, you don't know whether you can play anymore." The Tigers lost both games of their doubleheader that afternoon, as if watching Hank struggle to be his old self completely demoralized them. His old club finished fifth in 1943, just another season going nowhere while they waited for Hank. On his way out of the ballpark, Hank took a heavy breath and admitted what he feared most: "You might have forgotten how to play."

A few weeks later, Hank softened and realized something about his own comeback. Maybe he wasn't going to be the same ballplayer he used to be, but neither would anybody else. So that would even the playing field. If they were all not as good as they used to be, at least they would be not as good as they used to be together. That went for all of them in the war—Hank, Joe D, Williams, Feller, the whole gang. They'd all struggle to regain what they used to be. Maybe it would take a couple of years for the league to catch back up to speed. So as embarrassed, frustrated, and angry as Hank felt in those damn war-bond games, he decided that one day he, too, would make a comeback, no matter how lousy he looked or how sore he would inevitable feel when he returned. "I see no reason why fellows like myself shouldn't be able to step back into our old jobs after this is over," he concluded. "I may be past my peak, but I'll still be playing with and against a lot of men who, like myself, have had their careers interrupted by the war."

Hank was proud of his stateside service, if not at what it did to his baseball condition. But he was tired of doing nothing. He hadn't quit baseball to stay out of the fight. He was competitive by nature, just like any other player, and he thought that if he was in the service, he should go somewhere dangerous. Hank requested a transfer from Waco to Washington, DC, in October. When his request was granted, he marched up the chain of command in the Pentagon. Greenberg was no stranger to fighting for his convictions. He wanted to contribute more to the war than photo opportunities and gym workouts. A shrewd and savvy sense sharpened by his years of haggling over annual contracts with Walter O. Briggs served him well. What were a few brass suits in the Pentagon? After a few months of red tape, Hank finally talked his way into his combat assignment. On December 29, 1943, it was announced that "the nature of the assignment was undisclosed."

Hank knew exactly where he was going. He was leaving for India, with the XX Bomber Command, also called the Twentieth Air Force, to establish airfields for the first B-29 Superfortress, the next-generation heavy bomber, which was designed for the sole purpose of incinerating Japan. Hank waved at the photographers when he left San Francisco on his way to the far east. More than two years after he left the Detroit Tigers, Hank Greenberg was finally going to war.

CHAPTER 12

Time for Miracles

In February 1944, J. G. Taylor Spink, the editor and publisher of *The Sporting News* and perhaps the most powerful newspaper voice in baseball, rang the White House doorbell. No official permission had come from Washington to start the third wartime season. Though the baseball industry operated under the assumption that the green light was still on, Spink spoke for the uncertain establishment when he sought an answer.

All winter long, many ballplayers thought there was no chance for a 1944 baseball season because the war had degraded the game so badly. Rudy York, the first baseman and only home-run hitter in the Detroit Tigers lineup with Hank Greenberg and Dick Wakefield in the service, expected he would soon be called, though his draft board eventually rejected him. York spoke for many players when he said, "With the loss of such mainstays, I don't see how baseball can expect to interest fans for another season." Servicemen were plenty worried that their favorite distraction would be taken away from them. Letters flooded into newspaper sports departments around the country urging the game to go on. *Yank* magazine, the official GI weekly magazine, comically assured servicemen, "There's absolutely no truth to the rumor that Yankee Stadium will be turned into an induction center."

The jitters were enough to elicit a reply from the White House from Stephen Early, the president's spokesman. The answer was yes, but from now until the end of the war, baseball's continuation was delicately conditional. "I am not sure it would be in the best interests of the war effort for the President to make a supplemental statement at this time," he wrote. "We have traveled a long way since the President wrote Judge Landis more than two years ago. It might well be that the President would prefer to leave the matter from now on for determination under the regulations laid down by the Selective Service Act and manpower situation generally."

It wasn't quite as convincing as what Spink and the rest of the baseball business hoped for, but it would have to do. The good news was FDR was allowing the 1944 season to continue. The bad news was that for the rest of the war, as the fronts expanded and the manpower needs increased, baseball would not be safe until Germany, Italy, and Japan were officially out of the race, and even the small pool of replacement ballplayers might not be exempt from future military service.

Nobody could blame Roosevelt for having no time to devote to baseball. Not even Clark Griffith had Oval Office access in 1944. For the first time in eleven years, the president could not see him at the White House. Griffith handed FDR's pass to Early instead, who said, "I know the president is pleased to see baseball continuing."

The years when Roosevelt threw out the first pitch on Opening Day seemed an eternity ago. With every passing month since the end of the 1943 World Series, the war had intensified. From the Pacific, stories trickled home about the costly invasion of the Gilbert Islands and the bloodbath on Tarawa beach in November. A Marine and former Philadelphia Phillies pitcher, Jim Bivin, the last man to face Babe Ruth in the majors in 1935, narrowly avoided death on Tarawa while running supplies on D plus 1. "Those machine-gun bullets whipped past us a lot faster than the line drives I used to duck in the pitcher's box," he quipped, making light of how insanely dangerous Tarawa was.

The big winner of the 1943 Series might not have been the Yankees, but Marine fighter squadron VMF-214, commanded by Major Greg Boyington, a former Flying Tigers pilot and double ace in the Pacific whose Corsair pilots broke so many rules that they called themselves Boyington's Bastards before choosing the more print-friendly moniker the "Black Sheep." Boyington cooked up a great idea that the press loved, because if Boyington loved anything more than flaming Zeros, it was newspaper articles written about him and his squadron, but mostly about him.

Boyington wanted baseball caps for his pilots, so he offered to trade one Japanese kill for each baseball hat from the winning team. The Yankees won the Series, but the hats came from the Cardinals. The publicity officers had a field day, posing the men of VMF-214 on the wings of a bent-wing bird, the men wearing their new baseball hats and holding bats and balls. Without a doubt, some of those Cardinals hats made it into combat. Boyington wasn't the first Marine ace to mention baseball in the same breath as combat. Ace Joe Foss described dueling the Zeros in his Wildcat fighter over Guadalcanal in terms anyone could understand: "The Zero has a twenty-millimeter cannon that looks like Dizzy Dean's fastball when the tracer comes at you."

Navy lieutenant commander Richard O'Kane believed in baseball for the men, no matter if they manned guns on a battleship, served in a submarine as he did, or flew against the Zeros. "There is no question in my mind about the contribution of sports toward winning the war," he said. "The boys who were in good physical condition made good pilots. They got malaria and tropical diseases like the rest down around Guadalcanal, but the boys who kept in shape got over that stuff."

The boys in the Pacific liked baseball to help keep their morale up, because they knew beating Japan was a lower priority than defeating the Germans. Lighthouse Harry Wilson, a former star football player at Penn State now flying with a B-25 group, said, "Baseball is the big game. No matter how busy soldiers are or how remote, they always want to know the big league scores. Talk about batting averages, pennant races, and Dem Bums were just as eager in the jungle as they were on Broadway or Main Street."

Marines who endured some of the most brutal jungle fighting in the war loved nothing more than the camp games held between the different platoons and divisions. Gambling was frequent, Lucky Strike cigarettes the highest-priced currency. Baseball helped soldiers survive in far-flung places with extreme climates, and it always helped when there was a ballplayer helping them. There wasn't a single G.I. who served in North Africa who wasn't touched by Zeke Bonura. He was one of the most colorful characters the war produced and one of its most giving.

Once a highly prized amateur athlete from Louisiana State, he had plenty of professional offers to play basketball and football, but baseball was first. He was a great hitting first baseman who put together several solid years for the White Sox and Senators in the 1930s. Zeke was one of the most popular ballplayers in the league, among players and fans. He had a wide smile, Southern charm, and a terrific sense of humor. Fellow ballplayers nicknamed him "Bananas," because of his family fruit business, but there was truth in the pun.

When the war started, Zeke was on the downhill side of his career. His legs were shot, but his spirit remained. Sent out to North Africa, he spent two years organizing service leagues and service teams with ever-increasing fervor and complexity. To the GI's, Zeke was a big deal, an honest-to-goodness big league star stuck out in the sand and shit just like they were. He never saw himself as anyone special and they loved him for it.

Zeke Bonura probably did more to help the morale of the fighting man than anyone in the Mediterranean Theater. He convinced the Army to let him convert an airplane hanger into a full-service gymnasium for the troops. There was nothing else like it in North Africa or Europe. He organized basketball games and officiated them, even though he admitted he didn't know or care about the rules. He just wanted the boys to get exercise and have fun.

Bonura's farm system of service teams was a sight to behold. He had fully-equipped leagues in teams in a 200-mile radius around Oran, Algeria, where he traveled dusty roads driving his own jeep and was warmly received by common soldiers who knew and loved him. If he didn't have enough sporting equipment, he wrote letters to his old baseball friends at home and begged for more bats and balls. He might have been more popular than the beloved Major Gen. Terry Allen, and that was really saying something.

The soldiers loved Zeke and sparked his creativity. Once he found an abandoned racetrack in Oran where camel racing had been the premier event before the Germans came. Bonura turned it into a baseball diamond. Camels were allowed to watch the ballgames.

The French awarded him the Legion of Merit for his North African "World Series," in which he had 44 teams playing in 20 ball fields. They weren't only American ballplayers, either. He recruited the Brits who knew how to play Cricket and showed them how to play baseball. He recruited Americans, Canadians, French, and Algerians to play ball, showing through his efforts that he firmly believed the path to peace was through play.

His masterpiece was his New Year's Day 1944 sports spectacle. He planned a big football game, and to build up the excitement, staged a camel and donkey race through the main street on the morning of the big game. He somehow arranged for paratroopers to make a drop onto the field before the game, which the GI's loved nearly as much as the beauty contest he felt with five of the best looking WACs (Women's Army Corps) he could find. How he got swimsuits in Algeria is probably a story for another book. The main event was the football game he dubbed "The Arab Bowl." He made 10,000 soldiers very happy.

When Bonura's old friend, Al Schacht, the former pitcher turned baseball comedian, visited him in Casablanca, he was moved at how Zeke could even get shell-shocked kids into ballgames. Zeke's war was making young soldiers feel better. He fought it with every ounce of his charisma. He wanted them to go home happy, not scarred and shattered. He once wrote, "Guess I'll spent my holidays with the camels and the Arabs, but I'll be thinking of good old America and home."

When *New York Times* baseball writer Arthur Daley caught up with Zeke in 1945, and discovered how much he had done to help troop morale in one of the war's forgotten theaters, he wrote words the soldiers of Operations Torch and Husky would have surely agreed with: "His popularity is such that if the soldiers ever were called upon to elect one of their own a general, Zeke would be wearing five stars right now."

In late 1943, Roosevelt, Churchill, and Stalin met in Teheran to plan the invasion of Western Europe for spring 1944, while the rugged mountain campaign slogged through Italy, where General Omar Bradley, a former regular on the West Point baseball team, was such a fan that correspondent Ernie Pyle wrote, "Baseball is his greatest love." The bombing war in Europe raged on, with the Americans hitting by day and the British by night. In China and India, the Air Transport Command shuttled huge amounts of fuel and supplies to support Chinese fighters. In virtually every theater of the war, on land, air, and sea, former ballplayers engaged in the fight, boys whose playing days must have felt as distant as FDR's peacetime pitches.

When the 1944 season began back on the home front, no team embodied wartime baseball more than the St. Louis Browns. They were cobbled together with ballplayers rejected for military service who were perfectly suited to be wartime replacement players, but astonishingly they attained a winning balance elusive for most teams during the war. They possessed older, arguably more skilled ballplayers, whose experience compensated for their lack of raw, young talent. When the Browns began the 1944 season with a 9-game winning streak, the American League was stunned. It seemed as though the Browns sorrowful drought might be at an end.

For forty-two consecutive seasons, the entirety of their history, the Browns had never won the American League pennant. They were so bad for so long that it took the worst war in the history of mankind to make them winners. The Browns were a sixth-place team in '43 and a surprise third-place club in '42, which had been their best finish since 1928. Needless to say, winning seasons and the St. Louis Browns did not go hand in hand. Old-timers remembered the days when George Sisler was the best pure hitter in the American League, but that was a long time ago. The Browns were baseball's original lovable losers, so charmingly terrible and mismanaged on and off the field that they made losing comical and cute. Their adoring and long-suffering fans affectionately called them the Brownies.

Being a Brownie fan in St. Louis took a lot of guts, especially during the reign of the Cardinals. While the Cardinals rose to power in the late '20s and mid-'30s and resumed their assent under manager Billy Southworth during the war, the Brownies were coming off a disastrous few decades, bottoming out with four consecutive seasons of 95 losses or more starting in 1936 and ending in 1939, when they finished dead last at 43-111 and a humiliating 64½ games out of first place under manager Fred Haney, their dapper little dictator. Amazingly, a small band of St. Louis fans still swore their allegiance to the Brownies, win, lose, or . . . well, usually, lose. And lose some more.

It would take a miracle worker to save the Brownies, but war is a time for miracles. Owner Don Barnes convinced Luke Sewell, a twenty-year-veteran baseball man who was a major league catcher and part of one of the most illustrious baseball families of his generation, to take the money and run. He was hired to manage the moribund Browns. Sewell took the job for the salary, but he was still worried that this was career suicide.

But in 1944, Sewell picked up a little bit of the Cardinal confidence. When the season began with housing in short supply in St. Louis, Southworth and Sewell and their wives shared an apartment. It was a great arrangement. Why not? The two teams shared Sportsman's Park. One couple got the place to themselves while the other couple was out on the road. Sewell undoubtedly got to hear all about Billy junior's bomber exploits from the proud dad.

Southworth and Sewell were similar. They were both tightly focused, lifetime baseball men who knew nothing else and had the feel for using the right players in the right roles. Both men understood how wartime baseball operated, and both of them respected the times and the limitations in which they were managing. Billy junior was based stateside flying bombers as an instructor, so Billy senior still worried about him. Lots of kids got killed in stateside accidents, though Billy senior had tremendous confidence in his boy. Luke always lent him his ear, so Billy senior had a friend when he needed it most. He was pulling for the Brownies, who after their hot start sank into a close, summer-long pennant race with the Tigers, Yankees, and Senators. Billy kept an eye on the Browns while his Cardinals won 105 games for the second consecutive year and once again ran away with the National League pennant.

Perhaps there would be an all–St. Louis World Series in October, but to get that far, Luke Sewell would have to figure out how to manage the biggest bunch of idiots in the American League. Sewell's backup infielder Ellis Clary, a twenty-seven-year-old wartime-replacement player, knew poor Luke had made a deal with the devil. "Terrible job to manage that bunch of hyenas," Clary said. "Drank anything that poured."

Sewell needed his own buzz to tolerate this bunch of degenerates. The most screwed-up, misplaced misfit was right-handed pitcher Sigmund Jakucki, who went by the names Sig or Jack and was one of the most maligned wartime-replacement players. His quirky name didn't begin to tell the story of how screwed up he was. He had pitched in the big leagues in 1936 for the Browns and got bombed so badly that he drifted down into the minors. He pitched for the Los Angeles Angels in the Pacific Coast League, where he sold ghostwritten columns to the *Los Angeles Times* and furthered his reputation as a numskull, hotheaded, arrogant, half-drunk, bush league jackass straight out of Ring Lardner's *You Know Me Al* stories. Jack had a drinking problem for years. Most people assumed he was born a drunk, though his Army hitch in Hawaii in the early 1930s where he first learned to pitch probably didn't help him any. During the war, when the Browns were desperate for pitching, one of their scouts heard he was throwing for a mill team in Texas. The Browns tracked down old Jack, who was still knocking back the innings as if they were bottles of Scotch.

Jack became the face of the '44 Browns for all the wrong (or right?) reasons. A pure wartime-replacement ballplayer, Sig was all Texas and lacked compassion. If a hitter crowded him, he'd knock him down. If he gave up a home run, the next guy was going down. Jack was the most unpopular guy in the league, the kind of wartime busher that made the rest of the replacements look bad. But the Browns tolerated him because he was winning. In his grand return to the majors in 1944, eight years after he was never supposed to come back, he pitched with the confidence befitting his thirty-four years, went 13-9 with a nice 3.55 ERA, and, though he infuriated Luke Sewell on more than one occasion, did a fine job filling out the rotation and helped carry the Brownies through the pennant race. He could taste that World Series money coming.

Jack got the headlines, but the Brownies had other wartime anomalies. Pitcher Denny Galehouse was working six days a week at the Akron Goodyear factory when the Browns tracked him down and asked him if he would be interested in pitching on his Sunday off days. The money was too good to pass up, so after his Saturday shift, he hopped a train and commuted to the city where he was supposed to pitch. He showed up without any extra side work, usually pitched the first game of a doubleheader, and left the ballpark as soon as he showered and changed. Then he went back to work for the rest of the week. It was a smart piece of wartime baseball planning and it paid off, with Galehouse posting a 9-10 record and a 3.12 ERA despite that he was never in good shape and only spent one day a week with the club.

Another pitcher, Nelson Potter, said he would have done anything for the war effort, but the government let him do nothing. He was an old thirty-two with bad knees and worked in a print shop during the off-season. Potter was never any good until Sewell taught him a screwball. He was also a tough bastard. He once clobbered Senators outfielder George Case as he sped down the line, sparking a brawl so violent that cops and military police stormed the field. Sewell tolerated him because when the stakes were high,

Potter was good. He won 10 games in the final two months of the season, on the way to winning 19 games. He was never so good elsewhere in the majors as he was with the wartime Brownies.

The Brownies proudly fielded the infamous "all 4-F infield," a near wartime royal flush of four infielders the Army didn't want but who were actually good enough to win the pennant. The glue was second baseman Don Gutteridge, who at age thirty-two, had seen more in his baseball career than the rest of his teammates. He had been reared with Branch Rickey's Cardinals but released in 1940. He signed with the Brownies in 1942 and played a steady second base and noticed how empty the stands were. "You could have fired a shotgun into the stands and not hit anyone," he said. In 1944, he was Sewell's right hand, charged with keeping the knuckleheads in line. He got MVP votes for that job, and he deserved it.

The third baseman was the thirty-year-old Mark Christman, who originally signed with the Tigers in 1935 and was back in the big leagues only because of the war. First baseman George McQuinn, thirty-four, flunked his Army physical because of a bad back, but at least he didn't get drunk every night. An old dog, he was just enough of a hitter to be dangerous and was as effortless with his glove as he was with his dry wit. McQuinn needed every bit of his fielding ability to handle shortstop Vern Stephens, who was only twenty-three but already had one bad knee. He busted it up in the minors and the Army flunked him, so he returned home to Long Beach to work in the shipyards in the winter. He was one of the most heralded prospects to come out of Southern California in years, and when he made the majors, war or not, he lived the life. Nobody had more fun than Vern. He went through the girls like DiMaggio, but he could damn sure hit, and when a guy can hit, he can damn well do anything he wants.

Stephens was a scattershot off the field and a rocket on it. If you threw Stephens an inside fastball, he would turn-and-burn, and if you tried to nickel-and-dime him away, he'd rifle it to right. He was by far the best young position player remaining in the American League. He hit 20 home runs and led the league with 109 RBIs in 1944, and without him the Brownies would have been also-rans. There was a great debate about the wartime shortstops of St. Louis: *Who ya like better, Stephens or Marion?* That conversation was had inside foxholes, tanks, submarines, and airplanes, and on streetcars in St. Louis. Marty Marion, the Cardinals shortstop, got all the attention, but nobody on the Brownies thought Marion was better than Stephens, who had more power, was a better hitter, and had a stronger arm. Sure, Marty was a poet with a glove and Vern made 35 errors, but his arm saved him many a time, and Marion couldn't dream of hitting the ball as hard, as far, or as often as Stephens. He was a great ballplayer, until the broads and the booze caught up to him in the mid-50s and finally sank him. But he was just the right age to be a hell of a player in 1944.

Stephens was the youngest regular on the team. The rest of them were old men and spare parts. Outfielder Mike Kreevich was thirty-six. His bad legs kept him out of the Army, and his bad drinking got him released from the Athletics in 1942. Sewell took him in under the condition that he control his alcoholism and coaxed a few decent years out of him. Another Athletics reject (and that was saying something) was pitcher Tex Shirley, who was only twenty-six but also had a drinking problem and a nasty temper. Another player, outfielder Milt Byrnes, was rejected by the Army because of a bronchial condition. He couldn't field worth a damn and coughed a lot, but he could hit, which is all Sewell cared about. Catchers were so rare that nobody thought twice about employing twenty-six-year-old Frank Mancuso as the backup, even though he'd banged up his neck and legs in paratrooper training. The Army cut him, but he was good enough for the Brownies. He had one problem—if he tilted his head to chase a pop fly, he would black out. In the grand scheme of wartime baseball, carrying a catcher who might faint during a game was a minor inconvenience.

Billy Southworth Sr. may have been the most famous wartime manager, but nobody did more with less than Luke Sewell. "I never will forget him," Mancuso said. "He was a college graduate, a very intelligent fellow. He was very good at knowing what he had and what each guy had been through, good or bad, and what made him successful, and he was not judgmental of the guys who clearly had problems. All he saw was their role on the field and how it could help us win. When you have that focus every day, it really became easy to forget about the war for a few hours. I think the fans really liked that as much as we did."

The rivalry with the Tigers went down to the last day of the season, but even as the Tigers finally played their way back to within a game of the World Series, not a single guy on that team thought this would have been any race at all if Hank Greenberg had been there instead of somewhere in

China or India, last they heard. The Tigers also lost pitcher Virgil Trucks, a young, hard-throwing 16-game winner in 1943, and Al Benton, a crafty right-hander who won 15 games in 1941. Both pitchers joined the Navy. The Tigers almost had it all, and it started on the mound, where the duo humorously nicknamed Mr. Right and Mr. Left nearly pitched the Tigers to the pennant, but they would never have come close without the most important replacement they signed during the war.

Catchers were the hardest players to find during the war, so veteran minor leaguers long on wisdom and short on tools were in high demand. General Manager Jack Zeller dipped into the Southern Association to purchase the contract of Paul Richards from the Atlanta Crackers. Richards was a rough, thirty-five-year-old backstop with permanently discolored teeth from all the tobacco he chewed. He was rejected by his draft board on account of age and bad knees, but he couldn't resist the opportunity to return to the majors for the first time in eight years. Zeller made it perfectly clear to Richards that it was his job to spruce up the team's problem-child pitchers, Dizzy Trout and Hal Newhouser. Richards accepted the challenge with glee and set about unscrambling the eggs.

The right-handed Trout was obviously nicknamed Mr. Right. He came into his own in 1943, winning 20 games, but was even better in 1944, when he won 27 games and led the league with a 2.12 ERA, remarkable numbers considering he was a workhorse. Dizzy led the league with 40 games started and threw 33 complete games. Not surprisingly, he led the league with 352⅓ innings pitched, but he pitched as though fatigue could not afflict his twenty-nine-year-old shoulder, where he had inked a tattoo of a tiger.

Trout was a smiling storyteller full of hocus-pocus and happy bullshit. He stuffed a red bandanna in his pocket when he pitched and wore it under his hat when he did not, a nod to his Indiana farm-boy roots. He told tall tales about the time he turned a triple play by hiding a ball in his shirt and winding up with both arms and a ball in each hand. He bought drinks for sportswriters and got drunk with them. But he also had a mean streak.

Richards helped Trout learn that he didn't have to rip everyone's head off when he got mad. Trout used to go into the stands to have it out with fans who got on his case. He finally figured out that if he ignored the idiots, he was nearly unbeatable. He could be a screwball when the game was over, but while he was on the mound, he would never win if he couldn't control his desire to kick the living crap out of everyone and everything that pissed him off. Richards also taught him restraint on the mound, urging him to pitch with his fastball and change speeds instead of trying to blow the smoke past every hitter. Richards succeeded in settling Dizzy down, explaining, "He acts up, but not as much as he once did. He gets mad one minute and then forgets about it. He's liable to stay mad all afternoon without the fans knowing about it."

Mr. Left, Hal Newhouser, was another story. He finally came of age during the 1944 season, but it was a long road for the young pitcher. An immature kid with great stuff, he had no idea how to win or keep his cool. His outbursts alienated older teammates. He groused and feuded with them, so they slapped the condescending nickname "Prince Hal" across the boy with a rough-around-the-edges face and a thousand-mile stare.

When the war broke out, Newhouser wanted to join the Army, but his draft board classified him 4-F because of a heart defect. Devastated to be left out of the service, Newhouser tried again and was rejected. Fans calling him a draft dodger and questioning his toughness infuriated him, blurring his focus when he pitched. He never forgot the anonymous person who mailed him a yellow postcard with one simple word written boldly across it: BASTARD. He possessed a fierce desire to prove himself, but could not harness his great ability.

Richards helped Newhouser, who thought he had finally grown up in the first half of the 1943 season, when he pitched so well that he made the All-Star Game. But he collapsed in the second half when his summer slipped away, winning only once in the last two months. Game after game escaped him. After a frustrating outing in Washington, he roared into the dressing room, tore up his uniform, and broke several soda bottles by heaving them against the wall in a rage. Newhouser's season ended a miserable 8-17. Confused, he thought about quitting baseball, but couldn't because he needed the money. "It was just eating me up," he said. "I didn't know how to pitch. I didn't know how long I was going to stay in baseball, not with the record I had."

Richards had seen enough. He confronted Newhouser when nobody was watching and told him to grow the hell up. He was too good to be losing like this. He was a big leaguer and he should act like one and forget about the Army, because the Tigers needed him. Richards wasn't stupid, he had been around a lot of pitchers for a lot of years, and he knew Newhouser's left arm was something special, but the kid needed to believe in himself and quit giving the hitters so much credit. The hardest thing for a young ballplayer to learn is that he can only control what he can control, and as soon as he relinquishes his great zeal to manipulate outside inertia, the sooner he will come into his own.

Richards told Newhouser he was getting on the side of the ball instead of getting on top of it. "You've got to work on your fastball location," he barked. "You've developed a bad habit of letting the ball slide off your fingers, and it tails into a right-hander's wheelhouse." Richards saw also that the young lefty had no sense of timing and rhythm in his delivery. There was no groove, no tempo. Richards wanted Newhouser to get rid of the hurried, overexerted windups that made his fastball straight as a string. If he could do that, Richards preached, his stuff would get better, and at long last he would develop consistency with the curveball that everybody said was nearly as good as Feller's. "Find a groove and keep it," Richards preached. "Then you will win."

When 1944 began, Newhouser was a different pitcher from day one, and the Tigers knew it. Manager Steve O'Neill watched him and realized the boy was becoming a man, changing from a thrower to a pitcher. He finally listened to Richards, who told him that his arm was so strong and his stuff so good that he didn't need to worry about trying to strike everyone out. When Newhouser admitted early in the season that he didn't need all of his fastball velocity to win, Richards and O'Neill both knew the pitcher was going to win big.

And he did, blossoming in 1944. Newhouser led the league with 29 victories and 187 strikeouts, losing only 9 games, posting a 2.22 ERA. He won the American League MVP award, beating out Dizzy Trout and Vern Stephens. Newhouser was AL *Sporting News* Player of the Year, going 13-3 from the start of August to the end of the season, including an 8-1 mark in September with a 1.68 ERA. He wasn't just throwing good stuff, he was throwing great stuff, and he'd figured out how to keep an edge and not lose his composure.

One incident in particular showed Newhouser's maturity. A Browns backup catcher named Tom Turner wouldn't stop baiting Newhouser with verbal abuse. When the catcher came to bat, Hal calmly walked halfway to the box and announced, "You won't get a loud foul, loudmouth," and disposed of him with three fastballs. Behind the plate, Paul Richards smiled behind his mask. Newhouser always had his old catcher to help keep him straight. "When I feel like blowing sky-high, Paul walks calmly out in front of the plate, shoots the ball back with a grin, and cracks, 'Settle down, kid,' and I usually do."

Together, Mr. Right and Mr. Left combined to win 56 games for the Tigers, more than any other tandem in the majors since 1904. Trout and Newhouser were practically brothers, too, and as the Tigers battled the Brownies down the stretch, manager Steve O'Neill flogged his horses, pitching them almost every day. "They tell me when they feel like pitching, and I'd be a rock head if I didn't string along with that pair," he said.

The establishment wanted the Tigers, but the people were rooting for Luke Sewell's Brownies as sentimental favorites to upset the Tigers and win the team's first pennant in forty-three years. "The fans are pulling for them," the *Chicago Tribune* reported, while the *Hartford Courant* wrote, "An American League pennant for the Browns might be a good thing for baseball in general, but none too popular with owners and players of other first division teams." The Tigers thought it was such a lock that the team printed World Series tickets, though the fragile lead was only 1½ games on September 20, with twelve days and 13 games remaining in the regular season, and a 1-game lead on September 27 with 4 to play.

But then the unthinkable occurred on September 29, when the Brownies swept a doubleheader from the Yankees, and Dizzy Trout and the Tigers lost the second game of a doubleheader to the Senators to force a tie for first place. On September 30, Denny Galehouse shut out the Yankees for the Brownies, and Hal Newhouser pitched a complete game to win his 29th and beat the Senators. If both teams won on October 1, the last day of the regular season, it would force an unprecedented 1-game play-off to determine who would represent the American League in the World Series against Billy Southworth's Redbirds. Sig Jakucki pitched for the Brownies in St. Louis against the Yankees. Dizzy Trout started for the Tigers in Detroit against the Senators. War or no war, it was one of the greatest pennant races the game had ever seen, and the ending would join baseball's wartime mythology.

St. Louis was ready to back the Brownies to force an all–St. Louis World Series. A record crowd of 35,518 turned out, many adorned in straw boaters and sporting Mississippi River farmer tans. A large portion of these fans were undoubtedly Cardinals honks, but with the Yankees in town, everyone knew where the city's allegiance stood. Even if these were the no-name wartime Yankees, they were still as hated as if DiMaggio were playing. Another several thousand fans were turned away at the gate as the ballpark filled to standing room only. The excitement was loud and palpable, and moments like these reminded one why FDR wanted the game to go on.

The atmosphere was electric, but Luke Sewell was stoic as usual. His entire pitching staff was gassed or sore, and the only fresh arm he had available was Jakucki. Figured, Sewell thought. Get to within one game of the World Series and the last pitcher standing is the one who usually drinks until he falls down. Sewell made Jack swear he wouldn't get plastered the night before. Jack accommodated his manager and, under the spying eyes of several Brownies, apparently turned in early for the night. But he came to the park the next morning reeking of booze. When asked why he had broken his vow, Sig shrugged and said, "Nobody said nothing about the morning of the game."

Jack pitched better when he was drunk. Sewell shrugged his shoulders and said what the hell. At least Jack was pitching on normal rest. In Detroit, manager Steve O'Neill did not have that luxury. He had mercilessly pushed Dizzy Trout and Hal Newhouser through the last week of the season, and now Trout was pitching on two days' rest in his third start in six days against veteran knuckleballer Dutch Leonard, a break-even 14-14 pitcher in 1944 who hadn't beaten the Tigers since 1941.

The games started almost simultaneously, and the Yankees got to Jack first, when he gave up a two-out run in the first inning and a two-out unearned run in the third inning to fall behind 2–0. The park was quiet. The Brownies had done nothing against starting pitcher Mel Queen. Meanwhile, in Detroit, Dizzy and Dutch traded zeros through three innings, but in the fourth, Trout surrendered 3 runs, including a 2-run home run to Stan Spence. Spence murdered the Tigers over the weekend, his third home run in three days. The crowd of 45,565 grumbled. It was hard to swallow that the Washington Senators were on the verge of ending the Tiger season one victory short of the World Series. All eyes were focused on the happenings in St. Louis.

When the scoreboard was updated at the Browns game, the crowd at Sportsman's Park erupted. The Browns saw their chance. They needed to get Jack some runs, and they needed them now. In the fourth, Mike Kreevich singled, bringing up Chet Laabs, a stocky, five-foot-eight, thirty-two-year-old, part-time player. An all-star in 1943, he joined the team late in the 1944 season after leaving his full-time job in a war plant and was only in the lineup because Sewell had benched Milt Byrnes. When Laabs was announced in the starting lineup, the fans roundly booed Sewell's decision to play him batting third in left field. He entered the game hitting .230 with only 3 home runs in 65 games, but this was wartime baseball, and miracles happened.

Laabs settled into the box, and Queen made his first mistake. He tried to bury a low-and-inside fastball, but he left it where Laabs could reach it. He unleashed his short arms and lashed a line drive to left field, climbing as it went, settling eight rows deep into the stands for a 2-run home run, tying the score, 2–2, shaking the rafters, and sending a clear message to Detroit. In the fifth inning, the sequence repeated itself. Kreevich singled with 2 out and Laabs blasted Queen's hanging curveball some four hundred feet for another 2-run homer, giving the Browns a 4–2 lead. The crowd launched to its feet as the ball rocketed out to left center. Laabs trotted around the bases on a cloud. His teammates jumped to the top step of the dugout to cheer him around the bases. He would never again hit a home run so powerful, dramatic, or meaningful. Grantland Rice called Laabs "the chunky, hard-hitting outfielder" who "hit $100,000 worth of home runs for his mates against the Yankees."

The news reached Detroit, and the crowd at Briggs Stadium shuddered. Dutch Leonard had his knuckleball working and took a 4–0 shutout into the bottom of the ninth inning. Before the game, he'd received a phone call from a gambler offering him $20,000 to throw the game, but Dutch thought the guy was joking. It didn't matter. He was pitching to finish the season with a .500 record and was not overly concerned with the pennant race around him. He gave up back-to-back singles to the bottom of the order to start the ninth and surrendered a run on a sacrifice fly to leadoff hitter Doc Cramer. Then Eddie Mayo went down for the second out. Mike Higgins hit next. Everyone in the ballpark knew exactly what O'Neill was thinking. *If I had Hank, he'd be hitting right here, and we're back in this with one swing of the bat.* But Leonard fluttered one more knuckleball, Higgins did nothing with it, and Detroit lost, 4–1.

Unless the Yankees could rally and beat the Browns to force a 1-game play-off tomorrow in Detroit, the season was over. The players retreated in silence. A reporter commented, "The Tigers dressing room was full of woe and sad faces." O'Neill wistfully said, "We'll just have to wait and hope those Yankees do something." The quiet was painful, and most of all, they knew, damn this goddamn war, they'd be in the World Series if Hank Greenberg were here.

In St. Louis, the crowd erupted when the final Tigers score was posted. For the first time in their forty-three-year history, the Browns controlled their own destiny. Sig Jakucki kept their 2-run lead intact into the eighth inning, when in the Browns half, Vern Stephens unloaded on a pitch from Hank Borowy. Stephens clobbered the hell out of it, a towering shot that hit the roof of the right-field grandstand. "Junior" danced around the bases like a little kid. He never felt so good again. The Browns had a 5–2 lead, and Jakucki only needed three more outs to send the Browns to the World Series for the first time in history.

Jack had pitched his whole life to be in a game like this, and out of every pore of his body flowed every ounce of alcohol he had ever consumed, as if this game alone purged his past. He never expected to be here after all these years, standing on the mound with the ball in his hand in a sweat-stained flannel uniform with BROWNS written across the front, while nearly forty thousand fans swirled around him. Johnny Lindell was first up. He had 2 of the 5 hits Jack had allowed. He hit a hard line drive to right-center, but right fielder Gene Moore tracked it down against the wall for the first out.

Nick Etten was next. He hit a sharp ground ball that ate up second baseman Don Gutteridge, nearly tearing the glove off his hand, good for a one-out single and making Jack ever grateful for Moore's catch. "Pitching with every ounce of energy in his huge frame," according to one writer, Jack got Frankie Crosetti to line a hard shot to Mike Kreevich in center field. The ball hit right at the center fielder is the hardest one to handle, but there was no way Kreevich would disappoint a drinking buddy. He made the catch for the second out of the ninth inning. The Browns were one out away.

The crowd came to its feet. This was real noise, not only an ovation of anticipation that could be heard by the Tigers players somberly listening to the radio in Detroit, but from one coast to another, and past the shores of the States, to the Pacific islands and the European Theater; yes, into Tokyo and Berlin, to where the sleeping giant was steadily marching in the fall of 1944. The Americans were coming, and hopefully the war would end in the winter, but right now, all the energy was with the Brownies, the hopeless losers one out from being champions, and the gruff, stubbly-faced, goofy-looking, half-drunk journeyman bum on the mound whose throwing arm was hanging by a thread. He rocked up once more into his windup and threw whatever he had left.

It wasn't much, but it was enough. Oscar Grimes hit a towering pop fly deep into fair territory down the first-base line. You could run forever in the foul territory in Sportsman's Park, so that's just what George McQuinn did. There was nothing pretty about his route: he ran with his head kinked backward as far as it would go, squinting into the sun, paying no attention to the bull-pen mounds under his feet or the railings coming near him. He followed the ball even as his old-man legs wiggled underneath him, taking an unpredictable path, until finally, the ball returned to the earth, settled in the webbing of McQuinn's glove, killing the Tigers, driving a dagger into the heart of Hank Greenberg, wherever he was, and handing the St. Louis Browns the 1944 American League pennant.

Jack was too exhausted to throw his hands into the air. So were the Browns. They gathered around him on the field, sharing hugs, pulling their flannel shirts off. The crowd gathered around them on the field, and the players fled into the dressing room, where owner Don Barnes was waiting with tears in his eyes. No champagne or beer was waiting to be sprayed. That was considered too demonstrative and wasteful during the war and not at all respectful of fellow countrymen serving abroad. So the celebration was proud and subdued, but altogether tired.

The Brownies played like champions down the stretch, winning 11 of their last 12, sweeping the final 4 from the Yankees, while the Tigers split 4 with the Senators and were, once more, left waiting for Hank. The

Cardinals were coming home from New York to begin the World Series in a few days. When manager Billy Southworth stepped off the train, a porter told him, "Look out, don't let those red-hot Brownies get you." The Cardinals were such heavy favorites that *Newsweek* columnist John Lardner speculated, "From what I've seen of the Cardinals, it would take eight teams and a couple of cruisers shelling from offshore in the Mississippi to beat them."

The Cardinals were indeed the heavy favorites, but at that moment nobody bothered to worry. "Stoic Luke Sewell calmly greeted well-wishers as though he had been winning pennants for years," one reporter observed. Among the parade was Yankees manager Joe McCarthy, whose conciliatory handshake was short and professional. The longtime field boss of the Yankees could feel his career slipping away.

But at the moment, nobody felt better than the St. Louis Browns, as the war went on and more boys went away and some never came home again. Somebody asked Sewell for a comment, and though he was never one for emotion, what he said spoke not only for the attitude of his team but of his country, which for three long years had no quit. "We've been down but never out. We've been there fighting all the time. We didn't come up off the floor. We've never been on it."

CHAPTER 13

Satisfied to Be Alive

Bob Feller had been at sea so long that he was rarely mentioned in the States, but in the spring of 1944, his war finally came to him. He was a gunner now on the *Alabama,* part of Task Force 58, whose mission was to protect the flagship aircraft carrier *Yorktown.* The engagement in the Philippine Sea was fierce and frightening. Feller was there, firing his Quad-40 with the other gun batteries on the *Alabama.* His war, in his own words:

My men and I had to fight off two attacks in one night more than once, but the night during the Turkey Shoot was a very long night. For 13 hours, the Japanese threw every plane it could at our task force. All of us on the *Alabama* fought them off. I was gun captain on a Quad-40 with about 25 sailors throwing ammunition. We fired eight rounds a second and opened up at 4,000 yards. For all 13 hours, we stayed at our guns. We had our C-rations to eat and we just stayed there and waited for whatever was going to happen. On the sky just above the sea horizon, I spotted dots, four of them. Could be anything, could be Hellcats. I blinked hard. Nope. These were twin-engine, high tail. These were Betties. When they got close enough, we opened fire.

Feller's firefight stayed with him for years: "The sky turned black from smoke and bright white from tracer fire. The smell of cordite overpowered the sea air. The Japanese sent bombers, and we sent up a wall of white-hot metal to meet them. I didn't feel fear or a moment's indecision. I kept my four guns blazing. Two of the Betties disintegrated, and the others ran."

Not long after, a large fleet of torpedo bombers and dive-bombers went after the *Yorktown*, but were slaughtered by the *Yorktown*'s Hellcats, and the pilots gave the battle its nickname, the Great Marianas Turkey Shoot. On the decks, sailors looked up into the clear blue skies and had never seen so many swirling contrails all at once. The few bombers that made it through were cut to pieces by the guns of the *Alabama* and *South Dakota*. It was a horrendous wall of fire, so bad that Feller remembered the Hellcats backing off, he said, "to avoid being chewed up by our own guns."

The losses crippled the Imperial Japanese Navy, taking three carriers and six hundred planes to the bottom. Navy casualties were light, but close calls were not. Feller never liked to talk about it.

The story of the 1944 baseball season was good news for troops around the world, and it was about to be used as a morale builder, as many USO tours composed of major league players, coaches, and managers spread out across the globe when the season was over.

Luke Sewell boarded a troopship headed across the Pacific to the China-Burma-India theater, known to servicemen as the CBI. The CBI was the forgotten theater of the war, and in many ways the one Americans knew the least about, though it was the largest front of the war in terms of acreage and population. The central job in the CBI was to support the Chinese Army against the Japanese, in conjunction with the British Army and the Gurkhas, with a handful of forward American commando units. The voyage took several days and a passenger was in deep trouble without seasickness pills. The last leg of the journey, up through the Bay of Bengal, off the shores of Japanese-held French Indochina, Thailand, and Burma, were all dangerous waters where many ships were sunk. When the Liberty ships made land at Calcutta, Sewell and his companions lugged their duffel bags down the gangplank and into a world as far removed from baseball as they could possibly go.

If the seafaring didn't make them sick, Calcutta would. This rancid, overpopulated, poverty-stricken slum immediately culture-shocked most

Americans. Sewell and some GIs hopped an Army truck and drove through the city, the only way to make it through the crowded streets without being accosted by beggars. The daily dead—from cholera usually, GIs took pills to avoid it—were stacked up next to the famished, near raw meat for sale, swarmed by flies. Cigarette and opium smoke and truck exhaust choked the polluted air. It usually only took a few minutes for most American boys to wonder what in the hell they had gotten themselves into. Luke Sewell might have been the most stoic man in the major leagues, and he needed every ounce of his self-discipline not to use a government-issued puke bag. Another GI described his first visit to Calcutta in terms that many soldiers experienced: "the sickening odor, the heat, the tiny child with one hand behind and the other held out to you with pleading eyes, the dead left lying until evening when all are gathered up," all greeted the senses and burned inside minds for the rest of their lives.

Sewell had a mission, but he wasn't a solider. On this eight-week USO barnstorming tour, the group made four or five stops a day to tell groups all about the recently completed 1944 World Series between the Browns and the Cardinals. It would have been mind-numbing work but for the enthusiasm of the kids, which made it worth it every time. Along with his two ballplayer travel partners, veteran outfielders Dixie Walker of the Dodgers and Paul Waner of the Yankees, Sewell brought a little baseball to Burma. "Everywhere we found the fellows keenly interested in baseball," Sewell said. "They asked a thousand questions and we did our best to answer them. We showed them pictures of the 1944 World Series, gave them baseballs, autographed their short-snorter bills or anything else."

The movie reels of the 1944 World Series were always the most popular. Luke could talk about it all day long, and he did, for the entire trip. That season was close to his heart and always would be, especially the way his boys had rallied to win the pennant, and the satisfaction he felt in playing Billy Southworth's Cardinals. Luke liked to tell the story of how Billy told the papers, "I know the Browns deserve the pennant. I'm really glad they won. While I never wanted to be quoted on the subject while the American League race was on, I was pulling hard for the Browns all the time. And the same goes for my boys—they all wanted to see the Browns."

It was a hell of a World Series, and for the boys watching the movie reels in the company of real live big leaguers, it was the next best thing to paying in person the $5 to $15 above face value the ticket scalpers were getting in St. Louis for the 6-game Streetcar Series. George McQuinn hit a 2-run home run off Mort Cooper to win Game 1, 2–1. The GIs cheered at the image of the beaming McQuinn shaking hands with his teammates at home plate. The Game 2 image featured Ray Sanders sliding in safely with the winning run of a 3–2 Cardinals victory in 11 innings. The Browns beat up four Cardinals pitchers in Game 3 and scored 4 runs with two out in the third inning, and Jack Kramer pitched a complete-game 6–2 victory to give the Browns a 2–1 Series lead. Each time Sewell told the story, the GIs swore they could see a hint of remorse in Luke's eyes. The Browns were so close, yet so far.

The moment that defined the strength of the Cardinals and the weakness of the Browns occurred in the first inning of Game 4 when the young and talented Stan Musial hit a 2-run home run off the used-up Sig Jakucki, pacing a 5–1 Cardinals win. Musial had been great again in 1944, but he knew he would probably serve in 1945. He hit .347 during the season and led the league with 197 hits and 51 doubles. The newsreel showed Brownie George McQuinn hook-sliding into third base, but the series was tied, 2–2, and the Browns were out of gas.

Sewell's eyes always got sad the rest of the way, but he stayed upbeat for the boys. Their suffering was worse than his. Mort Cooper came back and struck out 12 to shut out the Browns, 2–0, in Game 5, and the Cardinals took a 3–2 lead. And in Game 6, Max Lanier beat the Brownies, 3–1, pitching the Cardinals to their second wartime World Series title. That made it official: Billy Southworth's Cardinals were the greatest team of the war years. Sewell and his troupe told this story all through India and Burma, meeting soldiers and airmen. There was the ball game with Merrill's Marauders, a precursor to the modern American Special Forces. Sewell and the gang saw the Great Wall of China and met the engineers, many of whom were African-American, building the Burma Road. They played an impromptu ball game on Christmas Day near the Ledo Road. You couldn't have blacks and whites playing baseball at home, most certainly not in St. Louis, but you could on the other side of the world. "We had quite a game with the engineers," Sewell recalled. "Christmas Day, we battled eleven innings to a scoreless tie."

When Sewell and his troupe first arrived, the Army sent a C-47 transport plane to pick them up and fly the short hops around. When the ramp dropped and the pilot came down, Sewell recognized the smile and the face, though he had never seen the man wearing a weathered A-2 leather flight jacket with a Chinese blood chit painted on the back and a .45 tucked into his shoulder holster. It was Buddy Lewis, the former third baseman from the Washington Senators, and, boy, did he have stories to tell.

Captain John Lewis was well versed in pilot-speak, the unemotional detachment from the extraordinarily dangerous. Nothing was routine about the life of an Air Transport Command (ATC) pilot in the CBI, except that John Lewis was better known as Buddy Lewis of the Washington Senators, one of the best hitters in the American League before he went to war. The ATC pilots were the grunts of the airmen. They were neither fighter jocks nor bomber boys, but they were the lifeblood of the Allied effort in the CBI.

The ATC was busy. By 1943, when the Japanese seized the Burma Road, the only way to get men and supplies across to China from India was aboard a fleet of C-46s, C-47s, and C-87s, their pilots creating aviation's first around-the-clock military airlift modeled on the domestic airline industry. The first batch of American fliers included former airline pilots, bomber pilots, crop dusters, and commando pilots. A former major league third baseman probably wasn't in the plans, but when Lewis won his Troop Carrier wings, he showed so well in flight school that Colonel Phil Cochran handpicked Lewis as one of the few rookie fliers among the veterans.

Lewis mounted up his C-47, a converted DC-3 airliner, and nicknamed his ship *The Old Fox,* in honor of Senators owner Clark Griffith, though Lewis never found a mechanic who could adequately paint the nose art he wanted. The flying was as rough and unforgiving as Lewis's sarcastic humor. The pilots flew out of the upper Assam Valley, off a muddy six-thousand-foot airstrip at Chabua to supply Chiang Kai-shek's army. It was pure guerrilla flying, and Buddy and his boys flew the most dangerous route in the theater, the five-hundred-mile ferry from Assam to Kunming and other points of China's Yunnan Province over the Himalayas, better known among the aviators as the Hump.

The Hump was a real son of a bitch. The planes flew round the clock through all kinds of bad weather. Hell would have to freeze over for a ship to be grounded. The pilots flew with virtually no navigation aides and were unarmed save for the Thompson submachine guns and Browning automatic rifles crewmen were known to poke out of open windows to jab back at marauding Japanese fighters. The pilots approached their jobs with macabre humor, nicknaming themselves the Dumb Bastards and the Assam Trucking Company. Pilots said flying the Hump was like playing blackjack against the house because nobody could win forever. More than a thousand men and four hundred planes were lost to enemy and elements during the war. Twisted carcasses of mangled planes were strewn across the Hump, and to a newcomer such as Luke Sewell, they might resemble silver crosses in a cemetery. The pilots had another name for this racket. They called it Aluminum Alley.

Buddy was fearless and took his friends right to the front. When he met Sewell and the rest of USO Troupe 418 in Burma, he had been grounded by a sinus infection, but he wasn't about to let that get in the way of seeing some old big league buddies. For the next few days, Buddy flew Sewell and the boys all around the CBI, mostly to desolate, little jungle outposts that weren't on the regular schedule and were so freshly scarred by the war that they scared the shit out of the civilian ballplayers. "We thought we were on a sightseeing tour but soon learned we were bussing an airstrip," sportswriter Whitney Lewis wrote. "That was a few days after the town had been taken and the field was still closed. We got down and trucked over to where Lewis guided us through a city leveled by bombers and artillery. A few dead Japs remained in some of the shell craters." The forward areas where Buddy took Sewell and the gang didn't all have electricity for the film projector, so Sewell just explained the story of the World Series and signed autographs. It didn't matter to the boys. Buddy brought loads of mail to the troops, saying, "A bag of mail from home is worth more than an extra meal."

While Buddy ferried the ballplayers, the stories rolled forth like the dice in the notorious craps games pilots played late into Saturday night while the radio played Chinese girls singing covers of American songs. The pilots never took off their jackets in the night's terrible cold or the day's hot sun, and the bravado never took a day off. The ground crews worked on the planes by torchlight at night because the metal was too hot to touch during the day. Elephants were trained to lift barrels and crates into the cargo bays. The airstrips were literally cut out of the jungle near peasant villages. C-47s, nicknamed Gooney Birds, and fat C-46s, chided as Dumbos, rumbled in a few feet above mud-and-thatch huts.

Buddy fit right in with the flying circus. ATC pilots said they "lived like dogs and flew like fiends," and he was no exception. Gambling pools formed over who could make the most jumps over the Hump with the heaviest amount of cargo loaded onto the plane. Pilots carried cocaine in their kits to bribe the indigenous folk to help them evade Japanese capture. One pilot's coke snorted so well that he not only made it back with his life, but a Tibetan fur hat and silk scarf.

But tales were told of guys who were shot down and never seen again, decapitated by headhunters at best or tortured by the Japanese infantry at worst. Bullet-ridden bodies were occasionally returned to the airfield via the locals, clear messages that the pilots had been strafed in their parachutes. Pilots sucked oxygen from hoses in the cockpit and resembled well-heeled maharajas in their silk scarves and aviator sunglasses. Pilots counted the bullet holes with pride. Sometimes the mechanics patched the planes with empty beer cans. Occasionally a squadron would take in a lion cub as a mascot. Buddy, as brazen as the rest, believed, "What the hell! A pursuit pilot has six .50 cals and four hundred mph in his engine. We fly the same shit with a pistol and a tommy gun."

But baseball was never far from Buddy's heart. His greatest moment came when he flew several sorties in the glider-tow invasion of Burma, when he cut loose his stick deep behind enemy lines and shouted to the paratroopers, "There's home plate! Good luck!" Then he circled *The Old Fox* around, landed, and went right back up. Buddy and other Hump drivers flew up to twelve hours a day for a week during the invasion, so taking Luke Sewell and a couple of ballplayers around "the town" was no big deal.

"The tougher the going, the quieter Buddy became," recalled former Phillies catcher turned ATC pilot Bill Atwood. "I remember one day when we landed on a hastily constructed clearing. The Japs had just given the field a severe bombing and strafing. Men were in their foxholes and Zeros were still visible. Buddy calmly set the ship down on the runway. You could still hear the drone of the Jap planes when Buddy finally spoke: 'Isn't anybody going to help me unload? I want to get back to the base for supper.'"

Lewis was awarded the Distinguished Flying Cross for his service in the Burma invasion. His citation read, "For extraordinary achievement in aerial flight during which exposure to enemy fire was probable and expected. Flying transport aircraft carrying a normal load, in addition to towing two heavy-loaded gliders, he took off at night for a point 200 miles behind enemy positions in Burma. Due to the proximity of the enemy and the necessity of surprise, the entire flight was made without radio aid, requiring the highest degree of piloting skill to avoid mid-air crashes either with aircraft in the towing unit or other nearby units on the same mission."

When Luke Sewell heard that, he wondered why more people wanted to talk to him than to Buddy, who put it, "My job is to drive a C-47 plane wherever they desire." One of his flights was to take Luke Sewell and the rest of his troupe back to Assam, so they could catch a ride back to Calcutta and get out of town. The 1945 baseball season would start in a few months. Luke had been asked thousands of questions on the tour, but he only had one question he wanted to ask Buddy. As they said good-bye, Luke knew Buddy did not know the answer. "I have no idea," Buddy said. "I guess I'll just have to sweat that one out, too." Luke watched his old friend slip away, a little older, a little grayer, and wondered if he would ever see him playing major league baseball again. Buddy Lewis might have an easier time if he were shot down over China.

When Hank Greenberg arrived in India in spring 1944, he immediately realized that he might be the tallest man in the CBI. Hank cast a long shadow wherever he went amid this melting pot of Indians, Chinese, British, Australians, New Zealanders, and Americans. It was said that a person could walk one city block and hear six languages and pray to three gods.

Hank saw how sports were a large part of GI life in the CBI. The engineers built a boxing ring in Calcutta and called it Monsoon Square Garden. Soldiers put on rodeos where GIs tried to lasso wild camels while driving jeeps. Rudimentary basketball hoops were commonplace in the jungle. The flamboyant Air Corps major general Claire Chennault played GI softball in the Rice Paddy League and was known to occasionally play shortstop in pickup baseball games, reminding the troops that he once played ball at Louisiana State. On a crude baseball field in Burma, Luke Sewell and his troupe played on Christmas Day 1944, a game on which thousands of rupees were waged. Right field was pockmarked by mortar-shell craters.

No sport meant as much in the CBI as baseball. When a local maharaja caught wind of the game, he invited two GI teams to visit his summer palace in the foothills of the Himalayas and put on a demonstration on his cricket pitch. The maharaja liked baseball so much that he indulged his fancies by playing first base in his traditional robes while removing his turban in favor of a GI baseball cap. When he took his turn at bat, the GIs were stunned to see that the maharaja could hit. The story made the *CBI Roundup,* the GI newspaper, which wrote, "The huge powerfully built ruler wanted to take a turn at-bat and he made the G.I.'s take notice by smacking out several powerful drives." A well-traveled GI would have been wise to identify that this maharaja must have already been handy with a cricket bat.

The maharaja was more worried about hitting than was Hank, who never played much baseball in the CBI or in the Army. He thought it was a waste. "I could have played ball with the camp teams, but I had my own ideas about it," he explained. "I didn't see any reason to use myself under bad conditions. I tried a couple of times and it was futile. I was hitting against wild, young pitchers who almost knocked my head off. The fields were bad and hard on my feet, which were never good feet. I wasn't going to get any good out of baseball in the Army unless I was playing against good teams and there were no good teams in my outfits."

Hank had performed too much soft work in the States to consider his overseas tour as anything less than a combat assignment. His main concern was to do his part to help finish the war and race home in time to find out if he could play again in 1945. Before that could happen, he needed to finish his tour and rotate out. Hank could be forgiven for not playing with the maharaja or another line-level company. He wanted to win the war so he could come home and win the World Series.

Over in Europe, the bomber boys had been calling the war against the Third Reich the Big Leagues since the war began. Now, the junior circuit was about to open, although the effort was anything but lightweight. Operation Matterhorn was the code name for this massive logistical effort. Hank was as minuscule as the millions of pebbles cleared by thousands of peasants who laid miles of runway for hundreds of American B-29 heavy bombers. Hank's CBI tour began in India, where the first American bomber stations were set up, a few months ahead of the airfields in China, where the bombers would transfer and from which the bombing campaign over Japan would commence.

In all his travels, Hank never lost his gentlemanly touch with ordinary people from the States. India was quite an experience for most GIs, but nothing compared to meeting Hank in the streets of Calcutta. A young GI named Mort Reichek remebered every detail:

> During my travels across India I got to see more of the country than most natives. I visited the Taj Mahal in Agra; the Hindu temples outside Madras; the holy Hindu city of Benares; the Towers of Silence outside Bombay, where the Parsis deposit their dead to feed the vultures; the caged prostitutes in Bombay's Red Light district; and enough other famous sites to fill a guide book to India. But the most startling sighting for me occurred in Calcutta one day as I strolled down Chowringhee, the city's main boulevard, while on a weekend pass. Walking alone on a street ahead of me was a tall Air Force officer. From a distance, he looked vaguely familiar. As he approached me, I was stunned to see that the officer was Hank Greenberg.
>
> He was visiting Calcutta on a furlough. We exchanged salutes, and he stopped to ask me for directions to some place. I apparently had the look of an old Calcutta hand. We conversed for about 15 minutes. The weather was brutally hot. In front of us as we talked was the Grand Hotel, which housed a club for British and American military officers. Greenberg was about to invite me to join him for a drink inside when he suddenly realized that I would be barred from entering because I was a mere staff sergeant and not an officer. He was clearly embarrassed by the matter of military rank and apologized. I told him that I was unconcerned and that I had been thrilled to meet him. I said that the Bronx, our mutual hometown, would have been a better setting than Chowringhee. We exchanged salutes again, shook hands, and said our good-byes. "It was a pleasure to meet you," he said as we parted. During three years in the Army, no officer had ever said that to me.

But then I had never met an officer who had been my boyhood idol.

When the newspapers at home heard Hank was in India, they played the patriotic slant, mentioning that Hank was simply in charge of physical fitness for the troops. But he had not come all this way to lead a bunch of guys through jumping jacks. He had been through bombardier school and was qualified to help crews on the bombing runs, though he knew the brass wanted him out of harm's way. Hank wanted a taste of danger, and he was determined to get it while he was on the other side of the planet.

Hank wasn't the only heavy bomber to arrive in India. He was attached to the 58th bomb wing of the Twentieth Air Force, established in April under secret order of the Joint Chiefs to conduct heavy-bombing operations against the Japanese mainland. The airfields cleared by peasants were for the B-29 Superfortress bombers, the Super Forts, which first flew in 1942 and were charged with the destruction of Japan. After staging the bombers at Kharagpur, India, Hank and the XX Bomber Command relied on the already-stretched-thin Air Transport Command pilots such as Buddy Lewis to ferry men and supplies over the Hump to China, where B-29 bases were being set up. Hank's initial Chinese airfield was Kwanghan, where he posed with a Chinese laborer, a coolie, in a famous wartime photograph distributed around the States.

One of the few times Hank picked up a bat was to play in a softball game at a hospital base in China. "When I stepped to the plate in Kumning, some of the kids yelled, 'Come on, Hank, hit one onto Cherry Street!' I knew they must be from Detroit. Luckily I really got hold of one that day and gave it a ride. A few days later, back at my own base in Chengtu, I couldn't get the ball out of the infield."

During the spring, Hank made several trips over the Hump, including one with Buddy Lewis as his C-47 pilot. That was Hank's first taste of danger, surveying the cemetery of Aluminum Alley as a passenger with the Dumb Bastards of the Assam Trucking Company. "Flying the Hump is a pretty nerve-racking experience. I went over it five times, and you're always worried about the weather," Hank said. "It's rare that you have a clear day. If you fly over the weather, you're sweating it out in fear you won't be able to find your landing field when you come down through it. If you fly through the weather, you're constantly afraid you'll hit one of those mountain peaks. Always in the back of your mind is the fact that if anything goes wrong, the plane can't be landed."

On a few flights he crossed the Hump in the B-29s, which were at least armed. But that didn't make them any safer. He was no war hero and he knew it, and he didn't want to be one. He didn't have to travel far to hear stories that Japanese fighters would jump the bombers. Some Japanese aces hunted B-29s like wild boars. If the crews were shot down, if they survived, if they were captured, they were as good as dead and would probably be decapitated. This was Hank Greenberg's war, but Hank Greenberg would be the first to tell you that it wasn't his war. It was just the war he was stuck in.

After months of preparation, Hank was on the flight line for the Twentieth Air Force's Opening Day, the first American B-29 raid over Japan. The target was Yawata on the southern-most island of Kyushu, the center of Japanese steel production. This was no easy hop. The bomber crews were told that it was as important as hitting Essen in Germany and was thoroughly defended by antiaircraft guns, searchlights, and fighter squadrons. The airmen were excited but scared. The B-29 already had a reputation as a rugged girl with a moody edge. "She's a good ship," one gunner said. "But some guys get killed on takeoffs." The airfield chaplain, Father Stack, blessed the bombers. Hank, who was working in the control tower, stood and bowed his head with one of the crews. He was Jewish and the chaplain was Catholic, but that didn't matter one bit. A prayer is a prayer during war. Hank always thought that the war had a way of making all those silly lines such as race and religion that people squabbled about at home melt away when men faced life-or-death situations daily.

On the afternoon of June 14, 1944, seventy-five B-29s, each carrying two short tons of explosives, took off from Kwanghan and Chengtu. The bombers needed every inch of the two-mile-long runways. An observer flying in one of the lead ships wrote in *Yank*, "It seemed like we'd been rolling down that endless runway at least ten minutes without leaving it. The end of the runway—where was it? Just as the dusty orange blur beneath us changed to green, we were airborne, skimming a few feet over the trees and rice paddies of China."

Hank remembered, "I'll never forget the first mission our B-29s made from our base to Japan. I drove out to the field in a jeep with General Blondy Saunders, who led the strike, and took my place in the control tower. Those monsters went off, one after the other, with clocklike precision. Then we spotted one fellow in trouble."

A fully loaded B-29 weighed 141,000 pounds and carried up to 20,000 pounds of bombs on takeoff. The huge, four-prop Wright Duplex Cyclones with two General Electric turbochargers made a fantastic roar and were prone to engine fires, especially when the props started cold, and in the early days the engineers were still learning how to properly mix the B-29's volatile fuel. Hank and the rest of the ground crew saw one of the bombers develop engine trouble and struggle to get airborne. Smoke was coming from one of the engines; she was clearly in danger. The captain tried to cut the engines, but the bomber skidded into a ditch, then into the rice paddies. Hank and others took off in jeeps, racing out to help the crew escape. Then Hank almost bit the dust. The bombs exploded, consuming the plane and producing a tremendous fireball. Hank and the other rescuers, who were now running to the crash scene, were blown off their feet. The heat roared over them. Hank had been knocked down by a fastball many times, but this was something else. He thought he was a dead man, and he was almost killed.

"The blast knocked us right into a drainage ditch alongside the rice paddies while pieces of metal floated down out of the air. I was stunned and couldn't talk or hear for a couple of days, but was otherwise undamaged. The miraculous part of it all was that the entire crew escaped. Some of them were pretty well banged up, but no one was killed. That was an occasion, I can assure you, when I didn't wonder whether or not I'd be able to return to baseball. I was quite satisfied just to be alive."

Dazed though he was, Hank longed to participate in one of the raids, though he would have to wait his turn. Seven bombers turned back from the Yawata raid, and for all the dangers, nobody wanted to miss the historic mission. When one of the bombers returned to the field four hours after takeoff, the crewmen deplaned and were practically in tears, crying, "Goddamned engines!"

The bombers that made it to Yawata arrived around midnight, greeted by searchlights and flak. When the incendiaries fell, the bombers climbed as if they'd got a kick in the pants, but one ship wasn't so lucky. The tail end Charlie of the formation was caught up in the searchlights and cut to pieces, going down with all four engines flaming. The crew was never heard from again. The fight over Yawata was pure misery. About a hundred fighters met about seventy unescorted bombers. The sky was filled with shrapnel and Japanese pilots who wanted to kill Americans to ensure their place in paradise. The B-29 bombing war over Japan never got the same attention that the B-17 war over Germany got, but it was every bit as fierce and is now forgotten. Bomber crews soon learned that Japanese fighters would ram them or kamikaze them. Anything was game for the kill, including suicide.

The rest of the bombers returned home after dawn, after the crewmen ate sandwiches and drank cans of grapefruit juice over the Yellow Sea, making landfall over Shanghai. The bombers were counted one at a time when they returned. Everyone knew there were missing crews. In the months that Hank was stationed with B-29s at the front lines, he saw the things that changed him. The people at home never heard about these things, not in the papers, and not when the veterans came home. Bombers limped to the field, burning and cut to pieces, some crashing and saved for scrap. Bloodied and burned boys were pulled out on gurneys. Some crews were captured and their dismembered bodies were returned to the airfield. The war in China, Burma, and India was a vicious hotbed of racial, religious, nationalist, and militaristic slaughter, every bit a war of ideology as it was in Europe. Nobody ever showed you the cemetery over by the rice paddies.

All of this moved Hank, whose deep sense of justice and human dignity could not allow him to ignore this, but whose self-effacing modesty, his own lack of ego in the face of something much larger than he was, never permitted him to speak about anything he had seen. Hank may have been a better ballplayer than the other guys, but in the war, he was just as scared, mortified, terrified, and as bothered by it all as any normal soldier nobody had ever heard of. In that respect, the war belonged where it happened, witnessed only by those who saw it occur.

Though the Yawata raid did minimal damage with heavy losses, it was enough to signal to Japan that a new phase of the war was starting. This was the start of a fire-bombing campaign of historical proportions, designed solely to incinerate cities and industry, to crush the Japanese war machine and break the will of the emperor and his subjects. There was nothing civil about it; it was no different from flushing the enemy out of the ground with a flamethrower. Hank's tour called for him to spend the rest of the summer and the fall of 1944 in China, enduring the heat and the monsoons, the mosquitoes and snakes, the bug bites and the intestinal sicknesses that eventually contaminated everyone.

Hank heard only sporadically about the baseball season back home and wondered like all the rest of the GIs if the game would go on. That question could only be answered by the course of the war in Europe. Everybody knew Germany had to be defeated first, so news from the other side of the world was vital. Guys such as Hank serving in the CBI only got their news from the newspapers and the magazines, which frequently took weeks to get there. The news was always old, but the news was important. So in late spring, newspaper accounts of what had transpired in Normandy on June 6, 1944, finally made it over the Hump.

CHAPTER 14

Guts of Our Kids

Dawn, June 6, 1944. Nearly 3 million men are under General Eisenhower's command. The paratroopers of the 82nd and 101st Airborne have already landed behind the lines, scattered and fighting their way to the beaches, where thousands of naval craft are headed. There are five beachheads in Normandy: Sword and Gold, which are allocated to British armies; Juno, which is earmarked for the Canadians; and Utah and Omaha, assigned to the American armies. The Omaha landing is a disorganized disaster that perseveres on the strength of numbers and the line-level leaders's picking up scared kids and making a run for the cliffs. The Germans mow down the first waves and the casualties are heavy, but by nightfall thirty-four thousand troops are on Omaha, though none of them are more than a mile off the beach.

Among those 3 million men in the huge D-Day invasion, ballplayers were everywhere and easy to find. On the morning of June 6, former Brooklyn Dodgers left-handed pitcher Larry French, who in 1942 was pitching in the pennant race against the St. Louis Cardinals, was rocking through the rough seas off the coast of Normandy amid the largest armada ever assembled. He was thirty-six years old, a veteran of fourteen major league seasons, and the winner of 197 major league games. He dreamed of coming back to the majors to win three more games to finish his career with

200 victories, which meant little to anyone except him. Once he came to Omaha Beach, all he cared about was survival.

On D plus 2, French dismounted with the Navy supply corps and engineers. He crouched in a foxhole once he came ashore, praying with a guy he had never met, vowing that if he made it out alive before the destroyers knocked out the Germans in the church steeple calling in mortar and artillery volleys—he would never miss another day of church in his life. He later wrote to his friend and former teammate Augie Galan:

I got ashore D-plus-two, days ahead of my expectations. This beach was plenty hot—88-mm fire and mines wherever you stepped and the darndest fireworks at night: our support against the air raids, which came in on schedule each evening. First few nights we dove for our hole in the sand to get out of the flak from the trigger-happy sailors in the bay. We now just stay in the tent, realizing if the number is up it will get you anyway. I had a good friend of mine blown up yesterday by a mine not 50 feet from me. He got off the road about 15 feet.

I went up front a few days ago and spent a day and a half in the lines, but my luck was all bad. All the Germans I've seen have been dead ones or prisoners. Frankly, I would like to get one in my sights. I shot around 500 rounds out of my carbine prior to D-Day. And by golly, my shooting has improved.

There is no way for me to describe this scene of a few days ago. If you can imagine barbed wire 60 feet through, mined every inch of the way, even hanging on the wire like presents on a Christmas tree; pillboxes, 20 feet thick that took a direct hit from 14-inch shells to knock out; sinking ships, dead, injured and living soldiers, [paper] flyers from all the Allies floating in the sea among every type of wreckage, you have a small picture of this beach. It was tough to take and nothing in the world did it, could have completed it, but the guts of our American kids.

Guess I've said enough about the war, but I'm just full of it, and it is all I know at present. Except that I think of you fellows often, and I want you to say hello for me to Davis and "Dixie,"

Webber, Wyatt, Owen and Johnny Corriden. Tell Charley Dressen I
thought of his coaching line whistles when I heard those shells whin-
ing overhead.

But pass up the left-handed pitchers. I'd like to have them all
over here and walk them ahead of me to clear out the mines. Then
I'd be the only one left, able to go back and get the three games I
need to fill out 200 wins for the book.

As ever,

Larry.

Ballplayers were fighting in Europe over land, sea, and air. One of them
was a paratrooper named Forrest Vernon "Lefty" Brewer. On June 5, his
stick took off in the darkness and crossed the Channel with a fleet of their
invasion-striped Gooney Birds. The overnight drop was fucked up beyond
all recognition. Flak was fierce and the C-47s were not armored. Bullets
popped against the flying tin cans, pilots panicked, came in too low, and
fast, missed the drop zone, and twenty-four thousand paratroopers, including Lefty Brewer, tumbled out of the madness and into the marshes. After
landing too far to the east, many members of the 82nd died in the darkness
when they drowned in only a few feet of water in the Merderet River, which
the Germans had intentionally flooded.

Lefty survived the drop and scrounged up ten errant souls, gathered
weapons and ammo, and rushed to the assembly point near La Fière manor,
about two miles east of the original drop zone and two miles west of Sainte-
Mère-Église, the first French village to be liberated by Americans. The manor
was a stone farm and the Germans were dug in. This is why Lefty Brewer
had wanted to become a paratrooper. He was a squad leader, and in the
words of fellow solider Bill Dean, "one helluva firefight erupted."

When the Germans counterattacked with tanks and heavy artillery
later in the afternoon, Lefty Brewer was caught in the cross fire. Dean was
running for his life. The paratroopers were outgunned, surrounded, and
completely fucked. "I took a quick look and saw Lefty, running like he was
going to stretch a triple into a home run," Dean said. He held his breath,
and in that moment his friend's life flashed before his eyes.

Six years ago to the day, June 6, 1938, Lefty Brewer pitched a no-hitter,
striking out 14 in a Class D game. He won 25 games that season and put

himself on the baseball map. He was signed by the Washington Senators and began climbing to the majors. He had every chance to pitch in the big leagues. Brewer won 23 games over the next two minor league seasons and was on the verge of making the big club when he discovered he was included in the first wave of players to be drafted from his team. A week before spring training in 1941, he entered the Army with considerably less fanfare than Hank Greenberg. After a year of training, Brewer signed up for the paratroopers.

The paratroopers were the cream of the infantry crop, and their aggressive attitude fit perfectly with a highly competitive and athletic former pitcher such as Brewer. He loved the $50 monthly hazard pay and the hardass, country-running, fearless training regimen. He loved the jump boots and the jump knives, the paratrooper jackets and the war paint, the semiautomatic weapons that folded up into canvas bags. Many former pitchers with arm strength were outstanding at hurling grenades for accuracy and distance. Paratroopers were trained with one idea in mind—they were to be the meanest goddamned sons of bitches the Army ever produced, and they were being groomed for the invasion of Normandy.

Brewer earned his jump wings at Fort Benning in 1942. When he made his first airborne training jump out of the belly of a C-47, he climbed into his stick and squinted with familiarity when he recognized the pilot in his cockpit. Sure as shit, it was another former Washington Senator, Buddy Lewis. Lefty made eighteen training jumps, pitched some Army ball to keep his arm in shape, and in early 1944, was assigned to the 508th Parachute Infantry Regiment (PIR) of the 82nd Airborne Division, the famed "All-Americans." He pitched in England while the 508th waited for what they knew was coming. In his last letter home, he expressed confidence that he would survive. The big jump nobody at home knew about would be no different from any ball game he ever pitched. At least that's what he told his parents. "Don't any of you worry about me, just keep your fingers crossed for me as you did at the ballgames and I will be alright," he wrote.

But on D-Day, Lefty's luck ran out. His friend Bill Dean watched in horror as a burst of fire came from a vehicle-mounted German MG 42 machine gun. The MG 42 made a hissing and crackling noise that paratroopers feared. It spat bullets into Lefty Brewer's back. He was shot from behind and fell face-first into the river, six years to the day after his no-hitter. He died that morning in Normandy. It was three years until his body was re-turned to the States.

The stories of the ballplayers fighting in Europe were as deeply con-nected as the paratroopers trying to link up with the beachfronts. Phil Marchildon was lucky enough to fly on D-Day, but the sortie was uneventful for the former Philadelphia Athletics pitcher. The air raids meant to soften up the German coastal defenses accomplished virtually nothing. Not until August did the war catch up to the Canadian pitcher, who hoped to resume his major league career when the war was over.

Marchildon spent his war huddled in the tail gunner's seat on a Halifax bomber affectionately nicknamed the Hallie. The tail-gun spot of a Halifax was one of the loneliest places to be in the war. Technically it was called a Boulton Paul Type E tail-gun turret, but the gunners called it a coffin. Marchildon saw his war in pitch-darkness behind the trigger of four .303 Browning machine guns as a tail-end Charlie. Charlie dodged tracers and flak and could identify the attacking German fighters by moonlight and the fire protruding from their nose cannons. Marchildon's last major league game was a distant memory. He pitched 8 ⅓ innings and collected 3 hits in his last game of 1942, so thoroughly and gleefully soaked with sweat that he never wanted to forget the feeling.

His memories kept him company through the dangerous nights. When an American observer flew with Marchildon's Hallie crew on a nighttime raid, he was terrified of what these Canucks had to endure. "Never again at night!" the American protested. "In the daytime you can see the stuff that's shooting at you. But at night, wow! It's tracers and rockets and it scares you to death." The Canadians laughed and handed him a roll of toilet pa-per as a going-away gift.

Marchildon's space inside the Plexiglas bubble was so small that gun-ners usually dropped their boots into place first before crawling inside, strap-ping into the harness, and closing the turret's sliding doors behind them. Once airborne, the tail gunners took the brunt of the elements, the g-forces, and the Germans. Many gunners removed the top layer of glass to improve their field of fire, but as a result sat at twenty thousand feet in pitch-darkness in temperatures as cold as forty below and were the first guys to see the bullets coming at the bombers. A tail gunner's primary job was to warn the pilot to take evasive action, calling out commands such as "Corkscrew port!" and "Corkscrew starboard!" The RCAF's gunnery-course manual instructed gunners, "Never fire until fired upon; if gun fire, search for fighter; take evasive action." Each machine gun had only 1,160 rounds, so bullets were precious. It didn't take long for tail-end Charlies such as Phil Marchildon to realize the obvious: *Son of a bitch, we're sitting ducks.*

The Canadian bomber boys of the 433 Porcupine Squadron based at Skipton-on-Swale slept by day and flew by night, so Phil Marchildon lived his war as a duck in the dark. On his first day in England, he was strolling down the sidewalk when a German fighter strafed the cobblestones and almost ended Marchildon's war before it started. From that moment on, he lived through one close call after another. The squadron was formed in September 1943 and waited for new planes, which finally arrived in January 1944, the brand-new Mk III Handley Page Halifax bombers. The squadron airmen called themselves the Porkies. The Halifax was a front-line, four-engine bomber, the primary heavy bomber flown by the Canadians during the war. The 433 Squadron focused on German-held targets in France. In RCAF speak, their bombing raids were called "gardening, planting vegetables." Leading up to D-Day, the Porkies conducted raids in anticipation of the Normandy invasion and against U-boat pens and V-1 launch sites. Marchildon stayed alive, counting the missions until he reached thirty, when he could go home. Through June and July, losses to the Porkies mounted. By July, they were going all out at the Doodlebugs, the nickname for the V-1 flying missiles, the "buzz bombs" raining on London. Every night there were casualties and captured, steady reminders that Marchildon might never make it. He intentionally avoided eye contact and making friends because he didn't want to be reminded of them when they died.

A little more than two months after D-Day, on August 16, 1944, Marchildon's luck ran out. The sortie's code name, ironically titled "Forget-me-not" meant the target was Kiel harbor. Marchildon's crew was to drop mines in the harbor. Airmen knew the German ports were heavily defended, both on the way in and on the way out. Kiel was routinely hit by both American and British bombers. Billy Southworth Jr. flew a raid against Kiel on May 19, 1943, so frightening he questioned how he would ever get out of Europe alive. Now it was Marchildon's turn, so it could be said that the National League bombed the Germans by day and the American League bombed by night.

That night, Marchildon's Hallie, *P-Peter,* was attacked over the island of Fyen, east of Denmark. The ME-110 came right at Marchildon's gun turret, attacking at full speed from below and astern. Marchildon knew it was a 110 by the way the cannons were laid out—six guns, all in the front, two 20mm cannons and four MG 17 machine guns. This pilot was evidently experienced and cunning, for he snuck up on the Hallie in the dark and only opened up before Marchildon could see the moonlight in the pilot's eyes. The cannon fire tore into *P-Peter* and Marchildon fired back, but he was hopelessly outgunned. Marchildon swore the pilot clipped the bomber on the way through the formation, knocking the plane loose, like a batter who had been hit in the head by a fastball and slowly collapsed as he walked to first base.

The Luftwaffe pilot, Oberleutnant Herbert Koch, was a night-fighter ace who eventually claimed the last German night kill of the war. He set the Hallie afire on the portside wing root, and the bomber quickly fell out of formation at eighteen thousand feet and almost 200 miles per hour. The fire could not be extinguished and the bomber fell into a fatal dive. There was no time to wait. In the pitch-darkness, Flight Officer Phil Marchildon experienced trauma and terror that stayed with him for the rest of his days. Maybe not even pitching again would be able to cure this, though at this moment, like Hank Greenberg on the other side of the world, he would most assuredly just be happy to survive.

Marchildon kicked out the glass and got out of the bomber, which crashed at 10:52 p.m. All time and space became distorted. The cold wind immediately blew off his hat and boots. Marchildon swore he was in his chute for twenty minutes, but he really drifted to earth in a few minutes. The explosion of the crippled bomber could be seen for miles around, before the plane fell into the water and was extinguished into darkness. Only Marchildon and his navigator, First Officer George H. Gill, survived. The fire blocked off the other crewmen from immediate escape, killing five, whose bodies washed ashore in the morning and were given a polite burial by Wehrmacht troops. Later on, Marchildon and Gill learned a few guys had made it into the water, but froze to death in the night.

That little office in the back of the plane, the one with the coffin-lid cover, saved Marchildon's life. But as he hit the water and inflated his Mae West life preserver, floating in the darkness, shivering cold and wet, drenched and traumatized, he wondered what life he had left. He struggled to get free of his parachute lines and not let the heavy flight gear drag him to the bottom. After a few minutes, he heard Gill's panicked cries and urged him to be calm, so he didn't swallow salt water. Gill said Marchildon kept him steady and credited him with saving his life.

Then, all they could do was wait. The Germans threatened any sympathetic Danes who refused to promptly turn in Allied airmen. All Marchildon could do was wait and blow his whistle and hope somebody would scoop them out of the water. Then, after two or three hours in which mild hypothermia set in, a Dutch trawler picked up the wayward airmen and brought them to a pier, where they were examined by a doctor and handed over to the Germans. Phil Marchildon was a prisoner of war now. The next stage of his war began, one that he would continue fighting long after the shooting stopped.

Bert Shepard never fired a shot during the invasion, though he surely wished he could have. He was just another of the thousands of former minor leaguers who hadn't played in a few years. As soon as he enlisted in the Army Air Force and applied for pilot training, he figured his baseball career was over. He decided he wanted to be a fighter pilot, even though he admitted, "I'd never been near an airplane. Hadn't been within a mile of one."

As he proceeded through flight training, baseball remained close to his heart, but when he went up for his first solo, he discovered a natural talent and affinity for flying. The same attributes that he used as a pitcher came into play. He was balanced and coordinated in his movements, and he had a feel for proper engineering, the way the plane worked with his hands and feet, much as he had been on the mound, when in his good days he and the ball were as one. Most of all, Shepard liked the feeling of being in total command in his cockpit, just as he could dictate the pace of the game from the mound. "You're the boss," he said.

Shepard trained with the 55th Fighter Group, which deployed to England in August 1943 with three fighter squadrons, the 338th, 343rd, and the 38th. The 55th FG was the first group in Europe to go operational with the new P-38 Lightning, the distinctive twin-engine workhorse fighter. Shepard arrived in England in February and was assigned to the 38th Fighter Squadron, based at Nuthampstead. He began flying combat missions in March.

Shepard loved flying the P-38. He could take it as high as forty-six thousand feet and put it in a power dive at 525 miles per hour. The Lightning brought the hotshot out in him. He buzzed the Nuthampstead tower and did a barrel roll, which got him grounded for a few days. He was in the company of many fine pilots in the 38th FS, among them one of the most celebrated American aces of the war, Captain John D. Landers, who flew a famous P-51 Mustang nicknamed *Big Beautiful Doll,* adorned with six Japanese kill markers won in 1942, and compiled a career in which he was credited with 34.5 victories. Shepard would have loved his own dogfight kill, but the P-38s were mostly assigned to ground targets when they weren't escorting B-17s into Germany.

On March 3, 1944, on only his fourth mission, the little-known minor league pitcher from Clinton, Indiana, found himself thirty thousand feet above Berlin, stranded with twenty other fighters from the 38th and 343rd squadrons. It was to be the Eighth Air Force's first raid over Berlin, the target the bomber pilots called Big B. But the bombers, which included Billy Southworth Jr.'s former group, the 303rd, turned back on account of weather so bad that two Flying Fortresses collided in midair with full bomb loads, killing both crews instantly. The escorts, including Shepard, did not get the return call in time. They arrived over Berlin alone. They had made history, but they were in a hurry to get out of that airspace. American airmen did not want to get shot down, especially over Germany, where Wehrmacht troops called pilots airborne gangsters, "Roosevelt's terror *fliegers,*"—the terrorists of the skies.

Shepard's skill and reputation continued to grow within the squadron. By May, he flew as Landers's wingman, was promoted to first lieutenant, and was often requested as a wingman by other senior pilots. He was awarded second and third oak-leaf clusters to his Air Medal decoration. Shepard never had an abort, which was a rarity and added to his reputation. When the weather thawed that spring, the airmen cleared out a parcel of countryside and turned it into a baseball field, and the base decided to organize a team. Everyone knew Shepard was a former minor leaguer, so he volunteered to be player-manager. He pitched and played first base. The date was May 21, 1944, and even though he wasn't scheduled to fly until the next day, he couldn't resist the temptation to go over Berlin again. He volunteered for his thirty-third sortie, even though he knew it wouldn't be a milk run. He promised the guys he'd be back at the airfield in time to pitch the ball game.

Cut loose over Germany, the Lightning was an excellent ground-attack fighter. The pilots hunted for targets of opportunity. Shepard's flight identified a German airfield northwest of Berlin and dropped to treetop level. The Germans heard the Lightnings coming and opened up machine-gun defenses. Shepard was in a hot zone before he could blink. "When you go in to strafe an aerodrome, they've got a hundred or two hundred automatic weapons and they're just setting up a cross fire," he said. "Some of our planes had already strafed the field and there were some German planes burning, so I had a good column of smoke to line up on."

Shepard flew into the crossfire, and the machine guns tore him up. As his Lightning raced to the target at about 380 mph, bullets crisscrossed his canopy from the bottom of his plane's nose. Shepard felt immediate pain in his right foot, and blood splattered his cockpit. "I'm probably a mile from the field and they shoot my right foot off," he said. "You can just feel the foot coming loose at the ankle." He was also hit in the chin, opening an inch-and-a-half wound, causing him to slump over his controls, hit his head against the gunsight, and nose the plane sharply down. Shepard knew he was shot down and had no chance to escape. He was desperately trying not to black out. "The next thing I remember is I'm about to crash at a slight angle, so I horse back on the wheel, but not in time. I understand the P-38 crashed and burned, but it threw me clear."

The official German report stated that Shepard's P-38 crashed and the pilot was seriously wounded from a gunshot wound and was transported to an Army hospital. The ball game at his airfield went on without him. He was still bedridden when he finally heard about D-Day.

Back home on D-Day, moments of silence and prayer were called all across the United States. Church bells rang and preachers and priests reported huge crowds for morning services. The reason was simple. With 3 million men involved, it wasn't hard for anybody to find a close connection. The same was true in Tennessee, where in the morning the congregations gathered in church and later that day gathered at Engel Stadium to see the hometown Chattanooga Lookouts take on the visiting Memphis Chicks. There was a moment of silence before the game and the flag was flown at half-staff. All of the games in the major leagues were canceled, but the Southern Association played on, and the fans were glad they did. Everybody needed a great ball game and that's exactly what happened. The score was tied 3–3 in the eighth inning when Pete Gray came to the plate for Memphis.

Pete was having a good year for Memphis, but he had never hit a home run since he became a professional ballplayer. The long ball eluded him and he wanted it badly. The pitcher was a right-hander named Bob Albertson, who probably worked in a factory somewhere and never played in the majors.

He threw Pete a waist-high fastball, a touch middle-in, where he could really reach it. He dropped the barrel of that big, 38-ounce war club and got into it. Pete didn't hit a lot of balls in the air, but this one he did, and it got up into the heavy Southern humidity. The ball carried, Pete dropped his bat and apprehensively ran down the line, Albertson craned his neck, and the fans rose. This was a ball hit all the way from Nanticoke, through Brooklyn, through countless rejections and scorns, and through the bushes, flying in the face of everyone who ever told Pete he was worthless. Albertson's head sank into his shoulders and he kicked a cloud of dust with the toe of his spikes. Pete Gray's home-run ball landed softly and safely over the twenty-foot fence, 330 feet down the right-field line. Pete took his damn sweet time around the bases. That was a hell of a blast. You couldn't wipe the smile off his face. He had lived, breathed, and would have died for that moment, but few people noticed what Pete Gray did that day in Chattanooga, Tennessee, and nobody ever remembered or asked him. It was just Pete's luck that the first home run he ever hit fell on June 6, 1944.

CHAPTER 15

Baseball in the ETO

The war hurried along in the summer of 1944. The British finally took Caen to cover the left flank while the Americans slugged their way through the Normandy hedgerows, until St. Lô was captured and the breakout started in July. An assassination attempt on Hitler failed just as President Roosevelt announced he would seek an unprecedented fourth term. At the end of July, forty thousand men of the 2nd and 4th Marines wiped out a small Japanese garrison and secured a small yet strategically important island called Tinian. Construction began immediately on a B-29 airfield for the 20th Air Force to conduct bombing raids against the Japanese mainland, not long after the B-29s of the 20th hit Tokyo for the first time. Soon after meeting MacArthur and Nimitz in Honolulu, Roosevelt green-lighted MacArthur's ground invasion of the Philippines over Nimitz's preference to invade Formosa.

While the Americans broke out of Normandy and penetrated inland, the front-line units brought baseball with them. When Paris was liberated in August, American troops celebrated by sunning in Parisian parks. With free time, wine, and French girls at hand, one of the GIs' favorite pastimes was playing shirts-and-skins baseball. They played with joy and glee, and they should have, because they had survived some of the worst fighting of the war.

A small group of tankers from the First Army, officially Company C of the 741st Tank Battalion, nicknamed Vitamin Charley, landed on the morning of June 6, and the rest landed nine days later, fighting forward, tankers supporting the 2nd Infantry Division "doughs," as the tankers called the ground troops, a nod to the old "doughboys" of World War I. Vitamin Charley fought through the best SS troops in the German Army and helped capture Hill 192, the natural barrier leading to St. Lô, the exit point for the Normandy breakthrough.

A little ingenuity helped the next step of the advance. Engineers welded the German tank obstacles from Omaha to the front of the Sherman tanks. The tankers called them "Jerry Cutters," and they worked quite well for a time, clearing the hedgerows for the doughs to scurry through. Vitamin Charley helped to liberate one French village after another, providing time for rest for the tanks to be fueled and fixed.

When the tankers got downtime, they went straight to baseball, teaching the game to the local Frenchmen, whom the tankers generically called Pepe. According to the unofficial unit history written a year after the war, "While at St. Georges d'Elle we took advantage of every chance to relax, as we did whenever we weren't in the lines. Pepe, optimist that he was, was always trying to win a game of baseball. No matter who made up the impromptu teams, Pepe managed to lose almost invariably."

A bitter four-day fight to free St. Lô followed, inflicting heavy casualties on both sides and creating the breakthrough for Patton's Third Army to run wild through the disorganized Germans, an end-run attempt to cut off an entire German army. Again, the unit history: "Our First Army had made the hole, Patton was carrying the ball." After another month of bitter, thankless advancing in which many men suffered combat fatigue, Vitamin Charley pulled up at Sainte-Marie-Laumont on August 3. Once more, the tankers got a break, and baseball was the game at hand: "We had been placed in Division reserve, and for several days we had no artillery to fear. Balls and bats were dug out, and we enjoyed some more baseball. When Pepe's teams lost, as they always had, we felt happily that we were pretty close to normalcy. If Pepe's team lost, we were O.K."

Finally, twelve weeks after D-Day, all spent in nearly continuous combat, the tanker boys of Vitamin Charley reached Paris. The Sherman tanks were spruced up and the men showered and shaved for the parade down the Champs-Élysées. The men never forgot the adoring French girls or the citizens who plied them with wine and cognac and wanted to peek inside their tanks. Before the big parade, the boys got another chance to play the ball game of a lifetime in the shadow of the Eiffel Tower.

The boys played a game of shirts-and-skins baseball in a Parisian park, really getting at it this time, against each other. One kid threw with a side-arm delivery, cutting it loose. Another of the tankers, Milton Stern, peeled his shirt off, grabbed a glove, and got behind the plate. He'd never played professional baseball, didn't have the talent to do so, and never thought anyone in his family would ever have anything to do with professional ballplayers. But there he was, snapped in action by one of his buddies, playing shirts-and-skins baseball in Paris in August 1944. He had landed on D-Day and never said much of any of it to his family, about fighting through Hill 192 and St. Lô, bad, ugly brawls against tough and well-trained German divisions where lots of kids were incinerated inside their own tanks. He was twenty-six that summer, an old man among the tankers, and bore a little resemblance to Abe Lincoln without a beard, but lean and fit with his shirt off. He enjoyed the sun. There was still a lot of war to go, but in that moment in Paris, playing a baseball game with their buddies was meaningful to the boys of Vitamin Charley.

The boys suffering and sweating it out in German prisoner-of-war camps hoped that the Allies would soon be coming to free them. The massive aerial armadas overhead, American bombers and fighter escorts by day, and British by night, rumbling to their targets, gave them hope. In the warm summer months, so did baseball.

When former minor league pitcher Bert Shepard finally woke up from his crash landing in early spring, he had no sense of time or place. He had no idea how long he had been sedated, but he soon learned he was lucky to have been shot down near a Luftwaffe airfield, where the unwritten rules of chivalry surpassed those of conventional war. The farmers who found him wanted to kill him, but airmen looked after airmen, a courtesy Germans and British extended to each other in World War I and continued, including some American pilots, in World War II. A Luftwaffe doctor sent him to a hospital to convalesce before he was processed as a prisoner of war. That simple act kept alive Shepard's chances to play baseball again.

Shepard remembered waking up fat, dumb, and happy, but he quickly realized something was wrong. His right leg had been amputated eleven inches below the knee. That would certainly make pitching again problematic. He also had one hell of a dent in his face, where the gunsight had crushed his skull over his right eye, forcing doctors to remove a two-inch-square piece of the frontal sinus bone over his right eye. Later, Shepard realized that if the hits on his plane had been clean or had simply sliced his oil line instead of his leg, and that if the gunsight hadn't hit his head, he could have glided the plane in and walked away from the crash. But his having had no such luck created baseball luck. "Then the Germans talked to me a little bit, gave me a shot, and I went back to sleep," he said.

It was reasonable to expect his baseball dreams were over, but by August, when Paris was liberated, Shepard was using the warm weather to help put his baseball life together again even as he lived behind barbed wire and had a long winter ahead in which the Allied advances would force him to be moved to five different prison camps, each one deeper into Germany.

While he was a prisoner, Shepard made a decision. He missed flying, but he could not live without baseball. As he settled into prison life, he had just one focus. Baseball kept him alive spiritually, emotionally, and physically. Even without a leg, as an amputee, he was determined not let this new disability define him. "I had been an athlete all my life, and when I first realized that my leg was gone, I resolved that I would still be an athlete," he said. "This is the thing I dreamed about in those prison camps for months—the day I could get back on the diamond."

To help Shepard along, a Canadian prisoner crafted a crude wooden leg. The thing fit like a charm. Shepard started playing catch on the makeshift prosthetic. He had enough balance to slowly work his arm into shape. Satisfied, he began running sophisticated drills, such as changing direction, as he would have to do to field his position and run the bases. A German doctor was so amazed that he asked Shepard to demonstrate his artificial leg and the exercises he had performed to other doctors. As far as POW life went, Bert Shepard had it pretty good. He could walk, he could run, and he could dream.

The same could not necessarily be said for Phil Marchildon, the former Philadelphia Athletics pitcher whose bomber was shot down in August. He had been awake for every terrifying moment of his ordeal. He remembered when he and his navigator, George Gill, were processed and separated. On the train platform at Hamburg, the guards warned them not to make eye contact with the German citizens, who hated Allied airmen for the bombing campaigns against civilians in Hamburg, Dresden, and Berlin. Marchildon felt remorse for the innocent, but not for Germany, which he felt deserved the punishment for starting the war in the first place. Somewhere in the back of his mind must have been the thought *If it wasn't for the goddamn Nazis, I'd be winning 20 games.*

Instead, Marchildon withstood a dreary interrogation and was sent to Stalag Luft III in Sagan, Poland. He was now a *Kriegsgefangene*, a POW, or in airmen slang, one of the Kriegies, prisoners who liked to play baseball to kill time. Their existence became a race of physical, emotional, and mental survival. An airman limerick went like this, best sung with a belt from the Kriegie still, which spat out a wretched formula that tasted like antifreeze but packed a punch: *How do we play ball without getting shot / How do we escape without getting caught? / Don't sleepwalk too far while in your slumber / Or the Jerry in the tower will have your number.* Phil Marchildon would drink to that because he was now the answer to a baseball trivia question he would have preferred to never have been: Who was the first former major league player to become a German prisoner of war?

His quest to survive was his own special hell. Over the next several months, Marchildon subsisted on the ever-dwindling rations provided by the Germans. His former navigator, George Gill, serving his time in Stalag Luft I, wrote, "Food was the biggest daily concern for us all." Marchildon's conditions, however, were the worst. Stalag Luft III was the most notorious and barbaric of the German POW camps. Marchildon could tell he was losing weight and even the occasional dinners provided by the Red Cross couldn't stop his slide. The POWs knew the war was going badly for the Germans by the increasingly angry moods of the guards. Inmates plotted escapes. "The prisoners had an escape committee that forged identification papers, furnished maps, and made plans," Marchildon remembered. "Sometimes an escape party would make it. Sometimes they'd be caught and killed. Out of scraps of contraband, the prisoners built a radio, using a piece of fat for a condenser. They kept changing its hiding place, burying it in the earth under a floor, for example, and it would be tuned in once a day for a British newscast. Rats kept finding it and eating the fat, but although the Germans knew there was a radio somewhere, they never found it."

Resuming his baseball career seemed an empty dream. Some guy had a ball, so the airmen played catch the best they could. None of them had any idea Marchildon had pitched in the big leagues, unless they were fans and recognized his name from before the war. Marchildon wasn't eager to talk about his baseball career because he thought it was a done dream. He was thin and sickly, he thought; even if he was liberated, he'd never be the same pitcher he used to be. The captives played catch the best they could, but hesitantly. Kriegie baseball was a favorite pastime at all the Stalag camps. At Luft IV, a former minor league outfielder and coal miner from Pennsylvania, Augie Donatelli, who broke his foot when he was shot down on his seventeenth mission as a B-17 tail gunner, umpired camp games, a skill he turned into his major league profession after the war.

But Marchildon thought he would be lucky to survive these barbarians, much less play ball. He remembered a corral with a low fence, beyond which prisoners were forbidden to go. They were herded like animals and not permitted to stray. The other side of that fence felt like freedom, but the reality was nobody could get past it. Stories were that POWs who quickly went to the other side of the fence to retrieve a loose ball were shot on sight, execution style. The SS guards were as cold and cruel as the winter. They baited prisoners for sheer entertainment. One SS guard in particular was a calculating, callous bastard. All of the prisoners hated him. Marchildon remembered, "That guard stood by while a German soldier outside the corral invited a prisoner over to the outer fence to swap cigarettes through the wire. When the prisoner stepped over the inner fence, the guard cut him down with a submachine-gun burst."

Such stupid cruelty made the prisoners hate the Germans, who knew American POWs had a soft spot for baseball, so some camps printed newspapers with major league baseball standings and batting averages from a month before. The SS was always working hard to propagandize everybody. Right next to the baseball statistics were hateful commentaries thinly disguised as news, urging the Americans to denounce Jews and Negroes and trying to convince them Hitler was a decent fellow and that President Roosevelt had hoodwinked them into a war. The Nazis wanted the prisoners to believe that it was Roosevelt's fault that they were prisoners in the first place. The prisoners read the baseball news and ignored the rubbish. The months dragged on in the stalags, and the former ballplayers turned POWs easily lost track of days, weeks, and months. It was as difficult to get additional news from beyond the barbed wire as bread that wasn't stale. Most of the baseball news got to the men from prisoners who had more recently been on the outside. When some guys heard that the St. Louis Browns played in the World Series, they thought it was another of Hitler's stupid jokes.

In October, the baseball-playing boys of Vitamin Charley rolled their Sherman tanks and crossed the Our River into Germany, right into the dragon's teeth of the Siegfried Line, the western wall of German defense, taking out hundreds of pillboxes in support of the doughs of the 2nd Division, First Army. Thoughts of home were not far behind, nor were thoughts of baseball. A dough wrote:

> I have moved over here to help buck the Siegfried Line, after taking a swipe at Jerry in Holland with the Canadians; so it appears that the only box I'll be stepping into this spring will be a pillbox, and I shouldn't have trouble finding one of those, Jerry has really dotted the landscape with them. The German is proving a resourceful and determined foe. This struggle is farther from a finish than a lot of people are prone to think. A hard fight lies ahead, but I am confident that we are equal to it. I was able to listen to the World Series and that was highly gratifying to me. I was in England then. But one of the biggest treats I have had over here came to me the other day, when the first of the bundles of sports pages my mother has been saving and sending reached me. It was surely a thrill to scan my favorite page once more.

After a few weeks of fighting and mopping up, the tankers had a brief rest before rolling to Belgium, into the bitter cold, where all was unusually quiet until December 16. The idea of a German surrender before Christmas came to a crashing end when German Field Marshal von Rundstedt launched a ferocious offensive. Tanks came out of the trees, well-armed infantry blitzed, and the sky was again filled with German fighters and bombers. The American boys were scared as hell. The Battle of the Bulge began, and the winter months proved to be terrifying and dangerous. That was the worst Christmas those boys ever experienced. The tankers of Vitamin

Charley found themselves hiding in the frozen ground just like everyone else. The unit's unofficial history recalls how they experienced Christmas in the Bulge. "We didn't sing and carol, but lay in our foxholes praying silently. Christmas Day was ushered in by an artillery duel that began at midnight and lasted until the morning. Von Rundstedt probably figured the attack would lower our morale. It did. We were thoroughly scared. We started to fight as we never had before."

That winter, the soldiers used baseball to save lives. The SS were sneaky sons of bitches. They sent over English-speaking troops dressed in captured American uniforms and carrying American weapons. The first few times, the ruse worked quite well, but when word spread that the next Yank a dough didn't know might be a kraut, then baseball trivia became a matter of life and death. According to Nat Frankel, a tanker in Patton's 4th Armored Division, the best way to screen out strangers was to speak baseball. "Our lines were constantly infiltrated by German soldiers wearing American uniforms and jabbering English. How did we trap them? We would ask them if DiMaggio was still pitching with the Cubs!"

Many ballplayers served in the Battle of the Bulge with distinction, but if the fighting didn't get them, the frostbite could. The cold and wet conditions ruined many careers, including that of former Washington Senators shortstop Cecil Travis, who hadn't played in the majors since 1941. He spent most of the war playing for Army teams, but he was in the wrong place at the wrong time. Hunkered down in his foxhole with no room to move for a long period, he contracted a horrible case of frostbite. It also ruined the career of pitcher Ernie White, who broke in with the Cardinals in 1941, but lost all feeling in his arm when he became trapped in icy water. He was never the same. Infantryman Ralph Houk, who later became manager of the Yankees, took a bullet through his helmet and somehow survived. Paratrooper Jocko Thompson, one of the 101st's Battered Bastards of Bastogne, turned his toughness into a pitching career with the Philadelphia Phillies. Pitcher Murry Dickson jumped into a foxhole for cover with Patton himself. Patton thought Dickson saved his life and asked him to be his driver. Dickson declined.

Boston Braves pitcher Warren Spahn landed on Omaha Beach six months after the invasion and served with the 276th Battalion Engineers. He spoke for many of his contemporaries when he recalled the conditions:

"We were surrounded in the Hertgen Forest and had to fight our way out of there. Our feet were frozen when we went to sleep and they were frozen when we woke up. We didn't have a bath or a change of clothes for weeks."

Black ballplayers were out in the Bulge, too, though the fact that they were ballplayers went unknown to white troops. Hank Thompson was one of them. He turned nineteen that winter, twice arrested and thrown in the stockade for brawling with bigots. He already had a drinking habit, but, damn, he sure could hit. At home he was a great young hitter for the Kansas City Monarchs, but out here he was just one of the engineers, trying to keep warm and stay alive. Another player, Leon Day, could throw smoke in his days as a star pitcher for the Newark Eagles. He served with an armor battalion that came ashore on Utah beach on D-Day, and when the manpower was scarce, some generals had no trouble letting the black troops kill Germans. Black soldiers wanted to prove themselves, and they thought Negroes shooting at Nazis would scare the hell out of the master-race bastards, even as the Germans pumped out radio broadcasts ridiculing the Americans for fighting alongside each other, calling it *ein schwarz schmach,* "a black outrage."

When the Americans finally began counterpunching, one of the finest and least known moments connecting baseball to the Bulge occurred. Major George Stallings never played in the majors, yet his name was well-known in the game's history. He was the son of the former Boston Braves manager of the same name who led the Boston "Miracle" Braves, the team that rallied from last place on July 4 to sweep Connie Mack's heavily favored Philadelphia Athletics in 4 games and win the 1914 World Series. His son played only briefly in the minors before the war, but he inherited some of his father's tactical abilities.

According to *The New York Times,* Stallings advanced with little difficulty other than that of the terrain until he reached his objective. "There the Germans made a determined stand. They turned the ruins of the village into a strong point with dug-in infantry, artillery, and mortar positions. They also had established strong machine-gun posts and had self-propelled artillery dug in. An open field a thousand yards wide lies just to the north. The Germans also had this mined and also covered it with machine gun, mortar, and artillery fire. Major Stallings, accordingly, divided his force into three columns. One of these approached the hamlet from the west through the woods and another from the east along a sunken road. The third came down from the north, partly protected from observation by a finger of the woods that stretches diagonally across the open fields. The three columns converged on the village. They knocked out the self-propelled guns and rushed the Germans in their cellars and machine-gun posts. Besides the Germans killed, two hundred were routed out as prisoners of war." Stallings and his men fought house to house to clear the area, resulting in four hundred total prisoners taken and the village secured by nightfall. Such was the push across the European countryside, one battle for one town after another.

Baseball lingo was part of GI humor. With so many troops trapped and cut off, doughs called themselves proud members of the Foxhole League. But it was winter, with no fresh baseball news to discuss, and even so, the situation was just a little too fucked-up to worry if there would be a 1945 baseball season back home. Baseball tried to do its part by sending a small USO tour, comprised of National League ambassadors. While Luke Sewell and his American League cronies were flying around the CBI, established National Leaguers Frankie Frisch, Mel Ott, Bucky Walters, Washington Senators knuckleball pitcher Dutch Leonard, and St. Louis sportswriter J. Roy Stockton toured the European Theater of Operations (ETO), bringing with them tales of the 1944 season from the NL perspective.

The trip started with a bumpy B-17 flight over the North Atlantic so terrifying that Bucky Walters went to the cockpit and meekly asked the captain, "Couldn't you throw a curve and go around the next squall we meet?" The pilot scoffed and told him this was nothing. After twenty-four hours of flying, the group landed and posed with General Patton and General Bradley before they went to the front lines, expecting their December journey to be uneventful.

But the ballplayers and the lowly sportswriter quickly found themselves in the middle of the shit. They were three miles away from the front when the Germans split open the bulge. "When the Germans broke through, it was every man for himself because the Nazis were coming," Stockton recalled. Artillery shells rained around them. German fighters attacked the troops. The ballplayers were terrified. "Hey, Dutch," Frankie Frisch said to Dutch Leonard, the old knuckleball pitcher. "I'm going to stay near you.

Take good care of me, will you, Dutch?" Sure, Dutch said. But who was going to take care of him?

The answer was the boys with the machine guns. The tour must go on, come rain, shine, snow, or Krauts, so the troupe often played in front of small groups of doughs because commanders would not risk amassing (and losing) large numbers of precious men where German artillery was in range. Baseball was so vitally important to the morale of the front-line troops that nobody considered calling off the tour and sending the ballplayers home. They wore fatigues, and if worse came to worse, they could fire rifles, too. This was a lot more dangerous than the ballplayers had anticipated. When the civilian ballplayers signed up after the World Series, the war was supposed to have been over by Christmas. Instead, the ballplayers could see the V-1 buzz bombs roaring through the sky on the way to London to indiscriminately crash and burn.

The ballplayers continued on, but one day stood out among the rest. A show was held in a barn right on the edge of German territory, close enough to wrecked Panzers and burned-out Sherman tanks to see dead and bloated bodies on the side of the roads and hastily made German graves. About forty doughs were in the barn. Frankie Frisch, former Gashouse Gang St. Louis Cardinals second baseman who was now manager of the Pittsburgh Pirates, could liven up any room. But he was terrified, visibly shaken at the shelling so close to him. The doughs told him he would get used to it, and to tell them more about all the times he baited the umpires.

Mel Ott, the star slugger of the New York Giants, well past his prime, was traumatized. He had a hard time talking about what he had experienced. One memory stayed with him for a long time. It was a young G.I., battered and war weary. He couldn't have been even 20 yet. He approached his boyhood hero with his helmet in his hand. He knew everything there was to know about the ballplayer nicknamed Master Melvin. He could probably imitate Mel's big leg kick, tell you he broke into the big leagues as a seventeen-year-old rookie in 1926 and led the National League in home runs six times. He had grown up watching Mel play in the Polo Grounds in the 1930s. This boy had seen horrors he would never forget, but being in the company of his idol wiped clean his weariness. "Just think," he told his hero, "I had to join the Army to meet Mel Ott!" In that moment, it was as if Ott wore his blue Giants jersey with his famous number four, signing an autograph for a kid hanging over the railing.

Ott was the player-manager for the Giants. They weren't good during the war and hadn't been competitive since the 1930s, but that didn't matter to the doughs stuck in the Bulge. They wanted to hear all about the 1944 season, so Ott told them what they'd missed. He hit 26 home runs for the Giants and was closing in on 500 for his career. In need of wartime pitching because of the manpower crisis, the Giants brought up a quirky rookie pitcher named Bill Voiselle, whose jersey number became his nickname, Ninety-Six, which at the time was the highest number in major league history and the name of his hometown.

Voiselle had a terrible winning percentage at Jersey City in 1943. Classified 4-F for hearing loss, he was nearly deaf, which would have been perfect for an artilleryman and certainly beneficial for a pitcher who lost 21 games. Made it harder to hear the Jersey jeering that way. Most pitchers who go 10-21 in the minors don't get called up to the majors, but what the hell, the war was on, and the Giants needed pitching.

What did it say about the quality of play when a guy who lost 21 games in the minors came to the majors and won 21 games? Welcome to wartime baseball, doughs! Voiselle came to the big leagues for keeps in 1944 and went 21-16 with a league-leading 161 strikeouts, despite allowing a league-leading 31 home runs at the rotting, old Polo Grounds, which was such a dump that why would the Germans try to bomb it in the first place? The ballpark had underground bomb shelters for fans and local residents, but nowhere to hide for pitchers. Voiselle didn't give a damn. He couldn't hear the bombs off the bats anyhow. He was so happy to be in the big leagues that he pitched the Herculean total of 312 2/3 innings, leading the majors and becoming the first (and probably last) rookie pitcher to throw 300 innings in a big league season.

Frisch described his best pitcher, Truett "Rip" Sewell, a cousin to the Sewell brothers, Luke and Joe. Rip Sewell won 21 games for the Pirates in both 1943 and 1944, throwing his famous "blooper" pitch, a big, slow, soft curveball he also called his eephus pitch. To put that pitch in perspective, it was like a guy throwing slow-pitch softball in the majors. It wasn't changing speeds. It was throwing no speed with less speed. A guy could get away with that in the NL, especially against utterly horseshit teams like the Brooklyn Dodgers.

A lot of Brooklyn boys in the Bulge wanted updates on Dem Bums, but the news from the borough was not so hot. Branch Rickey was a genius when he led the Cardinals, but under his tutelage, he tanked the Dodgers, who finished in seventh in 1944. The only good news was that popular outfielder Dixie Walker led the league with a .357 batting average, but there wasn't enough time to tell the troops how many strange scrubs were playing for the Brooks and in the rest of the NL.

The Dodgers actually had a pitcher, Hal Gregg, who walked 137 batters. But compared to the seventeen-year-old outfielder Tommy Brown or the high school violinist Eddie Basinski playing the infield, Gregg was high-class. There wasn't much to tell about their season except for the time a knuckleball pitcher named Jim Tobin from the Boston Braves pitched the first wartime no-hitter against them in April. The Bums' third baseman, Frenchy Bordagaray, was so used up that he inspired Rickey to call him "the best bad third baseman in baseball history." When they heard that, the doughs roared with laughter.

Frisch explained how Billy Southworth Sr.'s Cardinals won the pennant again and mentioned that his son, Billy junior, was home from the war, the survivor of twenty-five bombing missions as captain of a B-17. Frisch told the kids about Bill Nicholson, a big slugger for the Chicago Cubs, who in 1943 and 1944 had the two biggest offensive years in baseball. In 1943, the man they called Swish led the NL with 29 home runs and 128 RBIs, and in 1944, he did it again, with 33 home runs and 122 RBIs. With Stan Musial set to join the Navy, Nicholson was set to give the Cubs their best chance to pry the pennant away from the Cards in 1945, if FDR, who had recently won his fourth term, green-lighted another season.

After every session, the ballplayers took questions from the soldiers. They would answer all sorts of mundane questions, but usually they were basic, homesick questions, because baseball news was so hard to get on the front. Most boys knew the Cardinals had won the World Series, but a few questions came up often.

How is Hank Greenberg doing?

Fine, the ballplayers said. He spent all of 1944 in China helping the big bombers go after Japan. That was all anybody in the States had heard about him. Nobody heard much about Hank during the war; it was as if he were forgotten. Some people thought he was dead, but that wasn't true. The ballplayers assumed he was in fine shape, but nobody heard anything about a bomber blowing up on takeoff and nearly killing him. After this answer, the next question was invariably:

Is he gonna play ball again?

Lot of guys from Detroit out in the Bulge! Nobody knows. He'd been in the service an awful long time. You stop playing ball for so long, who knows what it will do to a guy. But if anyone can do it, big Hank can. The Tigers were actually pretty good this summer, especially this kid Newhouser. He always had a good arm, but finally got his act together and led that other league in wins and strikeouts. Really good pitcher, wouldn't matter if there was a war or not, he was a winner with great stuff. Next question.

Who is this guy playing in the minors with one arm?

A guy named Gray, played for Memphis in the Southern Association on account of the lack of manpower. Spent his second year there and had a nice season. Actually won the league MVP award now that you mention it.

Is he gonna play in the big leagues?

That question made the ballplayers a little uneasy. None of them wanted to think that the majors were so worn-out from the war that a guy with one arm was actually going to play up there, or what was left of up there. In truth, none of the guys knew. None of them had seen him play, but they had seen his story in the papers. Pete got a lot of ink for a busher, but he had said something that was pretty moving. When presented his MVP award, some sportswriters gave him an award for courage, but Pete wouldn't have it. He said, "Boys, I can't fight. And so there is no courage about me. Courage belongs on the battlefield." That line got Pete a round of applause from the soldiers who heard that story.

Will there be a 1945 baseball season?

Beats the hell out of us. We're just ballplayers and managers. Probably depends more on you boys than anyone else. If Uncle Sam says the war is going good enough for us to keep playing, we'll play. But if he shuts us down, if FDR says red light instead of green light, we'll shut it down and be out here with you boys or working at home in the factories.

We heard Judge Landis died a few weeks ago?

Yes, that is true. The old Judge died in late November, leaving baseball without a commissioner at the worst possible time. Nobody knows who will replace him or what that will do to the 1945 season. This is gonna be a long winter, boys.

Does President Roosevelt still love baseball?

Dear Lord, we hope so.

CHAPTER 16
One Man Short

In the spring of 1944, Judge Kenesaw Mountain Landis finally made a concession to age. He moved out of the Chicago hotel he had lived in since becoming commissioner and into a small house in Chicago, where he and his wife planted a victory garden. In the summer, while the radio was tuned to the local broadcasts of the Cubs and White Sox games, Landis spent more time outside than he had in many years. He fell quite in love with tending his soil, raising vegetables to eat, just as millions of other families did during the war. It was difficult to imagine the old Judge out in the sun babying his tomato vines, but that's just what he did, taking in the hot and humid Chicago summer in relative peace.

He was pleased with the direction of the game, satisfied even in its less than perfect wartime state. Landis was proud of the two large checks baseball had presented to the war effort, one for $362,000 in 1942 and another for $308,000 in 1943. Landis never lost his public scowl, but in private he was as worried as any other grandfather. Both World Wars were intensely personal to the old man, who had once volunteered to surrender his seat on the federal bench to serve in World War I before President Wilson told him he was too damn old.

Landis's son, Reed, was a decorated pursuit pilot in World War I, becoming a twelve-victory ace for the famous No. 40 squadron of the British Royal Flying Corps, made famous by aces Mick Mannock and George Mc-

Elroy. Reed survived the war and quietly helped his father build baseball by serving as the chairman of the American Legion, which for years sponsored thousands of baseball teams that produced hundreds of future pro ballplayers. Reed served stateside in the Army Air Corps during the war, where he and the old man worried about Reed's son, Keehn Landis.

Something about flying was in the blood of the Judge's boys. Keehn Landis was a P-51 fighter pilot in the European Theater, serving in the red-and-yellow-checkered-nose 363rd Fighter Squadron of the famed 357th Fighter Group. The pilots called themselves the Yoxford Boys. Among the pilots in the 363rd were two well-known Mustang aces. One, Bud Anderson, flew a Mustang nicknamed *Old Crow* and became a triple ace. The other was a country boy from West Virginia named Charles E. "Chuck" Yeager, who in 1947 broke the sound barrier.

Worrying about his grandson in the skies over Europe did not help the old Judge's health. He stayed out of the public eye during the war years, so it was not common knowledge that his health was gradually declining. There were signs, though; rumor had it that Landis had declined a new five-year contract extension offered by the owners. Turning down guaranteed money wasn't like the Judge. Then, something was wrong when he didn't come to the World Series for the first time in twenty-one years. The last ball game he ever saw was in late August, when he witnessed the Great Lakes Naval Air Station defeat the New York Giants in Chicago.

In the early fall, Landis collapsed in his garden. He was admitted to the hospital and hated every second of it. He was eager to leave and was generally his belligerent self to the doctors, who didn't trust his heart and wouldn't let him leave. "It makes me so damn mad to feel old," he moaned. After about fifty-five days, his breathing became labored and the doctors placed him in an oxygen tent. He silently slipped away in late November, peacefully saying good-bye to his family and a small number of friends. He died of a coronary thrombosis on the morning of November 25, five days after his seventy-eighth birthday, just a few weeks before the crucial winter meetings.

Landis was hard and stubborn, and once he made up his mind, he usually closed it to arguments counter to the decision he had already made. But even with his enforcement of baseball's institutionalized discrimination, he had to be regarded as an effective commissioner because he guided and grew the game through the two greatest traumas it experienced in his lifetime, the Black Sox scandal and the war.

But that's not to say that the Judge didn't keep secrets. When he died, he left hundreds of boxes of his personal papers, letters, writings, diaries, correspondence, and news clips from both his baseball career and his time on the federal bench. Landis hoarded all his papers, which were assigned to the executor of his estate, his longtime secretary, Leslie O'Connor. When O'Connor died, he left the papers to his son, who burned all of the Judge's baseball papers, for reasons unknown, lost to history, going up in smoke like everything else during the war.

In death as in life, Landis had no personality. He didn't want so much as a flower sent to his grave. "They always can think of the most wonderful things to say about a man after he is dead," he groused a few weeks before his death. He had no taste for cordial formalities. He instructed that there be no funeral, and he wanted a private cremation and burial. But his timing was brutal. Everyone could see how much manpower the war was taking, and the window for playing ball seemed to close tighter each wartime season. How could there be a 1945 baseball season if Germany wasn't finished and there was no timetable on the defeat of Japan?

Landis might have had to reach out to the White House again, but alas, the stubborn old Judge died instead of asking Roosevelt for anything. The baseball owners did a good job keeping Landis's illness a secret, but not surprisingly, their contingency plans weren't exactly organized or efficient. They had never replaced a commissioner before and were willing to keep him on until his eighty-sixth birthday. The problem with baseball owners was they were always looking for somebody to save them from themselves. They hoped for a clean and smooth transition of power to a new commissioner, but the war didn't make the baseball decision easy because it would involve the federal government. *The New York Times* praised Landis in his obituary, but cautioned that without him baseball was in uncertain times. "His death left the major leagues without a guiding genius and placed tremendous importance on the National and American winter meetings on December 12 and 13 when a successor probably will be named."

Shortly after Landis died, the War Department ordered commanding officers not to issue medical discharges to publicized performers—ballplayers—and took over that function itself. This development meant that players could no longer be deemed 4-F by local draft boards. Every decision on every player was now a federal decision. Without Landis, and even without his disdain for Roosevelt, the baseball owners wondered if they would have the necessary power to override the War Department. In addition, Roosevelt was less frequently seen in public, so asking Clark Griffith to approximate the situation did not seem likely. Griffith was getting old and sick himself, and besides, owners were tired of his influence.

In early December, the owners established a committee to elect a new commissioner. They announced their confidence that there would be a 1945 season, but the reality was they had no idea if they would have the ballplayers to play the season. Two days before Christmas, the Office of War Mobilization ordered all 4-F personnel to be reexamined and reassigned to either the armed forces or war jobs—the work-or-fight mandate. This potentially meant that every single 4-F major league player could be pulled out of baseball for the greater good without any recourse.

As Christmas 1944 arrived, there had never been more uncertainty. Most troubling of all was the silence from the White House. Another green light was needed, and without FDR's vote of confidence, it wouldn't matter who was picked to be commissioner because there would be no season to govern. Some writers called it the most important off-season in baseball history. They would be proven right. The seeds of change in the postwar baseball business were planted the moment Landis was in the ground.

One bit of big positive news that winter was indirectly related to the questions at hand. Hank Greenberg was rotated home. He was in no hurry to discuss anything he saw or experienced in China and India. He also had no idea when he might be discharged, when he might play again, or if there might be a 1945 season. He closely followed the developments of baseball's unsettled winter.

His first public appearance was at Madison Square Garden in New York City in December. He appeared with his old friend Joe DiMaggio, who returned home from Hawaii because of bad ulcers and sore ankles. They were both wearing their Army Air Force Class A's. Reporters wanted to know if Hank would ever play ball again. As the guy who had been in the service since May 1941, his number would have to come up eventually, and when it did, he would play ball again, right? Joe D had no idea. He wasn't lying when he said, "Hank's in the toughest spot of us all. I doubt if he's played half a dozen times since he went into the Army three years ago."

When people got their first look at Hank in more than a year, he was a sight for sore eyes. Here was the long-lost hero, the very symbol of strength and fortitude, Superman jumping out of the comic books. Hank looked tall, strong, and healthy. He looked as if the war hadn't touched him one bit, but Hank knew that wasn't true. He had the scars. You just couldn't see them. "The big fellow, who has been in uniform for four years, looks fit, lean and ready to pick off where he left off," observed *The Washington Post*.

Hank's return forced many other questions, and they were all connected to what baseball would do without Landis, how it would appease the government's manpower demands, who would become the next commissioner, and what that commissioner would do during and after the war. Hank had seen both sides of the issue now, because now he was an Army man and a baseball man. He'd performed his duty, but he had a fair demand for the owners: if the war ended in 1945 and players were mustered out of the service, they should be given their jobs back with a forty-day window at the previous salary to prove their worth, as was the federal law for any other occupation. A team such as the Tigers would gladly make that exception for a guy like Hank, but what about the thousands of other guys who weren't as talented or famous? Would baseball discard the players who served just because they weren't good ballplayers anymore, which in effect spat in the face of their service and allowed baseball to put a few dollars over doing what was just? Hank had his finger on the pulse of the right issue—don't tell a veteran "thanks for your service" and then kick him out into the street. It wasn't right to Hank and it was bad business. That question was of great concern to major league ballplayers and served as a precursor to the labor movement and unionizing of coming decades. Why should players who worked for the war effort take pay cuts if their talent regressed because of the years they served? They should at least get a small hint of back pay before moving on.

Owners were closely watching the war news and Hank Greenberg's timetable for returning to the playing field. If Hank succeeded and earned his previous pay, stocking rosters could be expensive in a cash-tight time. But if he struggled and could be docked pay after forty days, then owners could get fat off the profits of what promised to be booming wartime attendance coupled with lower payrolls. That is, if the war ended in the near future.

All of it came down to how ballplayers such as Greenberg, DiMaggio, and Feller would perform when they returned, but everyone expected Greenberg to be first up. The shooting hadn't even stopped, but a labor war seemed to be waiting. Owners sensed players wanted a union, and in searching for a commissioner to replace Judge Landis, they sought a leader who would fight to prevent any sort of players' association. The easiest way to choke off any discussion would be to see if their golden geese were not the same when they came back from the war. They would take their stars for the box office and make do with their lesser skills at lesser salaries, at least until a new generation of postwar standouts developed.

Hank realized that he wasn't just speaking for himself. He was speaking for all returning major leaguers and the generations after. He picked his words carefully: "Baseball talent's a funny thing. It runs out on you, whether you're playing or not. I think that where the situation is obviously unfair to the returning ballplayer, he should be given the courtesy of being made a free agent, so he can make the best possible deal for himself with some other club. However, the important thing right now and for some time to come is the war. Nothing else matters."

Free agency! Hank the heretic! Owners shuddered. Hank was suggesting correct market value for players of a certain standing. Before the war, Landis had made scores of minor leaguers free agents because he thought teams such as the Tigers and Cardinals were coercing them into signing. But what Hank was suggesting was much worse than the Judge's liberation of minor league farmhands. This was granting freedom to players, illustrating that the very premise the Nazis had argued—about the Americans being modern-day slave owners—was true. The owners didn't want to lose their property again, and they certainly didn't want to bid for players. They feared skyrocketing salaries would destroy the game.

The owners didn't like what the war was potentially doing to their business model. This meant they'd better get one of their own in Landis's job or this could become costly. No owners wanted to pay ballplayers more than they thought they were worth, but they also didn't want to be told what was a fair wage for that talent. How could World War II lead to free agency in baseball? What, are they going to have agents, too? Isn't it just easier to scare a kid into signing a contract for less than he's worth instead of working with some guy to make sure the player gets a fair shake? The lack of trust went both ways. Players believed owners would use anything—including their service to the nation in a time of war—to undercut their earning power, including ignoring federal laws under the game's antitrust exemption and reserve clause, which gave owners the ability to act within their own rules. Hank was the lightning rod. "I've always been treated right by Detroit, and I don't really expect anything to change," he said, though he qualified his answer. "But I guess there is a possibility that some former servicemen will be given big pay cuts when they come marching home."

Hank had the star power to say these things, but most players did not. As always, it came down to what happened on the field; if the war ended soon enough in 1945 for Hank Greenberg to prove he could still play. That was his private quest, but more was riding on Hank's shoulders than anyone realized. When asked if he thought he could still play, he offered an analytical reply: "If it's over [soon], say, I'm going to report back to Detroit. I'll still be able to hit a few, I think. I can't say what will happen regarding that salary." Then he went about his business and waited for his orders, which would probably involve morale tours to various factories.

When the War Department made it difficult on baseball, ordering commanding officers not to issue medical discharges to ballplayers, deciding instead to make those decisions itself, this represented a dramatic departure from how business had been conducted during the war. The government basically admitted that, yes, some ballplayers had been given a lot of leeway to stay home and play as long as they worked in a factory. But now that leeway was over. The Battle of the Bulge and the stubborn Japanese had scared more than the boys trapped behind the lines.

Nonetheless, the owners pressed ahead and said they expected to start the season and appointed a ten-member committee to arrange working arrangements for the 1945 season and to select a new commissioner. That's where the owners went wrong. If there was one guy in Washington you didn't want to cross, it was Jimmy Byrnes, who aside from Roosevelt might have been the most powerful man in the Beltway. As the director of the Office of War Mobilization, he had the call on all manpower decisions. Byrnes didn't like baseball owners making statements that contradicted the government or, worse yet, made it sound as if Jimmy Byrnes worked for baseball. The crusty old senator from tobacco row made it perfectly clear in his distinctive South Carolinian drawl: baseball owners would not decide if there would be a season, the government would tell them if there would be one. The owners overstated their position and infuriated Byrnes, who did not care about baseball and did not subscribe to any of the sentimentality Roosevelt had for the game. Byrnes sought to tighten the noose, formally ordering all players previously determined to be 4-F to be reexamined for either duty or war-industry jobs.

Unlike Roosevelt, baseball as morale builder meant nothing to Byrnes. He saw his job as numbers alone, and any industry that withheld its manpower, in Byrnes's view, was subject to the highest scrutiny. "It is difficult for me and the public to understand how men physically unfit for military service can compete in the most strenuous athletics," he said. Byrnes clearly thought these baseball owners were minuscule-minded minions without care for the big picture. "We knew V-E Day could not be far distant, but there was a danger that what was evident in Washington might not be so clear to the G.I., who still had to fight his way across the Rhine. I did not want to take any action, however desirable for domestic reasons, that would carry to the fighting fronts the remotest suggestion that there was a slackening of effort, enthusiasm or support by those in responsible positions at home," he wrote.

The owners hated this mentality. They wanted their season, antagonizing Byrnes so much that he fumed in *The Washington Post*, "Damn it, you'd think the biggest question of this war is whether or not we'll have baseball next season." Landis would have been amused from beyond the grave. The second he was dead, the owners couldn't do anything right without him, picking a fight with Washington they could never win.

Byrnes was a bureaucrat, not a baseball man, but he controlled the fate of the baseball season. Owners, again, hated that. Teams were sending out contracts to players over the winter, only to have them returned unsigned, with notification that said player was now in the armed forces. Byrnes thought the owners were whining, period, and he didn't care if he offended them. The start of the fourth wartime baseball season was a tremendous controversy, and the game's greatest dilemma since Landis wrote to Roosevelt in 1942.

Letters flooded home from the front, but this time not all servicemen were enthralled with the idea of a group of guys exempt from the job of finishing the war because they played a sport that was said to contribute to morale. There was animosity this time, something that did not exist when the war was fresh, new, and exciting. It was something that could not be quantified, which Byrnes, whose skill for allocating resources was a key factor in planning the massive invasion of Normandy, also shared.

A typical pro-baseball GI letter read like the one sent by an Army private: "A lot of men in the service like to hear the games over the radio even if they can't be there to see them." A veteran of Operations Torch and Husky wrote, "I think professional sports should go on because they are morale builders. I know men overseas get a big kick listening to the World Series over the radio."

But then some men who had seen harder combat and were sick of it complained. These guys thought ballplayers were getting a free ride, and who cared if there was a 1945 baseball season? A paratrooper who was wounded on Leyte wrote, with airborne mean dripping from his words, "If those diamond stars are husky enough to win games they should come right over here to help us win this one." Another vet wrote to the *Chicago Tribune* in equally angry tones: "Let's give these glorified 4-F's some combat training and see what kind of stars they are at killing Germans."

Baseball was fighting a war within the war. The discord was a publicity disaster for baseball. Another reader wrote, "My nephew in the Navy says that the boys from his ship razz the big league players in the Hawaii Sunshine League. Every sailor crabbed about big-name players getting away with mayhem." There was some truth to disorderly ballplayers in the service, especially in the Navy.

Bill Wight, a left-handed pitcher in the prewar minors, joined the Navy and played ball for the Blue Jackets. He admitted, "A lot of guys were playing so they would not get shipped out." As the war entered the homestretch, when every able-bodied man seemed to count, that excuse wasn't good enough for many servicemen anymore. The Army and the Navy were both proud of their teams, but after three years of fighting, the act was wearing thin. A sailor wrote to Grantland Rice, "We don't like the way men who have been in the service for two years or longer are still playing on service ball teams or giving exhibitions. We think that after they have finished their training, they belong with us, carrying a rifle or using a machine gun. We need them with us when the action starts, but they have to be where they are ordered."

As much as baseball had been a vital part of servicemen morale during the war, enough might be enough. The sailor complained, "The fault goes to the higher ups and we know it. We think this should be stopped. We haven't any interest in what happens to those service teams. They can win or lose and we don't care. We know it isn't fair to them or to us. We need them with us when it counts."

Well, now the Army and the Navy had a problem, because if servicemen started questioning the brass's judgment when crunch time was coming, that didn't bode well. This controversy was an example of why Hank Greenberg didn't want to play baseball for the Army. Now it was easy to see by Hank's decision to work for the Army rather than play for it that he felt service ball was superficial service. Maybe that wasn't the case earlier in the war, but it was starting to look and feel that way now.

The pressure on ballplayers at home grew. Ballplayers wanted to play, but they did not want to go to jail. Ballplayers even had their own code in the doctors' lines, *PA,* for "professional athlete." A PA used to get a lenient pass, but not so much this winter. One ballplayer, Ron Northey, who hit 22 home runs and drove in 104 runs for the 1944 Philadelphia Phillies, became the first major leaguer drafted after the new 4-F rules were initiated. Northey had every earmark of a wartime ballplayer. He was married with a young son and had previously been twice turned down in questionable 4-F rulings, once for a left-ear injury and another for high blood pressure. This time, he quit baseball and signed up.

If that wasn't bad enough, Stan Musial's draft number was about to come up. That wasn't just bad news for Billy Southworth and the Cardinals, but for baseball, the loss of its only surefire young star for the '45 season. When Musial knew the draft was about to get him, he did what many ballplayers did and joined the Navy before the Army could get him. "I'm glad I made it into the Navy," he said, as if he would have been turned down. "A lot of my friends are on the Navy and they like it. I know I will, too." That's the spirit, Stan, but baseball owners hated it. Losing a player like Musial this late in the war effort was considered an affront to their chances of survival.

In their own high self-estimation, owners thought they had bled enough.

They had given players, money, equipment, scheduling, and night games, and what else did they have left? They had done exactly what President Roosevelt asked them to do in 1942. They had kept the body but given the blood. Now the government wanted baseball's body on the sacrificial altar to the war effort, and they couldn't get a word from Roosevelt. They resented Byrnes, but without Landis they could fight dirty in Washington. So they did.

The first step was to fire back through the newspapers. Right there, you knew Ford Frick, the former sportswriter turned National League president, was calling the shots, even though Landis's former secretary, Leslie O'Connor, was acting as interim commissioner. Frick picked up the phone and called one of baseball's primary mouthpieces, *Washington Post* columnist Shirley Povich, and other media friends in baseball's war to win public opinion. Frick could toss lines to a reporter as if he were throwing feed to the chickens.

Povich soon rattled off a litany of contributions made by the baseball owners, which he said included millions of dollars raised and donated, hundreds of thousands of dollars' worth of equipment, millions of free admissions granted to servicemen, thousands of games played for Army and Navy camp teams, thousands of minor leaguers and aspiring professional players shipped out, and of course hundreds of active major league ballplayers.

Povich saved special anger for Jimmy Byrnes, hinting at just how angry the baseball establishment was at the man who became secretary of state later that year. "Contributions and sacrifices are words that shouldn't be confused," Povich wrote. You could almost hear Ford Frick dictating the copy over the phone. "All sixteen teams could be manned by a total of 230 men, drawn from those overage or physically unfit for military duty or medical discharges. Park employees are invariably unskilled and in over age and under age groups. Baseball's consumption of total war materials is nil, except for transportation."

Frick continued his behind-the-scenes offensive, turning venerable sportswriter Grantland Rice into a Garand rifle, who wrote, "In the job of handling sports, the government in Washington has been a badly and baffled and bewildered bunch with only a vague knowledge of what it is all about. We have 90 million people deeply interested in some form of sport." Rice fired again: "It doesn't require the brains of Aristotle, Plato and Socrates with a dash of Einstein to understand that baseball's man problem is what will be left and what can be done with it."

Frick was as cunning a young politician as baseball has ever known. Upon the death of Landis, he decided that one day he would become commissioner of baseball. In this winter of discontent, he saw his opportunity to pull off an unparalleled power grab. He quietly made a series of visits to the Capitol along with American League president Will Harridge. Their objective was twofold: they wanted the 4-F's to be allowed to continue to play baseball, and the Office of Defense Transportation (ODT) to allow baseball teams to travel from city to city at a time when the nation's railroad system was heavily impacted by the war effort.

Frick was the leader of the charge. About a dozen times that winter he went to Washington and succeeded in not drawing attention. For years, he had watched Clark Griffith horde White House access and cut it off from the other owners. Frick didn't want Griffith's influence with Roosevelt shaping the future of the 1945 season. He considered Griffith a publicity-monger who only cared about his team. Frick and Harridge also had one valuable piece of leverage to use that Griffith did not. Although Frick had aspirations of becoming commissioner, the job was up for bartering. Not surprisingly, those on the first list of rumored candidates were all from the halls of power. J. Edgar Hoover, FBI director, was rumored to be a candidate, but he felt comfortable in his present job with all of his self-created information-gathering perks. He also made it perfectly clear that his opulent files contained no incidents of 4-F ballplayers dogging service.

Also among the rumored commissioner candidates was Jimmy Byrnes, the sworn enemy of baseball owners. That was an interesting name to put on the street. Of course, Byrnes said he had no interest in the job. But the very mention of his candidacy was enough to suggest that he was offered the job in exchange for letting the 4-F's play.

Frick wanted allies in Washington. In February, he finally found one in Kentucky senator Albert "Happy" Chandler, a self-proclaimed baseball fan who liked to tell stories about his days playing semipro ball. Chandler, a Southern Democrat, was just the sort of political insider Judge Landis would have despised. But Chandler was useful for Frick. He was a fan, and he had power, which was even more important.

Chandler was the head of the Senate Armed Services Committee.

After months of Frick's and Harridge's clandestine visits to Washington, Chandler emerged as a powerful friend to baseball. He made the discussions of baseball's manpower crisis a matter of public record. He initiated hearings considering work-or-fight legislation. When that was done, the War Department backed off its previous determination to claim all 4-F ballplayers, saying it would "not counsel against" the continuation of baseball. Unofficially, the government permitted baseball to keep its 250 or so remaining 4-F players. It had backroom politics written all over it—Chandler brought the War Department to the floor at the urging of Frick—and the Army had no desire to dirty its hands with a matter as trivial as baseball.

In early February, about a month before spring training was to begin, Chandler was confident enough to pronounce victory for baseball. "I am encouraged to believe with a reasonable degree of certainty that baseball can go through this season and the War Department will not object," Chandler said. "Baseball has a right to continue because of its morale value." Chandler even defused baseball's dreaded F-word, saying the situation "isn't so bad that we couldn't spare the 4-F's to keep the game alive." It was a tremendous victory for Ford Frick, and he clearly owed Happy Chandler something. Chandler was an ambitious man with a thirst for baseball and a long memory. He did not forget when someone owed him a large favor.

With the manpower hurdle cleared, Frick and Harridge set their sights on resolving the transportation issue, which in light of the resolution of the manpower dilemma was comparatively easy. Conferences with the ODT resulted in approval from Colonel J. Monroe Johnson, but baseball had to give to get. The price was the cancellation of the All-Star Game, which was more of a symbolic sacrifice than a functional or practical give to the war effort. To get the final approval, however, Frick and Harridge, the presidents of the leagues, had to agree to begin the season without a definite commitment to play the 1945 World Series. That one hurt a little bit more because the World Series was worth a lot of money from a lot of revenue streams. But even starting the season without the assurance of a World Series was another major victory for baseball, and Frick's finest hour. *The Sporting News* hailed him, believing baseball needn't look any further than the aspiring former publicist for a second commissioner: "As the hour for naming a successor to Landis neared, there was a feeling that Frick, who had done such valuable work for baseball in Washington, would land the job."

Frick's power play seemed to have worked perfectly. Becoming commissioner required unanimous voting, but really it required support from New York City, the seat of baseball power. Frick had the support of Walter O'Malley and Branch Rickey of the Brooklyn Dodgers and Horace Stoneham of the New York Giants. The rest of the clubs usually fell into place. Harridge could gather the American League votes for Frick, including the Yankees in their time of transition. Larry MacPhail, now in charge of the Yankees, wanted an insider who knew the dirty, unwritten rules of the game. "I would favor a practical baseball man, one who understands the game thoroughly and would intelligently interpret our rules," he told *The New York Times*. "Frick is well qualified to hold the position."

Frick's candidacy seemed like a home run, but an unforeseen snag held up his coronation. Warren Giles of the Cincinnati Reds would not vote for Frick, instead insisting his friend John W. Bricker, former Republican governor of Ohio and 1944 vice-presidential nominee, get the job. Who knows what kind of deal Giles had with Bricker, but he wasn't changing his mind.

Frick was stuck. He realized, after his successful winter of behind-the-scenes campaigning to get the 1945 season open, that he would not be the next commissioner. To appease Giles, and to pay back another favor, he wondered if Chandler, the Kentucky senator who'd spearheaded the Senate's effort to keep baseball going, would be interested. Frick knew Chandler would be. Frick thought the senator might be suitable, but also knew that as an outsider he would never have the industry smarts to last long. Frick had already worked with the glib Chandler, who loved the cameras as much as Judge Landis hated them and loved politics as much as the Judge loathed them. Chandler was as much a baseball outsider as Landis was an insider. Frick still wanted to become commissioner, but he reluctantly accepted that now was not his time. So he wondered, perhaps, what would happen if the man who'd saved baseball for the 1945 season became the next commissioner?

How long would it take for the owners to revolt against him and seek to replace him with one of their own insiders? Nobody knew for sure, but one thing was certain: Ford Frick knew how the baseball business worked much better than Happy Chandler did. And he knew that when the baseball business wanted to blacklist somebody, Beltway insiders had nothing on the backstabbing abilities of those running the national pastime.

All of the machinations and all of the madness in baseball's longest, darkest winter might never have occurred if President Roosevelt weren't in failing health. In previous wartime seasons, baseball's fate had gone right to his desk, and even if the issue took several weeks to reach the top of the pile, Roosevelt would get around to it. That didn't happen this time, and without his presence, baseball fell into a dizzying void. After several months, Roosevelt finally took a cursory glance at the game he loved, which had been vastly overshadowed as he prepared the nation for a postwar world.

As it became clear that baseball had survived the most dangerous off-season in its history, the architect of the original green light wasn't about to lose the chance to speak up about his role in saving baseball during the war. FDR clearly was proud that he had insisted that the game must go on. Through the war, Roosevelt found subtle ways to keep his identity close to baseball, such as delivering one of his major reelection-platform speeches in Philadelphia's Shibe Park a few weeks after the '44 World Series, pledging a speedy demobilization and prosperous postwar America. Despite all the shadowy operations performed by Frick, the nation was waiting to hear from FDR. Only his ceremonial blessing would ease all fears. His voice was never needed more than it was now, even if it was clear he had allowed Washington politics to play out beneath him. He'd established that he wasn't going to get involved again, not the way he had when he wrote the Green Light Letter to Landis. It was of little concern to Roosevelt who became the next baseball commissioner or how an agreement was reached to keep the season open. He had much greater concerns in every aspect of his life.

The war was nearing an end on both fronts, and he was concerned with a postwar Europe and discussing reconstruction plans for Germany and Japan. He was also worried about the Russians. The war had taken a tremendous toll on his health, but it hadn't robbed him of his charm and personality. His feelings toward baseball and his position on its role in American life during the war never wavered. At his White House press conference on March 13, 1945, President Roosevelt, who'd saved baseball during World War II, spoke his last public words about the game he loved:

Question: Mr. President, would you care to commit yourself on the subject of night baseball?
FDR: Well, I am one of the fathers of night baseball, as you know,

and I am all in favor of baseball so long as you don't use perfectly healthy people that could be doing more useful work in the war. I consider baseball a very good thing for the population during the war.

Question: Do you think within that definition, Mr. President, it would be possible for the big leagues to operate this year?

FDR: Why not? It may not be quite as good a team, but I would go out to see a baseball game played by a sandlot team—and so would most people.

When FDR blessed baseball one last time, cash registers rang loud across the land. Virtually every owner and executive praised FDR and counted the days until the start of the 1945 baseball season. "Baseball will carry on with whatever men are available and do the best it can to give the fans a good show," Harridge said. Eddie Brannick of the Giants said, "Mr. Roosevelt said we should continue if possible without hurting the war effort or the building of the Army and Navy. That's the way baseball wants it, too, and I'm confident the game will go on under those conditions."

When Clark Griffith heard the news, he smiled. He knew Frick, who was always envious of Griffith's private meetings with the president, had maneuvered masterfully in Washington, DC, his own backyard. Frick put on a power grab and Griffith knew it, gaining more power within the game than Griffith ever had, even if Frick didn't become the next commissioner, and winning more sway for the National League. The Old Fox had to hand it to him. Frick outfoxed the Fox.

Griffith could have been angry, but he seemed resigned. He was getting older and just hoped to see his team win what he expected to be the last pennant of the war years. He was as fervently patriotic as ever. He certainly hoped his two stars, Buddy Lewis and Cecil Travis, could return in time to help the team, waiting, as the Tigers were for Hank Greenberg. "I think we can continue all right under Mr. Roosevelt's outline," Griffith said. He was proud of his boys who served, but he wanted them back soon.

When Opening Day neared, Griffith went to visit Roosevelt in the Oval Office, as he had for nearly every year in FDR's presidency, to present him with his annual American League pass. He had missed the President in 1943 and 1944, but Roosevelt granted him an audience in 1945. Griffith was pleased, but only when he saw Roosevelt for the first time in two years did he understand why FDR wanted to see him in person again.

It was so he could say good-bye.

Griffith was taken aback at how frail Roosevelt looked. The president had just returned from the exhausting journey to the Yalta conference. His smile was sweet and gentle, but his body wasn't the same. In times of such personal shock, Griffith went back to his baseball senses. Even in moments of pain, he could always understand what his baseball instincts told him about a human being. That never changed, not from the time when Griffith was a pitcher and not now. He stood behind the president to pose for the photograph handing him the annual gold pass. He saw how loose the president's bow tie looked around his tiny, thin-stretched neck, wasting away like the years the two men had spent bonding over the game they loved. "A person's neck has always been a barometer of his health to me," Griffith said. "And it was true this time. He had aged, he had withered, and he had lost his sharpness. I tried to compose myself as I walked the long distance from the door to his desk." Every step made him sad. He wistfully thought of all those Opening Days. Griffith remembered the details of the conversation.

"Hello, Clark," Mr. President said, offering his hand. "How are you?"

"I'm pretty good, Mr. President. How are you?"

Now they were just Franklin and Clark, no matter that one was the president and the other the owner of the Washington Senators. They were just two elderly pals sensing the end. Franklin shook Clark's hand, but he didn't let go. There was comfort in familiarity, and with the grip of his palm, he was one old man telling another how tired, sad, and miserable he felt, and yet rejoicing, remembering all the great times they'd shared. "He held on to my hand and looked at me for a full minute," Griffith said. "He was deciding, I guess, just how much he wanted to tell me."

Finally, Franklin found a way to tell Clark how he really felt. He was a man facing his own mortality. He knew he would not live to see the end of the war, nor the start of another baseball season. Roosevelt spoke in a haunting voice Griffith described as lifeless and remote. "You know how I really feel? I feel like a baseball team going into the ninth inning with only eight men left to play."

Roosevelt's words haunted Griffith, who couldn't get the phrase out of his mind. He thought it meant that baseball was about to be one man short when it mattered the most. He thought it meant Roosevelt was going to die. "I remember telling my son, 'The way President Roosevelt talked to me today, he had a premonition about his death.'"

CHAPTER 17

He Died on the Water

On April 12 at his retreat in Warm Springs, Georgia, President Roosevelt felt a sharp pain in the back of his head and slumped unconscious, the victim of a massive stroke. He died in the afternoon, eight days after his last meeting with Clark Griffith. News bulletins quickly spread throughout the country. Strangers cried next to each other. A day later, Roosevelt's body was placed in a hearse and driven through Warm Springs on the way to the train platform. Mourners lined the street and a military guard awaited him. The casket was placed aboard the train, escorted by a member from each branch of the service. Thousands of rural mourners gathered along the train tracks for the President's seven-hundred-mile journey to Washington, reminiscent of Abraham Lincoln's funeral train. In the morning, the train slowly arrived at Union Station in Washington, where the body was loaded onto a six-horse field-artillery caisson for the journey to the White House.

The funeral would have made European kings envious. Six white horses pulled the flag-draped casket, followed by a procession of soldiers and sailors, marching in rhythm past many thousands of mourners. Armored vehicles and deuce-and-a-half trucks motored down the road, and a large armada of warplanes roared above. The National Mall was filled as far as the eye could see. Across the street from the White House, Lafayette Park was standing room only. Blacks and whites cried together, young and old, until the horses pulled up to the White House and the casket was lifted inside. The body was given private holy rights. Cameras were not allowed to witness Mrs. Roosevelt saying good-bye.

The casket was placed in the East Room, where Lincoln's body had rested eighty years earlier. Soon after, the casket was taken to Hyde Park, New York, where Roosevelt was laid to rest in the rose garden of his Springwood estate. Taps was played and a 21-gun salute followed. Another fleet of warplanes rumbled above. The casket was lowered into the ground and the flag was presented to Mrs. Roosevelt. There was a final blessing of the body.

The public was stunned. The population had little idea of how sick FDR had been or for how long. They had not seen him in the same frail state Clark Griffith had. They had no time to absorb his loss, only to accept it. Many said it was like losing a member of the family.

The rest of the country attended President Roosevelt's funeral by watching newsreels of his funeral in the local movie theaters. Theater owners reported long lines around city blocks waiting to see footage of the funeral, as though they had to see Roosevelt lowered into the ground to believe it. Theater owners kept the projectors running twenty-four hours a day until the crowds were finally gone. When it was over, theater owners reported there'd been widespread weeping and wailing in the dark.

Harry Truman was sworn into office. In his first speech to a joint session of Congress, he famously laid down the law: "So that there can be no possible misunderstanding, both Germany and Japan can be certain beyond any shadow of a doubt that America will continue to fight for freedom until no vestige of resistance remains. Our demand has been, and it remains, unconditional surrender."

Roosevelt was gone, but the game must go on. Baseball pushed back the start of the season until April 17. Clark Griffith delayed his Washington Senators opener until April 20. He once hoped FDR could throw out the first pitch again. The loss of Roosevelt was as traumatic for baseball as it was for Griffith, who appeared tired and sickly that spring.

Writing in his *Sporting News,* publisher J. G. Taylor Spink called for Roosevelt's immediate induction into the Baseball Hall of Fame, to be enshrined alongside his recently departed nemesis Judge Landis. Roosevelt *should* be in the Baseball Hall of Fame for insisting the game had to go on during World War II, but Spink's call fell on deaf ears and was forgotten soon after. The war was still too close and personal in early 1945 to think in historical terms. It wasn't fair to say the war was in the ninth inning. It was more like in the seventh-inning stretch. The good news was that baseball had a friend in Harry Truman.

A few days before Roosevelt's death, Truman endorsed the continuation of the game, just another of the long list of items of Roosevelt's desk that was part of a possible transfer of power: "I want to join our enthusiastic sports fans and say, 'Play Ball!' The great American game of baseball is the most popular sport both at home and on the war fronts. Ninety percent of troops polled abroad are in favor of sports at home."

But from the days of the American breakout at the Battle of the Bulge in January and the push into Germany in the spring, reminders came daily that the war was not yet won. Death was always near. The ballplayers were still in the thick of it. Pitcher Warren Spahn survived the Battle of the Bulge with a shrapnel wound and a Purple Heart and went back to work with the engineers. Spahn cut his teeth with these unsavory characters, who were convicts and felons released from jail to serve in the Army because of the acute manpower shortage. The Germans were blowing up bridges as they retreated in an effort to slow down the Allied advances. The Ludendorff Bridge was captured in early March when the First Army took Remagen. The arriving troops were shocked to find it still intact. The bridge was built for railroads, which meant tanks could cross it into Germany. It was a prize for the Americans and a blunder for the Germans, who began counter-attacking in an attempt to destroy it.

A prolonged engagement between artillery and air forces broke out for the next two weeks, including attacks from German V-2 rockets and jet bombers. The bridge took a beating, but the Americans thought it would hold. Spahn was there with the engineers and spent many hours fortifying the bridge. But on March 17, he heard the horrible sound of the metal twisting and the girders giving away, like buttons popping off a fat man's shirt. Spahn was safely on land, but the bridge suddenly collapsed before his eyes, taking eighteen engineers to the bottom. The moment traumatized him, though he hid it beneath a humorous and boisterous façade. Spahn knew a lot of the guys who were killed. He knew it could just as easily have been him. He had just come off his own detail on the bridge. In the time it took him to light a cigarette or hit the latrine, those guys were dead. That's how close he came to getting it, as quick as the blink of an eye, or the time it took him to pick off a runner at first base.

Spahn never liked talking about it. The war made him a heavy smoker and drinker, and he could cuss with the best of them. He was competitive and cocky and resolved to live life to the fullest, if only he could survive the rest of the war. He did, but not until thirteen years later did he explain that day in any meaningful detail, and then he never gave another explanation so detailed again. When he did, it was only because the reporter, Lou Chapman of the *Milwaukee Sentinel,* had served in Europe, too, and had covered him for years. Chapman had been trying to coax it out of Spahn forever. Everyone wanted that story, especially before the 1957 World Series, but Spahn didn't want to talk about it. Finally, Spahn decided to get it out of the way, so he picked Chapman because he knew he would understand better than most. Besides, it made up for the time Spahn locked Louie in an equipment trunk, or so went various versions told around old County Stadium.

Chapman cleaned up the more grizzly aspects of the story, writing:

It goes back to a spring day in 1945—to a spot on the map called Remagen, on the Rhine River in Germany. Spahn and millions of Americans like him were playing—this time for keeps—in the biggest world series of them all. A hard-bitten combat veteran of the 276th Combat Engineers attached to Gen. Courtney Hodges' U.S. First Army, Warren—previously a staff sergeant— wore shiny new second lieutenant's bars at this time. Because incessant German attacks had knocked out most of his company, he had been commissioned on the battlefield. He previously had been wounded by shrapnel—not seriously—and wore the Purple Heart with distinction.

Except for occasional harassment from the air and the usual evidence of war, this was a typical spring day on the Rhine. Hodges' troops had been the first to cross this important objective and established a two-mile beachhead deep in German territory. They

had achieved the feat by crossing the only bridge still standing—
the one at Remagen. Spahn's unit had been assigned the hazard-
ous task of building a steal tread over it so the vital sinews of war
could pass across and over to Hodges' advance guard.

On this occasion, Warren's men were to relieve the similar
unit on guard detail and he stood in the middle of the bridge
talking over the repairs necessary for the structure. The change
was to be made at 4 p.m. sharp. Moments before the change over,
Spahn and the other officer sauntered leisurely off the bridge and
just as they reached the end they heard a crash neither will forget. The entire bridge toppled like a deck of cards, carrying G.I.'s
from the other unit to a violent end.

That day in Remagen, as Spahn saw the twisted metal and the dead
bodies of guys he knew bobbing lifelessly in the Rhine, he decided that he
would never fear anything once he started playing ball again. In time, he
believed he was invincible on the mound, and even when he threw soft and
when people wanted him to retire from pitching, he laughed in their faces.
He was going to make V-E Day, hell be damned, and come back to play
ball again. Spahn devised a motto that stayed with him: "You either do or
you don't." That said it all: either you win or you lose, you live or you die,
you smoke or you don't, you drink or you don't. None of it mattered. Spahn
used to say, "Pressure, what's pressure?" He hated the word. He felt that
civilians didn't know what real pressure meant.

The Marines could tell you all about what real pressure was. While
the doughs in Germany fought for bridges, the Marines fought for beaches
in the Pacific. In February and March, the newspaper headlines about the
coming baseball season shared ample space with the invasion of Iwo Jima.
This sharp, volcanic, black rock of a hellhole housed two Japanese airfields
whose squadrons were beating the hell out of the B-29 formations. The island had to be captured, and for a few weeks the naval and air bombard-
ment paved the way for the Marines to land. Everyone figured it would be
an easy grab.

But when the Marines landed, they discovered the place reeked of sul-
fur. Marines said it smelled like shit. Even the farm boys who were used to
manure weren't ready for the stench. When the first waves of Marines came

ashore, there was nothing. The Japanese let the traffic jam build up on the beach. The Marines couldn't move in the loose, black volcanic ash. A guy took one step forward and fell two steps back. So they crouched on the beach and tried to hide in the soot. When the logjam had accumulated, the assault began, and the blood spilled. Many boys in the Iwo Jima invasion had baseball backgrounds, and in those dreary days baseball seemed like the furthest dream that could possibly come true.

One of them was Willie Greason. He was from Atlanta and as a boy never thought he would play professional baseball, until, as he explains, "It found me." Atlanta had no baseball fields he was allowed to play on, so he played in a fast-pitch softball league. "Played pretty good, too, and could also hit," he said. The kids used to call him Double Duty and the nickname stuck. He played pitcher and catcher (though not at the same time) for a funeral-home team that ferried its ballplayers aboard a hearse.

One day, he picked up a tennis ball and decided to throw it overhand, like a baseball. He had been flipping softballs for a few years and developed quite a keen wrist. He learned he could "turn the ball over," which means he could throw an off-speed pitch. Someone suggested that he try throwing a baseball. Willie threw it and saw what was there. He had a loose arm, a tailing fastball, and a mean slider. "I don't know how to explain it," he said. "It was a gift."

After high school, he was drafted into the Marines in 1943. He hadn't picked up an occupation and never thought baseball could be one. The Marines didn't think he could be anything but a killer. Greason became a member of the Montford Point Marines and experienced segregated basic training at Camp Lejune, where Greason still remembers (with a chuckle) a particularly nasty and foulmouthed D.I. named Goins. The Montford Point Marines did not became quite as famous to the general public after the war as, say, the Tuskegee Airmen who flew and fought in Europe, but in the Corps, the Montford Point Marines are famous to this day as the first black Marines. In 1945, as part of the 66th Platoon, assigned to supply, he landed on Iwo Jima. People thought supply meant you had it easy. Not so. Willie Greason ran through cross fire bringing ammo to the front lines, hauling the wounded, dodging the dead, and when it was over, he helped pick up the pieces of boys who weren't coming home. He remembered:

I was on Iwo Jima. I-W-O J-I-M-A. February nineteenth, 1945, never will forget it. It was awful. We went in on the fourth day. The Marines had only advanced three hundred yards in three days. So many of the Marines got killed and wounded over there, it's a shame. It was an island five miles long and three miles wide at its widest point, with a volcano on the other end. The Japanese had been there for years and they had every gun sighted. You couldn't even dig in volcanic ash. You'd dig it out and it would roll right back in. All you could do is put your face down. That's why so many of them got killed. And they had every area over there sighted. You had to go through mortars. In my platoon, there were forty guys, and we had thirteen casualties.

We had to unload weapons and ammunition and food. Some guys ran supplies up to the front lines. Some guys were on burial detail and had to pick up all the dead Marines. You see those crosses and you think that's one person under each one. But what they would do is dig out a trench, cover the Marine's body with a poncho, and take his dog tags. You may find just a leg or a head. They're not usually in the spot where they were killed. The Japanese would dig out a big trench and push them all in.

In the misery there were blessings. Willie Greason became a minister years after the war and believes he could never have guided his flock had he raised a rifle or fired a shot at another human being. "I wouldn't be a minister, I don't believe, if I had killed someone. I don't think God would want that. I'm thankful I never had to do that. I saw so much death. I thank God I didn't have to do that, and I pray now that I'll never have to."

On February 19, the same day Willie Greason came ashore, Harry O'Neill did, too. He was a first lieutenant in the 4th Marine Division who served at Saipan and Tinian. O'Neill played at Gettysburg College, where he was a three-sport star. He was a highly coveted catcher pursued by many teams, but he signed with Connie Mack and his hometown Philadelphia Athletics because Mack placed him immediately on the major league roster.

O'Neill played in only one major league game, July 23, 1939, against Hank Greenberg and the Detroit Tigers. Hank hit a double that day. O'Neill caught the ninth inning in a 16–3 loss, but he never came to bat. His life-less major league line ended right there—one game, one inning, no at-bats, a blank line for a .000 batting average, an eternal limbo. He played a little bit of minor league ball in 1941 and expected to become a high school teacher before enlisting in the Marines in September 1942.

When O'Neill got to Iwo Jima, he saw what Willie Greason saw. The lieutenants were always prized targets. On March 6, the Marines having made only small gains, O'Neill was killed by a sniper. He became the sec-ond and last player with major league experience to be killed in action in the war, joining his fellow poor soul in baseball lore, Elmer Gedeon, one of Clark Griffith's boys from the Washington Senators, who had been killed while piloting his B-26 bomber over Europe.

Nobody saw anything good at Iwo Jima. George Genovese was a feisty, little infielder from Staten Island who signed out of a Cardinals tryout camp before the war. Four brothers in the Genovese family played professional baseball. George played three years of minor league ball before joining the Army and missed three more years. When he came home, he played a good shortstop for the Hollywood Stars in the Coast League, then the Senators optioned him in 1950. He spent a month in the majors, drawing a walk against Allie Reynolds of the Yankees in his first at-bat. He grounded out against the Tigers and pinch-ran in another game. Three major leagues games and he was done. He wanted to go back to the Coast League to make bet-ter money. He became a successful scout, and he was lucky to be as far away from Willie Greason or Harry O'Neill's sands as he could. But the man who could talk about anything never liked to say a damn thing about Iwo Jima.

If you wanted to know how the typical Marine felt about finishing the war, Hank Bauer could tell you. Like Harry O'Neill, he was a former mi-nor leaguer fighting in the 4th Marines, and he went from Guadalcanal to Okinawa. Bauer spoke with Marine bluster, brutal honesty for a brutal war: "When you get into combat, everyone is scared shitless, unless he's lying, drunk, or crazy." Japanese troops would make desperate kamikaze charges against the Marines. Bauer remembered one such attack: "It was the crazi-est thing you ever saw. Hell, some of them were falling-down drunk. They were all laughing or cursing in this hysterical tone. We literally shot the shit out of those poor bastards."

Iwo Jima was finally secured in late March, complete with the famous flag raising. When the fighting settled, the start of the baseball season was never far from many minds. Among the first shipments of supplies from the rear to arrive when the island was secured was a bundle of about a thousand copies of *The Sporting News,* which were quickly passed out and eagerly consumed by anxious Marines. One leatherneck wrote home, "The sun is setting behind Mt. Suribachi and *The Sporting News* was the first stateside newspaper here." When the survivors of Willie Greason's platoon left Iwo Jima and regrouped in Hilo, Hawaii, he thought about how lucky he was to be alive. He didn't have any job or career lined up for when he came home, so he wondered if he could play baseball. But there was a problem. Willie Greason was black.

Dusty Baker, a longtime major league player and manager, remembered his father, Johnnie, telling stories about serving in "the black Navy." Despite military segregation in the Pacific during the war, black kids played pickup baseball games when they came ashore. Sometimes, black and white teams got together, and the social anxiety of racism back home in the States melted away. The war helped develop the next generation of black ballplayers, with plenty of stories told of black ballplayers who learned to play in the service. For many black kids, serving in the Navy or the Marines was the first time they had access to bats, balls, and gloves. In the Pacific, many black players began developing themselves as ballplayers. Some discovered natural ability they never knew they had, such as Bob Thurman, who found out he could hit and pitch. A youngster from Birmingham, Jehosie Heard, figured out he was a left-handed pitcher with a natural ability to spin the baseball.

The process of integrating both baseball and society began during the war, and Alabama was the cradle of baseball's new civilization. Before the war, no state produced more Negro League ballplayers. During the war, the Tuskegee Army Air Field in Alabama, the base from which the Tuskegee Airmen originated, had segregated sports teams for whites and blacks, including a baseball team that played games at Rickwood Field.

Birmingham, a steel-industry hub, was one reason alone Hitler should never have declared war. No German bombers could touch it, and the city produced massive amounts of raw metals during the war, all the while providing an industrial-league feeder system in which fledging young white and black ballplayers developed. Birmingham itself was such a hotbed of baseball talent, and the hometown Black Barons sent eleven players into the service, a sizable percentage of its sixteen-man roster. Breaking in with the Black Barons was a big deal for a young player, as Dan Bankhead did before joining the Marines. He was a right-handed pitcher gifted with a lively, loose arm that was eventually discovered by the Brooklyn Dodgers. When experienced players such as Bankhead and Lyman Bostock joined the service during the war, the Negro League teams faced the same manpower shortages the white major league teams did. "Owners of teams in organized Negro baseball are having the same manpower headaches that big league owners are suffering," *The Pittsburgh Courier* wrote. In Birmingham, that meant searching for younger players to replace the vets when the war ended. One of those little boys playing in the industrial and sandlot leagues during the war was a kid named Willie Mays.

The same was true in Mobile, where night baseball games at the local, white minor league park had proven not to promote absenteeism. President Roosevelt would have been proud, justifying his trust in people, who wouldn't work less because they had baseball, but more. The Alabama Drydock and Shipbuilding Company was pleased with baseball's role in worker morale. And so it helped a boy of ten years old named Henry Aaron, growing up in World War II Mobile, to see that baseball could be a part of his adult life.

When Willie Greason, who later went by Bill Greason, came home to the States after the war, he was always proud of his Marine service. In time, the black players who learned to play in the Pacific war became among the first generation of black players in the majors, and they groomed the second generation of black players, who instead of spending their best years in the segregated Negro Leagues helped define major league baseball for the next several decades. Bill Greason was one of that first generation and was one of two rookies on the 1948 Birmingham Black Barons. The other was the now teenaged center fielder from Birmingham, Willie Mays. In 1950, the New York Giants signed Mays. In 1952, the Boston Braves signed Aaron. The rest, as they say, is history.

History became possible as the war ground on. As a new baseball season came into focus, so did the issue of black ballplayers playing in the major leagues. The war caused seismic ideological shifts even before it was

over. When Judge Landis died, vocal supporters of baseball integration believed the time had come. They all believed Landis had been the staunch-
est obstacle, but truly, even if he didn't want black players, he was still
following the mandate of the team owners. But now black servicemen had
proven themselves all over the world, and the wartime shortage of baseball
players should have opened up new opportunities. The black press became
very vocal, and while the white press didn't much bother with the story,
the question was working its way to the surface. The argument went like
this, expressed around the country in black newspapers such as the *Los
Angeles Sentinel:* "If a boy from 43rd and Central is good enough to stop a
bullet in France, he is good enough to stop a line drive." That argument
was made by J. L. Wilkerson, the white owner of the Negro American
League's flagship team, the Kansas City Monarchs. He said Negro baseball had its best year of attendance in 1944, citing a "big demand for it. It's
the only amusement that a lot of folks seem to get."

The Pittsburgh Courier wrote, "There are plenty of good Negro players
either over the draft age or honorably discharged from the Army who could
step in tomorrow morning in major league company and more than hold
their own. Baseball has bemoaned the fact that it might not be able to carry
on because of player shortages. But not once have we seen an instance or
suggestion or even hinting that baseball could sign a few Negro players to
take the place of their departed pale-faced brethren."

It was a battle waiting to be had, but it wouldn't happen until the war
was over, or at least until a new commissioner was in place. That's not to
say Branch Rickey wasn't already thinking ahead, as he had likely been since
the early days of the war, when he saw the government drain the once-
prosperous Brooklyn farm system. So he scuttled his Dodgers the way the
Germans detonated their own bridges, so badly that doughs everywhere in
Europe complained how bad the Dodgers were. When manager Leo Durocher returned home from a USO tour through Italy, he wrote a worried
letter to his boss, Rickey: "Italy is full of Brooklyn boys and the paramount
question is: What happened to Dem Bums?" The answer was coming.

The Pacific campaign was as tedious and unglamorous as the rush
through Germany was exhilarating. Ballplayers everywhere, white and black,
wanted the damn thing over. One of them was a Navy pilot, Jake Jones,
the former Chicago White Sox minor leaguer who walked away from his

promising major league career to train for aviation. So many ballplayers wanted to be fighter pilots, from Billy Southworth Jr. to Buddy Lewis to Ted Williams, but only Jones actually got to fly naval air-to-air combat in the war, and he put up better numbers against the Japanese than he ever did against American League pitching.

Jones was a Hellcat pilot, the front-line, Navy, carrier-based fighter. He was assigned to Air Group 3 (AG 3) aboard the carrier USS *Yorktown*, affectionately nicknamed the Fighting Lady. AG 3 began combat operations in October 1944 during the invasion of the Philippines. On November 14, while striking a Japanese airfield, Jones homed in on a fighter trying to take off. Big Jake jumped the Zero and flamed it, his first confirmed kill.

Jones flew with skill and savvy. His finest moment came on December 14, when he attacked three Japanese fighters at the same time. The Hellcat was a nimble beast, better armed and better armored, and he flew circles around the Japanese, shooting down one and badly damaging another. The third guy got away. In February, Jones flew in the Navy's first strike on the Japanese home islands. He shot down three Zeros that day, giving him six kills, making him the only major leaguer in baseball history who was also a confirmed fighter ace. Finally, in late February, Jones was credited with another probable victory, his seventh, and the last victory claim of squadron VBF-3 during the war. Jake Jones was going home, but to what kind of baseball career, baseball season, or baseball business, he had no clue. He had no idea what it would be like when he tried to swing the bat again, but he knew that when he folded up his Hellcat's wings, that would be the end of that. He wanted to come home to baseball.

Billy Southworth Jr. knew flying was where he belonged when he walked away from baseball five years earlier. "Since my hands have gripped an airplane stick, they don't care so much about holding a baseball bat," he said. "I once had ideas of someday managing a club as Dad does, but from now on, I'm just a fan." The last several months had been blissful, though he spent a good deal of time emotionally recovering from his twenty-five bomber missions in Europe. He lived the single life of a war hero in Los Angeles for a time, spending time at the airfield in Santa Monica, driving into Hollywood, and entertaining offers for a postwar movie about his life. He had been to Berlin and back and had plenty to brag about, but that wasn't his style. He was still in the Army Air Corps, learning his way around the B-29 cockpit and training new bomber pilots. He figured his combat flying was over, but he would never say never until the Japanese surrendered.

His bond with his father was stronger than ever. Billy junior went to the 1944 World Series and spent Christmas at home in Dayton with the family. He was talking about flying for the airlines after the war, maybe even starting one up. He worried about the Cardinals, who were in for a rough year without Stan Musial and catcher Walker Cooper and the others in service, depleting the roster.

Billy couldn't wait for the war to end because he didn't feel comfortable in the new bombers. Flying the B-29 was completely different from flying the B-17 and took some getting used to. The B-17 was a darling. She flew like a truck, but always got you where you were going. You could shoot the shit out of her, take away three of her four engines, blow holes in her elevator, shred her body with shrapnel, bullet holes, and flak and she would still limp home, or at least close enough to ditch in the Channel. The B-29 wasn't as forgiving. She was more complicated and computerized, and the gremlins wouldn't go away, even for the experienced B-29 pilots. The troublesome engines still tended to flame up, and when they did, the B-29 was a death trap. So Billy counted his points and watched the war, hoping that both would lead him back to civilian life soon.

But Billy's luck ran out during a routine exercise on February 15, 1945. Southworth took off from Mitchel Field on Long Island, bound for Florida. As he took off, one of the B-29's engines flamed out. Southworth tried to abort. He had flown through flak and fighters over Berlin, flown formation with scared rookies who couldn't keep their ships straight, had seen German fighters pinwheeling toward his nose with cannons firing, and he had survived it all. But now he was suspended in the air around New York City, not an enemy aircraft in sight, yet with a horrendous engine fire that ate away his bomber's stability and controls. He nursed the silver beast back to the nearest strip, attempting to make an emergency landing at LaGuardia Field with his left outboard engine stopped. Billy battled the beast, trying to stay on top of her controls like a cowboy fighting a bucking bronco, trying not to be thrown.

He tried to shake the bomber's instability, it's refusal to obey his commands at the controls, and at that second Billy Southworth Jr. was standing in the batter's box against a fastball he could not hit. For all his experience, all his flying hours, he was overmatched by a mechanical failure. He lowered the nose to the horizon and put his gear down, hoping to make the short runway at LaGuardia, but knowing that little civilian airfield wasn't built for a bitch that needed two miles of runway. He inched the bomber lower, trying to trim it out, but it wouldn't respond. He could see the waters of Flushing Bay at the end of the runway and thought he would have to ditch in the drink. It was too late to reconsider now because he was committed to the landing. He had no power left in the engines and he could not climb and make another pass. This was it. Fire trucks and ambulances were waiting. The shadow of the B-29 raced over the runway, but the veterans inside knew they were too high. Billy tried to push it down, but he ran out of runway. He hoped he could skim Flushing Bay, but at the last moment Billy's wing dipped into the waves.

The water and gravity sucked the B-29 to her side. Billy wasn't flying anymore. The ocean was flying him. The B-29 flipped into the bay, front first. Witnesses said it fell over like a big, tall, awkward giant performing a clumsy somersault. The B-29 pilots who flew them in the Pacific, from flight lines Hank Greenberg helped establish, and from airfields where men died in the sand to secure, could tell what went wrong. Billy Southworth Jr.'s last flight ended with a fireball and an explosion that echoed across New York City. Even in the Bronx, Hank's hometown, and in Brooklyn, where Pete Gray once played, the boom could be heard in the distance. The flames burned all the way to St. Louis. At that moment, Billy Southworth Jr. and four other men in his crew joined the Bomber Boys they'd left behind, but in his final flight he would surely have found solace. Five of his ten crewmates survived. In his last game, Billy batted .500.

Billy Southworth Sr. was getting ready for spring training at home in Dayton when the telephone rang. He thought he was never going to be one of those fathers who got a phone call or a telegram from the War Department. He was dumbfounded and speechless when he heard the news, saying nothing, but his wife knew immediately what was wrong. The message was the same for Billy and a million other distraught wartime dads. The President of the United States regretted to inform him that his son was officially missing and presumed to be dead. Billy senior couldn't get his head around that. His boy had survived Nazi Germany, he had flown over Berlin, and now his body was missing in, of all places, Flushing Bay?

Billy senior had to see the scene for himself, so he was on the next flight to New York City. When he arrived at the crash scene, the B-29 wreckage was still scattered across the water like large pieces of shiny silver scrap paper. The Army sent a barge to scrape the debris off the waves. But there was still no sign of Billy junior's body, not even when the burned-out fuselage was found underwater. Billy senior just couldn't leave without his boy, so he asked the engineers if he could ride along on the barge while they combed the crash site. The Army said yes, so for the next week, the distraught manager of the St. Louis Cardinals rode the angry waves of Flushing Bay, searching the cold waters for his son's body. The engineers noted that Billy senior was frequently drinking from his flask. After a while, one body was pulled from the water. Billy senior was asked to identify it. He turned away in repulsion. No, that was not his boy. That was somebody else's son.

After a few weeks, that was the only one of the five missing bodies that turned up. The salvage crewmen, especially the ones who had served in Europe or the Pacific, knew the odds of finding bodies grew more distant by the day. But every day Billy senior was out on the water, hoping and praying that his boy would surface. By now he knew there was no way his son survived. His world was gone.

Billy had to leave for spring training soon to get the Cardinals ready for the season, but he had no interest in baseball right now. He didn't care about the standings, didn't care about the pennant, and didn't even care about winning the World Series again. If Billy junior was gone, baseball was just a job now, and he would do it because he was getting paid, but his soul was vacant. Everything hurt and felt empty. The things he'd always loved about playing and managing baseball, those felt like parts of another life now. His grief was deep and his eyes distant. After eighteen long and agonizing days, the Army wanted to call off the search, but first asked Billy if he would agree. Billy looked out over the water, felt the light breeze blowing through his thinning, gray-blond hair, and silently nodded yes. He died right there, out on the water.

Bad Check Goes to War: Copilot John Dillinger, Pilot Billy Southworth Jr., and bombardier Milton K. Conver in 1942. (Tim Conver)

Redbird over Germany: St. Louis Cardinals inspired nose art of Billy Southworth's B-17. (Tim Conver)

Proud Dad: Manager Billy Southworth Sr. welcomes home junior in 1943 after twenty-five missions. (Associated Press)

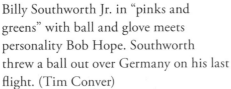

Billy Southworth Jr. in "pinks and greens" with ball and glove meets personality Bob Hope. Southworth threw a ball out over Germany on his last flight. (Tim Conver)

The Ghost on His Shoulder: Pete Gray played before the war in New York City's Metro League. (Tim Conver)

"One-Armed Wonder": Pete Gray's 1945 rookie season captivated the country. (Associated Press)

The Wounded Warriors of '45: Former fighter pilot Bert Shepard, who lost a foot in combat, greets Gray, who lost his arm in a childhood accident. (Associated Press)

Pilgrimage to Pete: Wounded soldiers flocked to meet Gray. (Associated Press)

Joe DiMaggio signs for eager servicemen in 1942. (Associated Press)

Flight Cadet Ted Williams (Red Sox), Navy officer Charlie Gehringer (Tigers), and Flight Cadet Bob Williams (White Sox) pose by a Marine Corsair fighter, like the one Williams would have piloted in the invasion of Japan. (Associated Press)

(L to R) Big Leaguers Dario Lodigiani, Walt Judnich, Mike McCormick, Joe DiMaggio, and Jerry Priddy stitch on Army stripes. (Associated Press)

Cardinals Manager Billy Southworth tutors rookie Stan Musial. (Associated Press)

Canadian Phil Marchildon shelved a promising pitching career with the Philadelphia Athletics to become the tail gunner on a Halifax bomber. (Associated Press and the Royal Canadian Air Force)

Stan Musial joins the Navy in 1945. (Associated Press)

Mr. Left & Mr. Right: Hal Newhouser was the best pitcher of the war years. Dizzy Trout was his able sidekick. (Associated Press)

Buddy Lewis traded a promising career as third baseman for the Washington Senators to fly 600 hours in a transport in the CBI Theater and win a Distinguished Flying Cross. (Author's Collection)

The Game Must Go On insisted FDR, throwing out the first pitch in 1938. (Associated Press)

Boyington's Bastards: Marine Fighter Squadron VMF-214 poses with Cardinal hats, gifts from '42 World Champs, and baseball gear on the wings of their bent-wing bird, the Corsair. (Associated Press)

GI's Play Ball: (Top) 8th Air Force GI's of the 398th Bomb Group play at Nuthampstead; (Below) GI's of Vitamin Charley, Company C of 741st Tank Battalion play shirts-and-skins in Paris. (Author's Collection)

Hank Greenberg, Slugger and Serviceman: He gave up the top salary in baseball in 1941 and stayed in the Army until mid-1945. (Associated Press)

The tallest man in China, Greenberg was a very small part of Operation Matterhorn, the strategic bombing campaign against Japan. (Associated Press)

Hank Greenberg returned to the Tigers lineup in July 1945, chasing the last wartime pennant. (Associated Press)

Throwing Smoke and Fire: Bob Feller, pitcher, and Bob Feller, sailor; manning his 40-Quad gun station on the *USS Alabama*. (Associated Press)

Bob Feller (left) and Hank Greenberg (right) took the oath days apart after Pearl Harbor, signaling the start of baseball's war. (Associated Press)

CHAPTER 18

One Arm, One Leg, One Nation

Billy Southworth's mood matched the color of the mud on the first day of spring training. Four feet of flooding from the Ohio and Mississippi Rivers saturated the practice fields in Cairo, Illinois. The Cardinals were only supposed to be in Cairo for a few weeks, but the rivers were flooded ten feet over the banks, the diamonds were a disaster, transportation was so backed up that players were arriving late, and when they did, the ballplayers were out of playing shape because of their factory jobs. This spring promised to be a total mess, and all his best players were now gone. When the fields were cleared off just enough to start practices, the players who knew him knew he was not the same. He tried to throw himself into his work, but the endless stream of condolences wore on him. He took to drinking again and just wanted the season to start. When reporters who had known his happy, gregarious style for years saw him that spring, they knew he was a changed man, like a ballplayer whose cap was blown off his head.

When Hank Greenberg heard the news about Billy junior's bomber crash, he truly felt sorry for the Southworth family. So much of that tragedy hit close to him. Hank knew all too well how temperamental the B-29 engines could be. That bomber was a thing of beauty when she was flying, but when her engines coughed, she was terrifying. His own B-29 mishap had almost killed him in China, and he thought again how lucky he must have been just to be back home in the States, alive and well, if silently suffering in agony waiting to play baseball again. He remembered the 1942 World Series, when he was in the broadcast booth watching the Cardinals play the Yankees. There was a lot of joy and pride when Billy talked about his son. Only later did Hank learn that the B-17 that memorably roared overhead and circled Sportsman's Park during the Cardinals rally had been piloted by Billy junior. That was one of Hank's favorite memories of the war; he was sad that the memory wouldn't be the same.

Hank looked like his old self when he was touring war plants during the spring. As always, he hid his anxiety with grace. He turned his focus to the war effort. He was masterful at shifting the conversation away from himself and onto winning the war. There was nothing disingenuous about it. His commitment to his service never wavered, nor did his belief that making a big fuss over him wasn't necessary. A few weeks later, when asked again about his future, Hank told *The New York Times,* "I never talk baseball. War's my business now and so I talk war, stressing the dire need for greater effort."

He visited factories, spreading his message. "The thing uppermost in the minds of your boys in the foreign theaters is to get the war over," he told workers at the Deep River glider assembly plant. "The way to speed that up is to give the soldiers the materials they need. Give them more gliders and give them quicker. If you could see, as I have, seventy-five thousand Chinese laborers building airfields with only their bare hands to handle the earth, then you would know the meaning of war."

He told the story of being caught in a blackout in Kunming when a Japanese bomber formation passed overhead. Hank was on leave and walking the city alone at night. He hid in an alley and found himself face-to-face with a seemingly menacing Chinese man. Hank thought he was a dead man, but it turned out that all the man wanted was his cigarette. Hank was also vague when discussing the B-29 missions. If he had more stories to tell, he wasn't eager to share them. If he had gone up as an observer, it was unrecorded, and he and his crew were sworn to secrecy. He understood how dirty the war was and understood the strategy for victory over Japan was to burn civilians alive.

Hank took great joy in visiting the war plants. Before he left for the CBI, he hated the hollow publicity work the Army had him perform.

But he acted differently when he came home. He was thrilled to be state-side, even if he was still in the Air Corps and was subject to recall. Compared to flying the Hump or worrying whether all the B-29s would make it home, this was easy. "I'm always amazed at the ingenuity of American production," he told workers in Hartford, where he once played minor league ball. "I see our workers doing things by machine that the Japs are doing by hand. It makes you realize why we can't possibly lose the war. I get such a kick out of seeing all this equipment pouring off the assembly lines. I'd seen it all before, of course, but I'd never paid any attention to it. Furthermore, everything we have is the absolute best. Back in China, for instance, you'd see more Chinamen under a truck than you'd see in it, trying to make the thing work. Yes, this war is a most interesting experience."

This war is a most interesting experience. That was a statement that Bert Shepard most assuredly would have agreed with. Fitted with his makeshift prosthetic leg, the former minor league pitcher and fighter pilot was part of a massive prisoner-of-war exchange in the winter and found himself on a George Washington ship headed home to New York Harbor. He was ever so glad to see Lady Liberty. He was another of those guys who didn't want to fly again as much as he wanted baseball back.

When he arrived on dry land, Shepard was taken to Walter Reed Army Hospital in Washington, DC, where he was fitted with a modern artificial leg. A lot of guys needed a few months to get used to walking on a prosthetic, but thanks to the wooden leg he wore in the German camp, Shepard took to his new leg right away. The doctors were astounded at how readily he adjusted, and all the nurses talked about the former fighter pilot who just wanted to pitch again.

If there was ever a man more lucky in World War II than Bert Shepard, nobody ever met him. He was lucky to survive his crash, lucky to be treated well by the Germans, lucky to have a Canadian prisoner to carve a makeshift leg, lucky to be part of a mass prisoner exchange, and, finally, lucky to be at Walter Reed while Undersecretary of War Robert Patterson was roaming the halls, searching for former POWs to interview about Kriegie life in the German stalags. Shepard happily volunteered for that duty.

When Patterson asked him what he wanted to do next with his life, Shepard beamed without hesitation. "I told him, 'If I can't fly combat, I want to play professional baseball.'"

Shepard was in just the town to make the statement. Patterson was a good baseball fan, a regular at Griffith Stadium to watch the Senators, and as a member of the cabinet privy to a cordial relationship with Clark Griffith. The Old Fox was trying to figure out how to cobble together a pitching staff for the coming season. He had the particularly devious, cheap, and sinister idea of rounding up four knuckleball pitchers and trying to win the pennant with a starting rotation that couldn't throw hard enough to make the flag billow. Patterson talked to Shepard, found out he used to pitch in the minors, and let Griffith know that he had discovered a most amazing lad. Here was a boy who had been a minor league pitcher before the war, was shot down and survived, and learned not only to walk again, but also to run and pitch with a crude wooden leg, all while interned by the Nazis! When Griffith heard about Shepard, he didn't care if the guy could pitch or not. That was a hell of a story, and a hell of a story would sell during the lean '45 season. Griffith told Patterson to bring the boy out to the ballpark as soon as he was comfortable on his new leg.

That didn't take long. Patterson asked the doctors to fit Shepard with a better, custom leg that would better permit him to play baseball again. Patterson had the same thought as Griffith—what a great story to have a war hero pitching on one leg in the nation's capital! You couldn't buy publicity like that! It worked on so many levels! The Army had a lot of guys coming home without legs, so selling Shepard's comeback to a skeptical nation hungry to see how broken men could have their old lives back was quite appealing. Griffith, for his part, was always looking for a new angle to drum up the box office.

The new leg was ready in March. Shepard met Griffith for a few minutes and got an invitation to the team's spring-training camp. Shepard's eyes hadn't been that wide since the German machine gunners were crisscrossing his cockpit with bullets, but this time, there was no fear. He couldn't believe his luck and of course, accepted on the spot. Shepard got his chance to thank Patterson, too, but once he realized how well he was getting around on his new leg, he thought about flying again. He even thought he could be a better pilot now with the artificial leg than he was with his original hardware. "You know," he hinted on the not so sly, "I'd like nothing better than to play baseball all summer and bomb Japs in the winter." Patterson lit up. The War Department loved this guy.

The spring was about one leg, one arm, and one nation. Excitement ran high as American armies raced deeper into Germany and Czechoslovakia in April. Fights broke out at every stop, but in the words of the baseball-playing boys of Vitamin Charley, the Germans were taking a healthy beating. "We were advancing at the rate of a town a day now," the unit's unofficial history reported. "Our Company optimists were prophesying a quick end to the war, some of them early in April. We could sense Jerry was weakening, that he was disorganized in his fighting and his supply lines. Our hearts were lighter, and somehow we didn't feel so tired, even after a day of fighting."

All that was left of the Germans were the fanatical, hardcore, and well-trained Nazis. The Vitamin Charley boys would surely have loved to have dug out their bats and balls to play a game in Germany, but it had to wait until surrender. It was still dangerous. Hitler Youths armed with *Panzerfäuste* lay in wait to ambush the Sherman tanks; a single shot could ignite the tank and destroy it. Many boys died this way, but still, the Americans pushed on and pushed back against the dying embers of the Third Reich. The Vitamin Charley kids saw it:

> We did know that the Kraut was being licked, and soundly, and we had a lift in spirits. He wasn't fighting with his old zest, and seemed to be falling back too quickly for his own good. His usually well organized warfare seemed a bit frayed around the edges, and in his rear-guard action he seemed much more anxious to get away than to stay and make a fight of it. Occasionally a small group would fight it out to the death, but this didn't happen too often. Almost invariably they turned out to be S.S. troops, or groups strongly laced with them. Where the enemy forces were Wehrmacht, completely or predominantly, he gave up when he found himself outmaneuvered or licked. But not the S.S.

As the baseball season neared at home, a great deal of attention was placed on finishing the war against Germany, but people still wanted their watered-down, wartime baseball. President Roosevelt was gone, but his spirit, and the game, must go on. Bert Shepard and his one leg was a big story of spring training. He was determined to make the major league team, and Griffith was just as committed to keeping him around, though his indifference showed what he would never say in public. He didn't think Shepard could pitch in the big leagues, not even in the drawn-down, worn-out last year of the wartime majors. But the owner darn sure wanted the attention Shepard offered, and so while Griffith waited for his real players, Buddy Lewis and Cecil Travis, to hopefully come home by the end of the season and lead the Senators to the pennant, he wasn't willing to farm Shepard out to the minors. He decided to keep him around the team as a batting practice pitcher during the spring and let him take batting practice and field ground balls at first base before every game.

Shepard got big crowds and big cheers wherever he went. He was big news, though he didn't have a big ego. A *Chicago Tribune* headline shouted louder than Shepard ever did:

LOSES LEG BUT NOT HIS SPIRIT

NAZI PRISONER YEAR AGO DRILLS WITH SENATORS!

Shepard himself was surprised; it was as though he were the only one winning the war. In his first exhibition game, Shepard struck out the side in the ninth inning of a 19–3 game and drew big applause from the crowd of two thousand convalescing soldiers. The first time Shepard took batting practice at Griffith Stadium, his sanitary sock kept slipping down and exposing his prosthetic leg, eliciting awkward laughter from his teammates, who suggested he place a rubber band on the sock around his leg. Shepard dutifully informed them that it would cut off circulation. Enlightened, his teammates told him they had never thought of that.

A few days later, Shepard got a letter from the boys of 55th Squadron, who hadn't heard about his baseball comeback yet. "The 55th certainly missed you," it read. "The boys all send regards and are sorry to hear that due to your injury your baseball days are over." Shepard read the note to reporters and then chimed, "Won't they be surprised when they hear about what has been going on in the last two weeks!"

Griffith made it official in late March, announcing that he was signing Shepard to a contract, but carrying him as a coach only. "We'll let him do anything he thinks he can do," Griffith said. He added Shepard would visit lots of Army hospitals, "whenever they want him." That was the deal Griffith made with Robert Patterson and the War Department. So really, Shepard was working for the Army more than he was playing for the Senators. The story caught the public's fancy, and there was one major league game everybody wanted to see in 1945: the game between the man with one leg and the man with one arm. When asked if he really thought he could play in the majors, Shepard glared through the reporter as if he were the gunsight of his P-38. "If Pete Gray can do it," Shepard shot back, "why can't I?"

Pete Gray had come a long way while America was fighting the war. He was ready to take the next step of his career and reach the goal he had always wanted when the St. Louis Browns purchased his contract from Memphis for the expensive sum of $20,000 and planned to bring him to the big leagues in 1945. He was playing the best baseball of his career, and his confidence was sky-high. Pete was convinced he was ready for the majors. His second season in Memphis was a career year, and as his statistics multiplied, so did the scouts in the stands. This time, they weren't rejecting him because he had one arm. They wanted him because he had one arm, because this was a ballplayer whose speed could help a major league team and, because of his condition, he would never be confiscated by the government, not even for factory work. They also rightfully recognized that he would be worth big box office, for a little while at least.

Pete's numbers would have been good enough for any two-armed player in the Southern Association to make the jump to the majors without any hesitation: a .333 batting average in 129 games, 167 hits, 21 doubles, 9 triples, 5 home runs, and, most important, a league-leading 68 stolen bases. He also led the league with a .996 fielding percentage and with 226 outfield putouts. During the war, these were top-level tools that were simply not available.

A flock of Ivory Hunters wearing wide-brimmed fedoras and blowing cigar smoke followed his every move that summer. Even the guys who were skeptical about Pete's hitting saw value in him because he was left-handed and could run. Two American League scouts were homing in on Gray.

"Wish" Egan, the man with the perfect nickname for a baseball scout, closely watched Pete through his thick bifocals. The fatherly chief scout of the Detroit Tigers had signed scores of big leaguers and wanted the Tigers to buy Gray in 1944. Egan recognized Pete's offensive limitations, but he wanted him because he could steal bases, envisioning a stolen-base specialist who could be a difference maker in the pennant race the Tigers lost to the Browns by one game. "We had a pretty slow club," Egan remembered. "If the Tigers had Gray to come off the bench to do some pinch-running in 1944, we might have nosed out the Browns for the flag."

But the Browns had a working agreement with Memphis and possessed the first option. The team decided not to sell him until after the season. The Browns' chief scout, Jack Fournier, reported, "War or no war, Gray is a big leaguer. Advise you to buy at once."

Pete Gray was too valuable for the Browns to pass up. Even though they went to the World Series for the first time in team history, the team finished fifth out of eight in overall attendance, struggling to attract crowds and alienating die-hard fans, who complained that everything was too expensive. By the time a fan paid between $1.65 and $2.55 for admission, then bought a 20¢ beer, 15¢ hot dog, and a 10¢ scorecard, you could be out up to $3 per person. For a family of four, that was too much money during the war. The fans were incensed when the price of the scorecard was raised to a dime just to see a bunch of replacement players. *The Sporting News* published a list of fan complaints. One man protested, "I'll be darned if I want to pay 15 cents for a five-cent bottle of coke or the same price for a hot dog. Bring down the prices and you will draw the crowds."

Or, you could sign a player who could draw the crowds. You couldn't buy the kind of publicity Pete generated. He was featured regularly in *The Sporting News* and appeared nationally in *Time* and *The Saturday Evening Post*. When a letter from the father of a young amputee in Los Angeles reached Memphis, the boy was invited to meet Pete. The local newspaper raised funds to bring him out and pose for photographs on the front page of the paper. Praising Pete was lucrative business, but when he saw the little kid's face light up, nobody had ever seen Pete's mug shine so brightly either. The kid, Nelson Gray Jr., planted a wet kiss on Pete's cheek and was reported as saying, "I am Pete Gray!"

Pete had a way of making fans love him. The war seemed to have softened many people, and perhaps that was because amputees, once reserved for the circus, were now flocking home from the war. It didn't matter that Pete hadn't been wounded in combat. He was easy for fans to identify with because he was a guy following his dream despite whatever obstacles life threw at him.

For Pete, converting doubters to believers was old hat, but he never once hesitated to remind people when they were wrong about him. The president of the Southern Association, Billy Evans, once told Memphis manager Doc Protho, "The manpower situation was pretty serious but hardly to call for signing a crippled fellow." When Pete became the best player in his league, Evans was singing a different tune: "I never tire of watching him and I think he has a chance to stay in the majors."

When rival managers refused to put him on the league's all-star list even though he was voted MVP, Evans overruled them and included Pete, who did not care one bit. "I'm not a freak, I'm a ballplayer," he spat. "I can play with those fellas in the majors, and I'd like to have the chance to show 'em what I can do."

When Browns manager Luke Sewell returned home from his USO tour to the CBI and heard that the club was going to buy Gray's contract and bring him to the majors, he knew it wasn't going to end well. Sewell had never met Pete and had nothing against him personally, but he knew how the other ballplayers were going to react. The Browns weren't exactly a bunch of well-schooled, politically correct, well-mannered guys. They were just old, proud, stubborn, and rarely sober dirt ballplayers who had just won the only pennant in team history. The ballplayers were going to feel entitled to a little respect, and Luke couldn't blame them, but he also knew this poor guy with one arm didn't know what he was getting into.

Much could be inferred from the decision to sign Pete Gray. Wartime baseball was dying a slow death at home, and perhaps the Browns simply weren't solvent enough to remain in St. Louis much longer. Either way, Sewell had no say in the decision. He felt the best thing for Pete would be to use him the way Wish Egan wanted to use him for the Tigers: as a pinch-running devil and a stolen-base specialist. Pete should be allowed to bat occasionally, but never when it counted, and he should never take at bats away from veteran major leaguers who'd already proved their abilities. Sewell thought it was the best solution for all parties: Pete could be a big leaguer and could help the Browns in the right role without causing great animosity on his team. The Browns could collect their box office. Sewell reasoned it could work out pretty well that way. But he knew he was getting Gray shoved down his throat. The order from ownership was Pete Gray would play every day, at least to start the season. Sewell protested, but only so much. He didn't want to lose his job in the middle of the war.

Sewell decided to do his homework. He began to investigate just what kind of ballplayer the famous one-armed wonder would really be. He called his friends down in the Southern League, the same managers who'd slighted Pete when they left him off the All-League list. "Some of them said he had no chance," Sewell remembered. "A few guys said he was real quick and a good drag bunter who could steal his way to first base and grab the ball. But I had serious doubts. When Don Barnes was running the Browns, he gave me a free hand. I could do whatever I wanted, buy and trade players, open and close the park, change the lineups. But all that changed when Muckerman took control. We'd always had trouble attracting fans, especially competing with the Cardinals, and Muckerman saw Pete as a drawing card."

Sewell immediately recognized that using Pete just for publicity was going to be a problem and highly unfair to everyone involved. But he also knew owners were owners. All they cared about was money, and they couldn't see anything from any point of view but the financial. It was the bane of working in baseball, and Sewell knew it. The guys cutting the checks knew nothing about scouting and team dynamics. So when spring training began, and the crush of newspapermen descended on Pete the very first day he walked into a major league camp, Sewell decided he would do his best to make this season work for everyone.

Pete did not recognize any of the factors that Luke Sewell did. He came in simply as a ballplayer who should have to earn his playing time, same as anyone else. But he also came in with confidence and thought that his minor league record at Memphis had earned him this shot. The first time he walked into the dressing room, Sig Jakucki took one look and shouted across the room, "Who let the one-armed bastard in?" Gray spun and wanted to go after Jack and kick the hell out of him, but he was a rookie and respected his place. He knew he was going to have to take some abuse and always expected it. But it didn't make it any easier.

Luke Sewell knew Pete could do nothing to change that. Sewell was also worried that it wouldn't take long for American League pitchers to find Pete's weaknesses and expose him as he had never been exposed before. When that happened, Pete was going to slump and slump hard. You needed both arms to hit successfully in the major leagues, wartime or not. That would kill his confidence and wipe out the curiosity factor that was supposed to boost attendance. "I was in the majors for thirty-five years and I only saw three or four guys in that time who were consistent draws," Sewell said. "Babe Ruth was the greatest. Bob Feller and Joe DiMaggio also drew big crowds. The rest? Maybe for a year, and then they'd be just another face in the crowd."

But Luke Sewell did not yet understand something about Pete Gray, and it would take the manager a few months to fully appreciate this about his one-armed outfielder. Pete didn't like being another face in the crowd. He liked to stand out and was quirky as hell. He knew everyone was watching him because he had one arm, but he didn't want anybody to like him because he had one arm. The fact that he'd taught himself to play baseball with one arm was why people loved him so, but Pete couldn't ever reconcile that. He just wanted to be seen as a good ballplayer, but as long as a ghost was beneath his shoulder, that was never going to happen. So Pete had to learn how to be accepted not for what he wanted to be accepted for, but for what he was accepted as.

At least he got good money. "I signed for a fifty-five-hundred-dollar salary," he proudly said years later, though it was certain that not a dime was left. "I probably could have made as much in the minors, but I wanted that taste of the big leagues." Before Pete even played a game for the Browns, the PR wheel was being greased. He went out on a stateside USO tour. The government distributed movies of how Pete functioned as a one-armed man in everyday life to the thousands of boys who came home with empty shirtsleeves. He visited hospitals and met with wounded GIs. This was particularly rewarding to Pete, though he never publicly attributed his opportunity to help the less fortunate to his baseball ability. When the USO tour was over and the Army had no more wounded for him to visit, he returned home to Nanticoke, satisfied, as Pete Gray the ballplayer, nothing more and nothing less, and waited for the season to start.

Pete had many memories of his road to the majors. He didn't like being seen as a one-armed man by people with both arms, but for kids who'd lost limbs in the war, he had no problem teaching them that anything was possible. He wanted and craved that responsibility, and his war was to help other amputees fight their new, intensely personal wars. Once when he was honored after the minor league season, he was uneasy in accepting accolades for the best year of his baseball career. But he was not shy in explaining why what he did in baseball was important for freshly wounded kids. He very much remembered how difficult it had been for him to get his life back after his own accident. "If I can prove to any boy who has been physically handicapped that he, too, can compete with the best, well, then I've done my little bit."

Before Pete Gray could play a big league game, and before the season could get full steam ahead, the next commissioner needed to be selected. The replacement players were safe, and victory against Germany was close at hand, so the time had come. Ford Frick wanted the job more than anyone else because he had seen how baseball had boomed after World War I, once Babe Ruth ushered in the golden days of the twenties and thirties. Frick believed baseball would flourish after World War II, with new stars yet to be discovered and with star servicemen, such as Hank Greenberg, who were bound to rediscover their prewar abilities, even if the war had chopped off a few years. But he also knew he lacked the Cincinnati support he needed for a unanimous vote.

So Frick went to Washington once more and looked up Kentucky Senator Albert "Happy" Chandler, who had been instrumental in getting the government to back off its demand for all of the replacement players for the 1945 season. Frick's move was cunning. He knew the baseball establishment already didn't like Chandler and never would. But Frick also knew the next wartime season could not start without a commissioner. For a man who aspired to be commissioner himself, backing an unpopular candidate who would win approval on desperation alone would seem to be the ideal formula for one day winning the job for himself. In February, *The Washington Post* described the baseball establishment's disdain for Chandler in condescending terms: "Senator Happy Chandler of Kentucky won't get Judge Landis' job as czar of baseball, partly due to the fact that the baseball people don't like Happy's war-built swimming pool or the [fight] he had with the photographer who tried to take his picture with a lady in a New York nightclub." (Translation: the lady was probably not his wife.)

After weeks of fierce infighting among the owners, Chandler was elected the second commissioner of baseball on April 24, a few days into the season. As Ford Frick correctly predicted, Chandler was hated from the start. Some owners lobbied to delay the election of a new commissioner for six months, until the war was over. But the decision was that the game needed a new leader to usher it into the postwar age and to lead it through the last days of the war. Owners worried that they would look weak if they could not decide upon a leader. Looking weak was worse than hiring somebody they didn't like.

Clark Griffith and Larry MacPhail of the Yankees pushed Chandler across the finish line. From the moment Chandler flashed his wide smile and said he was thrilled that his salary would jump from $10,000 in the Senate to $50,000 in the commissioner's office, the establishment despised him. They hated that he loved every photo op he could get, hated that he showed up at such mundane events as the Browns hoisting their 1944 pennant flag, hated that he loved to be seen and heard. Landis thought the commissioner should be seldom seen and firmly heard. Even in death, the old man ruled the game.

Chandler wasn't nicknamed Happy for nothing. The men who hired him hated his glib style. He was full of hot air, handshakes, and hyperbole. They were used to authority and consistency. "To me baseball is the greatest sport in the world," Chandler said at his introduction. "It has brought me probably the highest money of my life." The owners sneered. *Probably?* Did he mean to say there was something professionally greater than being commissioner of baseball? Fool. They already hated the guy and he wasn't even warmed up. Being a baseball owner meant acting like a gangster— never tell the public how much money we make and keep out of the press. Chandler thought he worked for the fans, but he had it all wrong. A baseball commissioner only works for the owners. It was like being elected pope. As old Judge Landis would have grumbled, Chandler was no pope. Don't it beat hell, he was a politician.

The problems started immediately. Baseball owners wanted those involved with horse racing banned from ballparks. They were the gambling scum of the earth, the cockroaches Judge Landis cleaned up after the 1919 World Series. But Chandler, being from Kentucky and a fan of the horses, had many wealthy friends in the sport and didn't see a problem with race-track life. He wasn't about to kick his friends out of the ballparks just because his new bosses, the owners, told him so. That was strike one.

Then Chandler said he wanted to take his time leaving the Senate. That was strike two. Then the big one: Chandler said black players deserved a fair look from organized baseball when the war was over. What the hell was this guy thinking? That was strike three and all hell broke loose. The old war had yet to finish, and already new ones were brewing.

But on the field, fans couldn't see past the excitement of Pete Gray and Bert Shepard as they waited for Germany to surrender and Japan to cave. "Griffith Stadium won't hold the fans who would want to be there when one-armed Pete Gray plays against one-legged Bert Shepard," *The Washington Post* predicted. This season, it was all about one arm, one leg, and one nation.

PART III

Waiting for Hank

1945

CHAPTER 19

Long-Lost Hero

On the most miraculous Opening Day of the war, Pete Gray walked to the batter's box in front of a disappointing crowd of 4,167 in the sunlit spring chill of St. Louis's Sportsman's Park. He heard his name announced as a major leaguer for the first time. Though he would never admit it, every step along the way in this long journey came surging back, all the way from the days in Nanticoke, to Brooklyn, to the many bush leagues, to Memphis, to all the happiness and hurt. The small crowd, including the giddy new commissioner, Happy Chandler, gave him a sturdy ovation, but Pete was locked in his own world. He didn't think to tip his cap to the crowd. He had waited far too long for this moment in his life to bother. He was finally here, defiantly proud, and the time had come to prove he belonged.

Everyone wanted to see Pete hit. The ballplayers inched toward the top step of the dugout, though with a great deal of skepticism. Pete had the highest burden of proof of any rookie who ever came to the majors. Detroit Tigers manager Steve O'Neill was an affable guy without a mean bone in his soft body, but he was on the edge of his pants. "If Gray can get his bat around fast enough to hit Newhouser, he will be a marvel," he said.

Then Pete looked out onto the mound, where the first pitcher he ever faced in the major leagues was Hal Newhouser. He towered there like a sentinel in high socks, muttering something nasty and generally not giving a shit if this guy had one arm or two. Mr. Left was the best pitcher in the majors, and that was Pete's first draw. Some luck. Now that was a hell of a way to come to the big leagues. Newhouser's personal catcher, Paul Richards, crouched behind the plate. The corner infielders, Don Ross at third and Rudy York at first, inched in a few steps, anticipating a bunt. Pete Gray, batting second and playing left field, was ready. Finally, after the longest few months of the war years, it was time to play ball.

Newhouser rocked into that big, over-the-top windmill windup and whipped his arm toward the plate. He made throwing hard look easy, and the ball exploded out of his hand. April smoke. The fastball bore down on Pete and was on him in a flash. Pete watched it all the way into the glove and didn't say a word, but the reaction was obvious: *Holy sweet Jesus, what the hell have I gotten myself into?*

Strike one. Holy Mary, Pete had never seen a fastball like this. Pete loved the heat, but he was overmatched. He managed to lightly swat a little ground ball to shortstop and was handily thrown out. Putting the ball in play was a moral victory, but now his first big league at bat was finally out of the way.

In Pete's second at bat, Newhouser jumped ahead in the count with the fastball and then finished Pete with a curveball that made him want to cry. It was the nastiest hook he had ever seen in his life and struck him out looking. In his third at bat against Prince Hal, Pete decided he wouldn't allow Newhouser to throw that breaking ball again, so he hunted the fastball early in the count. Newhouser challenged him with the first pitch, and this time Pete found his timing and got the bat off his shoulder, making solid, hard contact, the whippy crack of his bat awakening the fans.

Pete knew he got it good and took off running, thinking two at least, maybe three if it got into the gap. But the Tigers center fielder, Doc Cramer, a veteran outfielder who could still run, got a good jump on the ball. He dove before it could split the gap, tumbling to the wet turf and making the catch. Pete shook his head. Bad luck.

Finally, in his fourth at bat, facing bespectacled sinker-ball specialist Les Mueller, Pete hit another hard ground ball to short. He ran like hell and beat Skeeter Webb's throw, racing through the bag, safe with his first big league hit, an infield single. Pete was, without question, a big league runner, but his hit wasn't a big deal to anyone but him. There was no standing ovation. The ball wasn't thrown out of play as a keepsake. The Brownies didn't give much of a damn. Asked after the game how he felt, Pete simply said, "I've been turned down by more big league managers than any other man in history. I spent more money trying to get into baseball than I've earned in the game."

But Pete found some joy in finally being there and facing a guy like Hal Newhouser. There was nobody like him in the minor leagues. Pete couldn't wipe the smile off his face when he described facing him: "That left-hander was really rough. He threw me every pitch in the book. When I was called out on strikes, he used a fast curve that was almost by me before I figured out where it was headed." That's what Pete loved, that he was finally competing against the best players in the business.

Over the previous months, nobody knew where the baseball business was headed. The most tumultuous off-season the game had ever known started with the death of Judge Landis in November and ended with President Roosevelt's funeral procession in April. The mood in St. Louis was sad, just as it was in many other cities around the country, including Detroit, where thousands of mourners braved cold winds for a public memorial to FDR.

The winter had been long, but the hopeful spring promised the end of Nazi Germany and the continued bombing of Japan, though GIs were terrified that a massive invasion would keep them all in the Army for much longer than they wanted to be.

The war was grinding to a conclusion, and the postwar world was taking shape and so was baseball. The embryonic stages of two new baseball dynasties in New York City, one built with cash and another conceived with the currency of social evolution, began. All-new questions were looming, and they all had to do with manpower. How was the 1945 season going to play out with such diminished manpower, sometimes holding team rosters to as few as sixteen players? What would happen to the returning players? Would their skills have been lost in the war? What to do with the replacement players when the war ended? What about the black players who believed the time was now? Every day that the war came closer to ending, more social changes occurred. Despite these changes, baseball owners stubbornly held on to horse-and-buggy beliefs as the atomic age neared.

No team felt more frayed by the war than the Detroit Tigers. Having lost the pennant to the Browns on the last day of the 1944 season, the Tigers were determined not to repeat this heartache. They were the favorites to win the pennant in the war-ridden American League, but they couldn't score runs if they didn't have Hank Greenberg. He finally came home from China that winter, but he was still in the Army, touring war plants stateside. The Tigers were waiting for Hank, along with all of baseball and the rest of the country, waiting for the end of the war and waiting to move ahead into a new world to forget the past four years. But until then, they would all have to make do with an imperfect society and a flawed major league season, seen best through the life of the one-armed rookie outfielder of the St. Louis Browns, whose dreams slowly died in the season when they all came true.

One of a major league record 120 rookies playing in a season that almost never happened, Pete Gray would never have debuted without the war. He battled long and hard for this moment, and only the circumstances outside his control made it possible. At the start of the season 247 American League players were in service and 244 more in the National League. By the time the season was over, 384 total major leaguers served, while the sixteen teams cobbled together rosters with only as many as twenty-two players each. The total number of major leaguers in military service had gone up each year during the war. Pete Gray had practical baseball value.

Pete wanted no favors and resented the idea that he was in the majors as a publicity stunt, but it was impossible to avoid the speculation. Two conversations swirled around him. One was that he was only brought to the majors as a role model for wounded veterans. The other was that he was signed simply as a box-office attraction for a team whose attendance was so pathetic that they drew an Opening Day crowd of less than five thousand on the day they hoisted their first American League pennant. In reality, Gray was here for publicity and propaganda, which overshadowed anything he could do on a baseball field. Pete hated that more than anything else, but he quickly realized he could not do a damn thing about it. An anonymous club official told *The Detroit News,* "The Browns are trading on sympathy and capitalizing on affliction. I think it is in extremely bad taste."

Some people already thought he was a freak, and the tensions on his team mounted immediately. His new manager, Luke Sewell, was convinced Pete needed help fielding, though it's hard to imagine he would have had complaints with a two-armed outfielder who led the Southern Association in putouts and in fielding percentage. Pete had done this before. Someone hit him a thousand fly balls and he'd run them all down. Sewell tried the same routine and came away convinced that Pete was a major league out-fielder. "I thought I could help his fielding, but he has been showing me tricks instead," Sewell said.

Gray's spring training had been a media circus. Veteran baseball writers thought he got more publicity than any rookie outfielder since Joe DiMaggio. Though people respected his minor league record, Gray was welcomed with a hearty dose of skepticism. He was an immediate magnet for controversy and publicity, which rankled many of the St. Louis Browns. Gray was going to get a chance to play. The $20,000 purchase price from Memphis guaranteed it. But the veterans from the 1944 pennant-winning team resented him being handed an Opening Day starting job without earning it in the majors. The only question ballplayers asked about a new guy was if he could help them reach the World Series, where the bonus money doubled or tripled their annual salaries. When they saw Gray, they saw a guy who was not a $20,000 ballplayer. A defensive replacement and a pinch runner, yes. But not a guy who could play every day and be expected to hit enough to help the team win.

Pete didn't understand any of these dynamics. He had been dealing with skepticism his whole life, so why should the majors be any different? In the City Series against the Cardinals before the start of the season, Pete went 6-for-20, batting .300, but that wasn't good enough. The Tigers, the first team to face him in the regular season, had their doubts. Harry Heilmann, the Tigers radio announcer and a former All-Star outfielder, identified holes in Pete's game immediately: "He can bunt and he can run, I'll say that. How he'll hit major league pitching is something we'll have to wait and see."

Al LaMacchia, a Browns rookie pitcher who became a scout after the

war, sensed the Brownies were not sold, even as the fans seemed to be enthralled with the biggest story of the new season:

> The fans loved Pete and you could understand why, but the fans
> don't know what they're looking at. Pete was what they consid-
> ered a good ballplayer, but they were judging him with their hearts.
> Ballplayers, we don't judge ballplayers with our hearts. All we give
> a shit about is if he can play.
>   Pete could bunt and run, and that tells you he had no power,
> so he can't beat you with the bat, because unless he chinks one
> and runs like hell, he can't hit one over a guy's head and he can't
> hit one out of the park. So if he's a guy who can't hit and can run
> and play the field, then he's a fourth or fifth outfielder, and that's
> really what Pete was. If he had been the same guy with two arms
> that he was with one, nobody would have given a shit. But every-
> body knew they were going to play him and prop him up to be
> something he wasn't, and that bothered a lot of guys. As a ball-
> player, I always wondered if it bothered Pete, too, but I never got
> to know him well enough to ask.

Sewell tried to politic his way through his team's discord. He knew
his Brownies well. This surly bunch of crude bastards were proudly the black
sheep of baseball. They wore that with pride, but when they found a guy who
was an even bigger outcast than they were, they revolted. Sensing trouble,
knowing he needed his team to play for him and not convinced Pete was
an everyday player, Sewell tried to make ownership happy and did his
best to bridge the communication gap. "I tried to get close with him, but
he had kind of an inferiority complex," Sewell said. "The only one who could
make him happy was his mother."

That reputation didn't help, and soon Pete's own worst enemy was on
his own team: pitcher Sig Jakucki. He was back with the Browns for the
1945 season and beat the Tigers and Hal Newhouser, 7–1, on Opening Day,
but he was disgusted when Pete misplayed the first ball hit his way. Pete
made it up the next day, when in the second inning, he raced from left field
well into foul territory to track down a fly ball. Jakucki, who was always
drunk on the bench, was pissed off that Gray couldn't make that play when

he was pitching. Jack had seen enough. He was going to ride this guy for the rest of the season.

Gray went 0-for-2 against another tough customer, Dizzy Trout, before Sewell pulled him for a pinch hitter. It didn't matter. The Browns lost 11–0, and Pete had seen this before—when the team doesn't play well, blame the guy with one arm. The next day, Tigers right-hander Al Benton returned from his two-year stateside Navy hitch to make his first major league start since 1942 and beat the Browns and Nelson Potter, 1–0. Pete did not play. He silently bitched. Pete wasn't used to not playing every day. The Brownies lost two out of three to the Tigers, who looked like a pretty good team. Pete could already tell. It was three games into the season and the fans and the players were waiting for the rest of the ballplayers to come home. Al Benton was just the beginning. And when they came home, Pete Gray knew he was gone.

When the season started, Hank Greenberg was still touring war plants around the country. He followed the Tigers religiously and rooted for them, but he was also curious to see Pete Gray, the one-armed rookie outfielder he had first heard about when he was serving in China. Hank kept a strict wartime touring schedule, though on occasion he would slip into baseball talk out of natural habit. When he did, it was easy to hear his passion. He remembered his last game in May 1941 against the Yankees, almost down to the detail of each pitch. He hadn't forgotten that he was stuck on 249 career home runs, which probably bugged him more than he admitted. "I'd really love to get back and hit my 250th home run," he said. But he knew it was out of his control. "It all depends on the length of the war."

The length of the war, not the outcome, was now the biggest factor for all servicemen who wanted to come home to baseball. Joe DiMaggio was a fine example of such uncertainty. He was back stateside, but still in the Army, with no clear idea of when he would return to civilian life. He harbored hopes of playing for the Yankees again in 1945, but he was worried that the war had taken too much away from him. He'd lost thirty pounds over the past few years. When he tried to swing a bat, he was alarmed at how weak he felt. When asked what kind of player he would be when the war was over, Joe D admitted he wasn't sure.

The best thing DiMaggio did during the war was play a lot of service baseball for soldiers and sailors in Hawaii, who saw him play in a memorable summer season for the Seventh Air Force baseball team. Once, playing in front of twenty-six thousand spectators at Honolulu Stadium, he hit a home run that traveled 435 feet and, in the next at bat, hit one that went 450 feet. Joe liked playing in Hawaii so much that he suggested the big island might be an ideal site for a future major league team.

His Seventh Army team won the Hawaii League pennant with 31 consecutive victories before they were upset in the Pacific World Series by a Navy team so loaded with big leaguers that it was no stretch to say that the best baseball played in 1944 wasn't in the majors but in the Pacific rear. The Army-Navy Series was such a big deal that Admiral Chester W. Nimitz threw out the first pitch. Navy Seabees built three baseball fields at Kaneohe Naval Air Station, Hickam Field, and Furlong Field to accommodate the big crowds of sailors all over the islands who wanted to watch the big series.

But when the Seabees arrived at Furlong Field and discovered that all twenty-two thousand tickets had been distributed before they got even a single seat, the agitated construction battalions took matters into their own hands. The Seabees rolled a bulldozer into the ballpark they'd built, piled up a bunch of dirt hills behind the best seats in the house, and then built bleacher seats on top so their boys could have the best seats in the house. Then they cracked open their beers and had a good old time.

They saw better ballplayers than anyone was seeing at home. The Navy team had former Yankee Bill Dickey managing a team that had Virgil Trucks, Pee Wee Reese, Johnny Vander Meer, Johnny Mize, Phil Rizzuto, and Joe's brother Dom DiMaggio. Joe D shook his head; he wasn't used to losing a World Series. Joe D hadn't played much lately and missed baseball every waking moment. "I've got my heart set on coming back," he said. "The Army sees to it that your legs stay in good shape, but your timing goes right out the window. I guess it all depends on how fat or bony I am when the war's over."

It was fair to call the major leagues skin and bones to begin the 1945 season. At the start of the season, only 30 of the 144 players active on the 1941 Opening Day rosters remained in the majors, representing a dramatic 80 percent turnover in just four seasons. Among the newcomers were 50 new starters, with 22 of them, including Pete Gray, making their major league debuts. But it wasn't fair to complain about Gray's rise to the majors because all sixteen teams were populated with physically deficient play-ers. "I know of one ballplayer who has such defective vision that when he follows the course of the ball, he looses all muscular control. Fly balls drop behind him and in front of him and fans wonder why the club keeps him on the roster," the *Hartford Courant* reported.

The strategy was unspoken but simple. Teams wanted their box office so badly that they would take as many disqualified players as they could possibly get. If a guy couldn't run in a straight line, couldn't run the bases without falling down, couldn't track a fly ball into his glove, couldn't throw a pitch hard enough to hurt a fly, and couldn't hit, that was fine, because if he couldn't do those things, chances were he couldn't shoot a gun or be useful in any other way. But that didn't mean that the relatively healthy players weren't more terrified than ever. Some guys just didn't want to serve, period.

Nobody was safe from potential military service now, frightening the older players for the first time during the war. Mel Ott, who was thirty-six on Opening Day, was worried that he wouldn't be allowed to keep his job with the New York Giants. "I'll have to study up on the new 4-F rules," he said. A lot of ballplayers kept their fingers crossed, hoping the war would allow them to stay in the majors long enough to finish the season. Just get-ting the season started was a miracle. But getting through it was an en-tirely different story.

The opening weeks of the 1945 season for the Detroit Tigers were marked by murky rain and ceaseless cold weather. The schedule already in-cluded an absurdly high number of doubleheaders, previously planned to help cut down on travel demands, and the rainouts that often caused four- or five-day delays between games threatened to make the looming sum-mer months a merciless grind. But in those first few weeks of the season signs were that the war in Europe would soon be over, and with that came the hope that some semblance of normalcy could return to the diamond and the country by the end of the season. The excitement was building ev-ery day, every hour.

In Detroit as in other cities around the country, the local team's ex-ploits shared front-page billing with the bold headlines from Europe. Hal Newhouser got his first victory of the season when he beat the Cleveland Indians, 3–2, in 11 innings. He pitched the distance and responded with the winning hit when a fan shouted at him, "Win your own game, Harold!" Only 4,374 fans were at Briggs Stadium that day because it was forty-two degrees with a bad wind chill. The next day, warm weather brought thirty-three thousand to the park to see Dizzy Trout beat Allie Reynolds and the Indians. The pitchers nicknamed Mr. Left and Mr. Right shared newspaper headlines with such pulse-racing news:

TWO RED ARMIES JOIN IN BERLIN.

PATTON 35 MILES FROM AUSTRIA

A few days later, Al Benton, continuing his successful return to the Tigers from the Navy, beat the Indians and the papers announced:

MUSSOLINI EXECUTED BY ITALIANS

While the Tigers were in Cleveland, GM Jack Zeller traded for Indians outfielder Roy Cullenbine, a proven hitter. That trade said it all: the Tigers had no guarantee Hank Greenberg was playing this year. Zeller knew he had to make the trade. There was no Hank and no Dick Wakefield, who was in the Navy. Tiger pitching was so good that it didn't allow a home run in April, but the lineup could barely hit one, either. Zeller was a shrewd baseball man who sensed his team had a window to win, even when Rudy York, the gentle giant, started the season in a horrible slump. Daily life in Detroit was balanced around the ball club and the bulletins as April ended and May began. It was getting easier and easier to smell the end of the war in Europe. When the Tigers were shut out by the White Sox on May 1, the headline blared:

SOVIET FLAG FLIES OVER BERLIN!

Al Benton won again the next day, which is more than the Germans could say:

NAZI ARMIES IN ITALY GIVE UP;

BERLIN FALLS TO RUSSIAN ARMY;

YANKS CAPTURE VON RUNDSTEDT

Phil Marchildon was sleeping exhausted in the tall grass some-where in Germany on the morning of May 2 when he heard noises in the woods. He slowly woke up to the sounds of clanking guns and boots. He thought the German guards were coming to rouse the prisoners from a hurried slumber to resume their death march. As the Russian infantry had been advancing from the east, the Germans had forced their prison-ers to retreat along with them. Every day had become a constant fight to survive.

There was nothing left to eat. Men were digging for worms and eating shrubs. Marchildon was sickly and frail, skeletal, malnourished, and down more than thirty pounds. He was wasting away and wondered when the SS guards were going to say the hell with it and shoot them all. He felt so awful that he probably wouldn't have protested such a quick end. He knew he was breaking down physically and mentally. He didn't know how much more of this he could take, but he knew he was near the point of no re-turn.

Marchildon had taken to sleeping outside when the weather warmed because at least he could see and hear the Allied bombers overhead, and that brought him some comfort and knowledge that the end of the war must be at hand. But when he heard the soldiers rustling in the woods that morning, thoughts of a simple shot to the back of the head entered his mind. Everyone knew the SS guards were a bunch of sore losers. He had made it this far on sheer willpower, but determination wasn't enough to stop a bullet.

But then there was the most beautiful sight he had seen in ten soul-punishing, body-beating months incarcerated in one of the worst of the stalags. It was the lovely camouflaged gents of the British 12ᵗʰ Armored, who moments later were heating up a spot of tea for the tired and exhausted airmen. A few of the Tommies wanted to know about the German guard the prisoners mentioned and, after a time, hunted down the fleeing Ger-man guards. A few hours later, the SS guard who had shot the man for sport when he walked over the line to the outer fence was presented to the prisoners. The Brits asked if this was the guy they were talking about. The prisoners said yes. So, the SS bastard got the bullet instead. Marchildon had no sympathy. You live by the war and you die by it.

Now, at last, he knew he was going to live, but all sense of month and day was long since distorted. The Brits told him it was May 2, 1945, the very day the Russians captured Berlin. If the British troops had ever asked him what he did before the war, Marchildon might not have remembered that, oh, yeah, he used to be a ballplayer, but that seemed like some other guy's life now, not his. He was too hungry, tired, exhausted, and traumatized to fully feel his freedom. He was so frail that when he boarded the ship bound for Canada, he was given enough meal ration coupons to feed two expecting mothers.

When he finally did put weight back on, it was just flab, not muscle weight. He was down to his sagging skin and coal-miner bones. A return to baseball seemed improbable. He was too weak. His confidence was shot, and he didn't want to play, anyhow. He wanted the memories to go away. On his first night home, he slept outside because he could not stand the thought of sleeping indoors. He'd slept many nights outside while interned, with the endless drone of nighttime Lancaster and Hallie bombers lulling him to sleep. Sleeping outside at home was the only way he found calm. He slowly began to peek at the baseball news now and then, but he really didn't think he would ever pitch again.

While Marchildon recuperated, the Tigers pitching roared. Al Benton was so good early in the season that he allowed only 1 run in his first 27 innings and won his first three starts. With Hal Newhouser, Dizzy Trout, and Benton, the Tigers had the makings of a pennant winner. "If pitching in the early games tells the story, the Tigers and Cubs are headed for an October World Series date," *The Detroit News* reported. Nobody rooted harder for the end of the war than Tigers fans, as they eagerly followed the headlines such as this blunt gem:

HITLER DEAD!

On May 6, the Tigers swept the Browns in St. Louis with Newhouser beating Sig Jakucki and Al Benton improving to 4-0 with a 1–0 victory, courtesy of Roy Cullenbine's ninth-inning home run. Benton was so good that his ERA was 0.25 and *The New York Times* called him "currently the outstanding hurler in the majors." The headlines just kept getting better and better:

SURRENDER DOCUMENTS ON WAY TO ALLIES!

Finally, on May 7, all major league games were canceled for the news everyone had been waiting for:

WAR IN EUROPE IS OVER! UNCONDITIONAL GERMAN
SURRENDER AT EISENHOWER'S HQ!

President Truman addressed the nation, beginning, "The Allied armies, through sacrifice and devotion and with God's help, have won from Germany a final and unconditional surrender. The Western World has been freed of the evil forces which for five years and longer have imprisoned the bodies and broken the lives of millions upon millions of freeborn men." Crowds gathered around the country, but in Detroit, as in other places, the celebrations were subdued. When the baseball-playing tankers of Vitamin Charley got the news, they were in Pilsen, Czechoslovakia, the last town they liberated.

"We entered Pilsen, Czechoslovakia on May 7th, and that night had a mild celebration of the ending of the European war—not a real party. We stayed at Pilsen about a month, during which some of the tanks went to neighboring towns for security purposes. There the boys at last had the chance to get acquainted with their Russian allies, and to try out their beloved vodka. When they could first talk after drinking it, the usual remark was 'Oh, my God!' "

The Tigers were rained out on V-E Day, which was quite a problem so far in the season, with 27 percent of the entire major league schedule having been washed out. There was still the matter of the Japanese surrender and the millions of men still overseas, but on May 8, which was officially V-E Day, the tension finally came flowing out along with the streams of paper thrown out of buildings in celebration. Bars were packed. People danced in the streets. Catholic schoolchildren genuflected in prayer. The war first came to Detroit the day in 1941 when Hank Greenberg left to join the Army, and now the city rejoiced. The conflict had always been close and personal for Detroit, a major center of war production. The local newspapers kept close tabs on the war dead and wounded and never failed to celebrate the heroism of local boys. The Tigers had always been near to the town's heart, and now the town could dream that Hank would come home soon and the Tigers might win the first peacetime World Series.

The Detroit News followed the celebration, but wasn't oblivious to the somber reminders of the war, observing this scene: "The only spot really jammed was the downtown newsreel theater, showing those German atrocity pictures. It was encouraging to note that the churches did more business than the night clubs." The *News* also told the story of a local GI who had a rosary blessed by the pope at the Vatican and mailed it home to his friend. The reason the GI didn't keep it on his person? The GI was Jewish.

Across Detroit, Tiger fans were waiting for their own Jewish GI to return, their hopes expressed by this *Sporting News* headline:

V-E DAY TO EASE GAME'S PLAYER SHORTAGE

Now that the war against Germany was over, Hank Greenberg might be discharged. The Tigers didn't care if he wasn't the same ballplayer he was before he left. They were willing to take what he had left. Hank Greenberg coming home to Detroit would be the very symbol that the war was over.

The St. Louis Cardinals were on a train on the way from Chicago to Brooklyn when the good news of the war's end in Europe broke, causing much happiness in the Pullman cars. The Cardinals were in the middle of the pack with a team less powerful than at any other time during the war years, but they still thought they had as good a chance as any to win the pennant again, especially after sweeping the Cubs at Wrigley Field. But in the front of the train, manager Billy Southworth felt mixed emotions. He was proud of his boy for doing his part to win the war, but he missed him every day. Billy senior had been a hard drinker from the 1920s, but now he took his misery straight. The war had been cruel to him. He still wanted Billy junior's body back. Now the war he'd fought in was over, and the first game Billy senior was going to manage was going to be in Brooklyn, not far from the waters where his son's body was still missing. The misery flowed freely. He did not tell anyone but he rented a rowboat and went out into Flushing Bay alone many times, searching for junior's body.

His ballplayers knew Billy was managing with a hole in his heart, so they resolved to try to win this year for him, in memory of Billy junior. But when the Cardinals got to Brooklyn the next day, Harry "the Cat" Brecheen lost to the Dodgers. When the game was over, Billy said nothing. In previous years, he was usually so upbeat after a loss. But now he just changed clothes, went back to his hotel, and closed the door behind him. He went back out on the water. His ballplayers had never seen a man suffer so alone.

CHAPTER 20

Another War Begins

The American League played a light schedule on V-E Day, and the only game that held any meaning was the Washington Senators against the St. Louis Browns at Sportsman's Park. Pete Gray, the one-armed wartime replacement for the Browns, would get to face Bert Shepard, the one-legged pitcher and former fighter pilot and prisoner of war. But the matchup never came to be. Neither man was playing, and Gray was fuming to be benched so quickly into the season. On many days it seemed more reporters than fans were at Sportsman's Park, and the reporters all wanted to see Pete play. Manager Luke Sewell had enough. He shooed them away from his bench and told the writers to quit managing the team for him. Gray never played in the three games against the Senators, and when the Browns went to Washington a few weeks later, Sewell finally granted Gray all of one unremarkable at bat, in which the flustered Gray grounded out.

The photographers were crawling around Griffith Stadium, so they rounded up Pete to pose with Bert Shepard for a photo. Shepard was up for that and warmly welcomed Pete and put his arm around him. Gray smiled and appreciated the warmth. They had led two different lives before their paths crossed in the strangest major league season. Pete was smiling about as much as he was playing, which was about once every few weeks, but he beamed for Bert, who had one of those big, electric grins. The boys posed on the top step of the dugout and the photographers got their shot, but they forgot to clear the background. Sitting on the bench is an unknown Senators ballplayer glaring up at both "ballplayers" with disdain and disinterest, as if quietly wondering who let these crippled bastards into the league. Each time a flashbulb popped, the ballplayer had his answer.

The flashbulbs popped in Branch Rickey's office in Ebbets Field the day after V-E Day. Now that the Allies had conquered Europe, Branch Rickey was sending his scouts into the field to invade Negro League baseball. His breathtaking announcement came as sudden news to the gathered press, but this was not random. Nothing about Rickey's career in scouting and player development had ever been random, nor had any decision been made on a whim. He was a master organizer and planner, a schemer if you asked some, but in the coming years it became clear that Rickey had calculated and waited for this moment. The surrender of Germany meant the time was right. He knew baseball's new commissioner was more progressive than Judge Landis, and regardless of whatever Rickey liked or didn't like about Happy Chandler's politics, his rise to power would give the Brooklyn Dodgers theirs.

Rickey announced that the Dodgers would undertake an ambitious scouting program to stock a new team of black-only players called the Brown Dodgers. This team was a ruse, as phony as the fake armies built to confuse the Germans. There was practicality and purpose. The Dodgers were brutally bad on the major league level. Rickey bottomed out his roster and made his fans yearn to win again. Rickey knew the majority of the returning major league players would find jobs again, but not with him. He knew they would be older, but he wanted to win with youth. He also wanted to be the first man to tap a new resource in baseball, which for him meant signing black players. If he taught some of his ballplayers racial tolerance in the process, so be it, but he wasn't after black ballplayers because he wanted to teach a Bible-study class. He wanted to win and he didn't want to wait.

Rickey wasn't after black players simply because he was a warm and fuzzy guy who wanted to change society. The baseball historians got this one wrong. No, he needed players because the war had gutted the Dodgers. According to one count in *The Sporting News*, out of 147 Dodger minor leaguers before Pearl Harbor, 94 had since entered service, 50 were overseas, 3 killed in action, 17 retired, 24 missing in action, and only 12 still playing. Manpower was always the problem. So Rickey asked a practical question: Where could he sign good players that his competitors were not willing to sign, for next to nothing? For Rickey, the answer was the Negro Leagues.

But as much as Rickey wanted black players, he despised the Negro League business model. He didn't like the owners, whom he viewed mostly as criminals. And he was right. Many were numbers runners and morticians who ran the numbers, but they saw baseball as a way to better black people. Most Negro League team owners made their dough on the side and paid their players with profits from the rackets. But the Negro League owners came to despise Rickey, too. For all the talk that Rickey was some sort of holy-man biblical emancipator, he looted the black teams like the Nazis plundered Europe. Rickey refused to honor the validity of Negro League contracts, muscled owners when he wanted players, and was generally looked at by the black owners in the same light as a Gestapo storm trooper breaking their windows and stealing their merchandise.

Rickey always thought of baseball first. He had no concern for alienating Negro League owners. If he stole their fan base, destroyed their ticket sales, and put them out of business, then that was fine by him. This was a simple matter of winning and making money when the war was over. He knew the Yankees, who had recently been purchased by a group led by construction baron Del Webb, Dan Topping, and baseball operations chief Larry MacPhail, would never sign black players for fears of alienating their wealthy white fans. The Yankees were as white as their home uniforms, and Rickey knew they didn't see Yankee Stadium like some sort of Cotton Club, the place where whites came to curiously study blacks. They could keep whatever was left of Joe DiMaggio when he got home. Rickey wanted to find the black DiMaggio.

The white scouts Rickey employed had absolutely no idea how to cover the black leagues. The best way to get information was just the way Rickey did it. He had newspaper subscriptions to all the major Negro newspapers, which all had sportswriters and published some box scores, statistics, and schedules. Rickey built up a follow list from newspaper clips alone. When he sent his scouts into the field, he did not send them blind. He sent them with assignments. One by one, the reports came back to the office that spring. Rickey knew some of his scouts would have prejudices, but he reminded them to make this a baseball-only evaluation. How objective his men were, nobody really knows. It seemed as if Rickey already had an idea of which players he wanted to sign.

In April, three Negro League ballplayers worked out for the Boston Red Sox at Fenway Park. They included Jackie Robinson, then playing for the Kansas City Monarchs. They were summarily rejected. Columnist Wendell Smith, a leading advocate for integration, who acted as a birddog scout for Rickey, wrote in *The Pittsburgh Courier,* "Thousands of fans throughout the country are hoping that at least one of the major league owners will take an unprecedented step and sign a Negro player."

In midsummer, at the East-West All-Star game, the annual Negro League showcase, Robinson, who had Army service and was well-known from his football career at UCLA, batted second and played shortstop. He went 0-for-5, but Rickey was probably thrilled that Robinson didn't hit. He never wanted any of his competitors to know which players he wanted. The scouting reports would have read something like this: *Robinson— superathlete, strong, plus runner, aggressive base runner, plus contact hitter, good bunter, ordinary power, average arm, average range, average-to-plus infielder.* Hitting fifth for the East was Baltimore Elite Giants catcher Roy Campanella, who collected a pair of singles that day. *Plus, plus power! Plus arm! Can catch! Dumpy body, good athlete! Strength! Can't run, who cares!*

The beginning of baseball integration had everything to do with the manpower crisis caused by World War II. Scores of black kids had the ability to play professional baseball, and thousands more were introduced to the game by playing service ball at home and overseas. Likewise, the demand for fresh talent promised to undercut the returning white minor leaguers, who would be squeezed out of the game from every angle—by returning major leaguers, by younger minor leaguers, and soon by black players, who felt they'd earned the chance as much as returning white players.

Rickey was working both ends of the spectrum. While he was hunting for black players, he had scouts signing high school–age white kids during the war, even if they still needed their parents to sign the contracts for them because they were still supposed to be in high school. The high school players were of tremendous value to Rickey during the war because the draft couldn't touch these kids. So Rickey, to answer the war's never-ending manpower crunch, issued marching orders to his scouts to find the best players and get their parents to allow them to sign, no matter what it took.

Rickey had a scout in Southern California who was a master at this. His name was Tom Downey and he drove a Cadillac with a liquor cabinet in the trunk. Rumor had it he would often get the kid's old man drunk and then get him to sign. Sometimes, if Downey really wanted the player, he would offer the kid's dad the Cadillac in return and then expense the cost of a new automobile for himself to the front office. Downey knew Rickey was cheap, but he knew if the kid was a big leaguer waiting to happen, well, Rickey wasn't really so poor after all.

The tactics often worked. Downey signed two teenagers in greater Los Angeles. One was pitcher Erv Palica, who was seventeen when he signed. The other was outfielder Edwin "Duke" Snider, who broke into pro ball when he was seventeen. Downey outfoxed a lot of scouts to sign Snider, who was the best athlete anyone had ever seen come straight out of Compton.

The Dodgers signed so many high school kids that Jake Pitler, Rickey's rookie-ball manager in Newport News, joked, "When we took off on a road trip, our bus was filled with comic books, candy bars, and almost no shaving cream." Other teams shied away from signing youngsters during the war, fearing they would be lost to the war effort, but Rickey wasn't deterred. When criticized for taking in so many youngsters, he scoffed, "Some of them will be coming back and we will have them."

The manpower crisis reached its peak in 1945 and altered the way teams scouted and signed players. Before the war, signing high school players before they tasted low-level minor league baseball was unacceptable. After the war, it was habit. The same was true of Rickey's invasion of Negro League baseball. The Dodgers weren't pioneers; they were raiders. Instead of building up meaningful working relationships with Negro League teams and turning them into minor league teams, white teams, with Rickey's Dodgers at the forefront, destroyed them. The resentment from both white and black players was already enormous, and it was going to get worse before it got better. One war was ending and another was about to begin. Baseball, it seemed, was never happy unless it was fighting.

When Judge Landis died, black players saw the chance they had long been denied, the opportunity to overcome baseball's institutionalized discrimination. Their quest would be directly tied to the new commissioner and the way Branch Rickey sought to rebuild his team. Rickey's solution was to let World War II run its course and build for the future. He didn't want returning players like Hank Greenberg or replacements like Pete Gray. He wanted players who were still kids. Those were the players he was thinking about while the blood was still wet.

Rickey's plan was greatly helped by Commissioner Happy Chandler, who told the African-American-owned *Chicago Defender,* "After I take office, I would like to sit down with all parties interested in this question and talk it across the desk. I want to find out what is best for all concerned." The owners fumed. They elected a progressive! The Judge was always so dour and grumpy. Why'd it have to be a guy named Happy? In hindsight, if the choice had been to cancel the 1945 season in order to ensure that no blacks would play in professional baseball in 1946, the owners would probably have let baseball sunset until the war was over. Judge Landis was the immovable object, the man who said he would never take up baseball integration because owners wouldn't let him. They lost a Judge and gained a lawyer, what kind of trade was that?

The Sporting News loved Chandler's selection, thinking he was exactly what the modern game needed: "It is important to look into the future— efforts to unionize players, efforts to force the Negro issue in the courts. Chandler will be able to appeal to the public in a direct way. Judge Landis believed that the commissioner should keep himself aloof, that he should not give interviews on the record, that he should not go about making speeches, that he should show himself publicly only in ballparks. Senator Chandler is far too ebullient and effervescent a personality to keep himself under the restrictions which guided Judge Landis."

The owners hated Chandler, but they had only themselves to blame. They wanted their season, then resented that they only got it because Chandler made this dreary, dreadful, rainy and mucky, doubleheader-laden season full of cripples, gimps, and old men a reality. Chandler brought that point home every chance he got, typically chirping such things as "We are carrying on baseball with 4-F's. Baseball has not asked that a single able-bodied man be held back from the armed forces. Not a single man has been kept out of uniform because of baseball. Because of the great victory you are winning over our enemies, when you return home, we shall give you the greatest era of sport in the history of the world."

Yeah, the owners thought, the future looked great, but asked, Does it have to involve black players?

The Sporting News loved Chandler because he apparently had no enemies, a perfect leader for peacetime, writing, "Senator Chandler comes into baseball with no vendettas, without prejudices and with a tremendous amount of respect for baseball, those who play it, those who run it, for those who make the turnstiles click."

Chandler's problem was that he didn't understand baseball. He did not understand the difference between being a fan and being a servant of the owners. He did not understand that the baseball business works unlike any other business. Landis created the unwritten rules still governing the game decades after his death. While the national media generally hailed Chandler's selection, H. G. Salsinger, columnist of *The Detroit News,* understood that his tenure was doomed. "Baseball has selected a successor that represents by profession, nature and choice the main things Judge Landis fought against in his 23-year reign."

For years, Landis warned owners about hiring a politician as commissioner. He told them to select from inside baseball, because if they wanted to keep baseball the way it had always been, to maintain the unwritten rules, then they needed to appoint one of their own. What Landis was saying was if they wanted to keep black players out of baseball, then they needed to keep outsiders out of baseball. If Ford Frick had been made commissioner after Landis, he would have followed the old rules, and baseball's integration issue wouldn't have been resolved for years.

The war broke down the Judge's walls. The war made a politician necessary to keep the 4-F's, and so the war sparked baseball's massive social, geographical, and population changes in the following decades. Salsinger, an old-guard writer, knew Chandler would never last, because even if his ideas were good for baseball, they went against establishment rules.

Salsinger wrote, "Judge Landis knew politicians. He was one himself.

He was successful enough to achieve a Federal judgeship. He ceased being a politician after he ascended the Federal bench. He certainly never practiced politics after entering baseball. Another man going from politics to the commissionership might not be able to do the same thing. To carry politics into baseball, the Judge realized, could do only harm to the game. Judge Landis told the club owners to stay out of Washington and request no favor of any kind from the politicos. He himself remained out of the capital."

Landis was dead and could not look down with disdain upon Chandler, so Salsinger did it for him, writing, "Senator Chandler is one of the best-liked politicians in the country. Kentucky has never had one who excelled him in popularity. He came from the hills of his native state and he created a huge political following first by singing hillbilly songs at social functions. He will even today launch into song at the slightest provocation. He is always the life of the party and that may prove his main handicap in his new job."

Now it was too late. The owners had hired a man who thought black players deserved a chance to play, and worse yet, they gave Branch Rickey a chance to develop new players. They hired a commissioner who thought major leaguers returning from the war deserved a chance at unionization, a man who didn't want scouts signing players before they graduated from high school, and who probably believed that players had a right to ask for better money. Landis was right, no politician could survive in baseball if he tried to be everything to everybody. But Chandler sure loved to try to make everyone love him. The scorn flowed from Salsinger's fingertips to his typewriter as he struck keys that sounded future wars after this one ended: "Happy is a man who would much rather say yes than no and if he persists in this preference as commissioner of baseball, he will have nothing but trouble. He won't be running the show. The show will be running him."

The wartime manpower shortage was already succeeding in making baseball more completely reflective of America. But until that could happen, the war needed to end, and the 1945 baseball season, as dismal as it looked, churned forward like the volcanic ash on Iwo Jima. The public was catching on. "Baseball is not a monopoly of lily-whites or gray-greens," the

New York Post wrote. "It belongs to all the people. It is the typical American game. And so it is part of the American melting pot. Into this sport come men like Joe DiMaggio, an Italian; Hank Greenberg, a Jew; Lou Gehrig, a German; Sigmund Jakucki, a Pole, and others. There should be a place ready and waiting in it for the ten percent of Americans who are Negro." The funny thing was, Branch Rickey didn't want all the black players in the country. He just wanted the ones he wanted.

The 1945 season proved to be a tense and bittersweet time for many players. Nobody was going to want any of these replacements after the war, which created issues and tensions on a daily basis. Sig Jakucki knew nobody was going to want *him* when the war was over. He was pitching just fine in 1945, plodding along in mediocre fashion, but he knew his days were numbered, and so he drank accordingly. Jack was one of those guys who only pitched well when he was plastered. Hell, he wondered if he would lose his job to a black player, or maybe, just maybe, to some damn one-armed pitcher. Jack was crude and surly, hateful even, and he took out his anger on Pete Gray.

Pete had taught himself how to do everything in life, but for all his courage and resourcefulness, he still only had one hand, which made tying his shoes about the hardest thing he did every day. He always needed to ask one of his teammates to help him lace up his spikes. Even the players who didn't care about him didn't mind, until the day came for Jack to be a decent human being. He barked, "Tie your own goddamned shoe!"

Pete wasn't going to take that kind of abuse. Oh, no. It was bad enough that he wasn't playing every day; he didn't need to be treated like that. All the guys on the Browns thought he was just some surly loner, but Pete couldn't understand why having one arm meant he was less of a person. How the hell would they feel if they busted their asses to get to the big leagues, then got here after all those years and sat on the bench every damn day? Pete didn't have a lot of patience, and when Jack refused to help him tie his shoes, Pete was ready to string him up.

Pete thought he wasn't just standing up to Jack. He was standing up to anyone else on that team who didn't like him. He was no different from Hank Greenberg storming into the other clubhouse to demand the identity of who called him a "yellow Jew bastard." Jack used to say things like "You need both arms to play baseball!" Jack killed Pete every chance he got. It had been a few years since Pete got that kind of abuse, and, well, he thought that playing in the majors should have put that to rest.

Finally, Pete's frustration rumbled to the surface behind closed doors. One afternoon when the players got back inside the clubhouse before the writers did, Pete went after Jack. Nobody was around except the ballplayers. Punches were thrown. Pete made it clear: You didn't have to like him as a person, and, hell, you didn't even have to like him as a ballplayer. But you had to respect him for who he was, and to Pete, respecting him had nothing to do with his being disabled.

At times Pete might have wished that Bert Shepard was on his team, because even if Shepard hadn't lived his entire life disabled, at least he knew what it was like to have attention because he was missing something. But even that connection would not have provided complete solace because Pete had spent years trying to become a big leaguer, unlike Shepard, the accidental ballplayer. By the time the Browns played the Senators at Griffith Stadium, Pete's batting average had plummeted to .189. He was hitting everything on the ground. He wasn't driving anything.

Shepard was more understanding about his limited playing time than Gray was. Shepard loved being around the big leaguers after all these years, but he understood the hesitation to put in a guy with one leg to a pitch a game. He understood Pete's journey had been different from his, but he did not resent Pete for it as so many other players did. They both were here because of the war. Years later, Bert Shepard remembered how he longed to finally pitch in a major league game, but even as he yearned to play, he felt he had not earned it, and he felt bad for Pete Gray, who never seemed to be in a good mood even though he had finally played in the majors. Something, somehow, always seemed to be missing, and it had nothing to do with his arm.

But whatever Pete was missing, many other players in that long, last summer of the war felt they were missing more. Pete may have been a big leaguer with limited playing time, a big leaguer with a minuscule batting average, and a big leaguer with a grudge against the guys on his team who didn't like him, but at least Pete Gray was a big leaguer. That made him an easy target for resentment. As much as he was the public symbol of the courageous ballplayer whose determination had led him to the big leagues, he was also the bane of ballplayers everywhere, who watched the war against Japan drag out and take their chances of ever playing in the majors with it.

These ballplayers knew the war was leaving them at an awkward age in their baseball careers. When they came home, they would be too old to play in the majors, but hoped to find work in what promised to be a post-war boom in minor league ball. The servicemen ballplayers knew they were going to have to keep playing in the minors if they wanted to keep playing, and it at least beat working as a salesman. These were the nameless and forgotten ballplayers of the war years, but in the following decades, they became scouts, coaches, and minor league managers. They built the game from the ground floor, and the basis of their work ethic, their commitment to the game, and their life experiences was built from their war years, when they all waited and wondered what would become of them when it all ended.

Hundreds of ballplayers had a career like that of Al Kubski, who before the war played four years of minor league ball and was twenty-five when he went into the service. He hit .318 in his last minor league season before he was drafted into the Army in 1942. When he came out four years later, he was thirty, as good as dead for a pro ballplayer. Like many former minor leaguers, he'd lost the years in which he would have made the majors. He said he would have made the Army a career if the war had gone on much longer. Instead, he became a minor league slugger, four times knocking in more than 100 runs, including 144 as player-manager for the Blackwell Broncos in 1954. When he finished playing in 1957, he became a scout for the rest of his career, which is where old players and managers went to sunset. He signed a bunch of guys who played in the majors and smiled when his son, Gil, played in the big leagues in 1980 and later as a scout, signed his own big leaguers.

George Genovese was another ballplayer like Al Kubski. He was three years into his career as a minor league shortstop for the Cardinals when he was drafted. He didn't play again until after the war, settling into a nice career in the Pacific Coast League, where he played his best years for the Hollywood Stars. Genovese always believed that without the war he would have been an everyday major league shortstop. His double-play partner in Hollywood was Gene Handley, who played the war years in Sacramento while working at a factory. Even the players like Handley who played stateside but worked industrial jobs during the war said the lower quality of competition and fewer hours to devote to developing the craft took a toll on baseball skills. Handley got back to the big leagues for a touch after the war and spent the rest of his career playing in Hollywood. This old double-play combination used to needle the hell out of each other, and when they were done playing, they became scouts. Genovese signed so many big leaguers that he became the only scout in baseball history whose players totaled 3,000 career home runs. Handley had an eye for pitching and training younger scouts. His philosophy was simple, and in it you could hear the echo of the war years: "We're no smarter than the other guy, we just hope to be. Maybe we work a little harder and get a little luckier."

Plenty of midlevel big leaguers were waiting and wondering, knowing their playing careers would never again be the same. One of them was Dario Lodigiani, a San Francisco boy who grew up with Joe DiMaggio and was his best friend. Lodi, as he was universally called, was a solid .280-type hitter before the war for the Athletics and White Sox. He spent most of his Army career playing for the Seventh Air Force and was a mainstay on the Army Air Corps teams. Lodi, a jolly, good-natured Italian, loved to play but knew he couldn't possibly be the same player when the war was over. He was drafted when he was twenty-six and had already played 361 games in the majors. He would be lucky to be playing again by the time he was thirty. He was right, and soon the majors pushed him back to the Pacific Coast League, where he spent good years with the Oakland Oaks. He was done a few years later. After a short stint coaching in the majors, he spent the rest of his career scouting for the White Sox. He evaluated talent through the eyes of a World War II veteran, believing that "you must alert the boy that any possibility can happen. He has to know that he can expect the unexpected."

Sometimes players had no luck. Don Lindebergh was a low-level minor league catcher who played a few seasons before his career got off the ground. He joined the Army in 1941, but never played professional baseball again. That path was not uncommon. He eventually became a scout with a sound track record, the kind of crabby, old veteran who liked to brag about his players who made good and grumble about the boys he missed on. But like a lot of those low-level ballplayers, who in the last days of the war saw their careers end long before the war did, he was never eager to talk about it. Asked in his later years what he remembered of the war, he precisely offered, "I was in the service, let's see now, five years, eleven months, and twenty-eight days." Asked if he was overseas, he replied, "I don't talk about the war."

Some ballplayers had dumb luck. Billy Connelly had never played a lick of anything except sandlot ball when he joined the Marines as a teenager and landed on Iwo Jima at the age of nineteen. He was just a boy and too small-town and too naïve to really understand what he was getting into. Lots of stories were like that, especially in the Pacific, where the line-level sailors and Marines were practically all kids. Those veterans remembered cheering on their shooting as if they were at a football game or a baseball game. Connelly was all into it, too, but when he got tired of lying in the hot volcanic ash, he lifted his head. A Japanese bullet immediately punctured his jaw. The doctors fixed him up and he took his Purple Heart home. While Pete Gray and Bert Shepard were taking their first tour through the American League that spring, Connelly was quickly pitching his arm back into game shape. There was need for a boy like him in the majors. It helped that Connelly was right-handed, proving once more that baseball always has a job for a kid with a good arm.

Pete Gray was worried about keeping his own job. He was having an utterly miserable day against the Detroit Tigers on June 13, going 0-for-5 against three second-line pitchers. Gray was playing left field for the Browns when the big news swept through the small Briggs Stadium crowd of 7,246. Broadcaster Harry Heilmann read fans the bulletin that nearly brought the town to tears. The news was too big to wait for the game to end. Pete heard the commotion in the stands. He wondered if the war with Japan was over.

When he trotted back in between innings, the news was already in the Browns dugout. The guys on the other side of the field were practically dancing onto the field. Tigers GM Jack Zeller went downstairs and emerged in the dugout tunnel during the game, where he pulled aside his manager, Steve O'Neill, to break the wonderful news. Some kids in the stands were running up and down the aisles in pure glee, announcing the news Detroit and its hometown team had been waiting to hear for almost five long years: Hank Greenberg was finally out of the Army. As far as Detroit was concerned, it was V-G Day. Victory Greenberg!

CHAPTER 21

Waiting for Hank

The day Hank Greenberg walked out of the Fort Dix separation center, it brought back memories of when he'd first entered the barracks in 1941. He remembered how quietly he slipped into his bunk that night, such a far cry from the hotels with marble floors, brass bedposts, and mattresses that bounced. This time, there were a few newsmen waiting for him and some kids who wanted his autograph. He signed for the children, as he always did without fail, then sheepishly reminded the newsmen that this wasn't such a big deal after all.

But Hank was a big story. When he left for the Army, he became the symbol of the ballplayer who was about to risk it all for what became the war effort. Now, leaving the Army, Hank was a symbol all over again, the great shining hope of returning boys everywhere. Hank never thought anything he did was worth the fuss, but that was part of his charm. This time, his return to civilian life transcended baseball. It was more than just a question of how long it would take for him to get around the good fastball again or if he would ever have the same home-run power. The question around Hank was the same question everyone coming home from the war faced: How do I get my old life back?

When Hank walked out of Fort Dix looking as tall, as strong, and as impeccable as he ever had, boys around the world saw his image in their newspapers and asked if he could be the man he was before the war. Hank asked himself the same question as anyone else in uniform: Would he ever be the same person he was before the war? The answer was always, no, never exactly the same.

That was a difficult question for anyone to ask, but seeing Hank live through it, and exploring the question through the comfortable realm of baseball, immediately captured the public fancy. Hank hadn't played a single game, and already he was going to be the next big story of the 1945 baseball season. Everyone wanted to see him play, but Hank needed some time to figure out when he would be ready. He sought refuge from the press to gather his thoughts, so his first move after leaving the base was to go to New York City to see his parents and his family. Some of his nephews he hadn't seen since they were babies. A big Romanian family gathering was waiting for Hank in the Bronx, complete with home cooking, lots of hugs, a visit to temple with his parents, and probably his mother asking him if he was going to settle down and get married now that he was out of the Army.

When Hank checked Detroit's schedule, he found what he wanted. The Tigers would be at Yankee Stadium in mid-July, which would give him another perfect chance to see his family and friends from the old neighborhood. Hank decided he wanted to be as up to speed as he possibly could be when he got back to New York, so he decided he wanted to be ready to play by July 1. He never told anyone what his plans were.

Back at Briggs Stadium, GM Jack Zeller had no idea when Hank was coming back. All he knew was that when the big guy said he was ready, he was going to play every day, no questions asked. The thought of sending him out to the minor leagues to work his way back into shape never even crossed Zeller's mind. You just didn't do that to a player like Hank. When he said he was ready, he was ready, and that was good enough for Zeller and manager Steve O'Neill.

Just the news that their big slugger, their emotional leader, the rock they all looked up to, was coming home seemed to lighten the burden on the entire ball club and give them fresh confidence. The Tigers were 27-17 on June 13, the day Hank was cut from the Army, in first place by one game over the 27-19 Yankees, but they weren't running away with the race.

The American League was a tight pack, with six teams within 6 games of the lead, including the defending-champ Browns, who were in fifth place at 22-23 and weren't as sharp as they were the year before.

Hank's return threw another big question mark over the entire American League race. What if the Yankees got Joe DiMaggio back, what if the Red Sox got Ted Williams back, and what if the Indians got Bob Feller back? Now that Hank was on the way home, anything seemed possible. After four long years of war, that was a pretty good feeling. Much was riding on his return, for the Tigers, for baseball, and for the ordinary joes who wanted to believe that if Hank could do it, so could they. "It's the first big test of whether athletes who were out of sports competition for a long period can make the grade on their return," *The New York Times* reported.

Hank's homecoming was just the beginning. Pretty soon, the streets would be flooded with soldiers and sailors looking for their old lives in a new world. Hank was just one man of the first wave of 1.3 million to be mustered out of service in the next year. The war was an intensely personal experience for most American families, especially in a close-knit Midwest town like Detroit, where death notices were still commonplace in the daily newspapers and some forty-three hundred casualties had been reported since the start of the war. If Hank could come back soon and come back good, the Tigers might just win the pennant after all. And for one glorious summer, even as the B-29 bombers Hank recently served with continued burning Japan, it felt almost as if peace had finally returned.

But the truth was, the war was still going on, and nobody knew when Japan was going to surrender. The headlines made the war hard to miss in everyday life. There was no hiding the war news from the people, who lived this war as no other generation of Americans had ever intensely lived another war through their daily lives. The spring war news was loud:

GAINS ON OKINAWA IN STIFF AND COSTLY FIGHTING

500 B-29'S POUND NAGOYA

JAPS ON OKINAWA SHOW SIGNS OF CRACKING

TOKYO IN RUINS

SUPERS BLAST YOKOHAMA

TRUMAN REVEALS PLANS FOR VAST BLOWS IN PACIFIC

On the day that President Truman asked for a surge of war production, soldiers and sailors around the world thought that could only mean the invasion of Japan. Nobody wanted to think about it. The possibility of an invasion was dreadful and of no consolation to the old men in their early to mid twenties sweating out their full 85 to 100 points required for discharge. Entire American armies waited in occupied Germany expecting to mobilize at any moment. If that happened, all bets were off, and there seemed no possible way there could be enough manpower to play yet another season of dilapidated wartime ball.

Military intelligence estimated that a ground invasion could result in half a million US casualties. The lack of movement from Japan on a possible surrender seemed to indicate that the emperor would arm his people with sharpened bamboo poles Marines nicknamed "idiot sticks" to throw back the American invaders. The emperor knew the Americans had permitted two Russian armies to capture Berlin rather than absorb the casualties and drain their thinning manpower. Perhaps he suspected the Americans had no taste for this door-to-door urban street fight.

Baseball was a much more pleasant thought. Hank couldn't get back to the lineup soon enough, but he wasn't ready for what was waiting for him. The majors were full of bad umpiring, bad weather, bad players, and poor playing surfaces, all making every day at the ballpark a one-of-a-kind adventure. Players saw things they had never seen before and never saw again. The absurd was routine. On the day the news broke about Hank's discharge, Tigers base coach Fred Hoffman was hit in the head by a ball thrown by one of his own players. A rookie pitcher for the Boston Red Sox, Boo Ferriss, was discharged from the Army Air Corps and promptly pitched 22 consecutive scoreless innings. Clark Griffith succeeded in his bewildering idea of building a four-man pitching staff comprised entirely of knuckleball pitchers. His Washington Senators wore black armbands all season in memory of President Roosevelt. The Tigers lost pitcher Al Benton, who had been so good after returning from the Navy, when a line drive shattered his leg in two places. Attendance numbers were generally in the latrine, but occasionally the game could still surprise everyone. The biggest baseball crowd since before Pearl Harbor, 70,906, rocked Yankee Stadium's rafters to see the Yankees and Tigers split a Memorial Day doubleheader. The

Tigers scratched out merely 5 runs in two games that day, virtually causing Detroit citizens to pray for Hank to hurry it up.

The Detroit News was positive Hank would make an impact, even if the rest of the country, especially the big papers back East, were somewhat cynical that a man could be gone from the majors for four years and still be a hitter. When Ted Williams, serving at Pensacola Naval Station and expecting to fly combat cover in the invasion, was asked if Hank would ever hit again, he damn near ripped the reporter's head off. "Greenberg will hit, and you can count on that," he said. "Hank may not reach .350, but he'll swat that ball. At the end of the season, he'll be the most dangerous hitter on the Detroit team."

The Detroit News couldn't wait to see what Hank had left. Conjecturing about his return was delightful: "Three factors back Greenberg's projected bid to regain a place among the elite of the major leagues after about four years' absence: 1) physical condition that is a by product of Army life. 2) A native determination to excel. 3) The lowered quality of competition." And still, there was one big question. "Greenberg joined the Army on May 7, 1941. Nobody has ever attempted to resume baseball operations after so long a lapse." *The New York Times* offered, "Hank will be watched with more than ordinary interest because he is a real test case. At the age of 34 he can't possibly be as sharp as he once was. However it would be a complete delight if he accomplished the trick." Now all that was left was to see if Hank could be the miracle man of World War II. The next morning, above the box score of the Tigers-Browns game, *The Detroit News* headline said it all:

WAITING FOR HANK

Two days later, a Western Union telegram arrived at the offices of Hillerich & Bradsby Company, makers of the famed Louisville Slugger, addressed to chief bat maker Henry Morrow. The telegram, dated June 18, 1945, read simply:

PLEASE SEND TWELVE BATS MY MODEL TO DETROIT IMMEDIATELY. REGARDS. HANK GREENBERG.

Shortly thereafter, the bill for a dozen bats crossed GM Jack Zeller's desk. Zeller laughed. That's how he knew when Hank was coming. He was never so happy to get another payment-due notice. "I knew then he would be on his way soon," Zeller said. He quickly told his manager, Steve O'Neill, that the big guy was on his way back to Briggs.

A few days later, Hank Greenberg walked back up to the corner of Michigan and Trumbull. He arrived with no fanfare, intentionally so, when the team was on the road. Hank remembered his sad good-bye. He wanted to keep this sweet hello all to himself. He strode in the summer heat wearing a light, white cotton shirt with his travel bag in his hand, and as he crossed beneath the overhang reading BRIGGS STADIUM, he thought she hadn't aged a day in all the time he was gone.

The ballpark was peaceful when the team was away. Hank wanted it this way because he needed the room to himself to bleed his way back into shape, but he also wanted to say hello to her all over again. She still smelled like cooking grease, cigar smoke, and mowed grass. No girl ever smelled so sweet.

When he walked into the clubhouse for the first time, the first thing he noticed were all the names he didn't know. A lot of names were written on athletic tape, a sign of hasty and frequent changes. For a moment, this didn't feel like his old work space. The quantity of sheer strangers gave him the feel of the airfield back in Assam. When he looked for his old locker, he quickly remembered that it wasn't his anymore.

His old manager Del Baker was long since fired, which was too bad, because Hank liked him. He had never played for Steve O'Neill, but had met him a few times and figured it wouldn't be such a big deal. O'Neill, the jovial, overweight, and lumpy former catcher was the kind of manager who tried to make all of his players happy. Over the winter, he'd gone on a USO tour to New Guinea and the Dutch East Indies, way down in one of the war's most remote fronts. His experience moved him. "We just couldn't tell them enough of what has been happening in the game while the war is on," he said. The boys were so happy to see a familiar face that they crowded the affable O'Neill, who tried to accommodate them all. Upon returning home, O'Neill somehow estimated he had signed eight thousand autographs and jotted down eight hundred names of parents and girlfriends he was supposed to write to. How O'Neill handled all that mail was anybody's guess, but he sure couldn't wait to write Hank Greenberg's name into the Detroit Tigers starting lineup.

Pretty soon, Hank found his first old friend, the home clubhouse man, Ray Forsyth. Hank gave Ray a big hug, and the clubby went into his equipment closet and pulled out Hank's old uniform, still hanging on the same coat hanger he'd left it on in 1941. Ray also had a homecoming gift for Hank. Because it was going to take the bat company a few weeks to make his new lumber, Rudy York had left behind a few of his extra bats for Hank to get ready with. Hank smiled; old Rudy was still looking out for him, and he used virtually the same model. Ray, who was also the team's trainer and doctor, took one look at Hank and was astounded. "I wish I were in as good shape," he said. Hank was pleased with how good he looked. He weighed a firm 215 pounds and he felt solid. He said he tried on a suit he'd left behind in 1941 and found that it still fit perfectly.

But Army shape was not baseball shape. He ushered himself back into baseball exercises. He took batting practice again for the first time. The first ball he hit was a rocket, but that was a fluke, and Hank knew it wasn't going to be that easy. After only a few swings, he was already tired and sore. His legs felt like rubber and his balance was gone. Hank didn't say any of this in public because people were counting on him. Even though his comeback hadn't even officially started yet, he could already tell that there was no way he could be the same hitter he was before the war. Hank had to accept that he had indeed lost a lot of who he was. Now the question was if enough was left for him to make a difference, to make some of that lost money back, to win this pennant race, to get back to the World Series. He never thought of himself as a war hero and never thought of himself as a baseball hero, even though he knew he was a big star. All Hank wanted to do was make the best out of what he had left, and while he was certain some moments of great frustration and angst would lie ahead, he was also certain that the war had not robbed him of his professionalism. His pride demanded no less than his best, not to wallow in sadness over what the war stole. Hank had a job to do this summer, and even if he wasn't quite the same, he was going to gut it out and grind it all the way through to the finish line.

Then, Hank decided he needed to watch a few big league games to get a feel for the speed and flow of the big leagues. Maybe he hadn't done a lot of evaluating while he was a younger player, but he was certain he needed to now. He was not impressed with the quality of play. Simply put, he saw bad baseball everywhere around him. He saw guys who couldn't play and didn't know how to play. He saw pitchers who couldn't command the strike zone. He saw hitters who couldn't hit. He saw kids too green to be here and old men too washed-up. Hank looked around and wondered, did anybody care about the playing surfaces during the war? A lot of big league fields, including Briggs, were not kept up well during the war. A lot of that was because of water rationing, so you commonly saw brown patches of dead grass where it had once been green. The batter's box wasn't flat but cratered out, and the mounds were awful for the pitchers, who landed in huge divots.

Hank's postwar training was already starting, and he was developing his baseball mind in ways he never had before. These were all questions a general manager might ask himself. These were questions about evaluating players and asking where they were coming from, how they were being signed, and what they were learning before professional baseball and what they were not learning once they signed. Hank was learning what the war had done to the game, how it had in only four years caused changes in every way that were now here to stay and promised to rapidly proliferate. Hank figured out quickly that he wasn't the only person or the only thing that wasn't the same as it was before the war. The game was changing and hurtling toward the future in manners that seemed inconceivable only a few years earlier.

Hank sized up the wartime majors and decided that even if he wasn't the same player, he was still dangerous. Easing himself back into the swing of things, Hank thought he could make his comeback productive. "I have to catch up with the pitching and bring my timing around," he said. "That's going to be the hardest thing, hitting the fastball. I can follow a curve, but I've got to be able to get my bat around faster when they cut loose with that speed."

The wartime majors seemed strange to Hank, as did reacquainting himself with civilian life. A former Tigers teammate, Dutch Meyer, recently mustered out of the Air Corps and now playing second base for the Indians, told Hank it would be easy: "Don't worry too much about readjustment to civilian life. I know how strange everything seems right now. Pretty soon, you'll feel natural again."

As Hank labored through those first painful swings, he longed for the

American League he'd left behind, when the majors were so competitive that only the good survived and only the elite flourished. He didn't need to see too many games of wartime baseball to understand that the old days were gone, at least until the war was long over. He longed for the old days, when he could test himself against the best, but right now, the best were no more.

"You'd go into New York and get Ruffing and Gomez," Hank said, savoring the memory. "You'd get into Boston next and you'd have Grove and Ferrell. Then you'd go to Cleveland and Feller and Harder were waiting." God, the league was good! "They could all throw the ball past you. I don't see the good pitchers today that were in the league when I quit. A guy ought to be able to hit in this current league. If I don't, it will be my own fault."

When the Tigers came back in town, Hank came out for early batting practice and attracted quite a crowd of reporters, which he didn't like. He threw himself into the fire, hitting for four consecutive hours until he was soaked in sweat. He hit until his hands ached. He broke a bat and chipped another, which he never, ever did. Every swing frustrated him. He was under the ball. Or he was hitting on top of it. He asked for pitches to be thrown exactly where he wanted. Put it down and away, he ordered, where the slider finishes. Then Hank would try to rifle it to right field, but in those early sessions, he would more often curse under his breath, furiously berating himself as he pulled off and rolled over, grounding the ball to short. When he did hit one good, it was nothing but a line drive, a clean single, and that disgusted Hank as well. Nobody wanted to see a six-foot-four singles hitter.

Finally, Hank threw one of his new bats onto the grass and shouted, "That's enough." The reporters crowded him like a guy playing in the World Series. He was so annoyed he might have wished to be back in China. He was brutally hard on himself: "I'm bigger, stronger, and tougher, but I don't have the snap to my swing and I can't move as fast. Somebody would have to do a job on me, breaking down these muscles, before I can do myself any good. I'm missing balls I used to murder."

Steve O'Neill and Jack Zeller left him alone to determine his return date. "Hank is a tremendously hard worker, and one of the most aggressive and conscientious players I've ever seen," O'Neill said. He wanted Hank to hit fourth right away, which meant he wanted him to take his time and make sure he was ready. Greenberg talked to Zeller, who said, "I figure he will require ten days to two weeks to regain his timing. If he hits anywhere near his old clip, we're the club to beat for the flag."

Finally, the Tigers went out on the road to play Pete Gray and the Browns, and Hank again had the park to himself. He hired a personal batting-practice pitcher, thirty-seven-year-old minor league journeyman Bill Crouch, to throw to him. Crouch was a gem of a guy with a rubber arm, and he could throw any pitch, anywhere in the zone. He couldn't throw hard, but he was a masterful junk artist who could spin the ball, locate whatever he had left on his fastball, and change speeds. Crouch served up many made-to-order BPs for Hank. When Hank wanted fastballs on the outside corner, Crouch delivered. When Hank wanted the fastball up and in, Crouch obliged. Hank gathered some kids off the street and paid them each a dollar a day to shag balls in the outfield. The kids were happy to have Hank back. Would any other big leaguer have paid that well to stand there and shag?

No reporters were allowed inside the ballpark while Hank prepared. A few other neighborhood kids caught sneak peeks. Hank swung the bat until his hands were bleeding. Then he took his glove and headed to left field. Crouch grabbed a bat and hit everything at Hank—line drives right at him, over his head, into the corner, off the wall. Hank was satisfied he could play a competent left field as long as he didn't let any balls get behind him. He described himself as a "stumblebum" when he first came up, but he was proud of the improvements he had made defensively. He was, though, a little slow bending his knees on the ball hit hard right in front of him.

His personal spring training was crammed into only a few days. When his daily workouts were over, Hank took the ladle from the bucket and poured water over his head. When he was finished, he ripped the tape off his blistered hands. The blood soaked through the gauze. He went inside and stripped his shirt to let the trainer work on his shoulder, back, and triceps muscles. The treatment was forceful and left Hank with a string of bruises the size of baseballs across his body. He knew he was overdoing it, but he didn't care. He knew too much was riding on his comeback. The team needed him. The town needed him. The soldiers in the service needed him. The ballplayers who would emulate his comeback needed him. Hundreds of major leaguers needed him to perform well enough to protect their prewar salaries; he thought they might suffer if he failed. Everybody was waiting for Hank, who was too proud to admit that he felt like shit on a shingle. What the hell, it was time to find out how well he could play.

Hank announced July 1 would be the day of his return, a doubleheader against the Philadelphia Athletics at Briggs Stadium. He wasn't perfect, but he was as good as he was going to be. His throwing arm was sore from so little use over the last four years, and his hands would be in constant pain until his calluses formed again. A large crowd gathered around Briggs Stadium that morning, hoping to see Big Hank's big return. *The Detroit News* ran nearly identical photos of Hank from 1941 and 1945 and asked readers:

HOW HAS WAR CHANGED GREENBERG?

Well, that was the $55,000 question, wasn't it? After all, as a former GI, Hank was entitled under federal law to forty days at his former salary to prove his job skills were just as good as they were at the time of his enlistment. When Hank came to the ballpark that morning, he found that the corner locker he'd thought he would recover had somehow been assigned to a rookie pitcher named Billy Pierce, a teenager up from the Detroit sandlot leagues. Rather than throw a fit and demand his old locker, Hank gentlemanly said, "That's okay. When I first came to the Tigers, I had to work my way to that big locker. It's only right that I should do it again." Good luck finding another former American League MVP who wouldn't have been offended.

Hank unpacked his belongings, but he wondered, what kind of clubhouse manager would give the veteran's locker to a kid who was still in high school? He wanted to know what had happened to Speedy Brzezenski, who was one the younger clubhouse kids and batboys. When Hank asked around, he found out that Speedy had joined the Marines and come back to Briggs to visit the Tigers in May. Everyone noticed the large bayonet wound on his hand, but Speedy never said a word about it, so nobody asked. He had been in the fighting at Bougainville, Guam, and Iwo Jima.

He came back with three prized possessions—the baseball glove former Tigers shortstop Billy Rogell gave him when he enlisted, the Japanese flag he captured on Guam, and his life. Speedy was young at heart, but the players who knew him before the war thought he looked older. "I had ambitions to be a ballplayer, but on my next birthday I'll be twenty-five and that's pretty old to be starting out," Speedy said. Hank, who was thirty-four, suddenly felt very happy to be dressing in the locker that might have belonged to Speedy, who was still in the Marines, waiting for the invasion.

When Hank walked onto the field, the early crowd warmly welcomed him. Nobody had ever seen a player get a standing ovation two hours before the start of a game. Hank smiled and doffed his hat. He hoped the excitement would die down once the fans saw him play, but he never anticipated how this scene would repeat itself around the American League for the rest of the summer. The return of Hank didn't just spark speculation about what kind of player he would be. It made fans and writers hungry to see more players come home. Before Hank even stepped back in the box, rumors were that pitcher Red Ruffing would soon pitch again for the Yankees, Buddy Lewis might join the Senators, and Bob Feller could return to the Indians. The question became which players would make a meaningful impact on the American League pennant race. Hank didn't have the answers. He was just happy to be home, and it didn't take long for him to realize how everybody wanted a piece of him.

Connie Mack was delighted to see Hank again. They were each a sight for sore eyes. Mr. Mack patted Hank's big shoulders and said he looked fit. Hank might have demurred and cautioned the venerable Athletics manager and owner not to be so quick to compliment him until he watched him hit. They were old friends and hadn't seen each other for a long time. Hank thought Mr. Mack hadn't aged one bit, which was humorous, because he'd looked ancient before the war and he looked ancient now. He was the game's Grand Old Man, and the first newspaper serials about his life appeared in 1931, when he was already sixty-nine years old.

Mr. Mack, as people universally called him, said he felt younger than he looked. The days when he put on a chest protector, a catcher's mask, and a glove to catch pitchers warming up while he still wore his necktie and business attire proved that. Mack was long a proponent of keeping baseball alive during the war, and now that the end was in sight, he could discuss how the manpower shortage of the war years was going to lead to a postwar boom.

Mack had seen the game change numerous times in his eighty-two years, but he suggested that he had never seen anything like how the war was changing baseball, beyond anything accomplished by one scandal, one player, one team, one season, or one World Series. Writers and historians suggested that the Black Sox scandal or Babe Ruth or the Yankee dynasty were the most important elements in baseball history. Mack said they were wrong. The war changed everything, broke the game down and reinvented it. The war and how baseball adapted to and recovered from the manpower shortage were the building stones of the future game, and the Grand Old Man recognized that as the bedrock of baseball history. It was always going to be a question of manpower and how the game changed when the numbers were stripped and what happened when they rose again. He even believed diversifying the game was inevitable, despite the staunch opposition, telling black fans in *The Pittsburgh Courier* that integration would happen when "everything was agreeable," which was his way of saying, wait until after the war when the other owners have no choice.

"When the war is over, I look for better, more exciting baseball played by more skillful men before greater crowds than we have ever known," he said. "Attendance should soar after the war. Even now baseball is making millions of new friends, young friends and women friends. Night games have done much to popularize baseball."

Connie Mack, born in the second year of the Civil War, had seen it all, and that was no exaggeration. Mack was old enough to realize that the game he had known was now gone, and that it was headed toward a new, modern era. Mack recognized the mechanized age was coming. He foresaw economic expansion, population shifts, and geographic redistributions, and he believed his Philadelphia Athletics would one day have to vacate the Victorian-style Shibe Park, perhaps in favor of a new city altogether.

Mack saw the old wooden ballparks rise and would see them begin to come down before he died, and he knew the war would eventually spurn team owners like himself to demand new stadiums made of steel to boost sagging attendance, stadiums that were now going to be possible because of the huge manufacturing industry created during the war. New fans, the children of the servicemen from the war, would populate these new stadiums. They would flock to watch modern ballplayers, who would make fans forget Joe DiMaggio, Ted Williams, and Bob Feller as surely as those three had made fans forget Ty Cobb, Tris Speaker, and Christy Mathewson, just as that trio had made obsolete stars such as Cap Anson, John Montgomery Ward, and Old Hoss Radbourn.

Mr. Mack throught Hank's comeback was relatively small in scale but still appreciated what the slugger was trying to achieve. Every day, Hank, too, was realizing that the game he wanted to spend his life around when he was finished playing was starting to shift even as he sought to steady his legs beneath him. Mack had been around when ballplayers were considered so socially unacceptable that hotels would not accept them and when railroads were first used to transport teams from city to city. But Hank Greenberg could tell him that he had already seen the world's first massive airline in action, the Air Transport Command in China and India, and the B-29s bombers that carried out long-range missions that before the war were thought to be impossible. Hank could see the air transportation boom coming to baseball. He knew that instead of carrying bombs, the big planes would soon carry ballplayers.

He also knew some of those players were going to be black. Hank hadn't thought much about race before the war, despite the discrimination he experienced because he was Jewish. The war changed Hank's thinking. Now, he had seen murder, death, exclusion, and suffering in the name of ideology. He wouldn't stand for that, not in his modern world, not in what he wanted in his own team, and not in his idea of what the future of baseball should be.

When the small talk about such large topics was over, Mr. Mack congratulated Hank on his return and wished him luck. Hank, with a little, impish grin, asked a favor. "When your team is at bat, would you mind waving your scorecard to me in left field and direct me where to play for your hitters? I have never seen any of them before, it's going to be tough positioning for them."

Mr. Mack smiled. An honest answer might have been *Not to worry, none of my bums can hit the ball out of the infield.*

When Mr. Mack returned to his dugout, pitcher Bobo Newsom was waiting to bother him. Jesse Flores was pitching for the Athletics that day, but Bobo wanted the ball badly. Bobo was the biggest blowhard in the American League, so it was fitting that he ended up pitching for Mack, whose long history of dealing with troublesome pitchers could be traced to Rube

Waddell four decades earlier. Bobo won 21 games when he played with Hank on the 1940 pennant-winning Tigers, but wore out his welcome so badly that Jack Zeller traded him. Bobo demanded the chance to face Hank. "I want to prove that I still got my old power over him," Newsome said. So much for giving the guy his moment; old Bobo wanted blood.

Steve O'Neill filled in his first lineup card with Hank Greenberg's name on it, hitting cleanup, though Hank suspected he wasn't ready for that kind of responsibility. O'Neill insisted. His optimism often got the better of his judgment. Besides, too many people had bought tickets and wanted to see Hank, who, of course, felt obligated. When he came to bat for the first time in the first inning, his name was announced and the crowd rose to its feet and shook the rafters. The stands were filled with ordinary fans and servicemen in their uniforms.

The crowd of 47,729 longed for this moment. The city remained deeply touched by the war. Many of Detroit's GIs in Europe had already been sent directly to China in anticipation of the invasion. Local boys of the Red Arrow Division told harrowing tales of hand-to-hand combat against the Japanese. Marine Edgar Greene, the son of *Detroit News* sportswriter Sam Greene, was wounded on Okinawa. The last of 8,685 B-24 bombers rolled off the Ford Willow Run assembly line and was nicknamed *Henry Ford*, autographed by all the workers on the line, including the women. Five Michigan boys helped the battleship *Bunker Hill* survive kamikaze attacks off Okinawa. The killed-in-action list for local boys ran up to four thousand seven hundred, with more than seventeen thousand casualties. A B-29 crew in their ship nicknamed *City of Detroit* flew twenty-seven sorties over the Japanese mainland.

Hank always felt himself to be a small part of a large ordeal. He settled into the batter's box and bore down on Flores, a slight right-hander who was the first Mexican-born pitcher in the majors. Flores didn't throw hard. His best pitch was a screwball, and he was sneaky fast. Flores rocked into his windup, and for the first time since 1941, Hank Greenberg saw a major league pitch. He watched it sail into the glove like an old friend.

Old Hank or new Hank, Flores was a soft-toss specialist who didn't want any part of him. He nibbled the plate, throwing three pitches just out of the zone, but Hank wouldn't bite, and the count went to three balls, no strikes. Hank took a fastball for a strike, then hit a towering fly ball that twisted foul. Hank was late. His timing was missing. On the full-count offering, Flores pulled a string on Hank, who yanked a line drive to right-center field. He hit the ball on the screws but was easily out. The crowd loved it, but Hank could tell these fringy junkmen were going to nickel-and-dime him to death until he proved he could time the trash. Only then would he see the fastball.

In his next at bat, in the fourth inning, Flores threw him a first-pitch fluttering something. Hank's eyes lit up, he thought he saw a fastball. He took a ferocious cut but popped the ball up a mile high behind the plate, where the catcher made the putout. Hank hated popping up almost as much as he hated striking out. In the fifth inning, Flores fell behind in the count, 3-1, then threw something Hank could reach. He unleashed his long arms and drove the pitch deep to right field. The fans rose in anticipation, but Hank knew he missed it. The ball was caught deep in right center, not quite deep enough to land in those pretty blue bleachers.

His mind raced back to the last game he played in the majors, the two home runs he hit against the Yankees. In the sixth inning, Bobo Newsom got his chance to face Hank and succeeded only in walking him on four consecutive pitches. Bobo barked something pointless and inane at Hank as he walked down the line. Bobo's gibber-jabber sounded like one of the coolies speaking back in China.

Finally, in the eighth inning, facing left-hander Charlie Gassaway, Hank got something he could handle. Gassaway fell behind, 3-1, and the lefty came back with a fastball right into Greenberg's wheelhouse. Oh, thank goodness for a lefty. Hank saw the fastball all the way in. His bat roared to life like one of the big B-29 props, complete with smoke and exhaust spewing into the air.

Hank hit it well. He knew he didn't hit it great, but he hit it well enough. It wasn't the kind of gunshot he was used to, but he got that damn fastball down and away and rifled it to right field. Finally, Hank had put some air under the ball. The right fielder was Hal Peck, a wartime replacement from Milwaukee. Hank had been playing pepper with Peck all afternoon, but this shot was a little different. Hank thought he was at least going to get a double, assuming his legs didn't roll out from underneath him. He actually thought he might get stuck with a long single. The fans rose and watched the flight of the ball, and the more whimsical of sportswriters might have suggested that the fans willed the ball higher and farther into the air. At last Peck surrendered, dropping his glove to his side to watch Hank Greenberg's 250th career home run, four years in the making, land safely in the first row in the right-field pavilion. The most surprised person in the park was the guy who hit the ball.

Hank clanked around the bases, smiling as he went, soaking in the crowd, loving the feeling he missed so badly. Briggs Stadium seemed to sway him in her arms. Hank took in every sensation, from the dirt crackling beneath his metal spikes as he crunched around the bags, to the frustrated pitcher rubbing up a new baseball. Hank crossed the plate and gestured to the crowd. He took the happy handshakes and gleeful congratulations from the strangers who were now his teammates. But as soon as he sat down and exhaled heavily, Hank realized how sore he felt. Everything hurt, but the fans didn't know or care. They saw what they'd come to see. Hank Greenberg was finally home. He told Steve O'Neill that he wasn't strong enough to play the second game of the doubleheader. O'Neill told him he didn't mind. He told Hank to take it easy. He had a long summer ahead.

CHAPTER 22

As Large, as Strong, as Powerful

The summer was a tough grind for Pete Gray. His playing time significantly diminished in July as his batting average dove down to around .230, dragging his confidence along with it. He hated not playing regularly. Sitting didn't sit well with him. Pete got grumpy when he wasn't playing and flat-out intolerable when he wasn't hitting. He withdrew from his teammates, who thought he was a miserable loner with a drinking problem. But Pete was a ballplayer who wasn't playing, and no matter how much he drank, it's hard to imagine he was drunk any more than the rest of the bums on the Browns. His teammates thought he was a crabby recluse with one arm when they should have recognized he was upset because he wasn't playing every day. And for that, no amount of applause could change his mind.

One day, though, meant everything to Pete, the day the Browns came to Yankee Stadium. His family made the journey from Nanticoke to see with their own eyes, for the very first time, their son Pete Gray the major leaguer. Before the game, his father and brother, Tony, were allowed to visit him outside the dressing room. Peter senior hugged his son tightly. All those years he'd told him to get up and try again, to work harder when he failed, had paid off. Pete junior, though proud, could still only see through the impatient eyes of a ballplayer who wanted to play. He was excited to see his family, but embarrassed when he told them he was not in the starting lineup. Pete thought his family had wasted all this money to come this way just to see Pete Gray the professional benchwarmer. He felt humiliated, but his dad wouldn't hear any of that. Pete was not a failure. He grabbed his son, pulled him close, and whispered in his ear, encouraging him as he had so many years before, "You're somebody!"

When Pete came out to the field, his parents were waiting for him behind the railing near the dugout. His rural, working-class parents wore their Sunday best to Yankee Stadium. His mother, Antoinette, a thick woman of rugged stock, wrapped her arm around Pete's good shoulder and pulled him near. Pete beamed for the cameras. Pete's brother, Tony, the scratch boxer who'd taught him how to punch, told him, "This is it, this is what you've fought for your whole life!" Just for a moment, surrounded by his family, Pete showed the slight crack of a satisfied smile, just long enough to make his parents proud. Years later, he said no other moment ever meant as much to him as this one. He even had an extra $100 in his pocket from the Browns owner, Don Barnes, a gift, Barnes said, for bringing so many people to the park all season long, and money to take his family out to a nice dinner after the game.

When the writers got wind of Pete's family reunion and saw that manager Luke Sewell did not have him in the starting lineup, they jumped him. The press wanted to see Pete play in Yankee Stadium. That was a great story and they wanted it. Sewell didn't care if they thought Pete deserved to play because his family was here or they wanted to write it up. He resented that. This was his team, not theirs. "I didn't misrepresent anything," he said. "You're the guys who did the misrepresenting. I didn't say Gray would be in the lineup today. I'm not using Gray as a crowd puller when he's not hitting."

Those words said it all. Pete wasn't hitting, but he wasn't playing frequently enough to get rolling. Sewell's words sounded like those of a manager trying to keep his clubhouse support behind him, and knowing that if he ever backed Pete in public, he would lose his team's confidence. So instead, Sewell had to defy ownership, but it was easier to sit Pete on the road than it was at home, where the fans loved Gray and mercilessly booed Sewell when he wasn't in the lineup.

Not until a road trip to play the Senators in Washington and a trip to Walter Reed Army Hospital did Luke Sewell really get to know what made Pete Gray special. Pete and Luke were paired for the visit. Pete received a tremendous ovation from the wounded veterans, who gathered to watch him put on an informal demonstration of his baseball skills. The Army publicity guys set this up with the idea that Luke and Pete were the best of friends, not knowing how distant the two really were. The publicity guys set up a loudspeaker for Sewell to interview Pete in front of the crowd of soldiers. There, in front of the wounded warriors, the manager heard more about his player than he had ever stopped to learn.

Pete told about his journey from the sticks to play for the Brooklyn Bushwicks in hopes of being signed and of all the times he had been told NO in his career. He told of the people who had helped him in his career and how he finally made the most of his opportunity when he played at Three Rivers and then Memphis in 1943 and 1944. Finally, he spoke about how rewarding the journey had been when he finally zipped up that nice big league flannel with BROWNS written across it.

That's when Luke Sewell realized how he had been wrong. He realized he had looked at Pete through baseball eyes only. He hadn't looked at the totality of his personality or what he meant to the maimed soldiers. He didn't know anything about all the times Pete had been rejected, or even how long he had been playing. He watched in admiration as wounded soldiers approached Pete to tell him how much he meant to them.

Pete met wounded boys with grace. His value as a major league ballplayer could never be measured by his batting average or how often he played. It wasn't in how much his teammates liked or disliked him, or in how much he kept to himself, or in how many extra tickets he sold. Pete's perseverance meant everything to those wounded kids who came home from France or Germany or Iwo Jima or Okinawa missing arms or legs or both. One boy from the coal-mining country in Pennsylvania, Pete's backyard, lost his arm below his shoulder when a grenade exploded near him. Pete told him he was a brave man. Another kid said he had been a pitcher in the minor leagues before he lost his leg in France. He told Pete all he wanted out of his baseball career now was a chance to pitch batting practice to him. Pete said he'd love to see his stuff. Pete met them all equally. He was one of them, amputees just like him. He made them feel as if they could still achieve their dreams, too. Pete's father had been right after all. He *was* somebody. To the boys who'd nearly lost everything during the war, Pete Gray was as large, as strong and as powerful as Hank Greenberg.

Watching Pete inspire the wounded kids made Luke Sewell feel insignificant. He decided he had to keep getting Pete Gray into games, even if the Browns didn't win the pennant, even if they kept losing 1-run games, even if the rest of the players thought it was Pete's fault, even if the crowds dried up, and even if Pete couldn't handle the good fastball. He meant too much to too many people. Luke told *The Sporting News,* "So much fuss has been made over Gray that he'd have to be as good as Babe Ruth to live up to what people expect of him." Sewell watched in admiration as Pete met with one wounded soldier after another. Another reporter decided to ask Luke what he thought about Pete Gray now. The real answer was Luke didn't know how Pete was so good at comforting so many boys damaged in so many different ways. In his slow Southern drawl, Luke said, "He's a fine ballplayer, fast and courageous."

For the rest of the season, Sewell always made sure Pete had time for the wounded soldiers who came to the ballparks to seek him out. Luke thought Pete got along better with wounded boys than he did with the other ballplayers anyhow. So the wounded came in droves, bearing physical and psychological scars that somehow only Pete could help heal. They whispered in his ear and Pete kept their secrets. Before a game against the Indians, a boy who had been wounded in Germany asked to meet him. The boy was sad and crying. He couldn't imagine living his life with one arm. Pete met with him privately for an hour before the game and told him never to quit. He said the only way to survive was to never surrender. Then he hugged the boy and signed a ball for him.

One after another that season, the wounded boys, missing arms and legs, on crutches or in wheelchairs, flocked to meet Pete, who took them all in, far from the eyes of his teammates. The Brownies wondered why he never spoke and never smiled, why he kept to himself, why he drank so frequently and so heavily. They never stopped to think how Pete carried so many secrets of so many boys who had bits and pieces of them blown off. He was their guy and he thought he owed it to those kids.

Pete's playing time diminished, but the endless stream of wounded soldiers never did. Everyone was worried about what kind of ballplayer Hank Greenberg was going to be when he rejoined the Tigers, but did anybody stop to ask what kind of men these broken boys would grow up to be? Nobody asked what kind of ballplayer Pete Gray was going to be after the war. By the time the Tigers played the Browns, Pete hit safely in four of five previous games, collecting multiple hits each time, including another 3-hit game. He went 9-for-21, batting .428 in that span, raising his season average to .256. But even though Sewell gained a new measure of respect for Gray, he still didn't think he could play every day. Pete went 0-for-his-next 8. A few days later he was on the bench and his slow decline into misery began.

One arm or not, he was still a proud ballplayer, and never once had he been hitting as low as .234 on July 1. The hits wouldn't come, but the poor, wounded kids did. Pete never turned them away, but soon their combat stories became his. As he shut down teammates, his pride was further wounded when Sewell took to using second baseman Don Gutteridge, a career infielder, in left field. Pete had nowhere to turn. He blocked out his teammates and thought umpires had it in for him. Every ballplayer thought the 1945 strike zone was complete horseshit, but only Pete thought it had been made that way especially for him.

Pete complained in the papers. He said he was mad at himself for not hitting, but he was equally mad and insulted by Sewell playing an infielder in his outfield spot. Pete didn't want to bunt for hits, but he resented how infielders around the league crowded him anyway. Even if he made it clear that he was swinging away, the corner infielders still played in on him, which deeply insulted him. They were telling Pete, *You can't hit it past me you goddamned freak,* and that ran against every motivation Pete gave every wounded kid.

Finally, Pete asked if he was worth a damn at all. "I wonder if the Browns regret that they purchased me, though I know I have done them good at the gate," he said. He couldn't tell anymore. In helping boys find peace, he lost himself. He didn't know if the fans only liked him out of pity. The only people Pete knew for sure really loved and respected him were the wounded boys, whose secrets and horrors he collected throughout the summer. "If I couldn't make those catches, I wouldn't be out there," he said. "I never would have got my chance to play big league ball." He questioned his worth, even as the wounded thought he was the most valuable player they had ever seen.

Worse, a scouting report on Pete was getting around the league. He was a fastball hitter because he lacked the top hand. He couldn't control the bat enough to adjust to the harder breaking ball. That weakness had never been exploited in the minor leagues, where the stuff wasn't as good. But the big leagues are a vicious place for a ballplayer—every hitter has a flaw, a hole in his swing, and it will be discovered and mercilessly attacked. Pete lacked what he needed in order to adjust. He knew he couldn't hit the good breaking ball, like the one Hal Newhouser threw. He couldn't hit the best pitches because he only had one arm.

Pete could do nothing to fix that. He couldn't will himself to have two hands to be able to slow down the barrel of the bat, to wait that extra moment for the curveball to finish breaking. Pete had no choice. He could only hit one way, fast and aggressively, all-in, no doubts, and the strength of his character could not overcome this weakness. He was a smart ballplayer and knew he couldn't stay here now—not from a lack of effort, not from a lack of smarts—but because he was an amputee. That killed him, tormented him, and drove him to drink, pushed him to solitude. Only a ballplayer devoted to the craft for years can understand the torment Pete felt. All he could do was make the most of the rest of his season. When he heard Hank Greenberg was back in the lineup, Pete hoped Hank could do what he could not—hit the way he always wanted to in the big leagues. Hell, someone ought to be able to. Until Pete got the bat going again, no matter how many wounded soldiers he helped feel better, he just didn't feel better about himself as a major league hitter. He started to wonder how much longer it would be until the Browns released him.

Ah, for the summer of 1945, the only time in baseball history when professional ballplayers longed to hear their names and the word *released* in the same sentence. Usually when a guy got released, he was out of his baseball job; but this summer, *released* usually meant from the Army, which meant a guy could hurry back to baseball. Yesterday's heroes were coming back to town, and in the early days of Hank's return, legions of fans flocked to Briggs Stadium to see him play again for what felt like the first time.

Not many people wanted to know all about Hank's time in China and India, which was fine by him. It was one thing if another serviceman who had been in a forward area asked. Hank could easily have that conversation as one soldier to another, not as a star ballplayer to an ordinary fan.

When kids asked him what he did during the war, it was another altogether different question. Kids who grew up during the war knew guys like Hank, Joe D, Teddy Ballgame, Rapid Robert, and Stan the Man were off in the Army or Navy. But they actually thought those guys were doing the shooting. Hank always demurred. Yes, he had served, but many men were braver than he was. He wasn't ashamed to say that. In fact, if people never mentioned to him ever again that he had been in the service, he wouldn't have minded one bit.

Hank could do no wrong in front of these fans. In his first five starts, he went 6-for-21, batting .286. The duel between rookie Boo Ferriss and Greenberg captivated the public's fancy because both players were freshly released from the Army Air Corps. Three of Hank's 6 hits were home runs, two against a pair of good right-handed pitchers, Ferriss of the Red Sox and ace Hank Borowy of the Yankees, another sign that the old bat speed was returning. "GREENBERG GIVES NEW FLAG PUNCH TO TIGERS," *the Sporting News* headline shouted, alongside a cartoon showing a stretched-thin "GREENBERG THAT WAS" bridging a chasm to "GREENBERG TODAY." The Tigers were in first place as they embarked on Hank's first Eastern road trip, heading to Boston, New York, Washington, and Philadelphia. The first few days, Hank was surviving on adrenaline. Now, he had to survive the rigors of the road and the blistering East Coast heat.

The roadie got off to a rocky start. Doubt crept in at Fenway Park, where Hank went 1-for-10 and looked bad at the plate. The Red Sox fans cheered for him, but didn't want to see him hit against their Sox. They got their wish. Facing Ferriss again, Hank was overmatched and couldn't deliver with the game on the line. The Red Sox beat the Tigers 5–1 on July 13, with Ferriss improving his league-leading record to 15-2. Hank grounded out, struck out, hit into a double play, and struck out again in the ninth inning. Some of the writers wanted to know if Captain Greenberg was embarrassed to have been struck out twice by Private Ferriss. "Greenberg took the generous viewpoint that no personal affront was intended," *The Detroit News* noted. The following day, Fenway Park was nearly empty. Hank was hitless, the pitching-strapped Tigers were flat, and the Red Sox fans didn't seem to love the wartime aggregation of players named Johnson, Metkovich, and Tobin as much as they loved Williams, Pesky, and DiMaggio.

Next it was on to Yankee Stadium. The Tigers and the Yankees had developed a healthy hatred in the war years. Hal Newhouser wanted to shove the ball down their throats, but Steve O'Neill wouldn't dare let him pitch in that ballpark with the short right-field porch. Newhouser was older, but not always all grown-up. His baby daughter, Charlene, was the unofficial team mascot, but when it came to running the mouth, she was a peach compared to her daddy's screech. "I hope the Tigers finish first, but if we don't, I hope the New York Yankees won't win the pennant," he said. "Nobody likes them. They walk with the swagger as if they were something special."

There was nothing special about Hank's at-bats at Yankee Stadium, which Newhouser called "the softest park in the league, where a bloop fly ball to right field is likely to fall into the stands for a home run." They didn't call the joint the House That Ruth Built for nothing. Hank's first regular-season appearance there since 1940 was bigger news than General Eisenhower's recent visit to the Polo Grounds, where Ike showed up in his customary uniform, had a few snacks, and declared, "God, it's swell to be back," before it started to rain so badly that he ran for cover. The Yankees, 2½ games out of first place, drew 40,808 fans to the cold and wet misery. The locals saw it as a showdown series, but Hank's comeback meant more than the pennant race. The Stadium was not the splendid palace Hank remembered. The ballpark had become run-down during the war. The war had decimated the talent of the Yankees, too, but the new owners, who'd bought the team in January, promised to change that when the war ended.

You couldn't have a postwar boom without starting a new Yankee dynasty. Since taking power in January, Larry MacPhail had begun plotting the resurgence. The first step was getting DiMaggio back from the Army and into baseball shape. The Yankees were also ready to spend lavishly on repopulating their farm system, with an emphasis on buying the best young talent available. The plan was simple. They would find the next DiMaggio and build many pennant winners around him. The boy was out there somewhere. They just had to find him.

The Yankees already had a good number of kids coming back after the war and knew where to begin hunting anew. The farm director, George Weiss, called the shots. Someday, they would need to find the right manager for all that new talent, but first things first: painting the ballpark when the war was over and slapping brand-new advertisements all over the place so it didn't look like such a dump.

MacPhail was ready to be the biggest star in town, but he didn't anticipate how much the money behind him wouldn't like his being the center of attention. When Del Webb and Dan Topping put out the nearly $3 million to buy the team in January, it was clear that the war had made their purchase possible. *The New York Times* hailed their arrival, writing, "The New York Yankees, mightiest of all baseball empires, have a new emperor or emperors. This undoubtedly is the most momentous happening sports has had in decades."

That might have been an overstatement, but in New York City people couldn't wait to have the Yankees ruling the roost again. With Hank and the Tigers in town, the fans would take what they could get. Steady rain pelted the proceedings, but the umpires insisted the teams play despite horrendous conditions, which Hank thought was kind of stupid, and he wasn't the only one. "The field was a sea of mud," the *New York Daily Mirror* reported. "The pitchers, unable to work off the mound, almost slipped on every pitch they made. No one can recall when a game was played on a field in such poor condition."

The Yankees out-sloshed the Tigers, 5–4. The wet weather didn't help Hank any. The misery and knots built up in his legs and he went hitless. The second game was mercifully canceled. The *Daily Mirror* was appalled at the "conditions as miserable as ever have been experienced in the major league history of this city."

Determined to make good in front of his hometown fans, Hank wasted no time. In his first at bat the next day, he doubled to spark a 4-run first inning, leading the Tigers to a 9–4 victory to snap a 4-game losing streak. The double was a booming drive into the center-field cemetery, out where the monuments rested. That was a Greenberg gunshot like the ones the fans remembered, that big, loud, explosive crack of the bat. "It was the first time since the Tigers left Detroit that Greenberg's swing has been suggestive of years when he was the leading slugger of the American League," *The New York Times* suggested.

Hank started to feel a little more confident with the bat, but he wasn't ready to call himself all the way back. He realized he was playing ball in

an era unlike any other the game had known. If he wasn't the same, neither was anyone else. That would even the playing field at least for a little
while. He took into consideration all the variables and decided, "Most of
those who went into service are younger than I am. Maybe I have an edge
on the average in the matter of condition. I was always what they call a
'clean liver.' But almost all ballplayers have good physical habits, and a lot
of them in the Army and Navy have had a chance to play ball regularly in
the service, which I didn't."

Hank thought, "Most of the boys coming back will do all right for
themselves," but nobody could predict how long it would take for each
player or how rusty they would be. When the Yankee fans saw Red Ruffing, the former pitching ace recently discharged from the Army, they
were shocked at how much weight he'd gained. Nonetheless, they rose to
their feet to welcome home their long-lost hero, in his first game back
since he pitched against the Cardinals in the 1942 World Series. Ruffing
was so eager to get back into a game that he went up as a pinch hitter and
delivered a single.

The New York fans, a lot of them soldiers and sailors mixed in with
the civilians, alternated between cheering loudly for Hank and rambunc-
tiously for Red. The crowd "cheered these two Army vets to the echo," *The
New York Times* reported, roaring with "impartiality that was a testimonial to the individual popularity of yesterday's baseball heroes. There was
a strong sense the fans were cheering for the war to end."

Hank was feeling better, but he admitted he wasn't having much fun.
He'd never felt so slow in his life. He told writer John Lardner, "It will be
August before I or anybody else can be sure how well I'll come back. I never
figured I would come away from years of layoff with no baseball at all and
start right in to bust the pitching all over the lot. On the whole I'm well
satisfied, and nothing essential seems to be lost. My eyes are all right and
my legs do everything I ask them to. My timing will improve. It's just a
matter of playing as much as possible." Hank wondered if there was enough
season left for him to get good enough, fast enough, to be the difference
maker everyone wanted him to be.

The funny thing was, while people were waiting for Hank to hit bombs,
they were missing the point. On July 16, it seemed strangely fitting that
the Tigers were in New York when the Manhattan Project concluded. Hank

got 2 hits that day, including the double, but the big explosion was the top-secret detonation of the world's first atomic bomb, in White Sands, New Mexico. The Trinity test resulted in an explosion with the power of twenty kilotons of TNT. James F. Byrnes, the man baseball owners had so angered in the winter by protesting the work-or-fight mandate, was now secretary of state under President Truman. He hand delivered the message to Truman at the Potsdam Conference. The atomic age arrived the summer Hank Greenberg returned, hushed up amid all the news of baseball's strangest pennant race of the war.

The Tigers left New York in first place, but they looked like the worst first-place team anyone had ever seen. After an off day, they steamed into sweltering Griffith Stadium in Washington, DC, where the second-place Senators were waiting to trim that lead. Of all the places Hank wanted to see when he came home from the Army, this place was not at the top of the list. The Senators had a long history of being world-class Jew baiters. All that old stuff that Hank thought people would have moved past because of Nazi Germany? Nope, the Senators were still good at calling Hank Greenberg a Jew bastard. He hated the Senators and they hated him, and neither time nor distance had done anything to ease the mutual dislike. The Senators were right in the thick of the pennant race, and if there was one thing Hank didn't like the idea of, it was of not only losing the pennant, but losing it to these guys.

The other Tigers were well aware that the Senators hated Hank and called him names, and that only furthered their resolve to beat the Senators badly. When you wanted a pitcher to drive a dagger into another team's heart and then twist it around for fun, you wanted Hal Newhouser on the mound. He hated the heat, but he hated the Senators even more. He pitched a messy complete game where he walked more guys (6) than he struck out (4) and gave up 7 hits. He ran his record to 14-6, burying his head in a cold towel between innings, and beating pitcher Mickey Haefner, the minuscule, five-foot-eight lefty nicknamed Supermouse. The Tigers swept the doubleheader when Al Benton, who rushed back from his broken leg to pitch in July, won his second start in four days to up his record to 8-1, lower his earned run average to 0.93, and somehow draw comparisons to 1914 vintage Walter Johnson, the long-ago pitching ace of the Senators.

Hank had a tough time in the heat in those first few weeks back. He tried to pace and save himself, usually playing only one game if a double-header was scheduled. While the Tigers were in town, a small group of players, including Hank, visited Walter Reed Army Hospital. The soldiers naturally gravitated toward him. Hank talked with all of them, but he always bonded best with the boys who had been in the CBI. Sometimes people would ask him what the soldiers told him. Hank, like Pete Gray, never told anyone what the soldiers confided in him.

If playing one doubleheader in the heat and humidity wasn't bad enough, how about another one the next day? The Tigers were gassed out, swept by the Senators, losing to knuckleball pitchers Dutch Leonard and Roger Wolff, scoring only 4 runs in two games, peeling the lead back to 3 games again. Clark Griffith wanted to win the pennant, but he was asking an awful lot of his pitching staff. He was so worried about having enough pitching to win that the first time Harry Truman came to a Senators game, Griffith told him, "If I have nine pitchers this season, I'll be tickled to death."

One thing the wartime Washington Senators did impacted baseball long after the fighting ended. In search of ballplayers who could not be touched by the military draft, Clark Griffith turned to his favorite scout, Joe Cambria. "Papa Joe" was a little Sicilian who liked big cigars and wore a bright white fedora and a linen suit that gave him the look of an antiquities buyer roaming the streets of Cairo. He was also a world-class player runner, a man who knew talent and where to find it, where to hide it and where to buy it. During the war, he was the first "superscout" employed by a major league team to colonize a Latin country for the good of an American baseball team.

Cambria told Griffith something extraordinary: if he was willing to scout in Cuba, Cambria promised that he would find so many good ballplayers that he could replace this broken-down group of wartime guys with young, strong, fresh kids. Cambria spoke about Cuban baseball in loving terms, as if he were a great explorer who had discovered a rich land. Cuba had so many ballplayers, Cambria promised, that they were as plentiful as white sands on the beach.

And there were more promised lands, Cambria vowed. Thanks to the war, and the many outposts of the American Navy throughout the Caribbean, the natives were playing baseball more than ever before. He reported to Griffith that ballplayers were to be found not only in Cuba but also in

Puerto Rico, Venezuela, Mexico, and even the Dominican Republic, all countries where Negro League ballplayers had played winter ball for years. Cambria promised he could get a jump on the competition if Griffith let him. He had few competitors, and only one he was worried about, Alex Pompez. Pompez knew his way around the sandlots of Cuba as well as he knew his way around the Polo Grounds and the streets of Harlem.

All successful scouts are greedy. As cunning as Cambria had been in sending players to Griffith, he wanted to get more of them. He believed the Latin pipeline and the future of baseball went through his sources in Cuba. Cambria had a large network of birddog scouts who told him where all the good young players were coming up. In turn, he maintained a long follow list of players he wanted to see. One of the players on his follow list in 1945 would undoubtedly have been Orestes Miñoso, a teenager who could really swing the bat. But Cambria couldn't get him off the island and lost him to Pompez, who imported him to America a year after the war to play for his New York Cubans, who played right under the nose of the New York Giants.

Even though Griffith employed a steady stream of Cuban players during the war and continued the tradition of the first half of the century of major league teams' using a handful of light-skinned Latin players, the war allowed him to make his greatest breakthrough, but also his largest mistake. Griffith liked the Cuban ballplayers, but the problem with most of them was that they were too black. Not just black like the Negroes in the States, but dark, dark black. Griffith didn't really like that. He knew he couldn't sneak those guys into games even if he gave them phony names, falsified passports, lied about their ages, and claimed that he found them in Mexico. The other owners would never allow it. Besides, if his ballplayers didn't like Hank Greenberg because he was a Jew, then they probably didn't like Pete Gray because he had one arm, and so it was hard to imagine they would get along with a dark-skinned ballplayer. Griffith wasn't going to spend any more money on new players, so he would win the '45 race with what he had or not at all. Scouts like Cambria and Pompez argued that the wartime manpower crisis could have been solved by bringing Latin players to the mainland. Even though that didn't happen often, the idea migrated to organized baseball after the war.

Before and during the war, Cambria sent a slew of Latin American ballplayers to the Senators. Most of the players didn't add up to much, but a few signaled the future. Right-handed pitcher Alex Carrasquel was the best of them. A Venezuelan who came up in 1939 and was never touched by the services, he won 33 games over four wartime seasons. Infielder Gil Torres, a Cuban who came up in 1940 and was the prototypical flashy fielder who couldn't hit, was an everyday player for two years. Jose Zardon, another Cuban, spent the 1945 season plugging the outfield. Other Cuban ballplayers were on the Senators during the war years, men with names that sounded as strange to white kids in 1945 as the name Greenberg sounded in 1935.

Griffith also recognized that the few Cubans he had on the team didn't get along with the white guys. There were rumors of clubhouse tension, but nothing leaked into the press. He hoped it stayed that way. Griffith had been around the game long enough to know that his team's clubhouse was a ticking time bomb, and when it went off, he knew his only solution would be to side with his white players. So even as baseball struggled with what to do with black players when the war was over, a whole other issue took shape. What to do with the Latin players? They were coming, too. Once more, the war had made baseball change, and baseball made the country change.

Griffith was far more concerned with holding off the Tigers. He was only trying to fill his roster during the war, not revolutionize the game. But he inadvertently started the pendulum moving forward. The pipeline built by men like Cambria and Pompez created the future. World War II made the Latin American ballplayer a vital part of the American baseball industry. Old Judge Landis would have disdained this world, but his ashes were buried for good.

When the Tigers were in town, another war-vet ballplayer was out on the field in the early-morning sunlight looking for the man he used to be. Buddy Lewis was back in town, and it seemed as if only yesterday he'd been buzzing the ballpark in his Gooney bird on the way to the war. When Hank first saw him, he probably wasn't as shocked as other players were to discover that the hair that was blond before the war was now gray. Buddy was only twenty-eight years old, but his temples sported streaks of silver. Hank and Buddy had a lot in common and much to discuss. Buddy had been released from the Air Corps and felt all the same aches and pains Hank first felt when he started working out again every day. They were both vets of the CBI and knew all about things people at home didn't hear about, and certainly things the guys who stayed at home to play ball during the war couldn't fathom. Their war was larger in the sheer quantity of humanity than was Western Europe, but paled in comparison to the attention the war against Germany received. Back home in baseball, it was easy for Hank and Buddy to relive the old times that already felt distant yet were still so near. They had each other because the other players couldn't possibly understand tales that they knew from the Flying Tigers pilots or the B-29 crews; or from the British and American commandos in Burma; or of the Japanese looting of India's and Asia's cultural heritage that was every bit as disgusting as the Nazi thefts across Europe. The war Hank and Buddy lived was a dirty one, waged by peasants and professional soldiers alike, where a mule or an ox could mean as much and do more than a tank or a jeep. It was their war, their special piece of this special hell, and they had the gray hairs, the mud on their boots, and the blisters on their batting hands to show for it. Buddy missed flying, but he missed baseball more, and he was happy to never again risk his life flying the Hump as one of the proud Dumb Bastards of the Assam Trucking Company.

Buddy had seen all sorts of stuff he never wanted to think about again—the crazy Chinese soldiers wrestling each other and throwing themselves out of the windows of the planes for sport, the Flying Dumbos and Gooney birds with only a tommy gun or a Browning automatic rifle for protection jumped by Japanese fighters, and the charts marked by little black crosses where flight crews had died. Buddy was as proud of his flying numbers as he was of his baseball stats. He finished with 1,800 hours, 600 combat hours, 392 sorties, and a Distinguished Flying Cross.

But as in the old airman's drinking song from the First World War, all Buddy Lewis wanted to do was take the cylinder out of his kidneys, the connecting rod out of his brain, the crankshaft out of his back, and assemble the engine again. "I'm like a colt loose in the pasture," he said, yet Buddy was learning the hard way, as Hank was, that his body could not yet perform quite as well as his mind remembered. "I forget that I'm almost twenty-nine and not the kid of twenty-five who left here four years ago," he said. The best part about getting out of the service for the ballplayers who had been in for so long was just getting out. The worst part was realizing that some things on the baseball field would never feel exactly the same again. Their payment was their war memories and a strong sense of accomplishing something greater than baseball.

A rumor was going around that after the season, a tour of major leaguers would visit forward areas in the Pacific. When Buddy heard, he volunteered to fly the transport. Bert Shepard, Buddy's new teammate, who recently made news when he rounded the bases on his artificial leg in nineteen seconds, said he would be happy to fly fighter escort. He hoped to finally play in a major league game, but he considered himself the outsider. Hank and Buddy were the true big leaguers, the guys who belonged here. Bert Shepard was just happy to be here and wasn't at all angry when he realized that he would be gone when the war was over. All he wanted was just one game, one inning, one moment. He didn't want to make history, just peace. He never made noise, preferring to wait for the opportunity to be presented. He didn't like to ask and he wasn't going to complain if nobody wanted him to pitch. And, hey, he got to meet Hank Greenberg. That was a nice perk.

As for Hank, he was always happy and fascinated to hear from other ballplayers back from the war. His lifelong fascination with the war was beginning, but he just wanted his body to stop hurting. The problem was the damn schedule was a killer. It was one doubleheader after another, and when it was just supposed to be one 9-inning game, sometimes the game just wouldn't end. Hank got a break a day later in Philadelphia, when the Tigers and the Athletics played the second-longest game in major league history, trapped in a 24-inning purgatory resulting in a 1–1 tie called because of darkness and because Connie Mack was too cheap to turn on the lights at Shibe Park. That was wartime ball at its best (or worst?). Play forever and nobody wins. Tigers pitcher Les Mueller threw 19⅔ innings. Mueller said his arm felt fine after the game, but the former soldier with the bad headaches was never the same again. Four pitchers threw all the innings. Russ Christopher started and pitched 13 innings, allowing 1 run. The appropriately nicknamed "Jittery" Joe Berry followed with 11 shutout relief innings. The game was a bloodbath for batting averages and self-esteem. A bunch of guys went 1-for-10 or 2-for-10, but no hitter took it on the chin worse than young George Kell. The twenty-two-year went 0-for-10 (though he only struck out once), the kind of game that makes young hitters hate and curse the sport. Kell recovered in time, though. Connie Mack sold him to the Tigers a few years later, where he became a Hall of Fame third baseman.

Hank sat on the bench resting his bones and wondering how in the hell baseball came to this. He got only one at bat and walked. The game went seventeen consecutive scoreless innings before it was mercifully halted. A guy had to ask how the Tigers were going to have enough pitching to win if a guy like poor Les Mueller could be thrown on the sacrificial altar of pitching almost 20 innings in one day. It bordered on stupidity, even in the days when pitchers were supposed to finish what they started. If the Tigers needed an extra arm, they could have signed Satchel Paige, who that day pitched for the Kansas City Monarchs in a Negro American League game back at Briggs Stadium in Detroit. But that wasn't going to happen, and, well, if a club had a Hall of Fame arm pitching in its front yard and didn't want to sign him because of the color of his skin, they didn't deserve him anyhow.

Assuming the players actually got some sleep after 24 innings, they were back at Shibe Park the following day for (you guessed it) another doubleheader. Hal Newhouser did what an ace does, winning his 15th game, with a 4-hitter, walking 1 and striking out 8 tired Philadelphia Athletics. Ever the gent looking to raise a few bucks, Connie Mack begged Hank to play both games of the doubleheader so he could draw a crowd. Hank said, don't push it, old man. He only played in the first game and couldn't buy a hit, but a crowd of 20,341, a great haul for cheap Connie, did buy tickets. Mr. Mack got his profits, his pitchers shut down Hank, and his club split the doubleheader. Maybe it wasn't quite as nice as when President Roosevelt sent him a happy eightieth-birthday telegram urging him, "Long may your scorecard wave—FDR," but it was pretty darn close. For his part, Hank felt like a slow ox churning through the Chinese mud.

The road-trip workload crushed the Tigers. They also had to play an exhibition against the Navy team. The Tigers were starting to think that they knew how the guys on the Bataan Death March felt. Wartime ballplayers were baseball wage slaves who had no recourse over their masters. The final bill was enough to make a guy cringe. The Tigers played 67 innings in four days, not including the game against the Navy team.

Perhaps, in his offices in Philadelphia a few blocks from Shibe Park, a young labor attorney named Marvin Miller took note of what in hindsight would be viewed as egregious abuse of employees. In the coming decades, he helped the players form a union to fight against the mentality the owners fostered during World War II. But nobody knew at the time that the man who would be so instrumental in creating a union and free-agency rights was a few blocks away from the most tired, exhausted, and worn-out batch of wartime ballplayers anyone had ever seen. In games like this, it was tough to argue with the old Nazi propaganda line that slavery existed in America because of the way major league teams were able to treat players. The old model never went away; it just migrated to the minor leagues and lasted well into the next century.

The owners, including Connie Mack and Clark Griffith, never knew what they were creating in the summer of 1945 when they pushed their players like the mule and the ox on the Burma Road, hiding behind the war to abuse their players, to wear them down like poor Les Mueller's right shoulder, depressing their value and making them interchangeable. Modern ballplayers should never forget to look back before they look ahead.

The Tigers had a hard time not looking back at the standings, losing 8 of 12 on the road trip, earning the dubious nickname of the "winless wonders." Their lead was still 2½ games over the Senators, but it wasn't safe. This pennant race was indeed a death march. It wasn't the traditional race in which the strongest team was going to win. It was a matter of which team wouldn't break down first. Hank felt awful. He hated looking at his numbers during the trip. He looked like a busher who couldn't do anything to stem the tide of this slog, hitting only .187 on the road trip, 6-for-32 with no home runs. His season average tumbled to .226. A guy hated to say it, but that was Pete Gray territory. When a recently discharged Fifth Army dough was asked what he thought of Hank's comeback, he sheepishly said, "He looks the same as ever. Well, almost the same."

July ground to a close as the Tigers limped home, hanging on to first place, though they were hardly playing like champions. They were a circus of bad baserunning, bad fielding, injuries, and war vets trying to figure out which end of the bat was up. The league was full of screwed-up teams, so being in first place just meant the club was slightly less screwed up than the others. On the bright side, Hal Newhouser always pitched better when the Tigers were struggling. He won his 16th game when the Tigers returned home to play the White Sox and was really rolling now. He had great stuff and always something to prove. Had he been pitching for a club in the peacetime years, he might well have 20 wins, steamrolling to 30. But this was still a war year, and nothing played true.

Hank thought Newhouser's transformation from bratty prodigy to ace was greatly impressive. Before the war he was an immature kid. Now he was a young man possessing command of his emotions and stuff. The fans thought Hank was the key to the pennant, but Hank thought otherwise. Hal Newhouser was the single most important player in the American League, but the Tigers couldn't ask him to do it all. They needed help.

The good news was that another reinforcement was on the way. News broke that pitcher Virgil Trucks, a young, hard-throwing right-hander who was just coming into his own before the Navy took him away, was on his way back from Great Lakes Naval Station, hopefully in time to pitch before the end of the season.

The war against Japan seemed to be hopefully coming to an end in July. *The Detroit News* published an aerial photo of 176 B-17 bombers lined up wingtip to wingtip in Munich, like crosses in a cemetery. A squad of Michigan Marines were shown inspecting idiot sticks, the six-foot, sharpened bamboo spears rigged to look like rifles, which were carried by banzai chargers on Okinawa who were mowed down by the Marines. The B-29 firebombing raids on Japan continued daily, where a young boy, Sadaharu Oh, who grew up to hit more home runs than Henry Aaron or Babe Ruth, remembered being terrified at the sight of the big, silver bombers overhead. But despite the terror to the civilians, no amount of firepower from this endless summer of attrition changed the emperor's mind or seemed to deter his subjects from fighting on.

When a war correspondent for *Yank* magazine interviewed Japanese prisoners of war in the Philippines, he sought to understand the psychology behind their refusal to surrender. For the Japanese, surrender was a disgrace. For the Americans, the game seemed to be over. The reporter, with his translator, spoke to a sailor and surprisingly found baseball was a window into his thoughts:

Q: Why will Japan win the war?
A: Japan has never lost a war. She cannot be beaten.

Q: Do you think Japan can beat America at sports?

A: Yes.

Q: How about baseball. Didn't the Americans beat your pants off a few years ago?

A: You mean for the highest score, yes.

Q: You mean America didn't beat you?

A: Yes, Japan won. You got the high score, but there are more important things. Your players are not honorable.

Baseball, which had been a wartime escape, was now caught up in waiting for the war to end. Sure, it was nice to still have baseball, but even the fans who loved it were starting to think this had gone on long enough. If it was this bad in 1945, and there was an invasion, would baseball be worth playing in 1946? People loved the game and this was a symbol of what people were fighting for, but at some point, somebody has got to make baseball look like baseball. "With Greenberg and DiMaggio back in uniform, the American League would begin to look like its old self—and just in time, if you ask me," John Lardner wrote.

But other signs showed that the baseball business thought the war would soon be over, especially on July 27 when the Yankees shockingly sold pitcher Hank Borowy to the Cubs for the astounding sum of $97,000. That was by far the biggest monetary deal of the war years, and it proved that the teams who were claiming to be so desperate to stay in business weren't cash poor at all. Players wondered the obvious question: If the club says they can't pay any more each year, why can they drop one hundred grand at the drop of a hat?

Clark Griffith felt betrayed. Borowy passed through waivers, but no American League club claimed him until it was his team's turn to purchase the option. Griffith thought he was through spending for the season, but the opportunity to purchase a frontline staring pitcher in a pennant race almost never occurred. He was ready to spend handsomely, but Yankees GM Larry MacPhail sold the pitcher to the Cubs instead for less than Griffith would have paid, just so Griffith couldn't have the pitcher who might well have helped the Senators overtake the Tigers.

The deal said so much about the inner workings of baseball. Despite their pleas of poverty and how difficult it was to operate during the war, it was still very much business as usual. The owners were still making a ton of money and telling the players they were broke. This was the baseball oligarchy. Besides, MacPhail was the new guard and Griffith was the old. MacPhail wasn't going to help the Senators just because they were in the American League. No, he was going to bury the old man with his memories.

When the Yankees sold Borowy to the first-place Cubs, they also made it that much harder for the second-place Cardinals to catch them. Reading between the lines, the Yankees had exacted another measure of revenge on the Cardinals for beating them in the 1942 World Series and spoiling their last good wartime club. The Cubs ended the month with their best team in years getting the job done, leading the Cardinals and surprising the Dodgers by 6 games each. Adding Borowy, a sturdy, innings-eating, right-handed starter, was a boon for the Cubs, who were worried about Billy Southworth's team catching them from behind.

Larry MacPhail showed another side of his abrasive personality when he tore the respected pitcher apart on the way out the door, telling the press that Borowy was a terrible competitor who didn't know how to win, even though he led the Yankees with 10 victories. In this move of Yankee arrogance, they thought they were better off without a pitcher who'd won 56 games during the war. MacPhail took some of the money from the Borowy sale and hired scout Tom Greenwade away from the Brooklyn Dodgers, enticing him with a lucrative raise. Greenwade lived in Missouri and had birddogs everywhere, even out in Oklahoma, where one schoolboy athlete named Mickey Charles Mantle was a year away from starting high school, and a good young ballplayer could always be hoodwinked for cheap. The next Joe D was out there somewhere, and the moment MacPhail sold Borowy and used some of the cash to hire Greenwade, the Yankees came one step closer to their postwar dynastic dreams.

Some little moments were worth more than words. In the top of the eighth inning at Fenway Park on July 28, Buddy Lewis stepped into the box to face rookie right-hander Jim Wilson. It was Buddy's second game back and he was looking for his first hit. Finally he saw a pitch he recognized and reached. He put the bat on the ball and pushed a single into right field for his first major league hit since he doubled on September 28, 1941, at Yankee Stadium, nearly four years and about forty thousand miles ago.

He stood on the bag and took it all in. The Boston fans gave him a nice cheer. First baseman Dolph Camilli shook his hand. Both benches stood on the top step of their dugouts and applauded. Buddy was gray around the edges, but he still had that little-kid grin. He blushed and tipped his cap.

Some games felt so good that four years and forty thousand miles couldn't take the fun away. On the final day of July, the Tigers were at home to play the Browns. The pitching matchup, Hal Newhouser against Sig Jakucki, was a sign of the times. It was the wartime ace versus the wartime replacement. The alcoholic almost beat the ace. Jack scattered 11 hits in 11 innings, before the Tigers scratched out a run to beat him in the twelfth. Newhouser tied for the league lead with 17 wins and fanned 7 to up his league-leading total to 138 strikeouts. Jack never had great stuff, but he knew how to make it play better than it really was. He was just what Hank needed to help snap his slump.

He got hold of one of Jack's pitches in the second inning, putting a good swing on a ball that carried to deep center field. Hank hoped it would get out of the park because the home-run trot would be easier than running it out, but when the ball got over the center fielder's head, Hank knew he had to run for his life. His teammates egged him on, verbally flogging the big horse like bench jockeys as Hank turned second base, lumbering around the corner like a B-29 making a slow turn. He felt the pinch in his knees and his flat, heavy feet unearthing the infield dirt. The run from second to third felt as if it took forever, but Hank rumbled into the bag like the heavy bombers over Tokyo, landing safely with his first triple since April 1941. He was gassed and catching his breath, his hands at his hips, sucking heavy breaths, but with a huge, amused smile on his face. If the war hadn't killed him, the triple might have.

The Tigers ended the month with a 4-game lead over the Yankees and 5½ over the Senators. Hank, mired in an 8-for-46, .174 slump, thought the triple was a sign that he'd turned the corner. All he wanted to do was lead the Tigers as he always had before the war, when he threw his team over his shoulders and carried them to the finish line. The Tigers were at least succeeding in pushing the Browns out of the race. The Browns faded badly in July, falling into seventh place, 8½ games off the lead. They were disintegrating in every way, worn-out by the stress of knowing they were all mostly 4-F's who were only here as replacements, who would lose their jobs when the war ended. Some of the players were still angry with Pete Gray for no good reason, though he had barely played in July, angry that he kept his roster spot for nothing. Jakucki was a drunk, always bickering and baiting Pete, who jawed back. The bickering was endless, and so was the losing.

Pete began taking stock of what he'd accomplished and what he hoped to finish before the end of the war pushed him out. "I have one more ambition," Pete confided that summer. "I want to hit a big league home run. I'm hopeful I'll stick around for a while, but if I don't, and I hit that home run and I am sent back to the minors, I won't feel too bad. I'll have some pleasant recollections that I can look back on during the rest of my lifetime." When asked if he thought he really could hit that home run, Pete knew it was a long shot, and that broke his heart. "I guess you'll find the answer in my batting average," he said. Pete was hitting .235, but it was actually a lot better than Hank, who was hitting .209.

Pete didn't play at all the last week of the month. He grew more isolated as he played less. He drank more, but so did the rest of the guys. He didn't know that Hank wanted to meet him and see him play for the first time. Hank had been reading about him since Hank was in China. It didn't happen until the next game, when Pete got his first at bat in nine days and grounded out in the ninth inning. Hank saw Pete's struggles and felt for him; he knew what it was like to be the guy with something "wrong" with him. He wanted to walk over and tell him to perk up, but that wouldn't have been right just yet. In time, Hank decided, he would let Pete Gray know what he really thought of him.

CHAPTER 23

No Singing in the Shower

Billy Southworth Sr. was managing his ball club from the third-base coaching box on the night of August 3 at Forbes Field in Pittsburgh. The Cardinals, even without Stan Musial, weren't a bad team, but they were chasing the Chicago Cubs, the hottest team in baseball. The Cubs owned the National League in July, going 26-6, the best record in the league and the best month the Cubs had since winning the 1935 pennant, even bringing back memories of the September they had in 1908 when they wrestled the pennant away from the New York Giants and the Pittsburgh Pirates on the last day of the season.

Billy wondered if these Cardinals had the horses to beat these Cubs. The team just didn't feel the same. Pitcher Mort Cooper, the staff ace of their pennant-winning wartime teams, picked a nasty salary fight with owner Sam Breadon. He wanted a new contract worth $15,000, not the $12,000 he was offered, but the Cardinals weren't giving out any raises. Cooper argued that he deserved to be fairly rewarded. He pitched through immense elbow pain and piled up seasons of 22, 21, and 22 victories during the war. Breadon did not care if Mort Cooper thought he was a successful pitcher. When Cooper finally signed, Breadon punished him for his holdout by selling him to the Boston Braves, the worst team in the National League. Breadon was all too happy to receive $50,000 a few weeks after the start of the season. Cooper was the first big purchase made by Lou Perini, the primary owner of the Braves, who was already thinking about what the country would look like when the war was over. A construction man, he knew about logistics, construction engineering, travel technology, and emerging population markets. He was a Boston man who wanted to bring a winner to the Braves, but if that didn't work, he knew that when the war was over, there must be a move, even if no team had ever moved before, a move west.

Cooper was stunned when he learned he was moving East. He packed his bags and went to Boston, but he was never the same pitcher again. Breadon smiled comfortably. His tactics were a lesson to all his players: they were lucky that he paid them as well as he did, lucky to be major leaguers, and if they dared so much as suggest a contract negotiation, he would banish them, make it hurt, and splurge upon the riches of the player's labor. They should feel honored to be such well-paid slaves.

Billy's smile came by a lot less during the 1945 season. He still gave a good pep talk and his players liked him, but they knew his heart was missing. Billy junior was dead and his body was gone. The war would end, and when it did, his boy would just be another one of the missing that never came home. Billy hated that thought. He had only one wish, and that was to bury his son, his best friend. It haunted him as he managed his team, which was populated by younger players who weren't necessarily ready for the rigors of daily play in even the wartime majors.

Billy's spark plug, outfielder Enos Slaughter, was serving with other major leaguers on the far-flung islands Saipan and Tinian, working on ground crews for the B-29s when not playing baseball to entertain the troops. The ballplayers built their own fields, measured the distances of the bases, and laid down the chalk lines. They even built their own batting cages in an attempt to stay sharp before returning to the majors. It wasn't a stretch to say that the most baseball talent in one place at one time in the last summer of the war was in the Pacific with the B-29s. Slaughter swore that the Japanese troops holed up in the mountain caves used to emerge only to watch the baseball, and that was the only time their snipers weren't shooting.

While Billy was managing the Cardinals in Pittsburgh on August 4, a Saturday day game, a New York police boat discovered human remains in a thousand feet of water off Silver Beach, the Bronx. When the badly decomposed body was pulled from the water, the major's bars were still on the uniform. The dog tags were around what was left of the torso's neck:

SOUTHWORTH, WILLIAM B
0424797

The Cardinals scored 4 runs in the eighth inning to win the game. Billy was in a peppery mood as far as good moods went that summer, especially because rookie Alfred Schoendienst helped win the game with a 2-run pinch-hit single in the decisive rally. Young players always made Billy happy, and helping them develop into major leaguers was one of the few joys he still loved as much as ever. He predicted great things for the young outfielder, though he believed the boy would become a second baseman. Some guys gave the young redhead a hard time for the German surname and his hometown of Germantown, but the freckled boy laughed it off and picked up the nickname Red, for his shiny red mop resembling a victory garden full of carrots.

When Billy came back to the clubhouse in Forbes Field, two telegrams were waiting. One was from the War Department notifying him that his son's body had been found and positively identified. The other was from New York requesting he claim the body. Billy was stunned when he learned that the body was found all the way in Bronx waters. In the seven months Billy junior was missing, his body drifted from Flushing Bay, across the East River, and into the Bronx, about six miles away. The luck was astounding. Of the bodies of five missing aviators, only Billy's was discovered. Were it not for the small strand of Silver Beach, Billy's remains would have drifted into Long Island Sound, then into open sea, lost forever.

The ballplayers were loud and happy in the other room because the Cubs had lost in Cincinnati, cutting a game off their lead. Then, the ballplayers heard a loud, guttural cry from the manager's office and the room went quiet. In a few minutes, everyone knew. The baseball writers covering the game found out first and told the players, who dressed silently. They didn't care one bit about the pennant race anymore. Billy boarded the first flight to New York to claim his boy's body, but before he left, he changed his uniform and took his shower. The writers remembered Billy's old code: whistling a tune for winning, silence for losing. Today there should be whistling, but he did not sing. He sobbed, and his cries filled the silence in the Forbes Field dressing room.

Billy arrived in New York to claim the body. He composed himself and met reporters. Billy was gathered and collected, but distant. His boyishness was gone. "I have hoped and prayed we might recover the body," he said. "Only a parent can understand what it is to know that the body has been found. It gives me great consolation to know that I will be able to lay him to rest. Grim as that satisfaction is, nevertheless it is all I could hope for."

Billy thanked the policemen who discovered the remains and signed the necessary papers. The body was processed through Army graves registration. The casket was loaded into an Air Transport Command C-47 on the tarmac of LaGuardia Field. The big Pratt & Whitney Twin Wasps roared to life, and the Gooney bird taxied into position. Then the captain opened the throttle and the flying hearse lifted into the sky. On the same runway where Billy junior's last landing failed, the wheels went up on his last takeoff, escorted by Billy senior, who sat near the casket in the cargo hold.

On the bumpy flight to Lockbourne Airfield in Columbus, the air crew talked about the war news. The biggest day of the war for the Army Air Corps was right there on the front page of *The New York Times*. Billy senior had to smile. He had to. Maybe he could even laugh through the grief. Somehow, some way, the Southworth boys were together again on the morning of August 6, 1945:

FIRST ATOMIC BOMB DROPPED ON JAPAN

MISSLE IS EQUAL TO 20,000 TONS OF TNT

TRUMAN WARNS FOE OF "RAIN OF RUIN"

The Tigers were in Chicago splitting a doubleheader with the White Sox, and when Hank Greenberg heard, he knew the bomb had to have been dropped by one of the B-29s from his Twentieth Air Force, the fleet he helped get started in Operation Matterhorn. Hank always knew the Air Corps had something big in store, but he didn't know what. He just knew from the silence that they were working on something. Now he knew. From Matterhorn to the Manhattan Project, the news broke with the largest, boldest letters anyone had ever seen printed on the cover of *The Detroit News*.

ATOMIC BOMB
U.S. PULVERIZES JAPAN WITH BOMB
GREATER THAN 20,000 TONS OF TNT

President Truman's statement to the nation was delivered as the C-47 carrying Billy Southworth Jr. and his mourning father home to Columbus was airborne, making the five-hundred-mile haul in about four hours. The words changed history. "It is an atomic bomb," Truman said. "It is a harnessing of the basic power of the universe. The force from which the sun draws its power has been loosed against those who brought war to the Far East."

Even in the moment of the biggest news in history, a little bit of baseball language found its way into Truman's speech. When trying to place the magnitude of the bomb into perspective, he said, "It had more than two thousand times the blast power of the British 'grand slam,' which is the largest bomb ever used in the history of warfare."

Billy didn't know at the time that one of his favorite ballplayers, Enos Slaughter, was with the ground crews with another of the big leaguers serving in the Air Corps, Dario Lodigiani, on Tinian, from where the *Enola Gay*, took off. The ballplayers had been pressed into service and worked hard, refueling B-29s, changing out .50-caliber ammunition, and replacing hydraulic fluid. They would get the planes ready for their missions and watch them take off on their sorties.

Lodigiani never forgot when a few guys in Class A uniforms showed up for no good reason at all. Later, he realized these guys must have been from White Sands. The officers knew who the ballplayers were, and they wanted to give them a hot tip. "This friend of mine says, 'Dario, go out on the flight line this afternoon. History is going to be made.' Well, when you usually saw an officer, you didn't know who the hell he was, because in the war zone they don't wear bars. But these guys all had US on their lapels. We knew something was up. We didn't know it was the *Enola Gay* mission returning from dropping the atomic bomb. It went out before dawn and we saw it come home. When they told us what happened, wow. We knew we were going to get going home pretty quick."

And now, Billy junior was almost home, too. The C-47 landed at Lockbourne, and the body received a military escort. He was buried on August

7, the day after the mushroom cloud. There wasn't much national attention for Billy junior's good-bye, and he would probably have wanted it that way. His funeral got a few inches in the big papers in National League cities, but that was all. The news from a place called Hiroshima was much bigger than that of a former minor leaguer turned bomber pilot.

Six Eighth Air Force veterans served as pallbearers. Billy junior was laid to rest at Green Lawn Cemetery, with full military honors, in a wartime military funeral like thousands of others. Billy senior was presented with the flag from the coffin. There were no flyovers or anything like that. The headstone was adorned with only an Air Corps logo of wings and a propeller, reading:

Billy Brooks Southworth

June 20, 1916   Feb. 15, 1945

Then Billy senior walked away from his son's grave, knowing he would one day be buried alongside him. The war was over for father and son. Billy planned to take a few days with his family in Columbus before he rejoined the Cardinals in New York. The game must go on.

On August 4, the same day Billy Southworth's body was discovered, Bert Shepard's baseball dream finally came true. The Washington Senators were on a 7-game winning streak in which each game's starting pitcher threw a complete game victory, cutting the Tigers lead to 2½ games. Clark Griffith thought his Senators could catch the Tigers, so he pushed his pitchers to the edges of their ability. He had four knuckleballers, and a catcher, Rick Ferrell, who had recently become the all-time games-caught leader. Shepard had pitched an exhibition earlier in the summer against the Brooklyn Dodgers, held his own, and drew a big crowd. But he'd started to doubt if he would ever get the chance to complete his own comeback.

In the second game of a doubleheader against the Boston Red Sox, the Senators were shellacked for 12 runs in the fourth inning. A wartime replacement named Tom McBride drove in 6 runs in the inning. The Senators were losing 14–2 when manager Ossie Bluege decided not to waste another pitcher. It was Shepard's turn to get loose. He was going to pitch. It was the perfect time to use him, mopping up, where he could do no damage no matter what happened. Shepard got loose in a hurry. He could throw with ease and no pain, and he swore the last time he had been so nervous was when he tried out throwing again under the watchful eye of an SS guard with a machine gun. He could hear his heart pounding, but he was ready. Finally, Bluege called for him. Bert's smile could have lit up the Boston skyline. He damn near sprinted to the mound, where Bluege dropped the ball in his hand, patted him on the backside, and told the former fighter pilot to go mow 'em down. Shepard remembered saying to himself, "God-damnit, I'm in the ball game!"

The crowd gave him a hearty welcome. Shepard heated up in a hurry. He was thrown into quite a jam. The bases were loaded again with the Red Sox cleanup hitter, Catfish Metkovich, at the plate. Sure, the game was out of hand, but Bert didn't want to embarrass himself. Metkovich was a solid major league hitter. A lot of rookies might have been nervous, but Shepard was having too much fun. He nibbled and ran the count full. Metkovich was a dead-red fastball hitter, but Shepard knew what he had to do. "I said, 'Hell, now you got to throw the ball over the plate. You don't want to come in here and walk him." Shepard wound up, pushed off the leg the German gunners shot off, and put the fastball where he wanted it. He wasn't over-powering, but he put it in the right spot. Metkovich swung right though it. Strike three! Shepard practically danced off the mound. You'd never know that was an artificial leg under there.

Shepard stayed in that ball game for 5⅓ of the most wonderful innings in his life. He got to face 20 batters and gave up 1 run on 3 hits, walked 1, and struck out 2. He batted 4 times in the game, all against Boo Ferriss, who won his 18th game. Shepard didn't remember too much. "I think I hit a fly ball off him," but he actually walked, struck out, grounded into a double play, and bounced back to Ferriss. When the game was over, Shepard received plenty of congratulations from his teammates, including Buddy Lewis, who played right field that day. The newspapers didn't make a big deal out of Shepard's outing, but it was a momentous occasion in his life. He had lived the full experience of the wartime baseball player. He'd flown fighter planes in combat and he'd pitched in the majors. Most of all, he had lived, he had survived, and the rest of his life was in front of him. What more could he ask for? All it cost was his leg. He would make that trade any day. He could have been Billy Southworth Jr., and he knew it. Instead, he was home. A wire story said, "It was by far the most inspiring performance by a limbless veteran of World War II."

But Shepard knew that once that ball game was over, he was never going to play in the majors again. He was okay with that. "We were fighting for the pennant and we had some pretty good pitchers," he said. "It's hard for the manager to imagine that his best chance of winning is a guy with his leg off. You just can't imagine that. It didn't bother me, but I can see where the other person would have a problem believing that." Bert Shepard's war was over. Two days later, the A-bomb fell, and the end of war arrived for everyone else.

Baseball may have been insignificant, but it still fed people's souls. It was easier to think about baseball than it was to think that one bomb killed eighty thousand people, but might have saved more than a million Japanese and American lives without an invasion. While Truman waited for the Japanese surrender, and just a few pages after the biggest headline in human history, *The Detroit News* was worried about another matter:

WASHINGTON NOW ONLY HALF GAME BEHIND

Everyone was coming after the Tigers. Bob Feller, the best pitcher in baseball before the war, was eager to prove he would be the best when it was over. He spent the summer pitching for the Great Lakes Naval Station. His tour aboard the battleship *Alabama* ended, and now he was chomping at the bit to rejoin the Cleveland Indians. He closely followed the comebacks of Hank Greenberg and Buddy Lewis. Feller respected the replacement players, but he was a realist. He understood their valuable contributions to the morale effort, but a time would come when only talent mattered. He vowed to be ready. His catcher at Great Lakes was Walker Cooper, the All-Star Cardinals catcher, who promised, "He's lost none of his fastball."

The Tigers were trying not to lose their lead. They lost 5 out of 6 games from August 4 to 6, including an embarrassing series against the White Sox. Hank was mired in a 12-for-65 slump in which he was hitting .210. The Tigers limped home in the middle of the night, their lead down to ½ game on August 6, hoping their season wouldn't become the next mushroom cloud of the war. "Because of shameful deeds in Chicago, it was fitting that the Tigers returned home under cover of darkness," The *Detroit News* wrote, under their headline "TIGERS SLINK HOME IN THE DARK." Manager Steve O'Neill grumbled, "I didn't know there were so many ways to blow a ball game."

Hank took it upon himself to get the Tigers right. On August 8, playing the Red Sox in the 21st doubleheader of the season for the Tigers, he finally got it rolling, going 3-for-4 with 2 doubles. Playing in both games of a doubleheader for the first time since he returned, he had another 2 hits. The line drives were starting to come. In the tenth inning, facing Red Sox pitcher Jim Wilson, Hank hit a shot right back at Wilson so hard that the rookie couldn't get his glove up in time. The ball hit Wilson above his right ear, eliciting a sound like a cracking eggshell, dropping him to the ground. He was out cold. Hank ran through the bag and then turned around to see Wilson unconscious. After a long, few tense seconds, Wilson opened his eyes. Hank felt awful, but he was relieved. The last thing he wanted was to come home from the war and kill a kid.

The twenty-three-year-old was taken off the field on a stretcher and brought to Henry Ford Hospital, where X-rays revealed a fractured skull. After the game, Hank went straight to the hospital to check on Wilson. "They told me he could have no visitors now, so I'll wait a day or so until he feels better," Hank said. The people who knew him weren't surprised one bit at Hank's compassion. That's just who he was.

Hank was worried about Wilson the next day, but his swings gave him solace. He collected 3 more hits against the Red Sox, giving him 8 hits in the last three games, and the Tigers won again. As soon as Hank started to hit, so did Rudy York. The troubled slugger, whose power had been absent for much of the season, hit 2 home runs in a game for the first time this season. Detroit could dream again. The lead over the Senators was still only 1 game, but with Hank finding himself, the pennant was possible. *The Detroit News* sensed the excitement, reporting, "After Hank Greenberg returned to the Detroit lineup on July 1, he said that it might take him five or six weeks to regain his batting form. The only thing to do was keep on playing and, eventually, he hoped to be as effective as ever. It seems today that Greenberg had a fair estimate of the time he would need to come back. It also seems today that those who ventured the opinion that Rudy York would begin hitting as soon as Greenberg did, were not far off the line."

Seeing Hank swing the bat so well in Boston gave GM Jack Zeller the confidence he needed to aquire two pitchers off waivers in the next twenty-four hours. He acquired George Caster from the Browns and had to get the consent of six American League clubs before the Browns could officially wave the white flag and sell him to the Tigers. The rest of the teams in the league didn't mind. Everybody seemed to be rooting for Hank and the Tigers. Nobody wanted Clark Griffith to win.

Zeller finished his dealing when he purchased veteran junkballer Jim Tobin from the Boston Braves. Tobin pitched a pair of no-hitters in 1944 (one was a 5-inning no-hitter), and the Tigers only got him when seven AL clubs and seven NL clubs passed. Tobin had a lot of experience in the National League, and he knew the Chicago Cubs. That was how advance scouting was done in those days. If you wanted to know how to pitch to a team you had never faced in the World Series, you bought a pitcher from the other league who knew where to find all the holes in all of the swings.

There was still no guarantee that there would even be a World Series, but the manpower demands were easing, and news of the first atomic bomb gave hope that the Japanese would accept Allied demands for unconditional surrender. When Tokyo was silent following the Hiroshima bomb, another modified B-29 named *Bockscar* took off from Tinian hauling an orange bomb nicknamed Fat Man. After three passes over Kokura, where the cloud cover socked in the target, the bomb was dropped and detonated above a secondary target, Nagasaki, killing as many as eighty thousand. *Bockscar* limped back to Okinawa with only a few minutes of fuel remaining and nearly crashed. On August 9, manager Billy Southworth rejoined his Cardinals at New York's Polo Grounds, where Mel Ott had recently hit his 500th career home run, made possible only by the war stringing out his playing days. Billy could see the news of the second atomic bomb on the front page of *The New York Times*:

SOVIET DECLARES WAR ON JAPAN

ATTACKS MANCHURIA, TOKYO SAYS

ATOM BOMB LOOSED ON NAGASAKI

This war had gone on long enough, longer than it had to. The Army had more atomic bombs waiting to be dropped and planned to use them to support the ground troops in the invasion of Japan, which was scheduled for October, right when the World Series was scheduled to begin. At the same time, the Red Army invaded Manchuria with 1.5 million men and gained fourteen miles in the first day.

The Tigers played on, chasing the pennant, but like everyone else with a clear eye on what was coming next. There was a different kind of scoreboard watching that summer. This race wasn't simply about the Tigers outdistancing the Senators, or the Cubs holding off the Cardinals. This summer was a race against history. These were tense times when an invasion was still a very real possibility. Not until three days later did the Japanese offer to surrender, just as the Tigers were starting a series with the Yankees in Detroit on August 12.

Hank helped the Tigers win the first game in 11 innings with a double and a long triple to straightaway center field, 440 feet away. Newly acquired Jim Tobin beat the Yankees in his first game, pitching 3 scoreless relief innings. Tobin, too, was another sign of baseball's burgeoning future—the relief specialist. Hal Newhouser completed the doubleheader sweep, winning his 18th game and finishing off the Yankees in a tidy one hour, fifty-two minutes. Hank had 2 more hits, lighting up the lineup behind him, and the Yankees botched and booted around the ball so badly that their 133 errors in 101 games made them look more like they wore jail stripes, not pinstripes. The Tigers kept a 2-game lead over the Senators and the Japanese kept stalling.

The next day brought another doubleheader and a rematch against an old friend and memory. Hank faced Tiny Bonham, the starting pitcher for the Yankees on Hank's last day in the majors in 1941, the guy he hit 2 home runs against. Tiny wasn't the same pitcher he used to be, and the Yankees weren't the same team they used to be, either. Hank hit Tiny for a couple of singles, the Tigers got him for 8 runs, and the Bronx Bombers looked more like bumbling buffoons. Power-hitting outfielder Charlie Keller was coming back from the merchant marine soon, but he couldn't save the season. The war finished off catcher Bill Dickey, who was declining before the war and washed up when it was over. Joe D wasn't getting out of the Army soon enough. The aging, often-ill, and frequently inebriated manager, Joe McCarthy, was on his way out.

The Tigers finished another sweep, battering obscure wartime replacement pitchers, such as the dubiously named Monk Dubiel, to open a 3-game lead on the Senators. Tiny Bonham said Hank looked as good as ever. Maybe he wondered what Hank would have done if there had never been a war. On August 15, the time to wonder ended.

The Tigers were waiting for the Senators to come to town when the news hit *The New York Times:*

JAPAN SURRENDERS, END OF WAR!

CHAPTER 24

Take That, You Fuckin' War

The scene on the corner of Michigan and Trumbull was delirious. Crowds around Briggs Stadium were festive, joyous, triumphant, exhaustedly relieved, giddily drunk, pensive, reflective, and not at all reserved. Loud swing music played through the streets, from phonographs blasting at high volume. The scene was repeated in every big city across the country, where you could find servicemen kissing girls they had never before met and kids climbing up light poles. Paper streamed from office buildings, church bells rang, and the bars were packed. Newsboys stood on street corners selling newspapers. One reporter counted seven of them around Briggs. Six of them were howling with V-J Day news. The seventh little boy would not be deterred. His priorities in his young life were very, very clear as he shouted, *"TIGERS WIN TWO FROM YANKS!"*

People remembered exactly where they were and what they were doing when the war ended. Sportswriter Sam Greene was at the Fort Shelby Hotel smoking cigars with Detroit Red Wings hockey coach Jack Adams when sirens wailed downtown to announce the news. Adams asked Greene if he thought Virgil Trucks would be released from the Navy in time to help the Tigers. Adams said he hoped not. He was a Cubs fan who didn't want his team to face Trucks in the World Series.

Now that the war was over, the question was if the Tigers could win the pennant. The local fans wanted to find out. On August 15, an enormous crowd of 46,660 fans jammed into Briggs Stadium to see the Tigers play the Washington Senators in the first game of peacetime baseball. The fans came out early to watch a couple of war-vet ballplayers, Hank Greenberg and Buddy Lewis, take batting practice. Normalcy came charging home quickly. Gasoline and travel restrictions were the first to go, so fans could drive to the ballpark easily. The parking lots were full for the first time in years. Owners got a good idea: maybe they should start selling parking spaces to baseball games. The end of meat restrictions and other food rationing followed, which meant hot dogs were for sale at the usual price for the first time since 1941. Paper restrictions came off, which meant more newspapers would be printed and more baseball news than ever before would be distributed to the public, and baseball cards could be printed again, creating a younger generation of zealous, hero-worshipping young boys. Fans could even keep the foul balls hit into the stands again. The weather was perfect for a ball game and a federal holiday was declared. There was talk that the V-J Day game should be delayed, but GM Jack Zeller refused. "We decided that the Tigers would play the day war ended if the team was at home," he said. "We felt people wanted to be at the ballpark to celebrate." Besides, the team wanted the gate money.

The only bad thing about the end-of-the-war celebration was that Japan may have surrendered, but the Senators wouldn't quit. Dutch Leonard spoiled V-J Day for Detroit fans with his dancing knuckleball, pitching a 4-hit shutout, although two of the singles were courtesy of Mr. Greenberg. Buddy Lewis had 3 hits in his first game at Briggs Stadium since 1941 and was hitting .354 since his return.

Some players wanted to know what life had been like during the war for the players who served in combat theaters. Buddy Lewis got these questions all the time from civilian ballplayers, who asked about flying transports in China. Buddy said the strangest thing he ever saw was two Chinese soldiers so drunk when flying that one pushed the other out the plane door without a parachute and found it funny. Buddy was quick to mention that when he wasn't hauling humans, be they Chinese, Indian, American, or British, his cargo hold was packed with animals, which would always shit in the aisles and stink up the flights. Sometimes the animals would act up and the troops would shoot them and throw them out the door just to keep the rest of the pack animals quiet.

Hank and the Tigers figured out that it was going to take a long time to shoot the Senators and put them out of their misery. The Senators knew nobody wanted them to win. Hank's Tigers were the sentimental favorite, but the Senators had that rebellious spirit. When the teams played, the trash talk flew from one dugout to the other. Mickey Haefner and Roger Wolff, two of the knuckleball quartet, beat the Tigers in the series, and the Senators took 3 out of 4 games to trim the lead back down to 1½ games. The only game the Tigers won was Hal Newhouser's 19th victory, his 10th consecutive victory against the team he owned. The Senators hadn't beat him since 1943, when Buddy Lewis, who knocked in the only runs against Newhouser, was still flying the Hump. Hank Greenberg knew he was getting over his own hump now. He felt young and alive again, playing in front of big Briggs Stadium crowds for the first time in years. The Tigers drew 115,000 fans in just four days after V-J Day, and Hank soaked in the energy. He made a leaping, one-handed catch against the left-field screen in one game, pleased with the spring finally in his legs. He hit in all 4 games, going 8-for-15 to push his average all the way up to .326.

The truth could finally be printed. Everyone knew that wartime major league baseball had been a joke, especially in 1945. Everything else had been rationed, why shouldn't the quality of play? It was a worthy sacrifice. On V-J Day, columnist H. G. Salsinger of *The Detroit News* expressed the view of the baseball establishment when he wrote, "Even the most charitable and amiable of men must admit that the quality of major league baseball in the current season is the poorest in more than 50 years. Connie Mack said just that a few days ago and made it unanimous. The best that can be claimed for the 1945 competition is that it is interesting. Errors, tactical and mechanical, are as essential in the production of baseball drama as base hits, but the game has never known so many tactical and mechanical errors before."

Fans were too happy and relieved to be bothered with how shoddy the 1945 majors looked. It just didn't matter. What mattered was the war was won. On Guam, a B-29 crew in Hank's former XX Bomber Command hung a sign outside a cockpit window, humorously reading:

TOKYO TOURS, FREE FREE FREE!

SEE THE EMPEROR'S PALACE, FUJIYAMA,

RIDE THE WHITE HORSE!

NO ACK-ACK, NO ZEROES, NO KAMIKAZE!

16 HOURS ROUND TRIP!

Victory ships hauling thirteen thousand troops at a time arrived daily in New York and San Francisco from China, Europe, and other distant lands. The Tigers knew other teams would get their ballplayers back in 1946, but the one they wanted in time for the 1945 race was pitcher Virgil Trucks. "We would use Trucks," Jack Zeller said. "He'll be a starting pitcher right away."

Hank Greenberg was just like anybody else in those days immediately following the end of the war. He took it all in and thought about how much his life had changed during the war. It had taken a lot from his baseball career, but it had given a pride he could not replace. He would never brag about what he had done or what he had seen. That wasn't in his nature. As surely as he was proud that his batting average was back over .300 for the first time since he couldn't remember when, Hank was proud to have been a soldier. He did his part and nobody could take that away from him.

The world felt as if it was changing every day as servicemen streamed home and the realities of the postwar nation and world took shape. The baseball wasn't great during the war, but everything that made it great in the postwar years took shape while the best major leaguers wore service uniforms.

The manpower shortage changed everything, because in the war years, the sole question baseball struggled with was where to find players who couldn't be taken by the war. The first thing teams tried, signing bonus babies, created rampant postwar spending on unproven amateur talent and led to the creation of the amateur free agent draft. The untapped talent pools of Negro League and Latin players whose opportunities were created by the manpower shortage soon populated the majors and created multiple generations of star players. The war gave baseball travel and technology and population shifts, leading to new stadiums in new cities, and when new cities ran out, new stadiums were built in old cities. When players came home and saw how they had been abused during the war, they formed a union after a few flawed attempts, eventually getting what they all wanted the most when the war ended—free agency, the right to use their experience, staying power, and statistical accomplishments to negotiate with multiple teams at their own discretion for the most money without fear of retribution from the owners.

The war brought innovation by necessity to the playing field itself. With so many fresh replacement pitchers rushed to the majors, they brought strange tricks from the sandlots and different deliveries designed to create deception. The pitching was about to get a lot more sinister after baseball learned in the war years. "You hear mentioned the fade-away, knuckleballs, sliders, sailors, sinkers, butterfly balls, illegal spit balls, and other deliveries," *The Detroit News* wrote. The war created a new mentality among baseball men—nobody cared how pitchers got guys out, as long as they got them out. Some pitchers, it dawned on baseball men, were better suited to be relief pitchers. That came from the war, too.

Of course nothing played like a big fastball, and during the war scouts scurried to sign high school pitchers before they graduated. In one of his first acts before the end of the war, Happy Chandler banned the practice of cradle robbing, unknowingly and irrevocably launching the game toward the next phase of institutionalized, inflationary, and reckless spending on young talent. Within four years after the war, high school bonus babies were signing for more than $100,000, more than only a few major leaguers earned in a year, creating enormous animosity.

Everybody was thinking ahead now that the war was over. Baseball was no different from any other walk of American life. The Tigers were one of eleven major league teams who immediately signed an airline agreement with United Airlines, the beginning of the end of railroad travel and the dawning of the jet age, the spark baseball required for continental expansion. Suddenly, anything seemed possible, such as spring training in Arizona or moving a baseball team to some far-flung place, such as Los Angeles, or perhaps an obscure city such as Milwaukee. Fourteen of sixteen teams planned on spring training in Florida. Stadium lights, like the ones planned for Briggs, became commonplace. Replacing Victorian-style wooden ball-parks with stadiums made from steel and concrete, complete with elevators and escalators, was envisioned.

The war was over, but stories were told of Japanese soldiers who refused to surrender and of American aircraft attacked weeks after the surrender. You didn't have to convince Phil Marchildon, once upon a time a prewar pitcher for the Philadelphia Athletics, that the war wasn't over. Germany may have surrendered a long time ago and he may have been home in Canada following his prisoner-of-war experience that left him shaken and rattled, but the war was a part of his everyday life. He didn't want to pitch again, but Connie Mack wanted him in the majors before the summer was over. The Athletics were long out of the race, and that wasn't surprising news, any more than the thought that Mack thought Marchildon could bring a few extra fans to Shibe Park. Besides, now that the war was over, baseball men had to think about developing players, especially when that meant helping a war vet such as Marchildon salvage his livelihood.

Marchildon resisted Mack's overtures for several weeks, when he was tired, thin, and haunted by nightmares. He knew he wasn't the pitcher he used to be, but Mack told him he didn't have to be everything he used to be all at once. Everyone coming home from the war had to learn that lesson, not just the baseball players. Mack genuinely thought pitching would replenish Marchildon's soul as much as it would strengthen his body. Finally, the former Halifax tail gunner reluctantly agreed to join the team.

Some players who stayed home during the war didn't understand the ordeal of Marchildon and others like him. When Athletics pitcher and professional idiot Bobo Newsome asked him what day he was shot down, Marchildon told him, August 16, 1944. Bobo replied that the Yankees had shot him down that day. Bobo was delusional—he never pitched that day. Marchildon laughed because he was a good sport, but Bobo could never begin to understand what he was joking about. "In war," Marchildon tried to explain, "you play for keeps."

Marchildon had trouble thinking about baseball when the war was still so fresh in his mind. "You can't think consolingly of another game, another day, because in war there may not be another day," he said. "You know that the boys won't slap you comfortingly on the back after a tough break, or maybe you won't be there. That's the big difference. That's why war creates extra tensions that strain nerves. And it's why I think that baseball or any other competitive sport is the best and healthiest answer to the problem of returning some ten million servicemen to civilian life."

Connie Mack was right. Baseball was good for Marchildon. Going to the ballpark every day was good for him. Watching baseball instead of worrying about finishing the next mission was good for him. The war veterans who were back in the American League in 1945 all possessed a special bond. Marchildon, Hank Greenberg, Buddy Lewis, Bert Shepard, all had much in common, and all knew that they could, just as easily, have ended up like Billy Southworth Jr.

Even after V-J Day there were steady reminders of war dead. In Michigan, eighty-three Gold Stars were posted for athletes killed in action, with forty-seven from Michigan State, nine from the University of Michigan, three each for the Detroit Red Wings hockey club and Detroit Lions pro football team. The Tigers even lost a minor leaguer to combat.

Marchildon wasn't ready physically or emotionally to pitch when Mack told him the time was right on August 17 in Cleveland, but he lacked the strength to stand up to the old man. Marchildon entered the game in relief. He fidgeted and squirmed on the mound, endlessly tugging at the brim of his cap and his belt buckle, shrugging his shoulders in a uniform that felt too large. He pitched like a man with an SS guard lurking over his shoulder. Nobody can pitch scared and win. He walked 4, gave up 4 runs, and most troublesome of all struck out nobody. Marchildon thought the old zip was gone from his fastball. Worst of all, he hated pitching afraid. He feared he was permanently broken.

The Sporting News said Marchildon was "jittery and did not perform." He didn't feel like a man making a comeback. He felt like a man who was still a prisoner. He said simply, "I sure didn't feel like a kid anymore." He felt like a failure, a man consumed and discarded by the war, and he wasn't sure he wanted to continue. Connie Mack wouldn't let him quit, perhaps out of obligation, perhaps out of old-man stubbornness. Besides, Mark had a day planned for him in Philadelphia and wanted the gate money.

On August 29, Marchildon made his first start since 1942, in Philadelphia against the Washington Senators, with Buddy Lewis batting third. He was honored in a pregame ceremony arranged by Mack, who gave him $1,000 bond. The Senators were chasing the Tigers, trailing them by 1 game.

Honoring the integrity of the pennant race, Marchildon pitched his best game of 1945. He made it through 5 innings, walking 5, allowing 2 runs, and encouragingly enough striking out 2. He faced Buddy Lewis twice. Those were meaningful at bats for both men.

Marchildon needed to win a moment like this. He reached back for a moment and thought he felt the old fastball come out of his hand good the way it used to. Buddy, in his first at bat, put a good swing on it and hit a fly ball to left field. Picking up a little confidence, Marchildon got Buddy to ground out to second in his next at bat. Jogging on his way back to the dugout, Buddy slowed down in front of the mound. He found Phil, rubbing the sweat off his hand and the stress from his soul. In one of those slight moments only ballplayers understand, Buddy Lewis never forgot what it meant to Marchildon. "I wanted him to know I was with him," Lewis said.

Phil Marchildon pitched in one more game in 1945 and then went home to Canada to heal his mind and body. He gained enough confidence in the coming years to fight Connie Mack for more money, but he never shook loose the reputation that his value had permanently been damaged by the war. Players such as Hank and Buddy and Phil all knew the owners would talk out of both ends, praising them in public for their war service, then devaluing them in contract negations when they showed even the slightest sign of fragility. To owners, veterans weren't heroes. They were liabilities. It was professional baseball's version of spitting in a veteran's face. "We've already seen some war vets back in action on the diamond," *The Sporting News* reported. "Some of them, like Hank Greenberg and Buddy Lewis, are efficient as ever. Others like Phil Marchildon showed they were not quite ready and will need a lot of toning up."

Marchildon's return was another postwar comeback story that caught the public fancy. In the coming few years, plenty of guys would be trying to make it back, but few of them came back with as much psychological damage as Marchildon. In later years, he confessed his nightmares were haunted by memories . . . trying on his flight suit for the first time . . . closing the coffin door behind the tail gun . . . the dark nights and the chatter of the Browning machine guns . . . the tracers from his guns and from the cannons of German fighters . . . the engine flaming . . . the plane falling . . . faces of men he never saw again . . . falling through the darkness and waiting for the chute to open . . . splashing into ice water . . . picked up by the

Dutch . . . turned over to the Germans . . . the bastard SS guard . . . Christmas in a stalag . . . the British troops coming out of the woods. He had decided only one thing in the summer of '45: he would try to pitch again the next year. And that victory alone would have to do.

While Marchildon's return was courageous, Bob Feller was the guy everyone was waiting for. He had been toning up for his return for years. While he was at sea, he lived in the *Alabama*'s gymnasium and did thousands of push-ups, sit-ups, and pull-ups, running on the decks the best he could. He wore out the medicine ball and the punching bag. When he found a sailor who could handle his fastball, he played catch. When the ship reached land, he ran wind sprints barefoot in the sand. He played baseball occasionally, pitching in his Navy dungarees. He had the rare mental ability to block out the hitters he was facing and imagine himself on a big league mound. You could put a headhunter with a machete up at the plate and Bob would knock him down. When he finally came home to the States in spring, he attacked his time at Great Lakes as if it were a minor league season. He pitched 95 innings and won 13 games, striking out 130, but Bob wasn't counting the strikeouts. He was counting the days until he rejoined the Indians.

The day after Buddy Lewis hit his first big league home run since 1941, fittingly, against Hank Greenberg and the Tigers at Briggs Stadium, Feller was finally released from the Navy and declared he was ready to make his return on August 24, against the Tigers, at Cleveland. Feller absolutely wanted his first start to have significance. He alone decided when he was coming back. He wanted Hank Greenberg and the first-place Tigers. The end of his war had come and Feller had no fear. He wanted to test himself against the best. That was the Feller everyone remembered.

Feller's comeback captivated the country, but he adamantly refused to discuss details about his war experiences until he was much older. Feller's pride was as firm as his fastball. He would not compromise the men he'd served with. Serving on the *Alabama* meant that Feller's war occurred out of sight and out of mind. It was easier for the public to relate to the ballplayers sweating it out in Europe than with someone on the deck of a battleship a million miles away, but that didn't mean Feller was sunning himself on the deck.

He remembered well operating his Quad-40 gun emplacement against kamikaze attacks in the Mariana Islands and fought the ferocious naval and air battles between the Americans and the Japanese, when the crystal-blue water was smeared black by oil slicks with bodies bobbing in the waves like driftwood. Feller saw more fire than he ever cared to discuss. Sailors understood him. He saw flag-draped bodies pushed overboard. Above all, he would never, ever discuss the four men next to him who died when their Quad-40 gun battery, identical to the one Feller commanded, exploded when a spark hit the gunpowder. Those men disintegrated in their gun pit. He hated talking about that, as though that was the moment when he saw what could have been him burned alive.

Feller realized the war was going to cost him his chance to win 300 games, just as it had already cost Hank Greenberg the chance to hit 500 home runs. Feller was more than willing to make that sacrifice. "I didn't miss baseball at all, I wanted to do what little I could to help this country," he said. "I did what any good American should have done." The ballplayers of World War II were a different breed from any other generation, capable of believing in something more than their own careers and money. "We were getting pushed around, all over the world," Feller said. "We had a now-or-never mentality." He would not back down. He always said his greatest victory was winning the war, feeling a pride that he felt no baseball achievement could possibly match. Feller was proud that no Japanese fighter ever breached the wall of gunfire his battleship group, Task Force 58, put up to defend the aircraft carriers.

Now he wanted baseball back. He wanted all of it. He wanted every inning, every strikeout, every win, and every dollar. He paid his dues, now it was time to get his own. He watched the pennant race and followed the Tigers in their series against the Athletics. Feller still wanted to make a dent. On August 19, the Tigers led the Senators by only 1½ games. The war was over, but the pennant could still be lost. *The Detroit News* worried, "They are calling the Washington Senators a hungry team. That is what they called the St. Louis Cardinals in 1942."

Feller's impending return swelled fear that the Tigers could yet blow it. The Indians, still only 5 games back, hoped Feller would pitch them back into the race. It was a nice thought, but highly unlikely. The same was true for the Yankees, who learned that orders for Joe DiMaggio's discharge would have to come directly from the War Department, making his 1945 return impossible. Joe D would have to wait for 1946. Hank knew facing Feller was right around the corner. When he heard Feller wanted to face the Tigers his first time out, he smiled. He was excited. He knew Feller wanted to test himself.

Hank continued to find his swing after V-J Day, piecing together a 15-game hitting streak, the longest since his return. His stats were getting better, but he worried about how long he could realistically expect his body to hold out. Many times he wondered if he would be able to finish the season. His back, especially, gave him fits. It was always stiff and sore. Hank knew that was from the wartime layoff. There was nothing he could do to make it feel better, no matter what he tried. No amount of heat or ice soothed his vertebrae or calmed his nerves. He just played every day and hoped he wouldn't give out like a tire blowing on the road.

On the days when Hank couldn't carry the Tigers, Hal Newhouser did. He won his 20th game on August 20, shutting out the Athletics 4–0 at Briggs Stadium to become the first 20-game winner in the league, lowering his earned run average to 1.76. Newhouser was the best pitcher in the game, and it wasn't even close. His ERA fell below 2 runs per game in late May and never rose past 2 runs for the remainder of the season. He pitched 8 or more innings in every game he started since the end of May. He had fewer strikeouts than he used to, but he also issued fewer walks and had only given up 4 home runs, and none since the end of June, a span of 13 starts. He had learned the secret of being a truly successful big leaguer: when you put the team on your shoulders, other major leaguers admire you.

In every way, Hal Newhouser had become what Bob Feller was before the war, a pitching ace that starting rotations weren't just built around, but that entire teams were. Now, Newhouser was lined up to make his next start directly against Feller; that was the kind of game that made the war worth fighting. They were bound to have many battles after the war, but few would be anticipated as much as the first.

The majors following V-J Day created many once-in-a-career moments. A few days after his 15-game hitting streak ended, Hank faced rookie righty Billy Connelly of the Athletics, who was making his major league debut on August 22 at age twenty. The young pitcher had lived a lifetime in less than a year. In February, he was the young Marine shot through the jaw in Iwo Jima. The bullet wound was so clean and the plastic surgery so good that he looked as if he had nothing more than a shaving scar. When he got on the mound, Connelly pitched like he was more nervous to be facing the Tigers than he ever was terrified by the Japanese machine gunners. He walked the bases loaded and gave up a double to Hank and a triple to Rudy York before he was pulled. Hank hit his 7th home run later in the game and, when it was over, could reflect on how only in 1945 could a major league pitcher have been wounded on Iwo Jima in February and pitched in the big leagues in August.

The Tigers played the Athletics in eight more games over the next four days, with doubleheaders on three consecutive days. Even though the wartime travel restrictions that led to the scheduling of so many doubleheaders so close together had been lifted, the schedule wasn't going to be changed so late in the season. So the Tigers and the Athletics sweated it out, but none of the ballplayers who played the last wartime summer and into the postwar years ever forgot the abuse the owners put them through. The fans loved it, anyway, and the Tigers beat the Brooklyn Dodgers as the first team to draw 1 million fans for a season after the war. The Tigers took 6 out of 8 from the Athletics and held a 1-game lead over the equally exhausted Washington Senators as the Tigers headed to Cleveland to face Bob Feller on August 24.

Feller was waiting. As much as he missed pitching, he swore he was better now than he was before the war. He had developed better fastball control and a more consistent curveball. "I've got some surprises in store," Feller vowed. He promised to "pitch smarter ball." He was more worried about pitching under the lights than he was about the Tigers. When the Tigers arrived in Cleveland, Feller was damn good. Detroit manager Steve O'Neill was Feller's first manager when he came to the big leagues at age seventeen in 1936. O'Neill watched Feller warm up before the top of the first inning, saw how that arm windmilled like a thing of beauty, and how easily the ball came out of Feller's hand. O'Neill knew right away the Tigers were in trouble.

The Indians gave Feller a jeep as a coming-home gift. Then he promptly ran over the Tigers. He could still bring it, striking out the first batter of the game, Jimmy Outlaw. Then with two out in the first inning, Feller found the hitter he wanted. Hank Greenberg walked to the plate. He knew exactly how Feller was feeling.

Hank dug in with a little smile on his face and a wink back to plate umpire Eddie Rommel and catcher Frankie Hayes. Feller cranked into his windup. His fastball looked like it was shot out of a Quad-40. The ball exploded in the zone. *Son of a bitch still throws hard!* Hank loved it. Feller came back with a strike-one fastball, throwing it right at the outside corner. He'd promised better control and he delivered. Hank fired his hands, but the ball was past him before his foot was down. The swing was pretty, but Hank was late. Strike two. Feller had Greenberg exactly where he wanted him. Hank ran through the options. What would Feller do with two strikes? He might waste a fastball in the dirt or take something off a breaking ball on the outer half, try to get Hank to chase. Hank didn't think Feller would nibble. He had that killer look on his face already, which could only mean fastball. Feller was in get-it-and-throw-it mode. No screwing around. Hank really thought Feller was coming back with a fastball, but he thought for certain Feller would throw it on the inside corner. He choked up on the knob of his bat by an inch or two. Then he waited.

This was so much better for both of them, so much better than worrying about flying over the Hump, above the twisted-metal cemetery of Aluminum Alley, and so much better than being in the gun pits with the other sailors blasting the sky full of so much cordite that you couldn't smell the salt air anymore. Neither Hank nor Bob needed to worry about any other combat, any other death, other than the sheer joy of competition. Hank was all geared up for the fastball, and when he saw Feller rock into that fast windup, Hank was certain it was a heater until Feller threw a curveball that made him cry. On the 0-and-2, Feller dropped such a magnificent hammer that Hank could only watch in admiration. The helpless Hank had no shame as Eddie Rommel rung him up. Feller bounced off the mound, a little peek over his shoulder enough to satisfy him. It was as if he was saying, *Take that, you fuckin' war.*

Sam Greene, writing in *The Detroit News,* loved to go with full proper names when a ballplayer truly impressed him. He rarely did it for another team, but Feller wasn't any other player. "Robert William Andrew Feller convinced 46,477 more or less biased witnesses in Municipal Stadium last night that nearly four years in the Navy have not diminished the skill that made him the best pitcher in the major leagues before the war. As victims of his speed and curve, the Tigers will have to subscribe to the general verdict that Feller is just as good as ever."

Feller was great that day. He struck out 12, pitched a 4-hitter, and beat ace Hal Newhouser, 4–2. That was a polite way of saying, *Good season, kid, but I'm still Bob Feller.* Newhouser was worried when the game was over. His shoulder was suddenly bothering him. He iced it until he couldn't feel anything and hoped that the pain would go away in time for him to make his next start. When Hank and the rest of the Tigers heard Newhouser was in pain, they were worried more than their faces would allow or their newspaper quotes would admit.

Feller sat in an ice bath when the game was over and never felt so good. The only greater satisfaction would have been knocking the Tigers into a tie for first, but the weary Senators were granted a blessed day off, so he settled for trimming the Tigers lead to ½ game. He was a long way removed from the game he'd pitched out in the Marshall Islands where a kid from Brooklyn heckled him and a wild bore rushed across the field or the time a typhoon almost sank the *Alabama*. At that moment, Bob Feller felt so good that the end of World War II was already a distant memory.

CHAPTER 25

The Comeback Kids

Hundreds of Navy Hellcat and Corsair fighters roared low over the deck of the battleship *Missouri,* anchored in Tokyo Bay on the cloudy morning of September 2. The Navy called it S-hour, referring to the signing of Japan's formal surrender bringing the war to an official end. The peace ceremony took only seventeen minutes, with General Douglas MacArthur presiding.

MacArthur was not the kind of general who spiked the ball when he accepted victory, though of course he had longed for this moment. What most of the men didn't know about him was that he, too, had relied on his baseball memories to keep his sanity during the weary days of the war. He fondly remembered his time as the superintendent of West Point, when the cadet baseball team was coached by a feisty former major league infielder named Hans Lobert, who was full of vigor, humor, and passion. Once in 1943, while pondering the course of the war with one of his adjuncts, Lieutenant Colonel Red Reeder, MacArthur told him, "Red, when you go home, you tell Hans Lobert that at night when the pressure is on and it's hard for me to go to sleep, I'm able to rest only by thinking of those days at West Point when he was our jolly baseball coach."

Standing on the deck among the sailors was John M. Carlisle, *The Detroit News* war correspondent, who had been in the Pacific for more than a year chronicling the stories of Detroit boys. His descriptions of the surrender captivated his readers: "The sad, sallow, owlish looking Jap foreign minister, a funeral figure in a frock coat, slowly signed on the dotted line. Defeat registered in their dejected expressions, and the hopelessness and the lost dreams of the Japanese empire were etched in their lined faces."

When the ceremony ended and the dignitaries dispersed, Carlisle roamed the battleship talking with the sailors. More than once, he got the question he always heard when he met Detroit boys: How are the Tigers doing?

The answer was, just barely getting along. After losing to Bob Feller in his comeback game, the Tigers lost 6 of their next 10 games and stood with a 1-game lead the morning the photographs of the Japanese surrender on the *Missouri*'s deck was published in *The Detroit News*, accompanied by a howling headline:

FIRST TROOPS LAND IN SOUTHERN JAPAN

The war was really over now, but the Tigers had serious worries. They finished August with only an 18-17 record, hardly an overpowering month for a team that was supposed to win the race. The good news was that the end of the war meant the cancellation of travel restrictions, which permitted a World Series after all, but to bring the pennant home to peace-happy Detroit, the Tigers would have to navigate a September crucible unlike anything ever before experienced by any team. They would either survive or surrender. S-hour was upon them.

The September schedule called for 33 games in 30 days, 25 on the road, 10 doubleheaders, 9 on the road, and several on consecutive days. The four teams involved in the 1945 pennant races—the Tigers and the Senators in the American League, and the Cubs and Cardinals in the National League—all had to endure such torture down the September stretch. The wackiness of World War II baseball was to blame. In that last month, the war might officially have been over, but every single day brought reminders of it in the pennant races.

Players hated the schedule but in the war years wouldn't dare complain. The September stretch would inevitably wear down pitchers and grind down the replacement position players, who were short on talent to begin with and had to make do with poor field conditions, bad lighting, and an endless parade of train travel, hotel living, and road eating. Now, granted, it was still good work if you could get it, because a lot of soldiers and sailors coming home that summer were finding it tough to find a job or even a place to live. But it didn't change the fact that players felt abused.

The sailors from Detroit who craned their necks to watch the Hellcats and Corsairs fly over the *Missouri* had every right to worry. Hal Newhouser pulled a muscle in his back and complained of sore ribs and a sore arm. He had X-rays, but refused to pull himself out of the starting rotation. Another starting pitcher, Al Benton, got banged around the yard so badly in the second half that the Tigers were at a loss. "The mystery of Benton's collapse is as deep as ever. His fastball is no longer alive," *The Detroit News* wrote. The year after winning 27 games, Dizzy Trout was a break-even pitcher. The Tigers were so desperate for starting pitching that they rushed Army veteran Tommy Bridges back, literally walking him from the separation center to the mound. Bridges, a three-time 20-game winner from 1934–1936 who had 192 career victories before his wartime job as an Army clerk, tried to pitch again, but he wasn't the same.

After starting September by winning 3 out of 4 games from the White Sox at Briggs Stadium, the Tigers readied for the long haul that would make or break them. Between September 4 and September 20, the Tigers would play 23 games in 16 days, including 7 doubleheaders. "It is hardly necessary to mention that the championship aims of the Detroit club will rise or fall in proportion to its ability to meet the taxing demands of these 16 days," *The Detroit News* correctly summarized. Those sailors standing on the deck of the *Missouri* and every other soldier in Europe, the Pacific, and Indochina had fought so that the game would go on. Now it was up to the Tigers to earn their keep. War is hell, but so was this pennant race.

First up were 7 games in 5 days with 2 doubleheaders at Yankee Stadium, starting September 4 with the Tigers having a 2-game lead over the Washington Senators. When the Tigers needed a push, Hank Greenberg gave them a shove. With his father sitting in the front row, Hank wailed on a hanging curveball and sent it soaring as high as the Hellcats and Corsairs. The contact was good and loud, an explosion off his bat, another gunshot in the Bronx. The echo resonated through the Stadium, the hit described by *The Detroit News* as a "towering fly into the lower deck of the distant left field seats," which in the original Yankee Stadium was one of the greatest shots anybody had ever seen from a right-handed hitter. Joe DiMaggio went there before the war. Now Hank Greenberg had gone there in the late summer of '45, the 9th home run of his comeback, estimated at 425 feet. It would be thirteen years before the New York writers who covered the Yankees regularly said another right-handed batter hit a ball as far, when the next Hammerin' Hank, Henry Aaron, deposited one there for the Milwaukee Braves in the 1957 World Series. Even hard-boiled New York hacks were impressed. "A ball cannot be hit any longer than that in left field at the Stadium," the *New York Herald Tribune* reported of Hank Greenberg's gunshot. "The meeting of bat and ball made a terrible sound, more forceful than any heard in the Stadium for some time." Hank rounded the bases and crossed the plate. When he came to the Tigers dugout, he looked up into the first row, where his father was beaming.

After Hank's home run gave the Tigers a big lead, manager Joe McCarthy walked to the mound. The Tigers weren't the only team running out of pitching. McCarthy decided the time was right to bring in a forty-three-year-old right-hander who probably gave up more home runs than anyone else who ever pitched in the majors, in one way of thinking: Paul Schreiber. He was the team's batting-practice pitcher, who'd pitched almost 1,700 career minor league innings and whose last major league outing was in 1923.

The Tigers who had been stateside during the war were used to such absurdities, but to the comeback kids such as Hank Greenberg, the idea of a batting-practice pitcher actually being pressed into service in an official game, even to mop up, didn't seen possible. The Yankees didn't care. They were out of the race and needed the laugh. After all, nothing says surrender like a guy who doesn't belong there.

But Schreiber was a drinking buddy and one of the boys for all those years. The Yanks always voted him a full share of World Series money, which usually meant an extra six grand. Either Schreiber was baffling or the Tigers just didn't care, either. He finished the game in fine fashion, perplexing the Tigers with 3⅓ scoreless innings, even, yes, retiring Hank. It was about the funniest thing either team had seen in years, and in this September swelter, that humor was much appreciated. When Schreiber walked off the mound at the end of the game, both teams gave him good-natured, if mocking, applause. He lifted his rubber arm and doffed his ragged hat. "At least nobody got hurt," he said. And the funny thing was, he didn't get paid any extra, either.

The end of the war paid at the box office, where on September 5, the teams attracted 55,511 fans for a doubleheader. Once again, Hank did not disappoint. He crushed his 10th home run, a 420-foot blast to left field. The Tigers won the first game with 5 runs in the ninth inning against the nonexistent Yankee bullpen. Eddie Mayo, a tough little infielder picked up in the wartime scraps, hit a home run with all his buddies from New Jersey in town. But the Tigers couldn't finish the sweep in the next game, when Al Benton was hammered again failing to pitch his way out of the third inning.

September 6 was yet another doubleheader at Yankee Stadium full of dismal baseball played by tired and overworked ballplayers. Both starting pitchers, Jim Tobin for the Tigers and Red Ruffing for the Yankees, were atrocious in Game 1. The Yankees hit four home runs in a 14–5 victory, but the one that mattered most was hit by former Merchant Marine Charlie Keller, who belted his fourth since the war ended. Tigers pitching could be so bad when Newhouser or Trout were not on the mound that games like this could occur, when four Detroit pitchers combined to walk fifteen hitters. Did this team really deserve to win the pennant?

But the Tigers had the entertaining and uncanny wartime ability to stink and play good on the same day, thanks to all the doubleheaders. The Tigers bounced back to win Game 2, 5–2, behind pitcher Les Mueller, who proved that he could still get the ball over the plate even after almost pitching 20 innings in a game a month earlier. Hank did not hit much, but outfielder Roy Cullenbine picked up the slack and hit a home run in both games. The Tigers were playing the best bad ball in the American League, keeping a 1½ game lead over the Senators, who swept two from the Browns.

The Senators were entering their own special hell, playing 22 games in the next 17 days before their season was scheduled to end on September 23, a week before the Tigers. The reason? Money, of course! Clark Griffith rented out his stadium to the Washington Redskins, so his ballplayers had better win the pennant before the football players chewed up the field.

The Tigers had two games left in two days in New York, which was crammed to the hilt with soldiers and sailors fresh off the George Washington boats taking in the town before catching connecting trains and buses back home. The good news was that the Tigers had Hal Newhouser and Dizzy Trout pitching the next two days. Newhouser rose to the occasion, winning his 22nd game with a 4-hit shutout with no walks, so masterful that Hank's brother, Corporal Joe Greenberg, one of those soldiers just off the boat who made a beeline to the seats behind the dugout, blurted, "All I gotta say is that if Newhouser's got a pulled muscle, I hope every pitcher on the club gets a pulled muscle quick." He probably shouldn't have tempted fate or the schedule. Hank, happy to see his brother, whose own promising five-year minor league career ended when he joined the Army in 1941, gave him 2 singles and an RBI as a coming-home present.

The next day, September 8, Dizzy Trout beat the Yankees for the second time in the series. Even when Dizzy wasn't winning big, he still had a big mouth. He beat the Yankees twice, which wasn't saying much, then boasted, "You can blow the ball in there before they can get the bat around." That really said something about the power World War II had over baseball. If the New York Yankees weren't a fastball-hitting team, what was the world coming to? At least Hank could still hit a fastball. In his farewell to his family and friends for the season, he went 3-for-5 with five RBIs and his 11th home run, another towering shot deep into left field. As he rounded the bases, the New York fans cheered. Most in the crowd were servicemen. They didn't care that Hank played for the Tigers and not the Yankees. He was one of them, now and forever. The Tigers took 5 out of the 7 games and kept a 1½ game lead over the Senators. They had 21 games to go.

Pete Gray was counting the days until he went home to Nanticoke. He played even less in September than he had in August and grew increasingly removed from the teammates he was convinced didn't care much about him. He could tell manager Luke Sewell had no confidence in him anymore. Pete's average plummeted as he played less and less. He hit .184 in August, and September was off to another bad start. Speculation was fair play as long as Pete Gray was on the Browns bench. His feud with pitcher Sig Jakucki was cancerous.

Jack so despised Pete that on one sweltering-hot day, he left a raw, dead fish wrapped in newspaper inside Pete's locker. The message was clear. Jack thought Pete was the dead fish. Pete could handle no more. He bull-charged again. No amount of secrecy could contain stories about the wild fight between the drunken pitcher and the one-armed wonder, both wartime replacements throwing punches on their way out the door.

The season got away from the Browns late in the summer in a game on August 29 against the Tigers. Jack was getting hit around in the third inning when he saw the unthinkable, Luke Sewell coming to take him out of the game. Jack barked back when Sewell asked for the ball. He couldn't believe he was being pulled. He had 12 wins and had pitched almost 200 innings and his ERA was a respectable 3.51. So what if he drank his weight? His numbers spoke for themselves. After a long moment of confrontation, plate umpire Eddie Rommel went out to the mound. The question was for Sewell: Are you taking him out or leaving him in? Sewell did not hesitate to yank him. Rommel, a retired pitcher, wore a look that said it all. *You gotta go.* The war was over, and so was Sig Jakucki.

The demise of Sig Jakucki mirrored the downfall of the St. Louis Browns. Nobody could be a bum forever and keep getting away with it. All the bickering, all the booze, all the bad ballplayers finally caught up with the Browns. Jakucki was so upset when Sewell pulled him from the game that he got dressed and left the ballpark. He abandoned the team, went out and got drunk, and didn't show up again until the next day at the train station to join the team for a road trip to Chicago.

Sewell was waiting for him, and in a heated moment, the two had it out for all to see, including the reporters, who had Sewell telling Jack, "If you'd been in condition, I wouldn't have yanked you." That meant he was saying he was sick of managing a drunk. He was tired of Jack endlessly baiting and riding Pete Gray. The war was over, the Browns were out of the race and Sewell just didn't care anymore. Jack could go to hell, or back to working in a paper mill and pitching for peanuts, whichever came first. Sewell told his players to get on the train; they were leaving without Jakucki.

The old pitcher just could not believe his manager would fire him. He called the front office to complain and snuck aboard the train anyhow. When Sewell found out Jakucki was on board, he confronted him and fired him all over again. The manager told reporters, "He will never pitch for the Browns again." And he never did.

Sig Jakucki never returned to the major leagues. He bounced his way through the minors for a few years after the war, but he never lived down his days as one of the most glaring reminders of wartime replacement ballplayers of the dysfunctional St. Louis Browns. That other wartime ballplayer, Pete Gray, well, nobody asked him how he felt to see Jack go. But chances are, his feelings were quite simple: hit the road, Jack.

Jakucki was done and so were the Japanese. Now that the surrender documents had been signed, Harry Truman finally had the opportunity to cut out of the White House and rekindle one of Franklin Roosevelt's favorite traditions when he went to a ball game for the first time as president on Sunday, September 9, at Griffith Stadium, to see the Senators play the White Sox in a doubleheader, which they swept, while the Tigers played two in Fenway against the Red Sox. The Tigers won the first game, but the second game was suspended after 11 innings because of darkness, allowing the Senators to close the gap to 1 game at the end of the day.

Clark Griffith was always happy to welcome a new president to his ballpark, though he had to admit his heart was heavy for his old friend FDR. Griffith pulled the war maps down from his office walls and rolled them into a closet, including the map of Japan he had plotted for the invasion that never came. He still hoped the Senators would overtake the Tigers, but his players had no affection for him. They were tired and getting worn down, and they resented him for renting out the ballpark for the last week of the season. That would give the Tigers all the flexibility the Senators lacked.

None of this mattered to President Truman. Griffith could tell Truman was rather oblivious as a baseball fan, unlike many of the former chief executives. He was excited to be at the game, and before he threw out the first pitch of his presidency, he wanted to meet the two war veterans in the Senators starting lineup, Buddy Lewis and Cecil Travis. Lewis was holding his own in his first tour through the league since the end of the war, hitting .330. He recalled the time in 1936 when he was a rookie and, in his first opening day, caught Roosevelt's first pitch. That was a funny story Buddy liked to tell because it involved shaking hands with a Japanese dignitary and exchanging a few kind words with Roosevelt. After all he had been through in the war, Buddy looked back at that moment in his life as a harbinger of things to come. Now Buddy was a little older and grayer around the edges, but Truman told him not to worry. So was he.

Cecil Travis was having a much rougher go of it. The Battle of the Bulge veteran, who'd suffered severe frostbite, couldn't find anything about his old self. His first game back was the day before, when he went 0-for-4, but he knew already something was wrong. He went hitless in the first game of the doubleheader, which Truman stayed around to watch, gleefully munching peanuts and popcorn in the seats next to the dugout. Travis was happy Truman was having a good time, because he wasn't. He was already playing third base, instead of his natural position, shortstop, because he couldn't move the way he used to. He had been around the game long enough to know when something didn't feel the way it was supposed to. He also knew he wasn't going to find it in the last few weeks of the season. He was already thinking about 1946. He was scared that he would never swing the bat worth a damn again. Sometimes, the price to be paid for victory was the sacrifice of the rare gift of major league playing ability. He smiled and waved to Truman, but in his heart Cecil Travis knew he'd lost the best of what was left of his baseball talent in the Hürtgen Forest.

Hank Greenberg knew just how Cecil Travis felt, also going 0-for-4 in the first game of his doubleheader in Fenway. While Truman saw the Senators sweep the White Sox, the Tigers tried to split in Boston. In the second game, the Tigers trailed 3–1 before Rudy York hit a home run in the eighth inning that sent the game to extra innings. The game ended tied 3–3 in 11 innings halted by darkness. Hank went 2-for-3 to set himself straight, but in the fourth inning, he should have known better when he tried to stretch a single into a double. He hurt his ankle sliding into second base and limped off the field. Hank tried to play through the pain, but two innings later he took himself out of the game and dunked his scorching ankle in the ice bucket. Eddie Mayo, spark-plug second baseman, also banged up his abdomen sliding into third base. That led to this troubling headline in *The Detroit News*:

MAYO'S SIDE, GREENBERG'S ANKLE HAVE
STEVE O'NEILL WORRIED

That news was so bad it was almost enough to make a guy wish for the war to come back, but not quite. The problem was the schedule, where so many games so close together so late in the season and a lack of suitable replacement players thanks to the war made injuries and inconsistent pitching incredibly tough to withstand. The last pennant race of the war years wasn't racing to a finish. It was tripping over its own feet. May the best of the worst win.

If President Truman went from ballpark to ballpark to meet all the service veterans who were now playing in the majors again, he'd never get any work done. On the Sunday when he rewarded himself with his first ball game in Washington and all the major league clubs were playing doubleheaders, a former Canadian Army soldier named Dick Fowler pitched the second game for the Philadelphia Athletics against the St. Louis Browns. Pete Gray wasn't in the lineup for either game and got only one chance, a pinch-hit at bat in the first game, lowering his batting average to .219. Too bad, maybe he could have broken up Fowler's no-hitter, a 1–0 gem in which he threw the first no-hitter in the American League since Bob Feller on April 16, 1940. Had it really been that long of a war? Fowler said he fed the Browns "anything they couldn't hit," which was apparently everything.

Without Hank Greenberg in the lineup, the Tigers couldn't hit a lick. He showed up at Fenway Park before the doubleheader on September 10 walking with a cane on a heavily taped and swollen ankle. The good news was that there was no fracture, but the bad news was Hank didn't know when he was going to play again. But for once, the schedule did Hank and the Tigers a favor. After the final 3 games in Boston, the Tigers were going to Philadelphia to play the meandering Athletics 4 times in 3 days before arriving at Griffith Stadium to play the Senators in a series that could determine the pennant race.

Hank decided he would get off his ankle and try to be healthy in time to play the Senators. No way did he want to miss a chance to beat those guys. He had come too far over too many years to let pain get in the way of his finishing his comeback and leading his team, but he also didn't want to hurt himself so badly that he could never play again. So he sat on the bench for the next week, iced his ankle and swallowed painkillers, maybe wished for some morphine, and watched the Tigers sweat it out without him.

In Boston, the Tigers lost to Red Sox rookie Boo Ferriss, the discharged Air Corps man who won his 21st game and went 3-for-5 and knocked in 2 runs on September 10. The Tigers got the next two games back, thanks in part to Dizzy Trout, who stopped talking long enough to win his fourth game on the road trip and brag that he did it with the best stuff he had all year. While Hank healed and the Red Sox resigned themselves to not having Ted Williams, Dom DiMaggio, Johnny Pesky, and the rest of their regulars back until 1946, Detroit general manager Jack Zeller ordered the printing of World Series tickets and authorized the team to begin selling them. The prices for the 1945 World Series at Briggs Stadium: box seats (for all three games), $21.60. Reserved grandstand (for three games), $18 (tax included). Right- and left-field grandstands (for three games), $10.80.

You couldn't put a price on how much better the Tigers were with Hank in the lineup. Without him, the Senators were able to whittle the lead down to ½ game with 11 to play on September 13, before the Tigers arrived in Washington on September 15 for 5-games crammed into 3 days. The Senators were charging hard, starting September with a 7-game winning streak and winning 13 out of their first 19 in the month. They were bolstered by the return of former Navy man Walt Masterson to the pitching rotation, but they were battered and exhausted. Griffith pushed his tired pitchers on short rest down the stretch, flogging them like racehorses. If they didn't win, he might shoot them. The players hated Griffith, for his cheapness, for his stubbornness, for his old age, and his 1890s way of looking at baseball and the world around him.

They also hated him for importing so many Latin players, which represented a threat to their playing jobs now that the war was over. The ballplayers could hear boots marching behind them. Already in September, scores of guys were playing their last games in the big leagues. Thousands of former ballplayers would soon be competing for only a few hundred major league jobs. The rest of the guys would scramble for work, just like the rest of the servicemen.

The Senators were not alone in this anxiety, but perhaps they felt it more closely than others. On September 12, the powder keg Clark Griffith worried about finally exploded when a fierce brawl broke out among the players in the clubhouse. Pitchers Marino Pieretti and Alex Carrasquel, an Italian and a Venezuelan, fought over something as trivial as the possession of a baseball bat. Carrasquel grabbed the bat and took a healthy swing at Pieretti, who ducked and responded with a quick punch to give Carrasquel a black eye. The entire fight gave the weary Senators a bruising. Manager Ossie Bluege smoothed it over nicely, telling the press that the team was on edge because they wanted to take a bite out of the Tigers. But he was lying, knowing the tensions between the white guys and the Latin guys had been building for months. Such clubhouse discord was one major sticking point in the argument against black and Latin players coming to the majors in the next few years.

A new day was coming, but the Washington Senators felt like old outcasts. Their aging owner wanted them to win no matter how badly it hurt. All ballplayers get tired down the stretch, but the grind of '45 was especially painful and taxing. Asked decades later about that final month of 1945 and the frustration on the team, the genial and gentle Buddy Lewis tightened up. "Do you know the old saying 'What we see here, what we say here, stays here?' We had that sign in the dressing room," he said. "I still believe in that sign."

A lot was on the minds of both the Tigers and Senators before the start of the big series. The Senators were a team that was tired of wartime baseball and the exploitive nature of it all. Clark Griffith, who was always so obsessed with nationalism and hosting war heroes and presidents, completely ignored his players. When the players heard him say, "We'll win that pennant yet, call it a hunch," they cringed. Like a lot of major leaguers, they were tired of being recklessly abused just so the owner could make a few extra bucks and still treat them like property to be bought, sold, and traded with contract policies designed to drive them into the dust. The war vets felt worse. Even in Detroit, the tired Tigers related. Hank Greenberg could already sense his own salary dispute sometime in the near future, no matter how well he finished this season or next. The seeds of outrage, for change in the future, for creating a more modern game, were planted in Griffith's beloved ballpark, while the old man was still mourning FDR, the Tigers were still in first place, and the ink was still wet on the Japanese surrender documents.

On the train tracks from Philadelphia to Washington, the Tigers had plenty of time to ponder how the future was changing before their very eyes. All they were doing was playing in a little pennant race, but their world, their country, and their game were changing daily now that the war was over. *The Sporting News* predicted a golden age coming, when the game would be saturated with talent from the services. The papers were full of stories about ballplayers returning home. One of them was Boston Braves minor leaguer Warren Spahn, who survived the drive to Germany and spent the summer counting his points until discharge. He worked his arm back into shape pitching Army baseball and seemed to be on the right track. He had 73 strikeouts in just a handful of games and vowed to be ready to resume his career, eager to live to the fullest.

The black ballplayers who had for years toiled in the Negro Leagues sensed that the end of the war meant their well-earned time was at hand. The idea of competing with black players didn't sit well with most white players for all of the obvious reasons, but the one that bothered white players most was that they had been in the majors first and should have the first chance to make good before they were farmed out in favor of black players. It wasn't immediately obvious to these white players, but hadn't their country just fought a war to get rid of two dictatorships that hated everyone and everything that wasn't just like them? It seemed a little hypocritical, and it was, and it was going to take ballplayers a few years to get used to the idea that baseball talent was now going to matter more than race.

When the Tigers were playing in Boston, the Kansas City Monarchs visited Briggs Stadium again, as they usually did a few times each season, drawing a healthy crowd from the black neighborhoods in Detroit. Black baseball lived in a parallel world to white baseball, where Satchel Paige was as much of a celebrity as Hank Greenberg. Paige actually lost the game he pitched, but that didn't slow the tide of the new talent coming. Paige never actually thought he would pitch in the majors, and as a ballplayer it's easy to suggest that if he couldn't be the pitcher he was in the 1930s, he didn't want to pitch there at all.

The big Negro American and National League teams typically paid extortionist park-rental fees to the major league teams for use of their stadiums while the home team was on the road. For a few decades, this was a lucrative side business for the major league slumlords. They had no interest in signing the players, but the cash was always the right color. In the summer of '45 alone, Briggs Stadium hosted the Homestead Grays, Baltimore Elite Giants, New York Cubans, Birmingham Black Barons, Kansas City Monarchs, Chicago American Giants, Cleveland Buckeyes, Philadelphia Stars, and Newark Eagles. Future major leaguers such as Jackie Robinson, Roy Campanella, Joe Black, and Sam Jethroe played in Detroit, as did veteran stars such as Paige, Hilton Smith, Willard Brown, Piper Davis, Artie

Wilson, Willie Wells, Buck Leonard, Josh Gibson, and Cool Papa Bell. It's a good bet that the Brooklyn Dodgers scouts passed through the turnstiles at Briggs while Hank and the boys were on the road. In a few years, other teams started copying the Dodgers, including the rival New York Giants, who used their loose relationship with their Polo Grounds tenants, the Cubans, and their owner, Alex Pompez, to orchestrate the purchase of Willie Mays.

The Tigers on the train were elbow to elbow with servicemen coming home, but hundreds of thousands of guys were still in Germany. A lot of them were ballplayers, too. Army baseball had always been a big deal in the European Theater during the war, and it reached its pinnacle in early September when 200,000 soldiers witnessed the 1945 GI World Series, a 5-game spectacle played in Nuremberg, at a captured sports field the US Army renamed Soldiers' Field. Nuremberg Stadium was part of the former Nazi party rally grounds. It was an uncompleted sports complex that was once one of Hitler's favorite projects. He dreamed of constructing the world's largest sports arena at Nuremberg. In 1938, after the grand triumph of his deception in the 1936 Berlin games, he reportedly said that the Olympics "will be held for all eternity in Germany and in this stadium."

The war forced construction to be abandoned, and by 1945, all that was left was the ominous limestone façade. But around it was more than enough open space to line out a baseball diamond. Baseball was the thing to do in the American-controlled parts of Germany. A reporter noted that ball games were going on everywhere: "These days, you see baseball games of all kinds everywhere in the American zone."

A round-robin tournament was played through the summer to determine the participants in the GI World Series, and by the fall the teams were set. The obvious favorite was the big league laden 71st Infantry Division of Patton's Third Army. Patton was quite the collector of rare books, antique firearms, and major leaguers. His team had eight big leaguers and a slew of minor leaguers. Virtually the entire team had professional experience. The best pure hitter was outfielder Harry "the Hat" Walker, who played for manager Billy Southworth's pennant-winning St. Louis Cardinals in '42 and '43 before earning a Bronze Star in combat. But the most dangerous weapon in the Third Army arsenal was a tall, rangy right-handed pitcher from the citrus fields in Southern California, who threw hard sinkers from a deceptive sidearm delivery. The hitters hated Ewell Blackwell. They called him the Whip.

Patton expected a swift whipping, especially when he saw the opposition, the Overseas Invasion Services Expedition of Com Z, OISE for short. In other words, these were ordinary joes. Nobody knew who the hell these guys were. There was a pitcher from the Bushwicks, a bunch of college kids, some bushers, and a guy who'd pitched for the Pirates. The manager was Sam Nahem, a Jewish kid from the Bronx who wore glasses and saw the world with egalitarian eyes. He pitched rather pedestrian innings for the Philadelphia Phillies before the war, but he could spin a slider. He loved playing ball in the army. When it came time to put his team together, he found out that two Negro League guys were in the OISE. They both came ashore on D-Day and had both seen heavy fighting all the way to Berlin. Patton's team was all white guys. Nahem's guys were integrated. He was well aware that this took guts on his part. "A lot of teams were not integrated," he said. "And that was tough."

But Nahem wanted to win and couldn't say no to the talent. One player was Willard Brown, a power-hitting outfielder from the Monarchs. Brown wasn't a smart player, but if you left a pitch where he could get it, he could hit it all the way back to Kansas City. The real find was Leon Day, who was one of the best ballplayers who never played in the majors. He was built like a fire hydrant and threw smoke. When he wasn't pitching, he played second base. He was a tough out who could drive the ball and run. Nahem thought Day was the best ballplayer in Europe, and he didn't care one bit that he was black.

Game 1 started with 50,000 doughs sitting in the sun, consuming large amounts of local beer as well as the American stuff the quartermaster brought in. Now that the war was over, meat was available, so soldiers ate hot dogs and smeared on the mustard. They waved their short snorters and placed their bets. It was just like the States in a lot of ways, except that everyone had guns. Well, maybe it was just like the States. Ewell Blackwell's snappy delivery worked just fine. He was always at his best when he let his fastball do whatever it wanted to do. He threw so many sinkers and cutters that the 71st Infantry won, 9–2.

Then Patton's guys saw Leon Day pitch. They were astounded. He was stronger than Blackwell and he threw harder, overmatching them with a short-armed delivery and a hard, over-the-top curveball. He won game 2, 2–1, to even the series. The games shifted to Reims, France, where Patton's team was transported in style aboard a B-17. Blackwell was good, but Nahem was better, and the underdogs won Game 3, 2–1, to lead the series, 2–1. Patton's darlings took Game 4 to even the series when Harry the Hat hit the winning home run in a 5-0 win, sending the senior back to Nuremberg for the decisive Game 5. There on the field of Hitler's dreams, before a crowd of 71,000 soldiers and a few locals who remembered Hitler's speeches, Sam Nahem Bobby Keane beat Ewell Blackwell, 2–1, to win the GI World Series. Even Patton tipped his helmet. American intelligence officers knew all about how the Nazis felt about baseball during the war and how they used antibaseball sentiment to preach victory could look into the crowd and see citizens who once jeered the Americans now cheering for them. The officers looked on the locals with skeptical eyes.

The stadium crowds were enough to make the Nazi prisoners awaiting trial at Nuremberg jealous and yearn for the old days. Hermann Göring liked to chat up his guards, and when he heard about the commotion, he asked what was going on. Told it was a baseball game, the ex–field marshal asked to learn more about this American sport. Somehow, the conversation led to a man named Branch Rickey, the general manager of a team called the Brooklyn Dodgers, who planned to sign Negro players. Herr Field Marshal was alarmed. Told Rickey earned the salary of $100,000 to choose baseball players, Göring supposedly allowed a hearty scoff. His guards reported him saying, "That's a million deutsche marks! I was in the wrong business!"

Baseball was going to be big money after the war, and the Tigers knew it was coming as their train steamed to the big series in Washington. Commissioner Chandler sold World Series radio rights for $150,000 in the first major media deal of the postwar era, a precursor to his 1946 deal where he sold the rights to the next 10 years for $14 million. That, too, was significant, and yet another example of how the war propelled baseball and American sports into modernity. The war created a surge of demand for baseball, and the end of it loosened up the economy enough for corporate advertisers to make tremendous investments in baseball as media programming. The war made big baseball-media deals possible. In future years, the lifeblood of all professional sports teams became television contracts, and baseball created the model later imitated by pro and college football, basketball, and every other professional or college sports league that wanted a big-money television deal.

During the war, major league baseball teams made most of their money selling tickets at the front gate. When Chandler made the first big-money deal to sell media rights, he began to ruin that model and was letting the genie out of the bottle. Seven decades later, owners made all their money off TV, but were still greedy, making game tickets too expensive for ordinary people, whose children might actually be inspired to play the game if they could afford to go to the ballpark when they were young, choking off future generations of talent and diminishing the product. Even the technology that eventually made television affordable to the masses had its birth in the war. In the summer of '45, the demand for baseball was reaching new heights, and the boom was only beginning.

None of that future stuff mattered much to the tired and weary ballplayers headed to Washington. Hank and the gang were just trying to make it through in one piece, while the Tigers were printing World Series tickets and receiving ten thousand requests a day. Hank sat with his sore ankle because it still hurt to stand up, wondering what he had left. He wanted to win the pennant. He had no love for the Senators. As the world moved ahead, it was the guys locked in the past who had to win it all. It was up to the wartime birds to finish the job.

CHAPTER 26

The $300,000 Home Run

The Tigers arrived in Washington, DC, on September 15 to play the most important series of the season, 5 games in 3 days against the Senators at Griffith Stadium, perilously clinging to a ½-game lead in the American League standings. The schedule called for back-to-back doubleheaders, followed by a fifth game. Both teams were frayed and exhausted, but the eyes of baseball were upon them, even those across the Pacific, where thirteen divisions totaling 175,000 men were readying to land in occupied Japan. That news was buried in the newspapers; nobody wanted to know that we had really come that close to an all-out invasion.

Clark Griffith was pleased with the healthy crowd of 22,946 at his ballpark, including a four-man umpire crew instead of the usual three, the American League office's nod to the importance of this series. Griffith hoped for a clean sweep, which would push the Tigers into second place. He eagerly welcomed Commissioner Chandler, who got his first look at the Tigers. Major General Claire L. Chennault, hero of the CBI and frequent rice-paddy shortstop, was there to throw out the first pitch. Chennault was eager to meet Hank Greenberg and Buddy Lewis, veterans of his area of operations. The Senators were in a feisty mood. They wanted to win, but not for Griffith. A taste of that World Series bonus money would nearly match their yearly salaries. Bert Shepard remembered, "Sure they wanted to win the pennant, but what the hell, they sure didn't want to win it for the old man."

Hal Newhouser warmed up in front of the visitor's dugout, but he didn't feel right and couldn't get loose. He hadn't pitched in eight days. The ball felt flat coming out of his hand, and the cold, rainy weather wasn't helping his sore abdomen, back, or shoulder any. Nonetheless, he took the ball to start the game. The news was not so good for Hank Greenberg. His ankle wasn't getting any better. He tried to hit on it before the game, but the pain was too great, so he was not in the starting lineup. The field was in such soggy, shoddy shape that manager Steve O'Neill didn't want him to play anyhow. After one inning, it started to rain, and the game was delayed for more than an hour.

After the delay, Newhouser was cold and spent. After pitching only one inning he removed himself from the game. The Tigers were in trouble, but so were the Senators. Their starting pitcher, Dutch Leonard, aggravated his sore shoulder. He couldn't get his knuckleball working and removed himself from the game when the rain cleared. The last vestige of wartime ball was baseball in the dark ages, where the teams' most valuable commodities, starting pitchers, were run into the ground like a set of old tires.

When Newhouser's turn in the lineup came up, Hank gave it a go as a pinch hitter. Trying to find his swing in the cold and wet, he could do nothing more than hit a ground ball and roll into a double play. The other guys would have to do it. Reliever George Caster kept it close, and the score was tied 4–4 in the top of the seventh inning when Doc Cramer's triple scored 2 and Roy Cullenbine doubled home Doc to build a 7–4 lead. Caster closed it out with 3⅓ scoreless innings, and the Tigers went for the sweep.

Dizzy Trout put his money where he smoked his 35¢ cigars in Game 2. He moved up his turn in the rotation and pitched a complete game to win, 7–3, his 4th win on the long road trip. He salvaged his season down the stretch, improving his record to 18–14. Trout was helped by Rudy York's four-hundred-foot home run in the sixth and catcher Paul Richards, who hit a go-ahead sacrifice fly in the eighth. The unsungs got it done. That was how championship teams won in war and in baseball. The sweep badly hurt the Senators, who now only had 8 games to play, while the Tigers had 12 scheduled. *The Detroit News* told the fans back home:

TIGERS BEAT SENATORS, 7–4, 7–3, GO 2½ AHEAD

Hank tried out his sore ankle again the following day, September 16, but again it didn't feel right so he didn't start. Again, the Tigers would have to win without their rock. Newhouser tried again in the first game of the doubleheader and pitched courageously through pain, but the knuckleballer Roger Wolff outdueled him 3–2. Once more, the Senators needed every game.

The Senators cut the lead to 1½ games. The Senators had to sweep, and to do it they had to beat Detroit starter Al Benton, who had not won since August 6 and hadn't won a game this important all season.

Benton pitched his way out of trouble in almost every inning and the Tigers led 5–0 after seven innings, but the Senators wouldn't quit, scoring two runs in the eighth and two runs in the ninth to slice the lead to 5–4. With two out and the tying run at third base and the winning run at third base, Dizzy Trout proved that sometimes quirky and crazy is better than cocky and good.

The right-hander was summoned into a save situation on one day's rest to face pinch-hitter Mike Kreevich, the now thirty-seven-year old veteran who had been sold by the Browns to the Senators in August. Kreevich was a lifetime .283 hitter whose days were almost up, but he had been facing Trout for years and knew his nuances.

The moment was huge for the Senators. If Kreevich could scratch a measly single into the outfield, the run would score to at the very least tie the game and send it to extra innings. If he could manage to gap an extra-base hit, then the runner at first, the lightning-quick Gil Torres, could come racing home with the winning run.

It was the most important at-bat of the season for Washington. A win for the Senators would finish the double-header sweep and cut the Tiger lead to ½ game. A loss would push them back to 2½ games all over again, exactly where they began the day.

Trout sprinted to the mound and didn't even bother taking any warm-up tosses. His red bandana was stuffed into his back pocket and a huge chaw was rolled in his cheek, like a little kid with a lollipop stuck in the side of his mouth. He didn't care if he was on one day's rest. Never even entered his mind. He wanted the win, because the Tigers needed the split, and he wanted to pitch in the World Series.

Clark Griffith nervously watched. He bought Kreevich for a moment like this, hoping that the veteran's big-game experience with the 1944 Browns would help his team. Maybe he was hoping some of that Brownie magic would rub off on his Senators. But Kreevich's patience was about as thin as Dizzy's red bandana.

All it took was one pitch. Trout let it rip, but maybe he was fatigued just enough for his fastball to have a little extra sink. Or maybe he was demented enough to know exactly what he was doing and took just enough speed off the fastball to fool his old enemy.

Kreevich thought he saw a mistake. His eyes opened wide and he took a ferocious hack at a fastball in the middle of the plate and hit it hard on the ground. He knew right away that he missed the pitch. He screamed a profanity as he slammed his bat in the dirt and the ball rocketed on one hop to second baseman Skeeter Webb, who artfully handled the hop and threw out Kreevich to end the game and protect a 5–4 victory.

Griffith sulked in his seat as Kreevich fumed with his hands on his hips. The Senators ran out of steam. On the dirty brown grass in Washington, the tired Tigers stormed the field to thank Dizzy, who just maybe, was never as crazy as he led on. The lead was back to 2 ½ games with nine left on the Tiger schedule.

After the game, the giddy Dizzy said he was hoping to wrap up the pennant so he could hop in his automobile and drive to Chicago, buy a ticket, and secretly sit in the seats to scout the Cubs. After all, wartime fuel restrictions had been lifted, so Dizzy's little road trip wasn't out of the question. The Cubs were good. That day, they had beaten the Brooklyn Dodgers, sweeping their major league record 18th double-header of the season.

While the Tigers anticipated the World Series, the Senators were being written off. What a waste the war had been. Griffith's grand dream of a wartime World Series would probably never come true now. He would not achieve what the Browns had in 1944, and how that killed him. The Senators had only one game left with the Tigers and six games total remaining before their season ended September 23.

The Detroit writers saw the Washington writers writing their team's 1945 obituary. *The Detroit News* told readers back home:

WASHINGTON WRITERS GIVING UP ALL HOPE

On the last day of the longest road trip of the war years, the Tigers and the Senators played a forgettable game that showed every reason why wartime ball was so bad for so long. The weather was miserable, the attendance was minuscule, and the teams combined to use 35 total players. The Tigers lost 12–5, and manager Steve O'Neill used 6 pitchers, throwing his pitching schedule for the last week of the season into a mess. The Tigers escaped Washington with a 1½ game lead and headed to Cleveland on September 19 to face Bob Feller, with control of everything except for Hank Greenberg's troublesome ankle.

Hank made his first start in ten days and it was no coincidence that he wanted to test himself in a pennant race against Feller, who was making his seventh start since the end of the war and his third against the Tigers, the most he had faced any team. If the Tigers thought familiarity would be a factor, Feller quickly proved them wrong and trimmed their lead back to 1 game.

He was devastatingly good, pitching a one-hitter with 7 strikeouts to run his postwar record to 4-2 and earn his first shutout since August 21, 1941, when he whitewashed the Yankees also by a 2–0 score. O'Neill, who liked to joke that his catching hand still hurt from occasionally catching Feller's bullpen sessions when he managed him during his 1936 rookie year, noticed for the first time that the war might have sapped some of Feller's arm strength. He noted that Feller wasn't throwing as hard as he used to, but was better at locating his fastball and changing speeds with it. O'Neill thought the telltale sign was that Feller was throwing more curveballs than fastballs, which to him, said that the former sailor knew he was firing blanks.

If those were duds, they were still pretty good. Feller made the Tigers look bad, including Hank, who went 0-for-3 with a walk. Feller came so close to throwing a no-hitter that the only hit he allowed was a cheap flare off the end of Jimmy Outlaw's bat in the fifth inning. Feller was annoyed when right fielder Les Fleming let the ball drop in front of him without charging it harder. He wanted that no-hitter. Nothing infuriates pitchers more than fielders who can't catch fly ball singles before they fall. Other than that, Feller treated the Tigers like zeros.

The next few days should have been a joyous occasion for the Tigers to celebrate clinching the American League pennant in front of their home fans at Briggs Stadium, but instead the next eleven days turned into a desperate, hurried, and rain-soaked blur. The Senators were spent, winning only 2 of the last 5 games. The Tigers lost 4 out of their next 6, with frequent rain interruptions and little playing time from a very sore and creaky Hank. The only games Detroit won were Newhouser's 23rd and 24th victories on September 22 and 26, but he was just as tired and spent as the rest of the Tigers, who could feel the strain of a long season and a long war.

The best news was that pitcher Virgil Trucks was finally released from the Navy after a long delay. He was instructed to hurry his arm into shape and be ready to pitch at a moment's notice. When the Tigers lost 3–2 to the Indians in the second game on September 26, it meant they could not win the pennant at home. They would have to go back out on the road, and they would have to go back to the heartbeat of wartime baseball one last time, St. Louis's Sportsman's Park, to face the Browns, who were long out of the race and could force them into a 1-game play-off with the Senators if the Browns could sweep a scheduled doubleheader on what became September 30, the last day of the season.

Hal Newhouser's arm was falling off, and Hank Greenberg was sore and wasn't hitting anymore. O'Neill could see it now—great team suffers great choke, the Detroit Tigers, the war's last great joke. "One base hit," he lamented, "and this place would be a madhouse instead of a morgue."

It was raining in St. Louis when the Tigers arrived on September 27. It rained for the next three days, which became the luckiest three days of the war years for the Detroit Tigers. It allowed Hal Newhouser to rest his shoulder just in time to pitch again if needed. It gave Virgil Trucks time to meet the team in St. Louis and spend three days trying to hurry his arm into shape with catcher Paul Richards. He said he was in good shape thanks to pitching for the Navy, but he had no idea what kind of stamina or stuff he would have.

Hank Greenberg wanted to finish the season out, but everything hurt. It had been the longest short season of his life. He felt like a rookie again, gassed and bruised, exhausted mentally and physically. The crummy weather in St. Louis didn't help any. He spent three days in his hotel room, staring at the rain pelting the sidewalk. He had nothing to do but spend time with the boys, tell war stories, and remember the time during the '42 World Series when the B-17 piloted by the late Billy Southworth Jr. buzzed Sportsman's Park on the way to the war.

When Hank woke up on September 30, he peeked out his hotel window for just any opening in the sky and swore he could actually hear his legs creaking like wooden planks. He had hit well when he had been healthy and the heat loosened him up, but the cold weather was hell on his bones. He had seen bad rain in China during monsoon season and he wondered if experiencing the CBI might have prepared him for the slop of St. Louis. Then, a miracle: after three days of sitting around the hotel, the rain eased enough to allow the Tigers and the Browns to return to the field.

Once the players arrived, they discovered a muddy swamp. The playing conditions were as bad as anyone had ever seen during the war. The mud was three feet thick on the baselines. The batter's box was a sinkhole. The pitchers took a look at the mound and cringed. They didn't make spikes long enough to save a guy from sinking. Virgil Trucks looked at the mound and might have wondered why he left the Navy in the first place.

The Browns were already waiting. Chances are that if the decision had been theirs, they would just have gone home already. They were a third-place team going nowhere fast, and a lot of the players who'd kept them afloat in the war years would be going home for good after the season or sinking back into the minor league mud. Pete Gray was one of them. The summer had been long and lonely, filled with slumps and deprivation. Teammates sensed he grew sadder as September played out, and they were right. He rarely played and he wasn't in the team's plans. Even the steady stream of wounded soldiers had slowed, and soon he was described by one of his teammates as a man who was as lonely as a gravedigger.

When Virgil Trucks was trying to get loose, his cleats wouldn't catch in the wet turf and he grew frustrated, muttering profanities at the mud. He felt stiff and tight, and even though he had been throwing for three days, he didn't know how he could possibly pitch in a big game like this. Even though the war was over, this was the last breath of wartime baseball, and Trucks would try to gut it up and close it out.

When he was warming up, Virgil saw something he could not believe. Hank Greenberg lumbered out of the dugout and into the rain. There was no explanation for why Hank should be wading out into the cold. The grass was covered with a tarp and the teams weren't on the field. Hank's road gray uniform was firmly pressed on his muscular back, so impeccably hanging off his mountainous shoulders that he looked like he had never missed a game in his life. Virgil wondered what Hank was thinking. It was steadily raining and the game was delayed for another hour. The big slugger should be somewhere dry and warm, not out in this muck. But Hank strolled through the soggy grass, his spikes sinking as he walked, specking mud behind his legs, undeterred and singular in purpose known only to him. A few menacing growls came from the Browns bench, but Hank didn't give a damn.

"I remember so vividly," Virgil said, "how Hank went over to the other dugout looking for Pete. Back in those days, talking to the guys on the other team was something we didn't do. Hank walked over there and he bellows, 'Where's Gray?' Hank had this booming voice you couldn't miss. He always sounded like he was smoking a cigar. It takes some prodding, but Pete comes out and Hank shakes his hand and drapes that long arm around Pete's shoulder. What a moment! Hank shooed away a cameraman who wanted that picture. Hank wanted that to be between them two ballplayers. I think the fact that Hank saw him only as a fellow ballplayer must have meant the world to Pete. I don't know what Hank said, but I played with him for a long time, and let me tell you, there was no finer gentleman than Hank Greenberg."

Hank Greenberg and Pete Gray stood arm in arm in the steady St. Louis rain, talking softly for a few moments. This was the image of baseball in World War II. The serviceman was thanking the temporary worker for keeping the factory humming while he was gone. The hero got his life back. The replacement was swept out the door. Hank seemed to realize what few others could, that both of them had helped win the war in their own different ways. The magnitude of Hank's gesture was as grand as any home run he ever hit, at least to Pete Gray. Hank did not see Pete as a guy who shouldn't have been in the majors. He saw him as a fellow man and a ballplayer who deserved to be acknowledged for his effort. Hank knew Pete had done his part.

Hank and Pete shook hands. Then their moment together was over. Pete vanished into the dugout as Hank waded across the mud and returned to the visitor's side. Hank remembered what it was like to be told he didn't belong, but at least he had both hands to fight back. Pete did the best he could with one fist, but just once he might have wished for Hank's strength to hit a home run to shut up anyone who ever doubted his determination to be seen as more than the ballplayer nicknamed "the one-arm wonder." Then they each pushed their duffel bags deep into the past. Together, their experiences told the entire story of wartime baseball. A few minutes later, the rain eased just enough. The last great ball game of the World War II years was about to begin.

Virgil Trucks was throwing hard from the start, rifling his good fastball through the rain as if two years in the Navy never touched him. His opposite number, Browns pitcher Nelson Potter, had his screwball working. If the screwball had been a prisoner in a German stalag, it would have been shot. When it was working good, the pitch would start way outside against a right-handed hitter like Hank, and then just as the hitter gave up on the pitch, it would cut across the corner for a strike. Potter was a master at the screwball and a master screwball, who could make the pitch run around like a fall down drunk. When he faced Hank, the screwball was the only pitch he wanted to throw him. Potter wasn't stupid. He wasn't going to throw Hank a fastball, not if his life depended on it.

Hank knew that Potter always threw the screwball when he was in trouble. Hank got him for a hit in the third inning, but his bad ankle and big feet got stuck in the mud. He tried to hustle his way to safety, but was picked off third base to snuff out a big inning. Hank pulled himself out of the muck. He was filthy and furious at himself for what he knew was a baserunning mistake he could not afford at such a critical time. A lot of guys ran into mistakes during the soggy season, but that was no consolation. Mud was all over him—smeared on his legs and on his ass—and he dreaded the thought that he had just run the Tigers out of the pennant.

Trucks nearly pitched the Tigers into it. His stuff was better than anyone ever expected, especially his curveball, which he honed in the Navy with the help of former Tigers catcher Mickey Cochrane. Trucks was leading 2–1 in the bottom of the sixth inning when he ran into trouble. Manager Steve O'Neill almost never took his starters out, but this was different. Trucks had nothing left in the tank. He had come back from the Navy too late to be trusted to keep full strength in a moment like this. When O'Neill came to the mound, he didn't even ask Trucks if he wanted to stay in the game. O'Neill asked the catcher, Paul Richards, instead. Richards said no, Trucks had nothing left, and he needed to get out of this game.

So O'Neill made his bravest call of the season. He brought in the tired Hal Newhouser, with 310 innings on his arm and a body that hurt each time his cleats sloshed into the turf. In the bottom of the 8th inning with the score tied, 2–2, Newhouser was throwing fire in the rain when he gave up a one-out single to Lou Finney. Luke Sewell wanted that run to score at all costs, so he called for Pete Gray. This was the story of Pete's life in so many ways: nothing to it, come off the bench in the cold and pinch-hit against the toughest guy in the league, lefty against lefty, the guy with the great arm against the guy with one arm. His job was to advance the go-ahead run to second base, but he couldn't do it, instead forcing out Finney at second. Pete splashed through the mud, safe at first base, aboard on the fielder's choice. He was angry that he failed to advance the runner and determined to make good.

Newhouser was running out of steam. He gave up a booming double to George McQuinn that bounced off the right-field screen and sent Pete Gray running for his life one last time. Pete balanced so effortlessly as he pumped his only arm and ran on his two gifted legs, plowing through the puddles, turning second and rounding third as Roy Cullenbine cocked his rifle of a right fielder's arm and shot the ball home. Pete never stopped, never relented, never quit. Hank Greenberg in left field had a front row seat and his baseball instincts would have surely told him, *this field is muck and Pete Gray can STILL fly.* Pete slid in safely, the filth smeared across his face, his fury as dark as the clouds. "Gray, after streaking around the bases, slid home in the mud ahead of Cullenbine's throw," *The Detroit News* marveled. Pete stood up and didn't have to look at the scoreboard. He ran a dagger into Detroit's heart, and the Brownies led, 3–2.

When Newhouser came off the field, he had pitched 22/3 gutty innings, giving up 4 hits and striking out 5. O'Neill asked him if he had anything left. Tired, gaunt, sore, cold, and drenched in rain and sweat, O'Neill had his answer without a word. Hal pitched valiantly, as he had through the entire war. Now he was so tired he could cry. There was simply nothing left in his body to give. The teammates who watched him suffer and grind in those waning moments of 1945 knew there was never a doubt. Hal Newhouser was a man and he wasn't just one of the best of the war. He was one of the best, period.

With the Browns leading 3–2 in the top of the ninth in the first game of what was a scheduled doubleheader, Sewell pointed to Pete Gray and told him to play center field. Sewell's gesture could not be understated. The Browns were playing this game to win, and when it mattered most, he wanted his best center fielder in the game. Luke Sewell didn't always relate to Pete or understand what made him who he was, but he had been with him for a long time now. Putting him in center field wasn't the same as putting him in left field. If the other players on his team weren't going to tip their caps to the man with one arm, Luke Sewell would. Pete grabbed his glove. He got a smattering of applause as the raindrops fell on his bare arm. You could take the major leagues away from Pete, but you couldn't take away his desire to take every last moment the majors would allow.

Steve O'Neill sent Hubby Walker to pinch-hit for Newhouser, leading off the ninth inning against Potter. He was a pure wartime replacement, a thirty-nine-year old bench player journeyman who was back with the Tigers only because they needed help and they knew him because he broke in with them in 1931. That was a lifetime ago, and so was Hubby's last hit. Walker played in only 27 games all season, mostly as a pinch-hitter, but he wasn't very sharp. He had only 2 hits in 22 at-bats all season, a .090 batting average.

You could almost hear Potter scoffing on the mound, laughing at the idea that this old busher could possibly touch him. But Walker wasn't afraid and he singled to left field, his first hit since August 8, and his last regular season hit in the major leagues. The boys on the bench clapped for old Hubby, who hadn't even played in the minors in 1943 or 1944 when he was in the Navy. Hubby was happy. His batting average was now a robust .130, and more importantly, he was the tying run.

Potter, who was always emotional on the mound, cursed and kicked at the dirt. Then he looked into the dugout and shot a threatening glare at Sewell. He did not want to come out of this game and he would have killed his manager if he came out to get him. But Sewell wasn't worried about Potter's feelings. He just wanted outs and he was anticipating scenarios in his head, playing a game of mental chess with O'Neill, because he had three spots in the batting order before he had to face Greenberg.

Sewell was also worried about Hubby Walker, who didn't steal bases very much anymore, but he could still run just enough to be dangerous. The irony was he was exactly the same kind of player scout Wish Egan once thought Pete Gray could have been for the Tigers. When the Tigers rejected Wish's idea to sign Pete in 1944, the old scout didn't quit. Instead he scavenged the bushes looking for another left-handed hitting outfielder capable of pinch hitting and running and the wise old scout with the thick glasses, the thicker notebook, and the vast memory came up with Walker.

Pete and Hank might have been teammates, and at this moment, O'Neill only cared about getting Walker to second. Shortstop Skeeter Webb was next, the perfect man for this line of work. Sewell knew O'Neill would have Webb bunting, so as soon as Potter went into his delivery, he had his corner infielders charging. Webb was scrappy and skilled. He pushed a sacrifice-bunt attempt up the first base line. At first base, Hubby Walker was running for his life. He had to get to second.

First baseman George McQuinn was a fine fielder and a left-handed thrower. He charged the bunt and barehanded, and in one easy motion shifted his body and threw a bullet to second baseman Don Gutteridge. Walker spent his last moment in the majors splashing face first into the mud at second base, arriving just as McQuinn's throw popped Gutteridge's glove. The play was so close that Walker didn't know if he was out until he heard umpire Joe Rue call him safe.

Sewell was infuriated and ran out onto the field to argue with Rue, shouting at him nose-to-nose while Potter complained profanely. While the Browns argued, O'Neill waved Walker back to the dugout and replaced him with pinch-runner Red Borom. Hubby walked off the field doused in mud and rain, but he couldn't have been happier and he couldn't have been sadder. He was going to miss being a big leaguer.

Now the Tigers had a huge break, runners on first and second with nobody out. With the extra out to play with, O'Neill did not hesitate. He ordered Eddie Mayo to bunt, which he did successfully, moving the runners to second and third with only one out. Doc Cramer was batting next, with Greenberg on deck.

Then Sewell made the most unconventional move of his entire managerial career. He elected to intentionally walk Cramer to pitch to Hank, setting up a force play at any base. It made perfect strategic sense, but the move ignored the magnitude of the moment. Hank watched Potter lob four intentional wide ones. Sewell was saying everything Hank knew people were thinking all along. He was saying, simply, that Hank Greenberg cannot beat him: He was no longer the player he used to be. The war had ruined him. That's what he was saying. All the fuming, rage, anger, and frustration might have swelled inside Hank at this moment, but as he walked to the batter's box in ankle-deep mud, he was as serene as the Chinese countryside.

Nelson Potter stared down at big Hank. In Detroit, the fans were glued to the radio. In Washington, the Senators were huddled around the radio, guessing screwball and ready to hop a train if the Browns could help them out.

Potter wound up and threw his first pitch. Hank was a patient pro. He watched it all the way in and decided it wasn't for him. Ball one. Then he stepped out for a moment. Hank felt it all—the stories from the war he told and those he didn't tell, the men he had known and never saw again— he was a veteran ballplayer and a war veteran, like so many others now, and he had his career back, but he wondered every day how much of his baseball life the war had taken. Hank stepped back into the box, his spikes sinking into the mud, and he gripped the bat from his narrow stance and waited for Potter to throw the next pitch.

Potter wound up and flicked his wrist as hard as he could, the sure sign of a screwball. Hank's eyes picked up the hand movement before the ball left Potter's grip. Hank read the seams of a screwball spinning away from him. He was supposed to give up on the pitch, but Hank wouldn't surrender. He was going to wait this one out. He knew, he just knew, the pitch would have to get far enough down the runway and gravity would force it near the plate. When the screwball made its late turn, Hank dropped the barrel and connected with a thunderous gunshot.

Hank lifted the ball high into the air down the left-field line. His eyes scanned the sky until he found the ball, the way he once counted the B-29 bombers flying home. The Tigers spilled out of the dugout and slipped into the mud, craning their necks to see if it would land fair or foul. Pete Gray stood on his soggy center-field turf and watched the ball wondering if it would get out. Hank walked slowly, then trotted into a slow jog, and saw Potter jab his hands on his hips. Then Hank saw the ball land just fair in the empty grandstand, clanking against the wooden rafters and echoing onto the field. Hank's eyes widened and he felt alive again! It was a grand-slam home run. The Tigers exploded in cheers. Hank slowly put his head down. He was never one to let the magnitude of the moment overwhelm him. He dropped his bat and began the journey home.

Hank sloshed through the mud, the most perfect trot of his life, the mud specking up and sprinkling his cheeks, but he didn't mind. Pete watched him round the bases. He could have closed his eyes and ran right with Hank. Hank crossed second base, over the hump in the middle of the field, and turned for third as the Browns grumbled. Hank swore he heard one of the infielders mutter, "Goddamn that dirty Jew bastard, he beat us again." He savored the thought of the Washington Senators sitting around a hotel room listening to his grand slam on the radio, calling him every dirty Jew name in the book, and he loved the thought of how angry his home run must have made them. Luke Sewell ripped up his lineup card and didn't dare look at anyone on his team. He knew what they were thinking, and he could surely sense their disdain and disbelief, damning him, for at that moment he lost his ballplayers forever. They wondered and whined in unison, *Why the hell did you pitch to that big Jew?*

Hank reached third, proud of his diligence, determination, and deci-sions. As he said before the war, every home run was like hitting a home run against Hitler. And then finally, he came home, slowing to a walk as he crossed home plate with the biggest smile anyone had ever seen on his genial face. All his teammates were there to greet him and slap his muddy bottom. It was the biggest moment of his career, but there was nary a wit-ness. There were no film cameras, scant fans, and only a still photographer to capture Hank coming home. No other home run ever meant as much to Hank, but he might as well have hit it in China, for his home run was forgotten nearly the second the ball rattled into the seats. His struggle was over at last. Hank came back to the bench and exhaled deeply, blowing the last embers of the war from his soul.

Hank's grand slam won the game, 6–3, and clinched the pennant. The umpires called off the second game and sent both teams home. It was the first pennant winning home run ever to be hit on the last play of a season. The press called it a $300,000 home run, the estimated total pot of World Series money now at stake. *The Detroit News* headline at home said it all:

THERE'S YOUR PENNANT!

NOW BRING ON THOSE CHICAGO CUBS!

The *News* wrote, "To win a league pennant in the last inning of the year's last game with a jackpot homer is obviously the play supreme in baseball. To the best of our knowledge, Hank Greenberg's mighty clout at St. Louis stands unique in the game's annals. It provided an incredible climax to a league race in which the strangest things have been routine. It could not, of course, have happened to a worthier athlete than our Hank. His re-conversion to his old trade is surely complete, and many another player, back from the wars or presently to be released, will take heart from his experience."

Hank Greenberg's greatest day in the majors was Pete Gray's last. While Hank sat on the bench, he looked out to center field and watched the last wartime ballplayer of World War II play out the string to the bitter end. Roy Cullenbine batted next for the Tigers and, swinging aggressively to finish the game, skied the ball to right-center field. Pete gracefully glided over the puddles, his cleats sloshing through the grass until he called off the right fielder, Gene Moore, who relented. Pete reached up with his good arm and let the baseball fall into his hand like an apple dropping off a tree.

The last hitter of the inning for the Tigers was Rudy York, who hacked early and lofted a ball into left-center field. This time, Pete went the other direction, just as he had in a thousand tryouts before, chasing a dream only he believed in. Rudy put some air under the ball, so for one last time, Pete stretched out his legs and ran for what he wished would have been forever. The left fielder, Lou Finney, relented. Pete arrived under Rudy's fly ball in plenty of time, presented his glove to the sky, and caught the ball for the final out of the game.

Then, instead of rolling the ball up his chest to his armpit and shaking the glove loose onto his pinkie, Pete simply held onto the ball. He trotted off the sloppy field, a worthless piece of wartime surplus. He was going home to Nanticoke for good. Nobody remembered him anymore. He was just one of those bums who played ball during the war.

Epilogue: V-Mail

Many years after the fighting was over, Hank Greenberg was rarely reminded that he had once been a solider. People would stop and ask him about this baseball memory or that, and he would always be kind, but in time his days as a ballplayer were so far in the past that it seemed as though it were another life lived by another man. But Hank's time in the war, that always belonged to him, and the public never seemed to remember.

Hank's war years never felt as far away to him as all those home runs. He lost himself in reading history books about the war, though he would occasionally lose himself in a historical novel. His favorite book was *The Winds of War*, by Herman Wouk. Hank spent hours lost in those pages, reliving the old times with a thirst for knowledge that only grew as he aged. When he was done with a book, few things in life satisfied him more than sitting on the porch, wearing his white tennis shirt and shorts and sneakers, taking long drags off his cigar, and recounting to listeners the details of the book, the story, and the reminders of the life that nobody ever asked Hank Greenberg about.

Once his son, Steve—who was born after the war—asked a question that perplexed him. He knew Hank hit 331 career home runs in his war-shortened career. "I said to him, 'Dad, you would have hit five hundred home runs.' He said, 'I wouldn't have traded it.' But I don't know that it is unique among guys of his generation. The notion that he reenlisted after his initial stint, then missed the next four years, I never heard him complain once."

Hank wasn't the only player who never complained. He wasn't uncommon, only highly visible. He never thought he was any kind of war hero, even when people called him one. That always baffled Hank, and he was so modest that not even family members fully grasped how he came to be so selfless. Hank would have hated history remembering him as a hero. As a ballplayer, fine, but as a hero, as far as Hank was concerned, such a title was subjective, meant nothing at all to him, and could belong to anyone else who deserved it or really wanted it.

The war changed the guys who went away, but they also had a great deal of pride. Greenberg missed 500 home runs, Feller missed 300 wins, DiMaggio missed 3,000 hits, Williams missed 3,000 hits and 600 home runs, and Spahn missed 400 wins, but there were pitchers who missed out on 100 wins or 10 wins or even 1, or even pitching 1 inning more or their first inning in the majors. Some guys missed their first hit, and some never knew their first hit was their last. All of them were in the same boat, and this is one of the great miracles of World War II, that so many boys, from so many walks of life, from so many ethnic, religious, and economic backgrounds, all universally felt united and not divided, compelled to risk their careers for country.

Hank got to play in the last World Series he wanted so badly. The 1945 Series was an afterthought to the end of the war, but a hell of a Series nonetheless. The Tigers beat the Cubs in 7 games. Hank hit .304 and almost gave away the Series when a ball hit right at him in left field handcuffed him and got behind him. Hal Newhouser pitched the victory in Game 7, and the Chicago Cubs, cursed by the Billy Goat, are still fighting the war. As of this writing, sixty-nine seasons have passed with the epitaph, "The Chicago Cubs haven't been in the World Series since the end of World War II."

Hank Greenberg would want readers to know one part of his personality and accomplishments. That is how competitive his teams were at the height of New York Yankees dominance. He would ask family, friends, and fans the following trivia question. In the thirty years from the time Hank became a starter with the Tigers in 1933 to his tenure as Cleveland Indians general manager from 1948 to 1957 to his career as the vice president of the Chicago White Sox from 1959 to 1963, how many years did the Yankees win the pennant? The answer is twenty-one times. Of the teams that won the American League pennant in the nine years the Yankees did not, Hank's teams won the pennant seven times: the '34, '35, '40, and '45 Tigers, the '48 and '54 Indians, and the '59 White Sox. The last World Series ring Hank Greenberg ever won as a player was the one he earned on the rain-soaked field the fall after the war ended.

HANK GREENBERG, US Army Air Corps, 1941–45, led the American League with 44 home runs and 127 runs batted in 1946, before he ran into the postwar salary dispute he anticipated. He was sold to the Pittsburgh Pirates, where he played his last year in the majors in 1947, where he encouraged rookie Jackie Robinson not to let the bastards get him down. Hank settled down and married after the war and started a family. As general manager of the Indians, his experiences serving in the remote CBI Theater helped him grasp how strongly he disliked institutionalized discrimination in baseball. He would not let the Indians stay at hotels where black players were not welcome. He also continued scouting and signing black players, a practice honed by his creative friend and intelligent mentor Bill Veeck. Hank did well in business and played a mean game of tennis all the way up until the end, when he died of cancer in 1986 at age seventy-five.

PHIL MARCHILDON, Royal Canadian Air Force, 1942–45, found his old curveball again and became a career-high 19-game winner in 1947. He salvaged enough of himself to pitch in the major leagues until 1950. He did not escape his wartime memories easily, battling his demons for decades. But by the time he died at age eighty-three in 1997, he had made his peace. He wrote a book about his life, became far more comfortable discussing the war, and was inducted into the Canadian baseball Hall of Fame.

JOHN "BUDDY" LEWIS, US Army Air Corps, 1942–45, played in the majors until 1949, when his career ended at age thirty-two. A career Washington Senator, Lewis retired with a lifetime batting average of .297. He returned home to Gastonia, North Carolina, where he coached American Legion baseball and scouted for the St. Louis Cardinals for decades. Buddy was a friend to many young ballplayers, helping them come of age as young players and young men. He was an institution in Gastonia, where he lived to the ripe old age of ninety-four, dying in 2011.

BERT SHEPARD, US Army Air Corps, 1942–45, bounced around the minor leagues for a few years after the war, but never played in the major leagues again. He remains the only person to have pitched in the major leagues with an amputated foot. He died at age eighty-seven in 2008.

WARREN SPAHN, US Army, 1942–45, got the most out of life when he got out of Germany. He won 363 major league games, the most of any left-handed pitcher, despite not getting a chance to become a regular starting pitcher until age twenty-five. He was a 13-time 20-game winner and won his only National League Cy Young Award in 1957, the year he pitched the Milwaukee Braves to their World Series victory over the New York Yankees. He died at age eighty-two in 2003.

BOB FELLER, US Navy, 1941–45, never cared one bit that the war cost him a chance to win 300 games. He led the American League in strikeouts in his first three seasons after the war and struck out a career-high 348 in 1946. He was inducted into the baseball Hall of Fame in 1962. He always believed Harry Truman made the right decision to drop the atomic bombs. "It saved five million lives! Truman had guts. When you go into war, you have to go in to win." Feller finished with 266 career victories and died at age ninety-two in 2010.

BIG JAKE JONES, US Navy, 1942–45, is the only combat fighter ace to have ever played major league baseball. He returned to the majors after the war and hit 16 home runs for the 1947 Boston Red Sox, where he was teamed with Marine aviator Ted Williams. Jones played in the minors until 1949, but kept flying for another four decades. He and Williams were fast friends for many decades, engaging in their passions of fishing, flying, hunting, and hitting, until Jake died at age eighty in 2000.

HANK BAUER, US Marine Corps, 1942–45, broke into the big leagues and played 14 seasons, hitting 164 career home runs. He was a regular on the Yankee dynasty that won the World Series from 1949 to 1953 and again in 1956 and 1958. He later managed the Baltimore Orioles to the 1966 World Series title, but the players who knew him swore he not only refused to talk about his war career, but also asked reporters not to write about it. He never felt more guilty than the time he went to Japan with the Yankees on a goodwill tour about a decade after the war, sheepishly whispering to his manager, Casey Stengel, that he "might have killed somebody's brother or uncle out here." Bauer died at age eighty-four in 2007, always proud to have been a Yankee, but more proud to have been a Marine.

BILL GREASON, US Marine Corps, 1943–45, 1950–52, broke into baseball with the 1948 Birmingham Black Barons, where one of his main jobs was keeping an eye on fellow rookie Willie Mays. He pitched for the Barons in the last Negro League World Series in 1948, then pitched for the Barons until he was recalled for the Korean War, where he pitched Army ball. After his discharge, he was one of the first black players in the Texas League and became the first black pitcher in St. Louis Cardinals history when he appeared in 3 games in 1954. He pitched in the minor leagues until 1959 and later became a Baptist minister, shepherding his flock in Birmingham for decades. In 2013, he was presented with a Congressional Gold Medal, in honor of his service with the Montford Point Marines.

HAL NEWHOUSER shed the reputation of only winning because he was a wartime pitcher when he led the American League with 26 victories, a 1.94 earned run average, and added a career-best 275 strikeouts in 1946. He finished his career with the Cleveland Indians in 1954 and 1955 when Hank Greenberg acquired him. Though he never fired a shot or wore a uniform, the war still shortened his career, thanks to the back-to-back seasons of more than 300 innings pitched in 1944 and 1945. His pitching career was over at age thirty-four with a lifetime record of 207-150, and he was elected to the Hall of Fame in 1992. After the war he became a scout, where he followed in the footsteps of Wish Egan and covered Michigan. Newhouser remained passionate and opinionated well into his seventies, resigning from his job when his last employers, the Houston Astros, would not listen to his advice to select Michigan high school shortstop Derek Jeter in the first round of the 1992 amateur draft. Newhouser died at age seventy-seven in 1998.

PETE GRAY finished the 1945 season with a .218 batting average in 77 games and never played in the major leagues again. He played a few more years of minor league ball before he called it a career. He turned down financial offers to make a movie about his life, turning up his nose at the money he could surely have used, and told the producers that he would never allow them to cash in on what he meant to people with amputations. He retired to Nanticoke, where he lived, largely forgotten, until his death at age eighty-seven in 2002. He is the only amputee ever to be a position player in the major leagues. When he died, the neighborhood kids he still coached cried. Nobody from Nanticoke ever played in the major leagues again. For the record, Pete had to have been a good ballplayer, one arm or two. Nobody could have played baseball as well as he did with one arm if they didn't have the tools to start with. This scout says so.

MANAGER BILLY SOUTHWORTH and his Cardinals gave it a good try in '45, but it wasn't meant to be. The Cardinals won 95 games, but fell 3 games short. Billy was spent in spirit when the war was over. His ballplayers loved him, but knew that he was never the same after Billy junior died. Managing the Cardinals was always a tough proposition, where a manager had to keep his job. Billy was fired when the war was over and became manager of the Boston Braves in 1946. He guided them to the 1948 World Series, his fourth pennant of the decade. While with the Braves, he inherited ace Warren Spahn. Billy died at age seventy-six in 1969, but had to wait until 2008 to be inducted into the baseball Hall of Fame as a manager. Then, perhaps, Billy found the solace, rest, and sense of accomplishment he seemed to be missing in life. Billy was buried in his hometown of Columbus, right next to his son, the real baseball war hero, Billy Southworth Jr. You can still visit the father and son, together for eternity.

ACKNOWLEDGMENTS

I spent my boyhood summers in Wisconsin with my grandmother and grandfather, where the war wasn't something that was in a book. It was something that you lived and breathed. My grandmother married my grandfather after her first husband, a wartime Army serviceman, was killed in a stateside motorcycle accident. My grandfather, who was from the era of boys who wanted to grow up to be either big league ballplayers or aviators, was a pilot all the way. He served stateside during the war. My mom came along in 1948, the first of eight, and by the time I was a kid, the house in Milwaukee was populated with books, model airplanes, drawings, war board games, antiques, toys, and stories as thick as the pipe smoke my grandfather blew into the air and as loud as the ballgames he watched on TV.

For someone so young, I lived the years of the Great Depression and World War II through my grandparents and, in the never-say-die hustle of my mother, absorbed that generation's ethos. So while other kids thought World War II was something on TV, I knew it in a much more real, much more tangible way. The war was so personal and part of their regular life stories that it almost seemed as if it never ended. That allowed me, as I grew up, to better relate to all the old baseball men I got to know who lived the times in this book. I grew up alongside their worldview. I am a Gen-X World War II product.

When I was kicking around trying to find the right girl, I happened upon a lovely little thing whose grandfather was still kicking around. He took me used-car shopping one day and told me he didn't bite. There were stories that he landed on D-Day and went all the way to Berlin. Only after he passed away and we found his dog tags and photographs were we able to figure out what he never told us. He was the driver of a Sherman tank in a company called Vitamin Charley in the 741st tank batallion, which rode from Omaha Beach to Berlin and stopped to play baseball in Paris after its liberation. He saw a lot of fighting, which he never talked about, but his name on the unit's muster rolls proves Milt was just being coy. His granddaughter, Jen, the girl I wisely married, has his fight, compassion, and humor.

Milt would have told me to never tell this story, so I will anyhow. He left behind a stack of black-and-white photos that we found after he died. Sometime in late 1944 or early 1945, Staff Sergeant Stern of Vitamin Charley (741st Tank Battalion) posed while standing in front of a Sherman tank and one of the very rare M36B1 tanks with the big 90mm guns. Milt's sense of humor got the better of him. He poached a row of Nazi medals and pinned them to his Ike jacket. Then he turned up the collar of his jacket and slipped a German helmet over his head. He had one of his buddies snap a smirking photo of himself doing the old Seig Heil with an enormous, sarcastic grin. Why? Because he was a Jewish GI from Connecticut killing the Krauts with laughter when he wasn't actually killing them. He left the Army when the war over and like a million other guys, built a new life. Later, he took his little granddaughter with him to some of his Vitamin Charley reunions, until the years passed and there weren't enough tankers left to get together anymore. But she never forgot his past, how they made him and how they made her, and together, Jen and I never forgot how he helped make us.

Like the soldiers and sailors I wrote about, I was too young and dumb to understand just what I was getting myself into by writing this. I quickly realized that war is hell, and so was writing this book. The amount of research was enormous, and organizing and writing and rewriting it all proved incredibly difficult and painstaking. I had written two books about larger subjects that were framed around baseball before I got to this one. I had developed a great depth of knowledge of the game's history after the war, which is simply not common for a guy of my age and generation. The descriptions in this book are drawn from numerous historical sources and interviews I have gathered over the years. Everything is true and depicted as realistically as possible. Writing a book like this was like flying Billy Southworth's B-17. The first time he went up, he thought he was perfect. Then he landed and counted thirty flak holes in the bomber. I have done my best to ensure accuracy, and I hope to have patched all the holes before publication. Reader feedback is always welcome at klimaink@gmail.com.

Writing this book, especially about baseball and the war, meant that the bulk of the new material was going to come from period newspapers that I had never seen used in any other baseball or war books. The University of Oregon's fine collection of rare baseball books was a tremendous asset. The University of Wisconsin is where I found the bulk of what I used, hidden away in old cabinets. They don't call it the morgue for nothing. I can say that watching newspapers go away is like watching an old friend die, but I am glad I got out young enough to do something else with my life.

Before I go off and begin writing the next thing, a few special thanks are needed here. Gary Moncur and Tim Conver, whose fathers served with Billy Junior, helped me with information and photos from their excellent tribute to the 303rd Bomb Group Web site. The same thanks to Englishman Russ Abbey, whose knowledge of the 55th Fighter Group helped me to write Bert Shepard's story in better detail. Gary Bedingfield has done all readers interested in baseball in World War II a tremendous service with his *Baseball in Wartime* blog, a valuable resource.

Steve Greenberg is a good guy, no matter how many people ask him about Hank. The same is true of Roland Hemond, who once told me I reminded him of Bill Veeck, which is just about the nicest thing anybody in professional baseball has ever said to me. Rafe Sagalyn went through the back-and-forth with me for a few years on this before I just up and wrote the first draft, and Pete Wolverton made it better. My wife, Jen, got one mention already, but I think she deserves another. She's pretty awesome. And she sent me out to see a player we call the two-five, which turned out to be a really good idea.

Readers who like this book and the way I write things would do well to locate my other two baseball books, because I feel that these three books represent a unique trilogy of baseball and American narrative history. The joke is that I had no idea I had written a trilogy until I got to this book and realized how connected all three were. I suppose I always wanted a trilogy of my own, and I got one, in a strange way, written completely out of order and published over six years. Taken together, *The Game Must Go On* (2015) is part one, *Willie's Boys* (2009) is part two, and *Bushville Wins!* (2012) is part three of a trilogy spanning 1941 to 1957, telling both the story of baseball at war and postwar America and baseball. My apologies for this coming out of my head in such stranger order; honest writers will tell you they can't understand the way their own mind works.

I was happy when Steve Greenberg told me that Hank's favorite book was *Winds of War,* because I wanted to write the baseball incarnation of that book, something in Wouk style, with a lot of characters in a lot of places doing a lot of things over a long period during the war. I wish Hank could have read this.

SOURCES

Primary Newspapers

Birmingham News, Birmingham World, Boston Globe, CBI Roundup, Chicago Defender, Chicago Sun-Times, Chicago Tribune, Christian Science Monitor, Dallas Morning News, Denver Post, Esquire, Hartford Courant, Kansas City Star, Louisville Courier-Journal, London Times, Los Angeles Sentinel, Los Angeles Times, Milwaukee Journal, Milwaukee Sentinel, Newsweek, New York Amsterdam News, New Yorker, New York Herald Tribune, New York Times, Pittsburgh Courier, Sporting News, Stars and Stripes, St. Louis Post-Dispatch, Washington Post, Yank magazine.

Primary Interviews

Steve Greenberg, Roland Hemond, Virgil Trucks, Buddy Lewis, Al LaMacchia, Dario Lodigiani, Bill Wight, George Genovese, Lenny Merullo, Gene Handley, Spider Jorgensen, Greg Spahn, Bill Greason, Bob Zuk, Buster Staniland.

Primary Books

The Rand McNally Encyclopedia of Military Aircraft, by Enzo Angelucci (Gallery, 1980)

When Baseball Went to War, edited by Todd Anton and Bill Nowlin (Triumph, 2008)

The Mighty Eighth, by Gerald Astor (Dell, 1997)

The Encyclopedia of Minor League Baseball (Baseball America, 1991)

Semper Fi, Mac: Living Memories of the U.S. Marines in World War II, by Henry Berry (Arbor House, 1982)

Speaking Frankly, by James F. Byrnes (Harper, 1947)

Baseball in '41, by Robert Creamer (Penguin, 1991)

The Great Book of World War II Airplanes, by Jeffrey Ethell (Bonanza, 1987)

Now Pitching, Bob Feller, by Bob Feller and Bill Gilbert (Birch Lane Press, 1990)

Hank Greenberg: The Story of My Life (Times Books, 1989)

The Boys Who Were Left Behind: The 1944 World Series Between the Hapless St. Louis Browns and the Legendary St. Louis Cardinals, by John Heidenry and Brett Topel (UP Nebraska, 2006)

A Tiger in His Time: Hal Newhouser and the Burden of Wartime Ball, by David M. Jordan (Diamond, 1990)

Baseball's Pivotal Era, 1945–1951, by William Marshall (UP Kentucky, 1999)

One-Armed Wonder: Pete Gray, Wartime Baseball, and the American Dream, by William C. Kashatus (McFarland, 1995)

The Pastime in Turbulence: Interviews with Baseball Players of the 1940s, by Brent Kelly (McFarland, 2001)

Willie's Boys, by John Klima (John Wiley, 2009)

Bushville Wins!, by John Klima (Thomas Dunne, 2012)

The War in the Air: The Royal Air Force in World War II, edited by Gavin Lyall (Ballantine, 1968)

Ace: Phil Marchildon, Canada's Pitching Sensation & Wartime Hero (Penguin, 1993)

Even the Browns, by Williams B. Mead (Contemporary Books, 1978)

Masters of the Air: America's Bomber Boys Who Fought the Air War Against Nazi Germany, by Donald L. Miller (Simon & Shuster, 2007)

The Armed Forces of World War II: Uniforms, Insignia, and Organization, by Andrew Mollo (Crown, 1981)

Baseball Uniforms of the 20th Century, by Marc Okkonen (Sterling, 1991)

Nuremberg: Infamy on Trial, by Joseph E. Persico (Penguin, 1995)

The Fighting Lady: The New Yorktown in the Pacific War, by Clark G. Reynolds (Pictorial Histories, 1986)

Baseball's Forgotten Heroes, by Tony Salin (McGraw-Hill, 1999)

Country Hardball: The Autobiography of Enos Slaughter, with Kevin Reid (Tudor, 1991)

Can He Play?: A Look at Baseball Scouts, edited by Jim Sandoval and Bill Nowlin (SABR, 2010)

The Ballpark Book, by Ron Smith (The Sporting News, 2000)

Vitamin Charley: A History of Co. C, 741ˢᵗ Tank Battalion, in World War II, by George M. Smith, Richard Meacham, and George Hiller (Privately printed, New York, 1946)

Judge Landis and Twenty-Five Years of Baseball, by J. G. Taylor Spink (Thomas W. Crowell Company, 1945)

Once Around the Bases, by Richard Tellis (Triumph, 1998)

U.S. Navy Fighter Squadrons in World War II, by Barrett Tillman (Specialty Press Publishers, 1997)

The World Almanac of World War II, edited by Brigadier Peter Young (Bison, 1981)

The Army Air Forces in World War II, vol. 5, *The Pacific: Matterhorn to Nagasaki, June 1944 to August 1945* (Office of Air Force History, Washington, DC)

Official Unit History of the USS Alabama

Primary Archive

Franklin D. Roosevelt Presidential Library, Library of Congress, the Baseball Hall of Fame, New York Public Library Oral History Collections.

INDEX